MORE THAN CRICKET AND FOOTBALL

MORE THAN CRICKET AND FOOTBALL

International Sport and the Challenge of Celebrity

Edited by Joel Nathan Rosen and Maureen M. Smith

University Press of Mississippi / Jackson

www.upress.state.ms.us

The University Press of Mississippi is a member
of the Association of American University Presses.

Copyright © 2016 by University Press of Mississippi
All rights reserved

First printing 2016

∞

Library of Congress Cataloging-in-Publication Data

Names: Rosen, Joel Nathan, 1961– editor. | Smith, Maureen Margaret, 1967–
   editor.
Title: More than cricket and football : international sport and the challenge
   of celebrity / edited by Joel Nathan Rosen and Maureen M. Smith.
Description: Jackson : University Press of Mississippi, [2016] | Includes
   bibliographical references and index.
Identifiers: LCCN 2016020350| ISBN 9781496809889 (cloth : alk. paper) |
   ISBN 9781496809902 (epub institutional) | ISBN 9781496809919 (pdf single) |
   ISBN 9781496809926 (pdf institutional)
Subjects: LCSH: Sports and globalization—Case studies. | Sports in popular
   culture—Case studies. | Athletes—Public opinion—Case studies. |
   Fame—Social aspects—Case studies. | Athletes—Biography.
Classification: LCC GV706.5 .M667 2016 | DDC 796—dc23 LC record
available at https://lccn.loc.gov/2016020350

British Library Cataloging-in-Publication Data available

For David C. Ogden

Contents

ix   Foreword: International Sport in Context
        —Roberta J. Park

xiii   Acknowledgments

xv   Introduction: Drawing a New Map of the World in Sport
        —Joel Nathan Rosen and Maureen M. Smith

3   Suzanne Lenglen: Liberated Woman, French Revolutionary, or Both?
        —Nancy E. Spencer

25   Valentino Rossi: A Uniquely British Look at an Italian Motorsport Legend
        —Sean Bell

55   Andy Murray: Savior from Outside the Margins
        —Lisa Doris Alexander and Dan Travis

75   The Interaction of Personal, Local, and Global Forces: Yao Ming's Rise and Sustained Influence in Chinese Sport
        —Dong Jinxia, Zhong Yijing, and Li Luyang

99   Duke Kahanamoku: Racialized Colonization and the Exoticization of Aquatic Royalty
        —Joel S. Franks

123   Chad Rowan: Ritual, Religion, and One American's Pitch-Perfect Performance inside Japan's Hall of National Sport
        —Mark Panek

145   From Out of the Shadows of Invisibility: Brazilian Women's Football and the Pioneering Figure of Marta
        —Cláudia Samuel Kessler and Silvana Vilodre Goellner

163   The Many Faces of Samuel Eto'o Fils: (Re)Solving an Irascible Persona
        —Benn L. Bongang

186 Murali and Sanga: Forging Identity and Pride through Cricket in a Small Island Nation
—Gamage Harsha Perera and Tim B. Swartz

204 Grete Waitz: The Art of Hurrying Slowly
—Theresa Walton-Fisette

222 Rodney Marsh: The Making of a Maverick Footballer
—Dominic Standish

250 Ayrton Senna: The Legacy of a Global Racing Icon
—Viral Shah

278 Katarina Witt: The Many Faces of a Showcase Athlete
—Annette R. Hofmann

297 Afterword: The Wide Worlds of Sport Text
—Jack Lule

305 Contributors

311 Index

Foreword

International Sport in Context

—Roberta J. Park

Introduction

In the opening of his 2006 book *Sport, Culture and Society: An Introduction*, Grant Jarvie, who has written extensively about such matters, accurately observed: "It is impossible to fully understand contemporary society and culture without acknowledging the place of sport."[1] What was correct nine years ago has only become more so by 2015. Television, the Internet, smartphones, and other devices have made many sporting competitions *the* major international phenomena in today's world. According to the International Olympic Committee (IOC), it was estimated that at least nine hundred million people from around the world would watch the televised opening ceremony of the 2012 London Olympic Games.[2] Upon their completion, the 2012 Olympics were found to have been the "most watched event in TV history."[3] The London games also were the first in which every participating country fielded at least one female athlete. Two years later, Germany defeated Argentina by a score of 1–0 at Maracanã Stadium in Rio de Janeiro to win the FIFA World Cup. Even though questions would be raised regarding whether the numbers who watched these events were accurately reported, the games did indeed attract many millions of viewers worldwide.[4]

Women's international sport has seen a similar expansion in the past decade. In 1991, twelve countries sent teams to China for the first-ever FIFA Women's World Cup. Twenty-four would be represented at Canada in 2015. This is one of many indications of how much high-level sport for women have been growing. Declared the number-one sport in a recent online posting, "Top 10 Most Popular Sports in the World," soccer (or "football" pretty much everywhere outside of North America) is followed by cricket, basketball, hockey (field and ice), tennis, volleyball, table tennis, baseball, rugby, and golf in terms of global popularity.[5] These and many other sports hold competitions that also attract millions of viewers. Although their numbers are fewer in cricket, ice hockey, and rugby, women participate in all of these sports—and more. Such is the global landscape available to us as we seek to engage in conversations about sport in the twenty-first century.

Yesteryear

In antiquity, sport was about paying homage to certain gods, but not exclusively. The sheer physicality of athletics and their highly competitive nature were instrumental in fostering interest in the ancient Olympic events that began in Athens in 776 BC; it was more than just "bread and circuses" even then. The Roman Empire gave rise to different types of enticing contests, but athletes were more than mere vessels for enjoyment. They were virtual demigods, who, with a touch of flair—showmanship in today's lexicon—were able to capture the imagination of the people by virtue of their ability to transcend time and space and perhaps even gravity.

By the second century AD, gladiatorial and other events at Rome's Flavian Amphitheater (better known as the Colosseum) were attracting well over fifty thousand spectators. However, following Emperor Constantine's 325 AD edict criticizing such "bloody demonstrations," they began to decline and would end entirely less than a century later, although the impulse for sport in what we in the Western Hemisphere today think of as the Old World would not completely evaporate. During the Middle Ages, simple games like shinty and folk football enjoyed some popularity; however, it was jousting tournaments featuring the skills of the best knights that gained the highest esteem in many European kingdoms. Meanwhile, other parts of the world developed their own preferred contests, including a football-like game in China called *cuju*, and *kabaddi*, an Indian game that featured the act of crossing over a designated space to tag an opponent. In these types of contests as well as others, we can see that the spirit for competition stayed alive among people even when the official culture may have deemed it superfluous or even showed hostility to it.

During the nineteenth century, an expanding British Empire exported a number of popular English sports—soccer, cricket, the Rugby School's eponymous game, and others, which had become immensely popular among boys at such heralded institutions as Eton, Exeter, Harrow, and other English public schools—to Southwest Asia, the Far East, Australasia, and many other parts of the increasingly shrinking world. Moreover, what was occurring in sports among the British elite also profoundly influenced the French educator and historian Pierre de Coubertin and helped foster his creation of the modern Olympic Games. For more than a century, the Olympic Games have helped bring together countries from around the world. The Olympics have also been instrumental in promoting the development of such events as the Asian Games, which were first held in New Delhi in 1951, and the East Asian Games, which first appeared in Shanghai in 1993. By the time of the 2014 Asian Games held at Incheon, South Korea, 5,823 male and 3,678 females athletes participated.[6] It is interesting, and by no means inconsequential, that events such as these include many more sports that first rose to popularity in Great Britain and the United States than sport of local or even regional origins, including judo from Japan, tae kwon do from Korea, and Chinese wushu.

Direct colonial conquest too had a hand in the diffusion of sport, particularly given the broad scope of British colonialism in the nineteenth century moving forward into the twentieth. Beginning in 1930, the Commonwealth Games (originally called the British Empire Games and held every four years) have taken place in such diverse locations as Kingston, Jamaica; Kuala Lumpur, Malaysia; and Delhi, as well as in other former colonies ranging from Australia to Canada and even in Great Britain itself. The 2014 Commonwealth Games, held in Glasgow, included the participation of seventy-one commonwealth nations.[7]

Scholarship in International Sport

It is not just the number and extent of athletic contests such as these and other aspects of sport that have grown in many parts of the world. So too have historical and other studies related to these matters. When the *International Journal of the History of Sport* began publication in 1984, relatively few interesting and even fewer influential studies of the social, political, cultural, and economic history of sport had been undertaken. For a quarter of a century, the dedicated and insightful work of James Anthony (J. A.) Mangan, who was instrumental in starting up the *IJHS* and who guided it for decades, did much to foster important advances in this nascent academic field.[8] Soon, a growing number of scholars were researching and writing about important social, cultural, economic, political, gender-related, international, and other matters in which sport played a decidedly significant role. As only one of scores of sources that deserve attention, Amit Gupta's 2009 article "The Globalization of Sports, the Rise of Non-Western Nations, and the Impact of International Sporting Events" set forth valuable information regarding why, "with the advent of globalization[,] non-Western nations are increasingly asserting themselves in the decision making and economics of international sporting events."[9] Gupta urges us to consider the ways in which all of the world's nations have influenced the twenty-first-century sporting landscape and to stretch beyond the comfort of knowing sport only as it exists in the North American and western European contexts.

In what has become an increasingly globalized world, an understanding about other nations, their people, and their cultures will need to continue to improve. Greater opportunities to share such experiences in positive ways must also be provided. Certainly, events like the FIFA World Cup and the Olympic Games are highly competitive, but at least with regard to the Olympics, there have been opportunities to celebrate inclusiveness. This, after all, has been a major goal of the opening and closing Olympic ceremonies.

To help achieve such goals, we must develop a better understanding about sport's role. Understanding what sport meant in past centuries and what it means entering the twenty-first century is tantamount to gathering insight into the significance of competition wherever it exists. Thus, attempts to chronicle where sport has been and where it can go must extend beyond the boundaries, as C. L. R. James[10] has couched it, to delve more deeply into the nature of athletic competition. Insightful studies of sport, such as the one in your hands, whether strictly historical or transcending borders and cultural expectations, are absolutely essential for us all to fully engage in and expand the scope of sport scholarship in the decades to come.

Notes

1. Grant Jarvie, *Sport, Culture and Society: An Introduction* (New York: Routledge, 2006), 2.

2. "London 2012 Opening Ceremony Audience Hit 900 Million Predicts IOC," *Independent*, August 7, 2012, at http://www.independent.co.uk/sport/olympics/news/london-2012-opening-ceremony-audience-hit-900-million-predicts-ioc-8015361.html; and Lateef Mungin, "The London Olympics: 4 Billion People; 4 Billion Reasons to Watch," CNN, July 26, 2012, at http://edition.cnn.com/2012/07/25/sport/olympic-world-watches/ (both accessed June 4, 2015).

3. "London Olympics 2012 Ratings: Most Watched Event in TV History," *Huffington Post*, August 13, 2012, at http://www.huffingtonpost.com/2012/08/13/london-olympics-2012-ratings-most-watched-ever_n_1774032.html.

4. See, for example, "FIFA World Cup Breaks TV Viewing Records around the World," Live Production, June 30, 2014, at http://live-production.tv/news/sports/fifa-world-cup-breaks-tv-viewing-records-around-world.html; and Mike Mikho, "Brazil's World Cup Is a Marketer's Dream but Also a Potential Nightmare," *Adweek*, at http://www.adweek.com/news/advertising-branding/brazil-s-world-cup-marketers-dream-also-potential-nightmare-152890.

5. Khabir Uddin Mughal, "Top 10 Most Popular Sports in the World," Sporteology, at http://sporteology.com/top-10-popular-sports-world/.

6. "17th Asian Games, Incheon 2014," at http://www.incheon2014ag.org/index.

7. "Glasgow 2014, XX Commonwealth Games," at http://www.glasgow2014.com.

8. See, for example, Boria Majumdar and Projit B. Mukharji, "A Man for the Future," *International Journal of the History of Sport* 22, no. 4 (July 2005): 501–9.

9. Amit Gupta, "The Globalization of Sports, the Rise of Non-Western Nations, and the Impact of International Sporting Events," *International Journal of the History of Sport* 26, no. 12 (September 2009): 1779–90.

10. C. L. R. James, *Beyond a Boundary* (Durham, NC: Duke University Press, 1993).

Acknowledgments

As is the case with any endeavor such as this, we have enjoyed the input and well-wishes of a host of individuals and groups throughout this process, and we would like to acknowledge their hands in all of this. First and foremost, we are indebted to our conscientious and supremely talented contributors. You are the backbone of this collective effort, and your words and thoughts within are testament to your dedication above and beyond any of our expectations.

To the inimitable Biri Biri, who gave so much of himself, his time, and even his most cherished memoir—that extraordinary photograph that still hangs in his daughter's bedroom—thank you so very much for taking such an unexpected interest in a project that must have seemed as random as it did ambitious. You, sir, are a reminder of what sport is really about: great feats and perhaps even greater stories!

To Craig Gill, Katie Keene, and the entire team at the University Press of Mississippi, including Norman Ware, whose timely and sensitive handling of the copyediting made a quite good collection great, you have once again stood by and allowed us to do our thing while availing yourselves to us for any and all questions and/or concerns we might have had throughout this arduous process. We can also only imagine the challenge of standing semi-idly by while wrapping your heads around the specter of our collecting contributors from five continents writing about subject matter not typically found in works intended for North American audiences. For that alone, you are all to be commended and applauded.

To those of you who have read portions of the manuscript in various forms and offered substantive and perceptive commentary, namely David C. Ogden, Ellen Staurowsky, Earl Smith, Jeanmarie Jackman, Jonathan Clark, and, of course, Roberta Park and Jack Lule, we thank you for helping us to see the things our eyes prevented us from noticing.

As expected, our friends, families, and colleagues offered immeasurable support throughout. You are the silent contributors to projects such as this if only because you willingly endure the pitfalls and pratfalls of what are often quite bumpy rides. Most of all, you listen and do so strictly out of love and admiration, and we are of course grateful.

A particularly special note goes out to the aforementioned David C. Ogden. You were here from the beginning, and while your name may not officially adorn these pages, your spirit hovered about this work—a beacon in the darkness at many a juncture.

Lastly, a similarly special note of appreciation goes out to our counsel, Mark S. Gutentag. You always watch out for our better interests, so in actuality we dare not make a move without consulting you first. And for that, we are most grateful.

To all of you and others we may have thoughtlessly omitted, we offer our sincerest gratitude and hope that you will similarly revel in the fruits of this collaboration.

Introduction

Drawing a New Map of the World in Sport:
"Kickin' It in West Africa with a Football Legend"

—Joel Nathan Rosen and Maureen M. Smith

On a lovely late spring day in 2012, a rather conventional-looking senior citizen sat inside La Parisienne Pâtisserieon Kairaba Avenue in the Serrekunda section of Banjul, the Gambia. Just under six feet tall and noticeably slender, he sat quietly sipping his coffee while nibbling on a sweet roll and chatting casually with the people who would join him at various intervals around his table that morning, as if it were just any other day, which of course it was. A stranger happening upon this scene might never have known that in some parts of the world, this normal-looking chap enjoying a normal-seeming moment was at one time (and in many ways remains) nothing less than international football royalty.

He was born Alhaji Momodu Njie, although to the football world he is known as Biri Biri, translated from Hausa as "mischievous monkey," a nickname he claimed to have rightly earned for once being, in his own words, "the biggest troublemaker of all the children who attended [his] mosque!"[1] He was also

One of dozens of Biri Biri-related billboards on display throughout The Gambia. Courtesy the editors.

This photograph of Biri Biri and Diego Maradona hangs in Biri's daughter's bedroom and has never been shown publicly. Courtesy Biri Biri.

clearly the most talented athlete among the mosque's children, and still wears that moniker with obvious pride these many years hence.[2]

Now into his seventies, Momodu Njie remains the Gambia's most visible and most valued export, although to the men, women, and children of his home country, he is still simply one of them: Biri—the man who put this tiny nation on the world map as something other than just another former British colony struggling to keep afloat in a challenging postcolonial economy. To see him walk down the street, to visit him in his offices two floors above the Royal Albert Street Bazaar that he manages in downtown Banjul, or to merely share a beverage opposite him on a lazy morning in Serrekunda, one might never know that he is as revered a figure as there is in world sport.

Biri's biography is simple to parse. In the early 1970s, he was the first sub-Saharan African to successfully make the transition to European football, where he excelled in ways that few thought possible. After essentially rewriting the regional record books over several seasons playing in both Gambian as well as Sierra Leonean leagues, Biri broke into British football briefly with the First Division Derby County side in 1970, although he would return to the Gambia shortly after arriving in England, citing a lack of playing time and a touch of homesickness. His big break came in 1972, however, when he signed with

Denmark's Nykøbing Fl, which watched en masse as he sliced through the local competition while the Danish side trained in Banjul for their upcoming season. In 1973, however, he left Denmark to join the vaunted Seville side in the Spanish leagues, with whom he would star for the rest of the decade. Biri, the Gambian phenom who played heads above the rest, would be among the first imports to challenge European players for football supremacy alongside the likes of others with whom he shared certain non-European demographic characteristics, including the inimitable Pelé, Portugal's own spectacular East African import, Eusébio, and Argentina's Diego Maradona, who often cites Biri Biri as having a major influence on his own storied career.

It was certainly the dawning of a new age, one that would by the early twenty-first century see athletic talent emanating from all around the globe. In this regard, Biri may have been the first African to make such a leap, but he would hardly be the last. And yet, as far as celebrity goes, his remains a rather modest, localized version, and this is still the case for athletes in many corners of the international sporting world, although certainly there are exceptions.

As might also happen on that ordinary spring morning, a family of Spanish tourists, presumably from Seville, had similarly chosen to have their morning repast at La Parisienne and just happened to notice who was already there. Following an initial glance came an excited shriek, and from that shriek came a bevy of joyous utterances as this similarly nondescript family of four descended upon Biri, arms outstretched and pens at the ready. While the local Gambians casually went about their day, this Spanish contingent in one fell swoop elevated both the moment and this prototypical man of the people to an entirely different stratum. He was indeed a star among these faithful, and once the exchange of pleasantries turned into an inevitable stroll through myriad memories, the five of them were arm-in-arm and deep into quite animated and jovial discussions in Castilian, which took shape amid the other conversations taking place around them in languages ranging from Arabic to Wolof, Mandinke to Jola, and French to English, to name but a few. And this is really where our story begins.

Why a Book on International Sport Celebrity?

Part of what makes the above narrative viable for our purposes is that we get to imagine it far removed from an exceedingly Western context. Simply put, many people—and particularly those in North America—have a difficult time imagining celebrity—and particularly sport celebrity—that does not display an official "Made in America" stamp. As Jack Lule argues herein in his insightful afterword, North Americans display a level of sport chauvinism when it comes to games other than the ones they themselves have created and then marketed to the rest of the world. This is especially true in what the rest of the world calls "football," in which our man Biri once played so integral a role. And in so many ways, that is the most important tie-in to the story we are trying to present here—the meaning of athletic celebrity outside the confines of the Western world and in particular that which originates away from the commercial capitals of North America and where great athletic heroes are also fêted and featured, valued and certainly financed in ways in parallel to the American model, although such parallels seem destined to fly, somehow, well below the North American radar.

What the above narrative also recalls is that celebrity has always been a fickle if not downright capricious construct. Assumptions that celebrities serve similar purposes in an increasingly shrinking media-fueled environment are simply not accurate. In Seville, where spectators and supporters are still buoyed by the notion of all things Biri-related (and where there still remains a fan club named for him), and also in Copenhagen and perhaps even other parts of the football-mad world, Biri Biri is much more than a random name plucked from a random past.[3] In other parts of the planet, places where his star shines less brightly or not at all, where his name holds little or no sway, we would certainly expect a different outcome from what we saw on Kairaba Avenue in Banjul. But what becomes more clear through an examination of celebrity ever more broadly conceived is that its meaning, its significance, and its place in any given order, regardless of whether that place is cultural or political or economic or perhaps even spiritual, are accompanied by different inferences and consequences that will differ depending on geography.

As Biri's story further reminds us, the meaning of celebrity is often altered by nothing more than changes in temporal and spatial circumstances. The world certainly knows of the legends of Biri's immortal contemporary, Pelé, or the then younger star-in-the-making who once idolized Biri and Pelé both, Diego Maradona. Given that both Maradona and Pelé have since become household names of sorts, while maintaining a decidedly regal air long after their playing days ended, the question becomes: why they and not Biri?

Although they are among the greatest footballers of their or really any generation, neither Pelé nor Maradona were anything close to pioneering figures in the way Biri was. For all intents and purposes, Biri was international football's Jackie Robinson, taking the extraordinary leap across a colossal international divide fueled by racial assumptions while ultimately paving the way for the likes of others, such as Cameroon's Samuel Eto'o, whose story is chronicled herein, Liberia's George Weah, or Didier Drogba of Côte d'Ivoire, to name but a few, who prior to Biri might have never had the opportunity to transition from local phenom to regional superstar and ultimately to international icon. Biri's record as a player, his undeniable skill set, his reputation as a team player, and many other tangible and intangible qualities he brought to the pitch during his storied career suggest that he may have indeed gotten short shrift for all his excellence and path paving.[4]

To be sure, Pelé, as memorable a player to ever grace the playing fields, followed up his legendary career, one that featured a bevy of World Cups and too numerous individual awards and accolades to catalog here, with Hollywood films and the accompanying international acclaim. Maradona, with a more colorful reputation, to put it mildly, nevertheless continues to garner applause and opportunities that belie some of his more questionable life choices. This is not to suggest for a moment that celebrities should eschew "cashing in," as it were. Rather, it begs the question of who gets to cash in and why? Frankly, there is no blueprint for this. What we have, however, is evidence and an opportunity to explore such matters using whatever means are at our disposal, which brings us back to the work before you. What we can take away from these narratives—which feature a relatively small sample of celebrity athletes whose career trajectories and whose trials and tribulations are borne under the sometimes overwhelming weight of celebrity—are insights as to how celebrity, as viewed through the prism of international sport, works in many corners of the planet.

The international aspect of this collection comes at a time when North American professional leagues are feeling the pinch of globalization in their own bunkers. America's Major League Baseball (MLB), for example, serves as a sort of athletic United Nations, given that over 35 percent of MLB rosters, which already include large numbers of players from Latin America and the Caribbean, are made up of ballplayers from outside the Western Hemisphere entirely. Similarly, the National Basketball Association (NBA), whose first Asian-born top draft pick was China's Yao Ming (also chronicled herein) in 2002, has in the past two decades seen a remarkable spike in foreign-born players from Europe—Eastern and Western—as well as South America, Asia, and sub-Saharan Africa, all of which have made steady inroads into the American game, which was, perhaps ironically, invented by a Canadian.

The success of athletes from other countries in two of the North American big four, the list of which also includes the American brand of football and ice hockey, provides some of the better examples of how powerful sport has become as we continue to try to make sense of the increasingly shrinking distances between worlds. Therefore, rather than focusing on sports that are more typically viewed through the rather limited lens of the Western Hemisphere's experience, one that often relegates the notion of international athletic celebrity to resident aliens who have found their success in North America's uniquely branded pastimes, this collection serves as the reader's passport, as a means to cross borders into many of the other countries that make up this sporting diaspora where athletic cultures represent an even larger chunk of a sport puzzle that just continues to add pieces.

The Challenge of Hagiography

In working through our initial list of subjects while recruiting authors whose voices we thought absolutely needed to be a part of this endeavor, we had one particular concern that did not seem to plague previous collections on the subject of athletic celebrity and the forging and maintenance of reputation: the specter of hagiography. Perhaps owing to the notion that most of the continent's citizenry can be traced back to the "Old World," North Americans have demonstrated time and again that they can be at least somewhat objective, and even sometimes downright vicious, when reporting on the athletes within their own domains.

In sharp contrast, many of the athletes whose stories are shared in this collection are considered national heroes representative of their particular homelands and cultures, which leaves contributors caught betwixt and between the very notions of basic objectivity. Indeed, what North American athlete could be identified as such? Whereas in the 1940s, American soldiers could flesh out Axis spies by asking questions about Babe Ruth, in contemporary parlance, Ruth is much less a cultural icon than he is a cautionary tale regarding the demons of his excesses, which may have led to his falling out of favor with baseball's brass and which in turn may have led to his early death. If Ruth's legend is no longer sacrosanct—if the very notion of the minted-in-America adjective "Ruthian" could be challenged, along with the legacies of hockey's celebrated Maurice Richard or basketball's Bill Russell or Michael Jordan or perhaps even Chris Evert or the Williams Sisters of tennis fame—then questions pertaining to objectivity are no longer as much of a concern as they may once have been if only because these figures are not necessarily representative of any national character.

In terms of the international athlete, however, the inverse to North America is very much in play, rendering objectivity a much more difficult goal. It is no great secret to suggest that, given his circumstances, Yao Ming is as much a representative of China as one can find in the early twenty-first century, making his presence, or the presence of, say, Brazil's Ayrton Senna or Cameroon's Samuel Eto'o or certainly even Sri Lanka's once dynamic cricket duo of Murali and Sanga, a much more difficult matter to traverse when it comes to the basic expectations of academic criticism. Expecting Hawaiians to be harshly critical of Duke Kahanamoku or the French to suddenly turn on Suzanne Lenglen seems unrealistic, although indeed we do get to witness such impacting critiques via the following contributions when it comes to the complicated stories of Andy Murray and Rodney Marsh up against expectations of British life, Marta's challenge to the hegemony of male sport in Brazil, or the American Chad Rowan, who as Akebono took on the whole of Japanese tradition by achieving *yokozuna* status in Sumo. Despite such outliers, there was a concern that with so many contributors taking on subjects from their home nations, the temptation to romanticize or otherwise sentimentalize their subjects would just be too great. Fortunately, we can report, this was not the case. These authors whose work you will find within have worked diligently to move beyond such one-dimensional renderings of the athletes they write about to reveal engaging, compelling, and, yes, even flawed figures whose place in the broader sporting world extends rather than narrows the story that sport tells, as anthropologist Clifford Geertz once so famously reminded us.[5] And so, we offer up these renderings for your perusal and appreciation as we introduce to the world stories of athletes whose careers and legacies have been often overlooked, underreported, or simply, somehow, ignored.

Notes

1. Alhaji Momodu Njie, interview by Joel Nathan Rosen, Banjul, April 4, 2012.
2. Ibid.
3. Nanama Keita, "A Tale of Biri Biri," *Gambia News Community*, September 18, 2007, at http://wow.gm/africa/gambia/article/2007/9/18/a-tale-of-biri-biri.
4. Biri's former Gambian teammate Omar Sallah describes him still as "the best player Africa has ever produced," going so far as to insist that on the pitch, he was "a complete footballer" and "the best by anybody's standard." Mohamed Fajah Barrie, "Biri Biri: Gambia's 'Greatest,'" BBC Sport, May 23, 2005, at http://news.bbc.co.uk/sport2/hi/football/africa/4573729.stm.
5. This is a rephrasing of Geertz's now ubiquitous quotation found in this instance in Andrew W. Miracle Jr. and C. Roger Rees, *Lessons of the Locker Room: The Myth of School Sport* (New York: Prometheus Books, 1994), 9.

**MORE THAN
CRICKET
AND
FOOTBALL**

Suzanne Lenglen

Liberated Woman, French Revolutionary, or Both?

—Nancy E. Spencer

Introduction

Of all the living embodiments of sport's Golden Age, few stand out as vibrantly as France's Suzanne Lenglen. At a time when tennis was among the most popular sports in the international arena, this Frenchwoman's popularity surpassed that of some of the most heralded names of the day, including tennis's biggest superstar, America's "Big Bill" Tilden.[1] By the time she reached her first Wimbledon in 1919, the event was so highly anticipated that organizers were forced to move the vaunted courts from their original site at Worple Road to their current and significantly larger facility on Church Road.[2]

By 1925, Lenglen had become a full-blown athletic luminary whose star shone well beyond the courts where she had made her reputation, making her for all intents and purposes the first modern truly sportswoman.[3] Known as "the Goddess" as well as "the first diva of tennis," Lenglen continues to be thought of in some circles as one of the greatest—if not *the* greatest—female tennis players of all time, and certainly one who continues to cast an expansive shadow over the contemporary game.[4] Her playing style, a blend of power and pinpoint accuracy, can be found among players from Brazil's Maria Bueno in the 1950s and 1960s to Australia's Evonne Goolagong in the 1970s and 1980s to Martina Navratilova after that, and on to the age of the vaunted Williams Sisters. But long before speed and muscle came to dominate the women's side of the sport, Lenglen also demonstrated a balletic fluidity to her game that offered more than just a hint of spectacle, a feature not always present in twenty-first-century tennis.[5] While the verdict may still be out as to who really is the greatest woman player in tennis's modern era, a debate that usually comes down to Navratilova or Serena Williams, many observers unmistakably agree that well before Martina and Serena, and Steffi Graf and Chris Evert, emerged on the scene, Suzanne Lenglen had long since set the standard by which women's tennis was to be judged.[6]

But Lenglen's place in sport history was never limited to the courts. Mixed into her distinctive style of play was a movie-star quality and a flair for the spotlight that ultimately helped lay the foundation for the contemporary image of the women's tennis celebrity still in evidence today. In this regard, she was not only the first female athlete of the early twentieth century to put a dent in the male dominated post–World War I sporting culture; she was also among the first to be able to harness her celebrity into international stardom, which in turn translated into a vast array of opportunities such as publishing, product endorsements, coaching, and exhibition matches, and a comfortable retirement before her untimely death in 1938.[7] Thus, while her income may pale in comparison to that of many twenty-first-century stars, in many other ways she was opening doors to a more lucrative future by helping to turn the women's side of the tennis ledger into something much greater than merely a competitive B circuit clearly secondary to the men.[8]

This chapter examines Suzanne Lenglen's historic rise to international fame en route to becoming the first globally renowned female superstar athlete. Included are details about her formative years up to her initial appearance at Wimbledon, while exploring the role that her father, the infamous "Papa" Lenglen, played in her development. Moreover, we will examine Lenglen's career within the context of the Golden Age of Sport (which just so happens to parallel the period forever etched in the imagination by F. Scott Fitzgerald as the Jazz Age), when she became arguably the world's best-known athlete of either gender at a time when tennis was still largely the purview of elites and amateurs.[9] Integral to these deliberations will be ongoing discussions of Lenglen's influence on gender by virtue of her introduction to international audiences of what some have deemed a new style of sporting femininity based on her appearance, demeanor, and playing style, as well as a more critical appraisal of her legacy all these years hence.[10]

"Papa"

There is no doubt of the extent to which Suzanne Lenglen's tennis career was shaped by her father, Charles "Papa" Lenglen. By most accounts the world's first true *tennis parent*, Papa Lenglen was "a heavyset bear of a man" and "a businessman of some means" who was to be her "guide, business agent and hard-driving taskmaster."[11] Above all else, he was a master manipulator and strategist who taught himself just enough about the rudiments of both the men's and women's versions of the game to turn his daughter into a hybrid of both while ultimately making her a nearly unparalleled champion.

A retired pharmacist by trade and training, Lenglen moved his wife, Anaïs, and an eleven-year-old Suzanne to Nice on the French Riviera, which is where he introduced his daughter to the sport in which she would make her mark. Like many contemporary tennis fathers—Stefano Capriati, Peter Graf, and Richard Williams, to name but a few—Papa Lenglen was not at all an accomplished player, but he became a student of the game, learning its tactics while fashioning along the way a newer vision that could work for both male and female players.[12]

Papa Lenglen had ample opportunity to study the various games of the better players of both genders from his enviable vantage point as secretary of the Nice Tennis Club. In particular, he seemed especially interested in the serve and volley style of the English women, whose accuracy similarly intrigued him, but he was perhaps even more inspired by the men, who displayed a decidedly more aggressive way of addressing the ball.[13] As he studied both styles in their competitive contexts, he came to imagine the blending of the two and constructed his daughter's game accordingly, taking her already developing finesse game and adding muscle to it.[14] And he drilled her on both elements of this approach by having her repeatedly hit full strokes at strategically placed targets around the court, resulting in extraordinary levels of accuracy and consistency that would be equaled by no one else during her reign. As Mary Carillo explains in the HBO documentary *Dare to Compete: The Struggle of Women in Sports*:

> Papa Lenglen would drill her hour after hour after hour. And he would put handkerchiefs out on the court and ask her to hit the handkerchiefs. And she got so good at nailing them—just picking them off—that he would fold the handkerchief in half. And she would hit that one. And then he would fold it into quarters. She got so proficient at that. She could hit any shot from anywhere on the court. She had a total game.[15]

Young Suzanne's athletic development, however, was never strictly relegated to tennis—at least not at first. Superbly coordinated and stronger than she appeared, by age eight she had gained local recognition for her swimming, gymnastic, and cycling abilities as well as all-around skills typically found among track and field athletes—running, jumping, and throwing—all talents that would serve her well as she transitioned toward tennis full-time in the years ahead. She was, in the parlance of the day, a natural athlete, a strength that she displayed most conspicuously in how quickly she developed her tennis skills once she devoted herself full-time to the sport, while her father/coach put her through one grueling practice session after another.[16]

After only three months of training, Lenglen played her first set of tennis before a gallery of spectators. Encouraged by what was considered to be a strong performance, she was then entered into her first tournament, finishing a respectable second place. This breakthrough in turn convinced Papa Lenglen to further ratchet up the intensity of her training. Certainly, what he lacked in terms of formal training, he more than made up for in creativity and, according to some, cruelty. He had cobbled together a viable plan that would ultimately serve to make his daughter one of the premiere athletes of her day, and he seemed able, if not eager, to stick to the plan regardless of the consequences.[17]

Rise of a Phenom

Lenglen's development as a top-flight tennis player was indeed something of a family affair. Certainly, the Lenglens were an enigmatic bunch. Stories that first circulated about them and their training regimen told of this young girl perfecting her game under the tutelage of her father through an admixture of repetition and exhaustion. Putting all of his daughter's athleticism into the mix, Papa helped her wed the precision found in the women's game to the aggressive strokes he found in the men's, forming a graceful, almost dance-like cadence, creating a style that perfectly suited her overall skill set, which she would continue to develop throughout her childhood and on into her teenage years.[18]

Her graceful movements were thought to have resulted from a course in classic Greek dance she had taken at Papa's insistence at the Institut Masséna in Nice. This brought a ballet-like fluidity to her overall athleticism and allowed her to approach the ball from virtually any angle while being able to steer it to virtually any spot on the court regardless of angle. To be sure, Papa's use of such disparate and certainly revolutionary training techniques was based on his uniquely singular vision, which in the end was predicated on his stated belief that "with a well-directed course of training, any woman could be taught the game as it was played by the men, although naturally she would not be unable to play with the same degree of force."[19]

But Papa's altered approach to training did not end solely with physical manipulations, as he also employed some rather heinous means by which to turn an already emotionally fragile child into one who could be even more easily manipulated on the court and off. In session after session, Papa assaulted and battered her young psyche, ridiculing her in public, often to the point of tears. He would follow such abuse up with what Larry Engelmann calls "pandemics of deprecation" by which he would suddenly embrace and comfort her, but always return her to the courts to keep working. Even "Mama" Lenglen got in on the act by hissing at her when she missed a shot, blurting out such invectives as "Stupid girl! Keep your eye on the ball!"[20] This often callous treatment of the young woman took its toll, even while her game flourished. Her mental health continued to absorb one direct blow after the next, although in some ways the abuse would also render her rather impervious to most outside distractions she would face as she continued to climb steadily up the local and later regional rankings.[21]

Despite the brutality that underscored her training regimen, Lenglen was well on her way toward to stardom by 1912. She had won several select local tournaments as well as regional championships, including singles and doubles tournaments around Nice, in Picardy, and elsewhere. In 1913, she won the club championship at the Nice Tennis Club, which resulted in her being chosen to represent the club in a match against an Italian squad, where she again won multiple matches. With so much provincial fame coming her way so quickly, it was a only a matter of time before word began to spread of a thirteen-year-old tennis phenom who by the end of the next summer was laying waste to players, young and veteran alike, on the clay courts of both Italy and France.[22]

In 1914, Lenglen captured her first significant singles title by winning the World Hard Court Championship in Saint-Cloud, just outside of Paris.[23] But just as she was becoming a dominant player wending her way toward the brighter spotlights of the Grand Slam circuit, World War I intervened, resulting in cancellations of most major tournaments, including Wimbledon, for the duration of the war.[24] Interestingly, however, the Lenglens seemed to have taken the wartime lull as an opportunity to engage in what today would be called a bit of gamesmanship. Contradictory stories emerged—presumably originating in the Lenglen home itself—that offered competing assessments of how she spent her time during this long layoff from tournament play. Her parents maintained that she spent the war years "knitting socks or rolling bandages for the soldiers," while locals maintained that they observed her consistently if not constantly working on her game in ways that were thought to be even more rigorous than those undertaken during the prewar years.[25]

Once the war was over, however, and as a wave of sports mania swept across the West, with French athletes helping to lead the way, there was Suzanne Lenglen, primed and ready for the competition that followed. In France, this postwar competitiveness, as evidenced in the sheer number of athletic competitions being waged, helped further Lenglen's athletic prowess and resulting reputation, giving her battered homeland a national symbol that carried tremendous international appeal. Since French women were encouraged to compete in athletics, this extraordinarily talented young Frenchwoman would become the face of the recovery effort. Thus, by 1919, when she would make her first appearance at an international tournament, which just happened to be at Wimbledon, the tennis world eagerly awaited her debut on the hallowed grass courts.

Wimbledon

When Lenglen arrived at Wimbledon, she was already, as David Gilbert claims, "the focus of significant international media attention, not merely for the quality of her play, but also for her athleticism, fluency of movement, youth and style of dress."[26] And she would have a spectacular run to the finals, never dropping a set and losing only seventeen games as she defeated everyone in her path.[27] The women's singles final pitted the now twenty-year-old against Great Britain's Dorothea Lambert Chambers, the reigning women's champion, who was twice her age, had won the championship seven times between 1903 and 1914, and by custom was able to sit on the sidelines until the final round.[28] The contrast in styles between Lenglen and Chambers represented what many thought would be a changing of the guard in tennis. Here was an established professional, and a well-rested one at that, going up against a quite heralded but virtually untested newcomer whose game and flair for the dramatic were unlike anything anyone had before seen. In this regard, the 1919 women's finals became both a watershed moment in women's tennis and a litmus test for the future of the sport, which was itself evolving "from a more social game to a more 'popular public spectacle.'"[29]

Many believed that the much younger Lenglen would win the match handily, given the age disparity alone, but she and Chambers ended up playing three hotly contested sets. Lenglen won set one that took a staggering eighteen games to settle, at 10–8, while Chambers fought back to tie the match at 6–4.[30] The final set remained close until Chambers pulled to double match point at 40–15 with the count 6–5 in the third set, which seems to have sent Lenglen soaring into another gear. She started by saving those two match points, rallying to win the set and the match 9–7 in a tournament final that still ranks among the most memorable of all time and certainly one that would have implications moving forward as the sports world entered its Golden Age full-bore.[31]

Sport's Golden Age

Following her stirring win at Wimbledon, Lenglen continued to soar up the ranks of both tennis and celebrity. This era is typically referred to as the Golden Age of Sport, an age that was as much associated with the notion of "ballyhoo" as it was about the birthing of a newly minted sport-crazed landscape.[32] Dominated by American athletes, this vaunted age, generally thought of as a twelve-year period beginning with the end of World War I and extending through the start of the Great Depression, included some of sport's most legendary figures such as baseball's Babe Ruth, boxing's Jack Dempsey, Gertrude Ederle (the first woman to swim the English Channel), American football's Red Grange, and golf's Bobby Jones.[33] Tennis in particular was coming into its own during this age with the aforementioned "Big Bill" Tilden holding court on the men's side while Helen Wills found fame on the women's. But while it was an era devoted to memorable if not iconic personalities, it was also a transformative time when sport in its most general guise was moving beyond its pejorative reputation as the "toy department" of cultural interests, as American journalists had dubbed it, toward its present-day standing as an institution embraced around the world.[34] That Suzanne Lenglen came of age just as sport was actively changing the cultural landscape places her among those at the epicenter of the period, making her one of the seminal figures of the time.[35]

The few women athletes associated with the age tended to play individual rather than team sports, which was as much a matter of marketing concerns as it was the dearth of team sport available to women. The sports world, dominated as it was by men and controlled by public relations managers who typically marketed sport to what were perceived to be male tastes, contributed to this trend, highlighting those women athletes in particular who fit more traditional definitions of femininity.[36] Thus, for every Babe Didrikson willing to wear a false beard while dressing up to play baseball with the barnstorming House of David team, there were so-called glamour girls such as Helen Wills, who was known for powdering her nose between points, and skating's Sonja Henie, who typically wore quite revealing dresses on the ice back before that look was co-opted in the more modern age.[37] In this regard, sport could be easily wedded to the public's growing appetite for sex via the emergent publicity machinery of the times, which also gave rise to off-the-field narratives of personalities controlled by the same mechanisms that could be framed in quite ordinary terms, for instance the search for love and acceptance against a backdrop of the heroic struggle for victory against all odds. And yet, while women have historically stood subordinate to males in sport, having to resort to selling sex in order to gain notice, there have also been other women athletes who have asserted themselves in ways that disrupted "conventional images of femininity,"[38] with Lenglen serving in that particular capacity.

Lenglen, who was by no means conventionally beautiful though she has been routinely described as stylish in her own way, certainly disrupted traditional images in tennis insomuch as while she could put her own brand of femininity on display, her dominance on the court was what initially put her and ultimately kept her in the public eye.[39] Indeed, after Lenglen won Wimbledon in 1919, she would go on to capture five more Wimbledon singles titles to equal her six titles each in singles, doubles, and mixed doubles at the French Championships.[40] While her six French titles delighted the home crowds, her six singles victories at Wimbledon made her nothing less than a global sport icon.[41] Lenglen not only dominated play everywhere she appeared; she revolutionized the women's game in several obvious ways, ranging from the overall style of play to clothing styles, in what women wore on the court and perhaps even off it.[42] She was, in the words of sportswriter Sarah Pileggi, "this delightful, outrageous and quintessentially French woman" in addition to having been "the unrivaled queen of tennis from 1919 to 1926."[43]

Virtually Unsurpassed

Lenglen may have dominated the French Championships and Wimbledon, but she had yet to conquer the US Nationals at Forest Hills.[44] In 1921, Lenglen made her first and only trip to the United States as an amateur, where she played the defending champion Molla Mallory in the second round.[45] After losing the first set 2–6 and trailing 0–3 in the second, Lenglen walked off the court, claiming illness.[46] That would be the only match she would lose in a seven-year period.[47] When she next played Mallory at Wimbledon in 1922, Lenglen won easily. Lenglen never played in the Australian Championships, since it was largely an Australian affair until the Open era, although when she did participate in the other three Grand Slam events, she played very much up to form.[48]

The greatest challenge to Lenglen's supremacy over the women's game during the period came in the guise of the young American Helen Wills, who was six years her junior. Wills—later Wills Moody—had established herself as a legitimate rival to Lenglen by winning three consecutive US Nationals from 1923 to 1925.[49] Wills also captured the gold medal in the 1924 Olympics (in Paris) after Lenglen pulled out several weeks earlier. In February 1926, the twenty-year-old Wills took a semester off from the University of California, Berkeley, to travel to Europe, where she hoped to encounter Lenglen.[50] The two eventually met in the finals of a tournament at the Carlton Tennis Club in Cannes, in a match that was billed as the "Battle of the Century."[51]

The contrast between the two women could not have been more obvious, and the drama leading up to their match underscored their divergent personas. In one corner was a colorful yet explosive Frenchwoman, already tennis royalty, going up against Wills, a quintessential American girl-next-door, a scenario that ultimately generated hyperbole suggesting that the match represented the specter of an emergent albeit fledgling world power taking on the decadence of Old World Europe, though in the guise of the twenty-six-year-old Lenglen.[52] Makeshift stands were hastily built to accommodate the six thousand fans who attended the match.[53] Among those in attendance were the exiled Grand Duke Cyril of Russia, King Gustaf V of Sweden, the Duke of Sutherland, and the Rajah and Ranee of Pudukkottai, as well as the elite of Riviera society.[54] Reports indicated that people were literally hanging out of trees to catch a glimpse of this storied and, as it turns out, only match-up between the two players.[55]

The match stayed remarkably competitive, given that it was played on a red clay surface that clearly favored Lenglen. In the first set, Wills quickly took a 2–1 lead, but Lenglen went on to win the set 6–3. In the second set, Wills used her powerful forehand and backhand ground strokes to take a 3–1 lead. Lenglen evened the score at 3–3, but it became clear that the match was taking a toll on her. Instead of waiting until changeovers, Lenglen routinely walked to her side of the court following spirited points to take her customary sip of brandy.[56]

The match remained tight until Lenglen moved to a 5–4 lead at 40–15 for double match point. When Wills hit "a forehand crosscourt for an apparent winner," the players "heard an emphatic cry of 'Out!' from the corner of the court."[57] Believing that the ball was out and the match was over, Wills and Lenglen met at the net to shake hands. At that point, a linesman approached the chair umpire to report that a fan had made that call, and the match resumed. Lenglen was visibly shaken and proceeded to lose the next game, which tied the second set score at 6–6. While it appeared that Wills might have gained enough momentum to turn the match around, Lenglen was not finished. After breaking Wills in a hard-fought service game, Lenglen held her serve to win the second set, 8–6.[58]

Although tennis's two leading ladies would not meet again, it would not be for lack of trying. At the 1926 French Championships, Wills had to withdraw due to a bout of appendicitis, which paved a clear path for Lenglen to win the title easily. Later that year, when it seemed that they would have their rematch on the grass at Wimbledon, an unforgivable (if not unforgettable) communication glitch resulted in Lenglen missing her scheduled doubles match, which she was to have played in front of Queen Mary. When Lenglen was informed of the mix-up, she fainted and subsequently withdrew from the tournament. That would be her last Wimbledon appearance, since she would sign a contract to turn professional later that summer, a move that would ultimately disqualify her from playing in amateur tournaments ever again. While her decision seemed scandalous at the time, it would serve as yet another sign of the changing times, for which we can point to Lenglen's influence once again.[59]

Several factors contributed to Lenglen's decision to turn professional. For one, the global interest generated by the "Battle of the Century" alerted promoters to her potential marketing value, which piqued the interest of the legendary C. C. Pyle, the American promoter who single-handedly opened the door to professional American football through his marketing of famed college star Red Grange. Known rather pejoratively, though no less comically, as "Cash and Carry," Pyle sent his front man, W. H. Pickens, to France with the directive to sign Lenglen to a contract. When word reached Lenglen that a promoter wanted her to turn professional, she countered that she would not leave amateur tennis, claiming that it was, oddly, "simply too profitable." French journalists agreed, claiming that "amateur tennis paid well" in their country.[60]

Efforts to sign Lenglen to a professional contract might have ended there were it not for the "Jubilee Wimbledon disaster" that "changed everything."[61]

Feeling betrayed by Wimbledon fans who turned against her when she missed her doubles match, Lenglen realized that she could never return to Wimbledon. The final obstacle to her turning professional was her fear that she would become a social pariah, although Pyle convinced her that she could democratize tennis by liberating it "from the traditional aristocratic male-dominated associations and clubs," leaving her to "control her own destiny" and earn a profitable living from tennis, a scenario virtually identical to Billie Jean King's challenge in creating the Virginia Slims tour in 1970.[62]

The professional contract that Lenglen eventually signed with Pyle dictated that she would play at New York City's Madison Square Garden in the fall, followed by a cross-country tour of nearly forty other cities around the United States and Canada, before ending in Havana. Pyle told her that she would also star in a Hollywood movie and would receive endorsements for products ranging from perfume to tennis rackets to clothing. Pyle did not reveal how much money Lenglen would make, but when someone leaked the amount of $200,000 to the press, characteristically, he did not correct it.[63]

On Saturday, October 9, 1926, professional tennis made its debut at New York's Madison Square Garden with a match resulting from the Pyle-Lenglen partnership. His troupe of six professionals trotted out before a crowd of thirteen thousand, a remarkable turnout considering that amateur associations were actively discouraging fans, players, and officials from attending. Lenglen was certainly the star attraction and did not disappoint, as the crowds swooned to her elegant if not poetic style of play.[64] Her opponent, Mary K. Browne of Santa Monica, California, was ranked sixth in the United States at the time. But on opening night and each subsequent time they played after that, Lenglen defeated Browne handily.[65]

The overall success of the tour is difficult to calculate. Attendance fluctuated, ranging from the eight thousand who paid their way in to watch her in Boston to the three thousand fighting the elements on a late fall night in Philadelphia's unheated Sesquicentennial Auditorium.[66] Financially, Pyle made out quite nicely from the four-month tour, especially from Lenglen's endorsements of rackets, perfume, dolls, and clothing that were tied to the tour itself, leaving Pyle with profits in the $100,000 range and much more than his fair share of any royalties.[67] And although her earnings were not nearly on par with Pyle's, Lenglen fared better than the other players, pocketing an estimated $100,000 herself. However, when the tour ended, Pyle announced that he would not continue to promote professional tennis, leaving the six players who had relinquished their amateur status to have to reconfigure their own futures.

As Lenglen prepared to leave New York, she reported receiving and turning down several offers to appear in movies. Instead, she planned to play in exhibition matches as part of a tour of Europe, South America, and Asia. After returning to France, she continued to play professional tennis, but the exhibition tours failed to materialize, resulting in her retirement from tennis and a turn toward designing clothing supplemented by sales work in a Paris sports equipment shop, and eventually her own tennis school, where she coached the next generation of French players. When her tennis-wear designs appeared in photographs in 1930, it was clear that once again she was on the cutting edge of in terms of both timing and tastes, as her line, spurred on by the popularity of her Suzanne Shorts (later popularized as Bermuda shorts), showed her to be a visionary once again.[68]

A New Sporting Femininity

Before the 1919 Wimbledon championship, there was already a sense that a nascent brand of femininity was on the horizon, and it was certainly on display in the women's final.[69] In many ways—dress, comportment, on-court aggression—Lenglen represented this blossoming of a newer brand of femininity in this particular milieu while her opponent, Dorothea Lambert Chambers, clearly represented the more traditional variant.[70] Scholars have articulated that beyond the competition itself, this meeting also represented a symbolic battle between Lenglen, the upstart, and Chambers, cast in the more conservative role, as reflected by their contrasting styles across the board.[71]

As Jennifer Hargreaves points out, Chambers was certainly the more conventional of the two, "corseted in a long and heavy dress"[72] that forced her to remain along the baseline. Off the court, she was equally as predictable, remaining the epitome of post-Victorian respectability, which linked the classic notion of beauty with otherworldly concerns regarding "female purity, spirituality, and inner character."[73] Such a regimen would be a challenge for most women, let alone someone of Lenglen's ilk, whose entire public perception had been forged through a conscious rejection of the conventional. Thus, while most observers agreed that Lenglen did not represent beauty in the classical sense, the enthusiastic crowds who gathered to watch her caught on quickly that through her, they were witnessing a transition in terms of gender in which beauty now manifested itself in a display of physicality that seemed to move beyond mere image. As Susan Cahn suggests, her talent encouraged people to see "beauty in the way she melded quickness, agility, powerful strokes, and aggressive play with a leaping, pirouetting, apparently effortless style," leaving crowds with a much different impression of what a woman could do in the heat of battle, which had virtually nothing to do with her outward appearance or approach to competition.[74]

To many, this match was indeed a turning point, given that it represented what some consider to have been little short of an attempt to extricate female athletes from the constraints of prevailing gender norms.[75] What was less obvious, however, was the extent to which Chambers, although cast in the more traditional role, had already begun to challenge such notions of traditional femininity herself, but in a remarkably clandestine fashion. In terms of her dress and manners, Chambers seemed to reflect the expected continuity with the past, and yet her attitudes toward physical activity challenged these same attitudes, albeit subtly. Despite her outward bearing, in her own way, Chambers had begun to embrace more evolving notions of what it meant to be a woman—at least in the sporting environment. For example, she was thought to have encouraged talented younger women players to take a more conscientious approach to practice and the perfection of their games.[76] Furthermore, she advocated that women employ novel strategies such as the use of the drop shot to gain a psychological advantage over an opponent at a time when some in the sport continued to see the drop shot as an underhanded albeit legal blight on the game. This turn toward strategy and the psychological approach to competition, while typical of male athletes, was relatively new among women. As Gilbert notes, this "emphasis on tactics, variation, mental engagement and above all competitiveness marked a significant break with established notions of femininity."[77]

Whether Chambers had a hand in the revolution that brought about such integral changes to women's tennis remains unclear, although it is doubtful that her influence had as much impact on the development of the women's game as Lenglen's had. Recall that Lenglen was first and foremost a product of her father's tutelage, so there remains little to suggest that anyone else, let alone an Englishwoman noted for her gentility, could have had that much of an effect on her. Beyond that, even if Chambers did hold some sway over her young opponent, history remembers it much differently. What the evidence does suggest, however, is the extent to which Lenglen introduced dramatically new styles of femininity and feminine comportment to tennis, which she seems to have conveyed in three specific ways:

(1) Appearance and demeanor;
(2) Apparel; and
(3) Style of play and movement on the court.

These matters certainly do factor into this emergent form of sporting femininity, infused initially into tennis but later writ large into a sporting culture ripe for change.[78]

Appearance and Demeanor

As mentioned above, photographs, video footage, and narratives about Suzanne Lenglen reveal that she was fashionable and glamorous, yet she was hardly considered pretty in the conventional sense.[79] Her features were said to consist of "a strong and crooked Gallic nose, puffy eyelids, sallow complexion, and uneven teeth," all of which prompted the journalist Paul Gallico to describe her face as "homely in repose."[80] Hazel Wightman, a lifelong friend of Lenglen, thought of her as "homely," further saying that "you can't imagine a homelier face."[81] And yet tennis writer Al Laney would later write in her defense that "for an ugly girl, she had more charm and vivacity than a hundred pretty girls."[82]

Indeed, when Pyle sought to promote Lenglen's professional tour, he worried that her looks might be something of a hindrance to their collective efforts. In negotiating with her, Pyle acknowledged, "We'll have to get those teeth fixed up ... for the movies, you know"; Lenglen promised to undergo the dental treatment but only under the right circumstances.[83]

But not all media outlets seemed to fixate on Lenglen's facial characteristics. Indeed, upon her arrival at Wimbledon in 1919, the often notorious British popular press chose to emphasize her youthful appearance. Some British newspapers identified her simply as "Suzanne" and referred to her as a "girl," conveying an impression of her youthfulness, although in hindsight addressing her in such terms served to infantilize her as well. Commentaries in the *Daily Mirror* indicated that "Lenglen was not only 'winning matches and hearts,' but was also 'answering in the emphatic negative' the question: 'Does lawn tennis spoil a girl's looks?'"[84] Interestingly, the term "tennis face," a supposed malady that considered competition to have a deleterious effect on women's looks, had even been applied to Mrs. Chambers, Lenglen's opponent in the finals. A medical correspondent for the *Daily Mail* also was said to have linked physical exertion of tennis with the effects of war work and newfangled dance styles on the physical appearance of women. These claims, since refuted, fused with other existing misperceptions about women, their bodies, and the stress of competition to forge a rather formidable argument against strenuous exercise, although in actuality one could see that these suppositions were powerful allies in the maintenance of the traditional gender divide.[85]

But looks were not the only aspect of Lenglen's person under scrutiny. Her overall demeanor was also put to the test. Whenever she had the opportunity to play tennis, she became quite animated and fixated on the task at hand, which won her legions of admirers[86] although it led others to question her femininity. Regardless, in her first Wimbledon appearance following the end of the war, people packed the stands in record numbers partly just to get a closer look at her. However, many of these onlookers were shocked to watch her publicly touch up her makeup, as would many other women of the era. Some even walked out at the display, dismayed and disgusted, which demonstrates the limited extent to which the general public was willing to accept new gender-based standards of behavior.[87]

Lenglen's off-the-court style was too considered "equally flamboyant" to her courtside behavior. She has been described as having adopted all of the novel appearance elements of the day including "bobbed hair, vivid make-up, fashionable and expensive clothes, sparkling jewellery, and exotic accoutrements."[88] Other aspects of her look included revealing skirts, coats of various animal pelts, and her trademark bandana, as ubiquitous an accouterment as jazz singer Billie Holiday's omnipresent gardenia. Playing this diva role to the hilt, however, Lenglen was part of a movement of liberated women known as Flappers who flouted societal and sexual norms, as seen in period newsreels as well as in the more recent Hollywood film adaptation of Fitzgerald's *The Great Gatsby*, where Fitzgerald first delineated the period known as the Jazz Age. And indeed, despite her unconventional looks, Lenglen was by every measure the embodiment of this remarkable age. Moreover, she was most assuredly, as Gary Morley claims, "the darling of French society . . . a bold, free woman, an icon of the decade's 'Flapper.'"[89]

Apparel

Mode of dress was another way in which Lenglen would revolutionize the sport. Before Lenglen emerged on the tennis scene, women tennis players typically wore heavy, lengthy skirts with restrictive bodices. However, with her gracefulness and sensual presence, she sought to advance her game while, perhaps, highlighting her appearance by wearing what Michael Bohn terms "scandalously short and diaphanous tennis dresses," accessorized "with a gaily colored bandeau, or headband."[90] As Lenglen and Chambers entered the court for the 1919 Wimbledon finals, the contrast in styles could not have been more dramatic. Chambers sported a much more predictable and traditional look that included "a white gored skirt, reaching to just below the calf, worn with a long-sleeved shirt, buttoned at the wrists."[91] Meanwhile, Lenglen appeared in a soft linen hat highlighting a short-sleeved tennis frock with a white calf-length pleated skirt, and matching stockings.[92]

Some elements of the tennis establishment were shocked by what Lenglen wore on the court. It was feared that the manner in which she allowed parts of her body to be exposed, including her ankles, which up until then was considered to be the height of female immorality, would spill over into the fashions of the day.[93] The contrasting styles between Chambers and Lenglen were interpreted as being about deference, as well as competing interests between the forces of respectability and those of a more progressive nature bent on challenging such assumptions.[94] But while Chambers was so visibly tightly wrapped up in her more traditional sport-unfriendly attire, Lenglen, enjoying such unprecedented freedom of movement in her looser clothes, was actively redefining the look of a female athlete.[95]

Royalty was certainly aghast by Lenglen's appearance. Among the spectators who did not embrace this innovative style were King George V and Queen Mary, who witnessed the match from their royal box. They found Lenglen's taste in clothing to be overly revealing, and while she came to dominate their tournament, they thought it was despite, rather than because of, her attire that she was so successful there.[96] Of course, this would be the inverse of what actually transpired that fortnight.

Style of Play and Movement on the Court

But Lenglen's choices in attire did not merely emphasize her sensuousness. More importantly, they ultimately allowed her to move about much more freely on the court in ways that her predecessors (and opponents) could only imagine. She was not the only woman to believe that apparel should not hinder one's movements on the court. Owing to her more clandestine embrace of a newly minted sport sisterhood, Mrs. Chambers, too, believed that while at play, clothing should enhance rather than retard the body's effectiveness.[97]

At times, Lenglen's unrestricted movements on the court were likened to the way that men played, which should not surprise since "Papa" had patterned her game after the men he had observed on the Riviera. But Lenglen may have emphasized her style of play as well as her more fluid on-court movement with a strong degree of showmanship in mind. Some felt that her many leaps and pirouettes into the air were unnecessarily showy and were intended more for spectacle than tennis strategy, allowing her to show off her body while enabling the crowds to appreciate her more fully as she frolicked across the court.[98] Her long-time doubles partner, Elizabeth Ryan, was quoted as saying that "all those crazy leaps she used to take were done after she hit the ball," concluding that "she was a poser, a ham in the theatrical sense."[99]

And indeed, Lenglen was just as free with her body off the court. She frequently posed for photographers, standing with her right hand on her hip with her rackets tucked under the crook of her left arm, while holding her coat so as to reveal "as much of the tennis costume underneath as possible."[100] This celebration of a sense of liberation contributed to the notion that she had ultimately introduced sex to tennis.[101] As fans awaited Lenglen's first appearance at Wimbledon, much of the anticipation centered less on her revolutionary approach to the game and more on her fashion sense relative to the more typically "buttoned-down" image of the tennis female up to that point. Showing herself to have, in the words of one critic, a "flame-like precocity," her overarching appearance standards have been interpreted as reflective of her desire to expose her body, which freed her to pursue the game more vigorously while also perhaps inviting her objectification.[102] Looking at today's tour, one could argue that modern-day players' attire, based as much on fashion as on maneuverability, marks the logical progression from what Lenglen started, which further enhances her standing as a pioneering figure in the sport on several levels.

Contemplating a Complex Legacy

In the early twentieth century, Suzanne Lenglen was perhaps the most heralded female athlete in the world.[103] She conveyed a popular image that was based in part upon individual factors related to her style of play, her unprecedented fashion sensibility, and her overall personal demeanor. The changes she brought to tennis were in some ways quite visual, but she also transformed the style of play by moving with greater freedom and hitting the ball harder than the women who preceded her. Those individual attributes coalesced with societal transformations in which the roles of women were dramatically changing, which in effect brought changes to a game that had long been trapped in Victorian styles and practices. In this regard, she became a twentieth-century icon on several fronts, many of which remain apparent in the early twenty-first century.

The title of this chapter asked whether Suzanne Lenglen should be remembered as a liberated woman, a French revolutionary, or both. Based upon multiple narratives, there is sufficient evidence to suggest that she was all of it. Being "liberated" means to be free from constraints, allowing one to move beyond period expectations for socially governed behaviors, which in Lenglen's case could run the gamut from sexual attitudes to breaking free of gender barriers, both of which she most certainly did.[104] Proud of her standing in this regard, Lenglen demonstrated her liberation through her more modern choices and her rejection of traditional norms.[105]

Lenglen's style of play also lent itself to a level of liberation, as demonstrated by her on-court elegance, which has been described as acrobatic and even balletic; members of the media often reported on this aspect of her game, projecting it into a more far-reaching depiction of her overarching persona. Indeed, many fans wanted to see her play largely because of her graceful movements on the court. And it would be on the court where Lenglen could then demonstrate her liberation from traditional sex roles, which would manifest itself in, for instance, her propensity to throw her racket out of frustration, shout at officials when she received a bad call, or merely sip cognac during changeovers. She challenged such traditional gender roles by essentially refusing to be stifled by the expectation that women were incapable of aggressive play, by acknowledging that their freedom of movement was significantly hampered not by physiology but by sociology.[106]

In turn, a revolutionary is instrumental in fomenting significant change in contemporary social and political convention, and there are numerous ways that Lenglen demonstrated this, particularly in the way she materially altered the women's game, during her prime all but relegating men's tennis to the background, albeit temporarily.[107] Such evidence is especially on display at France's famed Roland Garros, site of the French Open, where the second show court is named after her, complete with a commemorative statue and a museum of images and artifacts. Lenglen has further been honored with an eponymous Paris Métro station and a sport center. Even her birthplace and cemetery plot have become tourist attractions.[108]

As unique an individual as has ever graced the courts, Lenglen has served as a model for many of her successors, although no one has really come close to demonstrating the complete package of talent and style, especially given the broad base of constraints in place in the time in which she starred. Some claim that the closest approximation was Monica Seles, whose once promising career came to a screeching halt after an on-court stabbing incident halted her momentum in April 1993. Fashion designer Ted Tinling had observed Lenglen's style when he was younger and maintains that Seles in her brief time in the public eye brought a similar panache and swagger back to the game.[109]

With her bobbed hair and regal air, Lenglen epitomized the Golden Age of Sport as so few would, playing this leading role into which she incorporated a unique albeit nascent brand of sport-inspired femininity. She was, in the words of one critic, "a leading actor in a newly internationalized culture of celebrity, '*the* player for the Jazz age, gay, brittle and brilliant,'"[110] thriving all the while in an environment in which fans adored her.

Given the context of contemporary global society, where social media spreads the most innocuous news like wildfire, we see a number of celebrities who jump back and forth between the role of hero and villain, given the vagaries of the twenty-four-hour news cycle and the telltale prurience that has turned gaiety into scandal. So perhaps it is safe to assume that while in all likelihood there will never be another Suzanne Lenglen, we remain, nonetheless, fortunate that her legacy lives on in modern professional women's tennis despite any perceived or manufactured controversy that cultural critics, then as now, have been able to construct around her narrative.

Notes

1. Michael K. Bohn, *Heroes & Ballyhoo: How the Golden Age of the 1920s Transformed American Sports* (Washington, DC: Potomac Books, 2009), 252.

2. Virginia Wade and Jean Rafferty, *Ladies of the Court: A Century of Women at Wimbledon* (New York: Atheneum, 1984).

3. Larry Engelmann, *The Goddess and the American Girl: The Story of Suzanne Lenglen and Helen Wills* (New York: Oxford University Press, 1988), 46.

4. Engelmann, *The Goddess*; Gary Morley, "Suzanne Lenglen: The First Diva of Tennis," CNN, last modified June 6, 2013, at http://edition.cnn.com/2013/06/06/sport/tennis/suzanne-lenglen-french-open-tennis/; Al Laney, *Covering the Court: A Fifty-Year Love Affair with the Game of Tennis* (New York: Simon & Schuster, 1968); Angela Lumpkin, *Women's Tennis: A Historical Documentary of the Players and Their Game* (Troy, NY: Whitson Publishing, 1981); and Wade and Rafferty, *Ladies of the Court*.

5. David Gilbert, "The Vicar's Daughter and the Goddess of Tennis: Cultural Geographies of Sporting Femininity and Bodily Practice in Edwardian Suburbia," *Cultural Geographies* 18, no. 2 (April 2011): 187–207, doi: 10.1177/1474474011399249, 195, accessed June 11, 2014.

6. See Larry Schwartz, "Martina Was Alone on Top," ESPN, December 1999, at https://espn.go.com/sportscentury/features/00016378.html, accessed July 27, 2014; and Kenny DeJohn, "Serena Williams Is Best Women's Player of All-Time after Resilient US Open Win," *Bleacher Report*, last modified September 8, 2013, at http://bleacherreport.com/articles/1766476-serena-williams-is-best-womens-player-of-all-time-after-resilient-us-open-win.

7. Gilbert, "The Vicar's Daughter," 191.

8. In 2014, for example, such heralded stars such as Russia's Maria Sharapova, America's Venus and Serena Williams, and China's Li Na earned upwards of US$25 million a year from com-bined earnings and endorsements. See Derrick Leon, "Maria Sharapova: Winner of French Open and Highest Earning Female Athlete," *Financial Buzz*, last modified June 9, 2014, at http://www.financialbuzz.com/maria-sharapova-winner-of-french-open-and-highest-earning-female-athlete-sports-92557.

9. Sarah Pileggi, "The Lady in the White Silk Dress," *Sports Illustrated Vault*, September 13, 1982, at http://www.si.com/vault/1982/09/13/624724/the-lady-in-the-white-silk-dress, accessed July 9, 2015.

10. Bohn, *Heroes & Ballyhoo*; and Gilbert, "The Vicar's Daughter."

11. Ross Greenberg, executive producer, *Dare to Compete: The Struggle of Women in Sports*, written by Frank Deford and Mary Carillo, HBO Sports, 1999; Engelmann, *The Goddess*, 7; and Pileggi, "The Lady in the White Silk Dress."

12. Pileggi, "The Lady in the White Silk Dress."

13. Ibid.

14. Engelmann, *The Goddess*, 9.

15. Greenberg, *Dare to Compete*. [Some have disputed this training regimen as apocryphal, although it does appear quite frequently in Lenglen-related literature—*eds.*]

16. Engelmann, *The Goddess*, 7.

17. Ibid., 8–9.

18. Laney, *Covering the Court*, 35.

19. Engelmann, *The Goddess*, 9.
20. Ibid., 13.
21. Ibid., 8–13.
22. Ibid., 14.
23. Laney, *Covering the Court*; John Parsons, *The Ultimate Encyclopedia of Tennis: The Definitive Illustrated Guide to World Tennis* (London: Carlton Books, 1998); and Pileggi, "The Lady in the White Silk Dress." See also Jeffrey Hart, review of *The Goddess and the American Girl: The Story of Suzanne Lenglen and Helen Wills*, by Larry Engelmann, *National Review* 40, no. 23 (November 25, 1988): 56.
24. Bud Collins, *The Bud Collins History of Tennis* (New York: New Chapter Press, 2011).
25. Engelmann, *The Goddess*, 16.
26. Gilbert, "The Vicar's Daughter," 189.
27. Ibid.; and Pileggi, "The Lady in the White Silk Dress."
28. Parsons, *The Ultimate Encyclopedia of Tennis*. [By 1922, the reigning champion would also be required to participate in the brackets—*eds*.]
29. Laney, *Covering the Court*, 45.
30. Gilbert, "The Vicar's Daughter," 190.
31. Parsons, *The Ultimate Encyclopedia of Tennis*, 89. Among those in attendance that day who were suitably impressed with Lenglen's excellence were King George V and Queen Mary.
32. Bohn, *Heroes & Ballyhoo*, 1.
33. This may have been in part because "the American public enjoyed unprecedented prosperity" (Bohn, *Heroes & Ballyhoo*, 1) during this time. Unlike Europe, where many countries had to rebuild from the devastation inflicted by World War I, the United States did not face the huge task of rebuilding.
34. See, for example, Jane Leavy, "Introduction: In Extremis," in *The Best American Sports Writing, 2011*, ed. Jane Leavy (New York: Houghton Mifflin, 2011), xvii. See also Bohn, *Heroes & Ballyhoo*, 249.
35. Bohn did not include Lenglen among his list of athletes who made up this Golden Age. However, several American sport history texts included her in their lists of key figures during the period. See, for example, Richard O. Davies, *Sports in American Life: A History*, 2nd ed. (Malden, MA: Wiley-Blackwell, 2012); Elliott J. Gorn and Warren Goldstein, *A Brief History of American Sports*, 2nd ed. (Urbana: University of Illinois Press, 2013); and Benjamin G. Rader, *American Sports: From the Age of Folk Games to the Age of Televised Sports*, 6th ed. (Upper Saddle River, NJ: Prentice Hall, 2009).
36. Gorn and Goldstein, *A Brief History of American Sports*, 202.
37. Martha Reid, "Folklore and Fairy Tales: Babe Didrikson Revealed," in *A Locker Room of Her Own: Celebrity, Sexuality, and Female Athletes*, ed. David C. Ogden and Joel Nathan Rosen (Jackson: University Press of Mississippi, 2013), 7; Donald J. Morozek, "The Amazon and the American Lady," in *From "Fair Sex" to Feminism: Sport and the Socialization of Women in the Industrial and Post-Industrial Eras*, ed. J. A. Mangan and Roberta J. Park (Abingdon, Oxon, England: Routledge, 1987), 294; and Gerd von der Lippe, "Henie, Sonja," in *International Encyclopedia of Women and Sports*, vol. 2, ed. Karen Christensen, Allen Guttmann, and Gertrud Pfister (New York: Macmillan Reference, 2001), 501–2.

38. Jennifer Hargreaves, *Sporting Females: Critical Issues in the History and Sociology of Women's Sports* (London: Routledge 1994), 116.

39. Greenberg, *Dare to Compete*.

40. Parsons, *The Ultimate Encyclopedia of Tennis*.

41. Morley, "Suzanne Lenglen: The First Diva of Tennis."

42. Lumpkin, *Women's Tennis*, 21.

43. Pileggi, "The Lady in the White Silk Dress."

44. Ray Bowers, "Suzanne Lenglen and the First Pro Tour," The Tennis Server: Between the Lines, October 31, 1999, at http://www.tennisserver.com/lines/lines_99_10_31.html, accessed July 9, 2015.

45. Collins, *The Bud Collins History of Tennis*; and Parsons, *The Ultimate Encyclopedia of Tennis*.

46. Parsons, *The Ultimate Encyclopedia of Tennis*, 89.

47. Pileggi, "The Lady in the White Silk Dress."

48. Collins, *The Bud Collins History of Tennis*; and Parsons, *The Ultimate Encyclopedia of Tennis*.

49. Steve Flink, *The Greatest Tennis Matches of the Twentieth Century* (Danbury, CT: Rutledge Books, 1999), 1.

50. Bohn, *Heroes & Ballyhoo*.

51. Parsons, *The Ultimate Encyclopedia of Tennis*.

52. Hart, review of *The Goddess and the American Girl*, 56; and Franz Lidz, "Tennis Everyone? When Helen Wills and Suzanne Lenglen Clashed on the Riviera in 1923, the Whole World Awaited the News," *Sports Illustrated Vault*, October 16, 1991, 90–94, at http://www.si.com/vault/1991/10/16/125154/tennis-everyone-when-helen-wills-and-suzanne-lenglen-clashed-on-the-riviera-in-1926-the-whole-world-awaited-the-news, accessed July 18, 2014.

53. Wade and Rafferty, *Ladies of the Court*, wrote that a crowd of four thousand people watched the famous match between Lenglen and Wills.

54. Lidz, "Tennis Everyone?"

55. Wade and Rafferty, *Ladies of the Court*, 47.

56. Flink, *The Greatest Tennis Matches*, 4. Multiple sources referred to Lenglen's practice of sipping brandy between changeovers. Michael Bohn acknowledges that "other tennis players in the 1920s often resorted to spirits in an attempt to lift a flagging body" (*Heroes & Ballyhoo*, 254). Others referring to Lenglen's practice of sipping brandy include Gilbert, "The Vicar's Daughter"; Parsons, *The Ultimate Encyclopedia of Tennis*; and Wade and Rafferty, *Ladies of the Court*.

57. Flink, *The Greatest Tennis Matches*, 4.

58. Ibid.

59. Wade and Rafferty, *Ladies of the Court*.

60. Engelmann, *The Goddess*, 243–44.

61. Ibid., 248.

62. Ibid., 252.

63. The amount of Lenglen's contract must be placed in context; at the time, Babe Ruth was earning $70,000 annually, which was more than the US president made in one year. Lenglen's tour would last only four months. See Engelmann, *The Goddess*.

64. Bowers, "Suzanne Lenglen and the First Pro Tour."
65. Ibid.; and Engelmann, *The Goddess*.
66. Bowers, "Suzanne Lenglen and the First Pro Tour."
67. Engelmann, *The Goddess*, 283.
68. Ibid., 327.
69. Gilbert, "The Vicar's Daughter," 191.
70. Ibid., 187.
71. Susan Cahn, *Coming On Strong: Gender and Sexuality in Twentieth-Century Women's Sport* (Cambridge, MA: Harvard University Press, 1994); Engelmann, *The Goddess*; Gilbert, "The Vicar's Daughter"; and Hargreaves, *Sporting Females*.
72. Hargreaves, *Sporting Females*, 116.
73. Cahn, *Coming On Strong*, 48.
74. Ibid., 49.
75. Gilbert, "The Vicar's Daughter," 188.
76. Ibid., 196.
77. Ibid., 198. This also brings to mind jazz phenom Louis Armstrong's behind-the-scenes approach to political activism; outwardly, he continued to appear traditionally subservient to mainstream expectations, while clandestinely he supported civil rights–related causes. See Max Jones and John Chilton, *Louis: The Louis Armstrong Story, 1900–1971* (London: Da Capo Press, 1971), 203–6.
78. Hargreaves, *Sporting Females*.
79. Bohn, *Heroes & Ballyhoo*; and Pileggi, "The Lady in the White Silk Dress."
80. Bohn, *Heroes & Ballyhoo*, 250.
81. Engelmann, *The Goddess*, 47.
82. Laney, *Covering the Court*, 88.
83. Engelmann, *The Goddess*, 254.
84. Gilbert, "The Vicar's Daughter," 191.
85. Ibid., 191–92.
86. Laney, *Covering the Court*, 36.
87. Wade and Rafferty, *Ladies of the Court*, 35–36.
88. Hargreaves, *Sporting Females*, 116.
89. Baz Luhrmann, dir., *The Great Gatsby*, starring Leonardo DiCaprio and Tobey Maguire, Warner Brothers, 2013; and Morley, "Suzanne Lenglen: The First Diva of Tennis."
90. Bohn, *Heroes & Ballyhoo*, 250.
91. Alan Little, *Suzanne Lenglen: Tennis Idol of the Twenties* (London: Wimbledon Lawn Tennis Museum, 1988), 21; and Gilbert, "The Vicar's Daughter," 190.
92. Gilbert, "The Vicar's Daughter," 190.
93. Greenberg, *Dare to Compete*.
94. Hargreaves, *Sporting Females*, 116.
95. Ibid.
96. Parsons, *The Ultimate Encyclopedia of Tennis*, 89.
97. Gilbert, "The Vicar's Daughter," 196.
98. Bohn, *Heroes & Ballyhoo*, 250.
99. Wade and Rafferty, *Ladies of the Court*, 44.

100. Pileggi, "The Lady in the White Silk Dress."

101. Ibid.

102. A. E. Crawley, "Suzanne: A Technical Study," *Daily Mail*, July 4, 1919, 4; cited in Gilbert, "The Vicar's Daughter," 192.

103. Morley, "Suzanne Lenglen: The First Diva of Tennis."

104. "Liberated," Merriam-Webster, at http://www.merriam-webster.com/dictionary/liberated, accessed July 8, 2015.

105. Morley, "Suzanne Lenglen: The First Diva of Tennis."

106. Ibid.; Engelmann, *The Goddess*; and Gilbert, "The Vicar's Daughter."

107. "Revolutionary," Merriam-Webster, at http://www.merriam-webster.com/dictionary/revolutionary, accessed July 8, 2015.

108. Morley, "Suzanne Lenglen: The First Diva of Tennis."

109. Curry Kirkpatrick, "Steppin' Out: In Her Third Season as a Pro, 17-Year-Old Monica Seles Has Fashioned Herself into a Cross between Suzanne Lenglen and Madonna," *Sports Illustrated Vault*, May 27, 1991, 58–64.

110. Gilbert, "The Vicar's Daughter," 188; and Hargreaves, *Sporting Females*.

Valentino Rossi
A Uniquely British Look at an Italian Motorsport Legend
—Sean Bell

Introduction

Having won world championships and broken several records in elite-class racing, the Italian Valentino Rossi is, internationally speaking, the most popular motorcycle racer of his day. Giacomo Agostini, who raced in the sixties and seventies, was the last Italian to be so heralded around the world for racing motorcycles. But since Agostini's run, Rossi has been by far the sport's most discussed rider, eclipsing various other stars in the field since his initial appearance on the circuit.

Clearly, stories about Rossi sell the most motorcycle newspapers and magazines, despite much competing coverage generated by British rider Cal Crutchlow (who finished fifth in the world rankings behind Rossi in 2013) and the emergence of an outstandingly talented new world champion, Marc Márquez of Spain. Indeed, the top story, even in Britain with its emergent local hero and the new young maestro to fascinate racing fans, remains Valentino. At nearly every track on the international circuit, Rossi draws by far the most loyal and overt fans. It is only in Spain, home to three of the top factory riders (Dani Pedrosa, former champion Jorje Lorenzo, and Márquez), that anyone else's fans outnumber the yellow-emblazoned hordes of Rossi devotees. In this regard, Valentino Rossi is an international phenomenon, a true sport celebrity by every measure with one foot firmly planted in the rich tradition of great motor racing stars of the past and the other in a space reserved, so far, only for himself.

A sense of this space requires a description of what MotoGP actually is. But rather than offering merely a thumbnail history, I will attempt to compare it with other forms of international motorsports as a way of demonstrating its uniqueness in this varied world. To be sure, fame is difficult to quantify in some respects. Rossi is one of the most famous and admired men in his native Italy, while he is merely "very famous" among those who follow motorsport in Great Britain, the United States, and other countries. And yet his is a fragmented sporting fame, dispersed throughout different nations in different ways, throughout the public, or publics, within those countries. He is nowhere near as famous as, say, Muhammad Ali, but the universality of international fame, spread however thinly, suggests that different nations must share some similar attitudes to the athlete or motorcycle racer and, therefore, some similar attitudes to international competition and motorcycle racing.

Motorsport itself is a peculiar kind of sport, as its genesis and development coincide exactly with the development of industrialisation and mass communications. The development of the concept of a public that is both actively engaged in these processes and actively observing them evolved into the concept of a section of that public that is most concerned with motorsport. These constituencies differ from country to country, and a useful exploration of the most important differences can be made by comparing Britain with America. To be sure, automotive culture differs substantially from one place to another. How roads and vehicles are actually used by the public, how they relate to public transport, and the prevalent social attitudes to both vary greatly across Europe, let alone further afield. I suggest that the appreciation of motor racing, while reflecting major cultural differences from country to country, is more universal and genuinely more international than it might look from the point of view of partisan fans.

Valentino Rossi's rise through the ranks of motorcycle racing began when he was a child, and his peak (or plateau) of performance coincided with historic developments in the sport itself in which he excels. MotoGP, the elite form of prototype motorcycle racing that replaced the previous era of two-stroke 500 cc Grand Prix, arrived in Rossi's third elite season, when he was at the height of his powers. He remains the only person to have won world titles on both the 500 cc two-strokes and the four-stroke MotoGP machines.[1] This and his seven elite-class titles have cemented his place among the greats, but whether he is the greatest of all time (GOAT) is hotly debated among race followers.

Rossi also has his critics. His continuing popularity looks set to be translated into a new career when he retires (should he survive his remaining seasons as a racer, given a typical career span in the sport). Arguably, his legacy as a businessman, corporate spokesman, and continuing ambassador for motorsport and motorcycling promises to be as unusual, if not as telling, as the career trajectory he has already demonstrated.

The high risk of serious injury and even death in motorcycle sport must also be addressed. Racers are not trying to get killed; they understand the risks better than anyone.[2] What cannot be denied, however, is that risk is an important aspect of both the sport and its appreciation. In an increasingly risk-averse era, particularly here in Britain,[3] interest in motorcycle racing, even riding a motorcycle on the road as a form of common transportation, is increasingly considered eccentric. This gives rise to the prejudice that racers are psychopaths bent on setting a bad example for others. Despite such prejudices, however, Rossi remains a public relations asset for both motorcycle racing in particular and motorcycling in general, and he is often credited with promoting responsible two-wheeled activity around the world regardless of the cloud of suspicion that has begun to linger over the institution.

Motorsport is a living example of how risk can be both admired and controlled, while simultaneously being embedded in a society that generally abhors risk. Like all sports, it has contested the borders between real life and the special conditions of a playing field or circuit of competition; therefore, its foremost personality is as an exemplar of the benefits of a sanguine approach to risk management. What some deem a *precautionary principle* suggests that one should consider both the risks of *doing* something, and those of *not* doing something. The litigious and blame-spreading culture of many modern societies encourages people to assume that the risk of *not* doing something will generally be advantageous, a conclusion that seems to increasingly plague sport, and motorsport in particular.

To be candid, writing from a British perspective about the international fame of an Italian may at first glance seem incongruous, but this vantage point may be useful for our purposes. To write the same story from Rossi's native land would require me first to adjust to his immense popularity and esteem in Italy and then peer toward the international horizon. It would be like trying to describe the international fame of British 500 GP champion Barry Sheene during the late 1970s. Sheene was a contemporary of Formula One champion James Hunt and a widely recognised mainstream national celebrity in Britain while also very popular abroad. An international perspective on his fame at the time might have best come from outside Great Britain.

In this chapter, I will examine why Valentino Rossi enjoys a peculiar kind of fame and why his reputation is greater than that of others who have also achieved great success in the same sport. To this end, I will explain what is unusual about Rossi and the sport of MotoGP from my own specifically British perspective, focussing on how we have arrived at the present situation before speculating on what the future may hold for the man and his sport. First, I must define the notion of international fame itself before I can dig more deeply into the specific Rossi mystique as it has been manifested through his years on the circuit.

The Contradictions of International Fame and Worldwide Renown

When considering an international reputation of any kind, one must consider one's own viewpoint and its relation to the many viewpoints across national and cultural borders. The many extant conceptions of the "public" used for various purposes in social, academic, and commercial analyses are partial and concerned with specific aims within specialised disciplines. They are, therefore, typically poor models to employ meaningfully in relation to a broad, subjective concept such as sporting reputation, even within a single national boundary, the realm of only one "public."

International fame of any kind suggests in this particular case a universal, perhaps even catholic appeal of an athlete to a very large number of people who may have little else in common. Given this, I will try to explain why Valentino Rossi fascinates me, and why I think he fascinates others of very different outlooks, cultures, and national standpoints, while harnessing in this effort my particular view of the globe from my home in Britain, rather than try to traipse too broadly out into a more general theoretical space.

Valentino Rossi's global persona exemplifies the contradiction between national and international sporting reputations. One's conception of fame depends on the conception of society that one employs to investigate it. Fame, understood beyond the national level, may consist of a broad or universal admiration for a given individual among the public across many countries, but it must physically reside in different nations. To say "universal" in this context is to employ the term in the sense of something broadly applicable, rather than actually everywhere. A ten-millimetre spanner (in lay terms, a wrench), for example, works on all ten-millimetre bolts, so they are universal, but not all bolts are ten millimetres, nor is everything bolted. If a good explanation of fame, in general or in particular, depends upon an analysis of a society, it follows that such an analysis would have some conception of the public within which that fame is communicated. Motor racing appreciation differs across Europe, in the Middle and Far East, and in North America; we consider the character of the publics in each country to differ broadly.

To assess someone's reputation, that individual's relationship to the public is the most important consideration. Unfortunately, the "public" as a concept is very difficult to pin down. For instance, the opening words of Jürgen Habermas's *The Structural Transformation of the Public Sphere* (1961) read: "The use of the words 'public' and 'public sphere' betrays a multiplicity of concurrent meanings." Habermas goes on to note: "Their origins go back to various historical phases and, when applied synchronically to the conditions of a bourgeois society that is industrially advanced and constituted as a social-welfare state, they fuse into a clouded amalgam." Here, he argues that "the very conditions that make the inherited language seem inappropriate appear to require these words, however confused their employment. Not just ordinary language, especially as it bears the imprint of bureaucratic and mass-media jargon, but also the sciences—particularly jurisprudence, political science, and sociology—do not seem capable of replacing traditional categories like 'public' and 'private,' 'public sphere,' and 'public opinion,' with more precise terms."[4]

Whichever method one uses to dissect a public at a national level will fail in one sense or another, because considering a national population simply as a mass is as pointless as considering it as a vast interface of individual atoms. Great blocs of taste, opinion, and commercial commitment can be sawn from the populace for various purposes. Western societies include many kinds of organisations that split and order populations according to purpose: marketers look at income bands, sociologically defined groups, and data that may help express preferences; medics can measure groups at risk of disease; and politicians, heads of charities, campaigners, and opinion formers may identify strategic groups of more or less influential components of public opinion on specific issues.

Increasingly, one can argue that the specialised, sample-based statistical methods of investigating large numbers of people are giving way to algorithm-based analyses of "big data," as deployed by Internet companies,[5] click by click; this can reveal all kinds of useful correlations. Both techniques may help academic study and the investigation of particular groups, but they are not very helpful in describing a whole public, in even a single country. The sense of public that exists across borders can be measured and compared, but it cannot be defined or schematised usefully with any currently available techniques. To simplify the public into interactive component spheres by one category, such as country, would naturally violate the attempt to integrate those spheres internationally. Conversely, to theoretically atomise the individuals of the world public would produce a mesh of existing concrete interactions that build into a map of the world that is many times bigger than the actual planet itself. So I first look at the world from where I exist and base my observations accordingly.

Inconveniently, I must also argue that, in another sense, there is no such thing as international fame. Of course there are imagined international communities and their objective expression in multinational crowds gathering trackside for MotoGP and other events. But, as with national markets within an actual global economy, fans, fan bases, and reputations must exist concretely within the constraints of a national perspective.

We speak of a global economy and can theorise and abstract from its vast interconnectedness, but to usefully and practically intervene in it, theoretically or physically, we have to think globally while acting locally. An international perspective can only be imagined, or abstracted, it being a Frankenstein's monster made of national parts, nowhere embodied in a living international person or population, except as the entire world.

Given these challenges, I will not attempt analyses of all the separate fames enjoyed by Valentino Rossi across all the different countries where he is famous, as they simply would not mesh. As a national hero, he cannot walk about unmolested in Italy, apart from in his hometown, Tavullia (in Marche), a special zone where the Italian and international paparazzi have (at least so far) enforced a curious pact of non-interference.[6] Certainly, this immunity may not hold true elsewhere.

American Admiration

The American portion of Rossi's fame may seem an insignificant drop in the ocean of sporting appreciation in that country. The United States' international motorsport fans have a strong component that appreciates world renown. I cannot find the origin of the rumour that Brad Pitt once said he wished that he were Valentino Rossi, but the multimillionaire Hollywood actor has visited Rossi on the starting grid and in the pits, perhaps corroborating the story, and has spoken several times, and reverentially so, of his admiration for the racer.[7]

Brad Pitt is much more famous than Rossi, but he is at the same time less admired than the racer, despite Rossi's constituency of fans being minuscule by comparison with such a successful Hollywood actor. Much as one might admire Pitt's movies and talent, he will not die from a bad performance on the screen, possibly unlike with a bad mistake on the racetrack. The activity of international sport, particularly such a dangerous one as MotoGP, will encourage people toward admiration in a way that acting or some other less dangerous activity simply cannot.

There is a universal, international admiration for great sporting heroes that inspires and encourages excellence through an objective appreciation of achievement. Certainly, while the followers of MotoGP are all citizens of one country or another, they can all watch and share similar (but not identical) feelings about the unfolding events, whatever their national perspective. However, how they interpret those events must surely differ.

Rossi's fans around the world appreciate human achievement, regardless of differences in how this appreciation dovetails with each fan's relationship with his or her national consciousness. For this reason, the ongoing received story of Rossi's rise, zenith, and something between a legendary stasis and a very cushioned fall is important toward understanding his peculiarity. Motor racing, like other American sports, diverged and created its own forms, many of them only now being practised outside America. American motorsport also has a class-cultural value that is far less prevalent in Europe. There is an American perception, however arrived at, that motorsport in general is a more proletarian or lower-class activity than American football, baseball, basketball, tennis, or golf—the sports Americans follow nationally and internationally across class and regional divisions.

Valentino Rossi comes from a middle-class background, albeit an unusual one. His father was a motorcycle and car racer, and he was brought up racing, riding, and driving at local venues with his father and his motor-racing friends. His middle-class status hinges on the affluent—but not rich—lifestyle his parents were able to give him, but the sport he races in has a working-class affiliation in both Britain and America. Motor racing in his native Italy is of course not class neutral, but it has a cross-class status. But before focussing on the making of a MotoGP champion, we should consider the development of motorcycle sport alongside the national perspectives of some of the places where that development took place.

Class and Culture in Motor Racing in Britain and America

The classic—and class—differentiation between motorsport in the United States and Europe is typified by that mythical and apocryphal comparison between NASCAR and Formula One. The supposed parallel development of the two sports can be summarised as follows: the American backwoods moonshiners who tuned big cars to outrun federal tax collectors, and then started racing them against each other; and, before and after this, European aristocrats who borrowed airfields, built racing circuits beside their country houses, and then gradually brought in mechanics, drivers, and manufacturers to run races for high stakes. Class in both places is much more complicated than that.

The cost of early, pre–World War I cars was astronomical compared to those of a few years' later, in both Britain and America. The post–World War I economies of both countries were clearly different, but both had large numbers of war-produced motorbikes and other vehicles on the market that were sold to a wider section of the public than had been able to afford them before. The same was true to an even greater extent in both the numbers of machines and the resulting social penetration after World War II in both Europe and America.

Car ownership was much more common in the United States than in Britain until the 1960s, for several reasons. The motorcycle, which often included a sidecar to carry the wife and kids, was the proletarian means of transport of the British working class for far longer than it had been in the United States, where the Ford Model T supplanted two- and three-wheelers out of some of its automotive class development. The British motorcycle champions of the 1940s, 1950s, and 1960s were working-class heroes in every sense of the word, regardless of their actual origins.

Around the world, lower-class race drivers emerged as soon as low-cost vehicles were made available to them. Pre–World War I forms of American motorcycle racing, such as board tracking, in which riders reached high speeds on wooden circuits, gave way by the interwar years to different disciplines such as short track (on prepared horseracing circuits).

Worldwide, as the available machines became more specialised after World War II, so too did the racers. Uniquely, American motorcycle racing's national championship[8] was multidisciplined for most of its history, combining short-track, off-road motocross, and enduro-style events and track and street-based races on asphalt, using a variety of machines. Indeed, the sideways skills that racers learned on the oval short tracks helped many great American champions, such as Kenny Roberts, develop their overall skills in the 1970s and 1980s, when the elite Grand Prix 500 cc two-strokes of the time spun their wheels, even on hot, fresh asphalt.

European riders today practice this American form[9] alongside motocross and supermoto[10] as part of their preparation for MotoGP. Cal Crutchlow and others have been coached in the controlled sliding the sport requires, while Valentino Rossi has built his own short track at his Italian home. Marc Márquez, granted the traditional elite champion's right to choose the form of off-season race, invited the short-track world champion Brad Baker along with international racing stars of many different motorcycle racing disciplines,[11] losing only to the American.

America has developed and maintained racing events run nowhere else, but it still competes in the elite international events such as Formula One (F1) and MotoGP, among many others. In the pre–World War II and immediate post-war eras, individual nations attached great prestige to their achievements in the elite Grand Prix. These sports now are internationally corporatist, moving world stages of branding erected in each country, whether on purpose-built facilities or on temporarily converted public streets.

While every country once diverged in its local forms of motorcycle racing, the international events provided a testing point for all the top riders, introducing the universal measure of all and the iron discipline of the stopwatch around a given distance. The standardisation of motorsport takes place at the international level as the races and their rules evolve while being distorted by the pressures of international finance and related manufacturers' and media interests. But success seems to breed success. A few years ago, all the top riders were Italian. By the early twenty-first century, most of them are Spanish. Once, Americans and Australians broke the Europeans' stranglehold, although long before that British riders and their machines set the standards.

The United States and Great Britain have at different times had a strong influence both on motorcycle racing and on international culture. The term "chopper," now associated with the Captain America bike ridden by Peter Fonda in the 1969 film *Easy Rider*, once referred to a Harley-Davidson that had been stripped down, lightened, and had its frame cut for better steering geometry. These practices tended away from racing and toward the customisation scene. Early chopper builders are thought to have exceeded the normal ambitions of home tuning, so that their local, relatively inexpensive Harley-Davidsons could keep up with the expensive imported 1940s and 1950s Triumphs and Nortons. Automotive culture is strewn with examples of vehicles designed for one thing being repurposed for something else; such modifications, serving both practical and cultural purposes, can be found everywhere. Thousands of war surplus Harleys still do taxi service on the streets of Indian cities, for example.

Harley-Davidsons are still the most successful racing bikes ever, but this is entirely due to their competitiveness on their home dirt, on oval tracks. They can also be very successful in drag racing, another quintessentially American motorsport,[12] but the lack of American manufacturers may have discouraged some US support for events in which only foreign machines take part, such as MotoGP and world championships in enduro and motocross. American motorsports may have siphoned some part of the audience away from international events; the American Grand Prix, at the new Circuit of the Americas in Austin, Texas, is as well supported as any other rounds in other countries. And there will be a big yellow contingent cheering for Valentino Rossi.

Cultural exchange between Britain and the United States is striking in its extent: America sends Chuck Berry and Elvis Presley to Great Britain, while the UK sends back the Beatles and the Rolling Stones. America creates the dominant film and television industries that made *Gone with the Wind*, *Ben-Hur*, *The Silence of the Lambs*, *Star Trek*, and *The Wire*, while Britain sends its best actors to play many of the key roles (especially the villains). And America sent—perhaps lent—its resources to rebuild Britain after World War II. But the sports cultures have stayed largely separate because one must be British to have a British attitude to sport. To wit, the British consider that their country is largely responsible for inventing international sport and sportsmanship, whereas Americans have invented their own sports, which the rest of the world seems at best ambivalent about.

The British Sporting Perspective

An important and unique feature of British attitudes to sport is that of international ownership. The British Empire, particularly in its final years, disseminated a vast amount of British culture across the globe, and it is no accident of history that the United States in large part brought about the end of that empire. American sports, especially basketball, are minority sports throughout Europe and are popular in Britain. But no British team can play for these sports' top honours. Talented basketball players from Europe or Africa, for instance, go to America to play in the NBA, in exactly the same way that American players of football, rugby, or cricket emigrate to countries with top-flight leagues in those sports, where they can better develop their talents.

The 2012 London Olympics opening ceremony featured a romanticised display of nurses and sick children, pleasing the British public with the notion of international admiration of their National Health Service. In a like manner, we offset the historical crimes of colonialism, empire, and imperialism against the positive contributions we believe to have been made by our sport: cricket is the national sport in India, Sri Lanka, Pakistan, and Bangladesh. Recently, Afghanistan also took up the sport after refugees fleeing to Pakistan picked it up. Cricket seems the only thing that (for now) can unite the disparate nations of the West Indies. It is also Australia's most important national sport, because it is played across the east/west divide of Australian Rules football (similar to Gaelic football in Ireland) and football (the global, rather than the American variety). Cricket itself was a partial template for the development of sport and ideas around sport all over the world.

Britain ceded ownership of football to the rest of the world a long time ago but retains the historical credit for inventing it. Tennis, golf, and rugby are positive by-products of Britain's formerly dominant military and cultural influence. Britain has recently bowed to reality and ceded pre-eminence in the administration of cricket to India, but that sport remains in some sense English, everywhere described as *quintessentially* so. Until Andy Murray, a British man had not won Wimbledon since Fred Perry in the 1930s, but the tournament itself, the only Grand Slam event held on grass, is world famous. Golf has also migrated from its Scottish origins into the international creative commons. Cricket players of all countries long to score a hundred or take five wickets at Lord's,[13] still known in cricket circles as "Headquarters," even though cricket central is now arguably in Mumbai, the megacity and Asian economic powerhouse formerly known as Bombay, and in the Middle East. A good performance at Lord's secures immortal fame, however, as the names are recorded on the wall at the ancient grounds.

The British perspective of international sport is therefore national and relatively objective, although in a curiously self-serving way. This also works the other way: defeat in cricket, tennis, rugby, golf, and especially football (particularly by the United States) is used as an example of social decline and the loss of the spirit of our sporting ancestors. Rare successes are thus made sweeter, except against the US football team, where it is expected.

Elite motor racing in Britain has a place in the national consciousness partly due to Britain's manufacturing pre-eminence up to the post–World War II period, and partly due to its ongoing engineering and creative contributions to the sport. Most F1 teams, for example, are based in England; all the gearboxes in IndyCar racing are made in England; and much engineering research and development of racing technology, which is transferred to both racing and road-going vehicles, also takes place here.

There are peculiarities in British attitudes to sporting fame. The British are the first to admit that they build people up only to tear them down, and they do not reserve this treatment solely for athletes but for almost anyone in the public eye, from entertainers to reality TV stars, politicians, and members of the royal family. This tendency does not seem to be exclusively British, however. International sporting success by British athletes will certainly see them being honoured, and will earn them money, even if those so honoured never make it to the top of their field. Tim "The Tiger" Henman was very famous and routinely honoured for his six Grand Slam titles, although he never won Wimbledon, his home country's most cherished tournament![14]

The British buy far fewer motorcycles than people on the continent, but they have historically accounted for a proportionately large slice of the European sports bike market, comprising the production machines that most closely resemble MotoGP prototypes ridden by Rossi and his competitors.[15] Motor racing has gotten deep under the skin of its enthusiasts in Britain, though a minority of the population, representing perhaps the ongoing reconstruction of the old national psyche. While many countries express their national consciousness through international sport, Britain has often invented or codified the very sport itself, thus extending the connection a British sports fan has with a particular sport's ongoing narrative and development. International motorsport is, in British eyes at least, partially a British creation. The Tourist Trophy (TT)[16] on the Isle of Man is among the most famous motorsport events in the world, for example, even though, because of its extreme danger, prototypes no longer race there.[17]

The section of the British public that follows, appreciates, or is concerned with MotoGP is not easily defined in obvious terms. Only a minority of motorcyclists are interested in it. Armchair fans of the sport (like me, although I have ridden motorcycles for more than thirty years) would not fall predictably into petrol-head categories.

F1 fans do not have to own or race cars. Similarly, readers of Britain's *Motor Cycle News* are not all motorcyclists. That organ's coverage of new road bikes, products, travel, and the like holds no interest for some of its readers. They read only the sport's coverage, especially MotoGP, World Superbikes (WSB), British Superbikes (BSB) and Speedway.[18]

The Spartan Upbringing of an Elite Motorcycle Racer

British motorsport fans have in their very DNA an appreciation and respect for those who seem to enhance, enrich, or progress the sport they take part in.

It is in this context that Valentino Rossi stands very much in the tradition of admired foreigners of the past, but his exploits could only have been accomplished recently. Whether one considers him the GOAT, his career marked both the end of one era in motorcycle sport and the genesis and development of another. As no one now looks likely to ever equal John Surtees's achievement of world championships in both the elite forms of motorcycle and car racing,[19] no one else could likewise perform the role Rossi did at the time he did. This "untouchability" probably enhances his reputation worldwide, but it is especially admired in Britain.

During a race (or qualifying round), the rider performs a set of cognitive activities, in much the same way that a practised classical musician performs a concert. The countless hours of practice and conditioning all lead to the performance, but performances are a minuscule part of the process of creating the musician. Similarly with MotoGP, the race weekend is the apex of much technical development, manufacturing processes, physical conditioning and damage repair, and practice on the prototype machines themselves and on other machines designed to promote particular forms of fine control. While a classical violinist may still use an eighteenth-century instrument, the fastest riders can only really race using the very latest parts.

MotoGP riders might be said to have a childhood that is both curtailed and extended. Most now at the front of the grid have been racing bikes in one way or another since they were five or six years old. Rossi rode his first bike before he was three. When, as young teenagers, racers compete in national or MotoGP support championships, known as Moto3 and Moto2, they may already be bringing a personal sponsorship to any ride deal they can negotiate. By their twenties, they must take their shot at the elite class, whether they come from Moto2 or WSB or elsewhere, and their career in MotoGP will not last beyond their late thirties, even if they win races and championships. From a very early age, these riders are chasing sponsorships, and practising and physically training very hard, because success is well rewarded.

Rossi usually ranks among the top fifty highest-paid athletes in the world. His competitiveness on the track notwithstanding, his company, VR46,[20] is a public relations and representative agency for upcoming talent, suggesting that Rossi will be a force and a personality in MotoGP for some time in the future.

In his autobiography, *What If I Had Never Tried It*, Rossi describes how he was introduced to racing as a small child by his father, Graziano, himself a former motorcycle and car racer. In 1991, Rossi finished fifth in the Italian national kart championship, but graduation to the 100 cc national and European competitions at that time would have been a big financial commitment. Rossi also joined the mini-moto craze of the time and showed good speed. "My plan was still [for Valentino] to race on four wheels because I was scared he would get hurt on a bike. But two things changed this. First, he really, really liked minimoto, he used to spend all his days riding. Second, we realised that karts were getting too expensive for us, and we knew that car racing is all about money,"[21] Graziano told British journalist, author, and broadcaster Mat Oxley.

Rossi's parents nonetheless had to increase their financial and time commitments exponentially as the youngster progressed to real motorbikes and road racing in 1993 and subsequently into the classes below the Grand Prix of the time. The machines, the travel, and the costs accelerated with his development as a racer. The sacrifices the family of a racer must make can only be subsequently offset by great success.

Double MotoGP world champion Casey Stoner, an Australian who retired at the end of the 2012 season while still in his twenties, is considered by many to have been the best-ever rider and the fastest-ever elite motorcyclist. The sacrifices his parents made were even greater. Because Stoner was ambitious and obviously talented from a very early age, he persuaded his whole family to move to Britain and live in a trailer so that he could take part in European competitions, a step he considered essential to his development into a world MotoGP champion. Stoner was the only person to win a championship on a fast but difficult Ducati MotoGP bike (in 2007). A seat on a Ducati has since been considered a career graveyard.[22] Rossi's two seasons on a Ducati (2011 and 2012) were disastrous and certainly damaged his fans' claims that he was the GOAT, but he also seemed to have emerged from a very different place.

Rossi first raced as a little boy with a plastic Teenage Mutant Ninja Turtle stuck to his helmet, and a little sticker of a turtle is stuck to the side of his helmets to this day. At the cusp of his childhood and adult careers, he was known as Rossifumi, in homage to the wild riding styles and eye-catching graphics employed by his favourite Japanese road racers. He had very long hair, and many of the other riders thought he was a girl at first. But his easy-going enthusiasm made him very popular with sponsors. He was fast, good looking, and apparently had no professional reserve with reporters. He built up a fan club as he progressed through national championships, which is unusual in one so young, and he eventually arrived at the 500 cc elite class.

But Rossifumi, wild and popular as he had been, was crashing too much. The fearsome 500s had to be mastered before they could be used with precision. Rossi became the Doctor, reflecting his belief that, to win on the 500s, it was necessary to be calculating and to bring a surgeon's approach to the use of the machine's controls, particularly the throttle. And indeed, by the time of his zenith, Rossi's fans did not believe that he could be beaten.

Stoner's trenchant views on Valentino Rossi's talents and fame, explained in his own autobiography, *Pushing the Limits*, elegantly express broader criticisms of the Italian around the world. During the 2007 season, which Rossi had been expected to win, the Australian switched from a satellite Honda to the previously unsuccessful and difficult-to-handle Ducati. Perversely, when Stoner beat Rossi, many assumed that it was because the bike's ferocious power down the straights allowed him to catch up and pass him. Stoner described his Ducati as "a real pig" after his first test and worked hard to find how it could be ridden competitively. In the first race of the season in Qatar, Stoner qualified just five hundredths of a second behind Rossi. The riders swapped first and second positions for the whole twenty-two laps, Rossi's well-balanced Yamaha overtaking on the slower sections of the circuit and Stoner's Ducati overtaking on the exits of fast corners and the opening of the main straight. Stoner said:

> At the time, people refused to believe that Valentino could be beaten in a fair battle, so all the credit went to the Ducati's top speed, rather than the hard work we had put into testing as a team or our performance around the rest of the circuit that was required to stay with [the] Yamaha through the sections where it was far better suited. It was frustrating to us, but I was happy.[23]

The Importance of Personal Rivalry to Legend

Valentino Rossi attracted similar criticisms early in his career. From an early age, he was spotted by potential sponsors as a personality as well as a talented racer, and as a result some people always felt that he was being rewarded with machinery that he had not earned purely with skill.[24] He kept winning championships, however. Rossi and his contemporaries, those who had also come through the same school of very hard knocks alongside him, provided a succession of rivalries that added drama, personality, and extra emotion to the last seasons of two-stroke Grand Prix and the first of the new MotoGP.

Rossi's many rivalries are a staple of the ongoing drama of MotoGP. Ron Howard's *Rush*, a movie about the competition between bitter racetrack enemies James Hunt and Niki Lauda, illustrates the importance of personal rivalry. The film traces the pair first crossing swords in Formula Three before moving up to Formula One to contest the 1976 championship. In that season, Lauda crashed and was trapped in his burning car for a minute as other drivers stopped and desperately, and bravely, tried to pull him out. He sustained disfiguring facial burns and, worse, appalling respiratory damage that required frequent painful vacuums of damaged tissue from his lungs. In the film, as in real life, Lauda said that it was his determination to beat his rival that spurred him on to compete again in the same season, just weeks after his crash, and to later win three championships to Hunt's single 1976 title.[25]

Rossi's rivalries with fellow Italian Max Biaggi, Casey Stoner, Spaniards Sete Gibernau and Jorje Lorenzo, and others through his long career have the whiff of legend to motorcycle racing fans. Because of Rossi's career longevity, he has been racing with, and been beaten by, younger men for some years now, men who used to have posters of him on their bedroom or trailer walls when they were boys.

Rossi's wild track celebrations after a win were famous, and he continued them in the new MotoGP class for a while.[26] His riding, exploits, and personality launched MotoGP, and he is universally regarded as having brought a bigger and broader audience to MotoGP and to motorcycling generally—a true international "ambassador" for two wheels. The sport and the pastime of motorcycling does need advocates, because of the different attitudes to risk assumed by racers and by broader society. Motorsport differs from earlier sports because it is not notionally a competition just between human beings but also a competition between their manufactured objects. All sports played internationally change with the times. Motor racing is different, because its entire existence is an expression of the Industrial Revolution.

Modernity in Motion

Motor racing is arguably the classical sport of "modernity," however one might describe that controversial term, and it might naturally be assumed to be part of the old order by those with a more rigid definition of postmodernism. That the late nineteenth and early twentieth centuries produced the modern codified forms, or organisational templates, of all sports, even for newer ones such as snowboarding, is broadly agreed to by all. The cultural significance of sport in general and of the codified forms it takes in particular are greatly disputed along many lines. One aspect of this is the development of technology in sports equipment.

In this regard, MotoGP is different from the pre-twentieth-century sports that dominate our conceptions of sporting contests. Elite motor racing has always been as much a test of the machine as that of the rider—"driver" in some depictions—a necessary condition of its existence that must be considered when describing the reputation of the athlete within the sport and outside it. The only ancient sport comparable is horse or chariot racing. We assume that the jockey or driver is largely in charge and responsible for coaxing the best performance from the horse(s), but a jockey's reputation might be damaged by the perception that he or she always gets the best horse. This perception can coexist with the understanding that the best jockeys tend to be selected to ride the best horses. This tension found in horse racing becomes even more complicated and contradictory in elite motor racing, because the rider's huge team and multinational factory backers have actually built the horse.

A tennis racket, swimming costume, or even running shoe may be considered a machine in many respects, but the regulation of those tools in the sports that employ them is ongoing, vigilant against what is seen as unfair advantage in a notional contest between human beings. Technological development intended to maximise performance proceeds alongside the evolving rules of oversight of governing bodies that make decisions. They decide what kind of equipment usage constitutes cheating within the traditions of a particular sport.

Tennis has not listened to John McEnroe and returned to wooden rackets, but swimming has banned the use of sleek pressure suits and codified the swimming costume. Athletics is currently undecided about the use of running blades by athletes with missing lower limbs[27] alongside athletes with feet and running shoes. Equality between them seems unenforceable, because a footrace has hitherto always been run by athletes who all possess two feet.

The cricket bat was not standardised to its current four-and-a-quarter-inch width until a player for Reigate in the late eighteenth century turned up to play with a bat that was wider than the stumps.[28] The modern cricket bat, although still made predominantly of English or Kashmiri willow, is controversial because the new treatments used in its manufacture have multiplied the force with which a cricket ball can be struck. This is understandably seen by purists as unbalancing the contest between batter and bowler.[29]

In many respects, the inevitable use of new technology in new, old, or ancient sports highlights the contradictions between the notional contests between individuals within a social context. Most sports aim to provide a backdrop of equality between human competitors, but technology can confer advantages or disadvantages that could never have been foreseen during the formation of that sport's traditions.

Motor racing has partially adopted those kinds of codes and regulatory forms at most levels, but its elite forms, Formula One and MotoGP, are intrinsically all about the technology. While motorsports of all kinds still change, they are regulated to test the competitive attributes of particular types of machines. Some series will seek to make the machines raced as nearly equal as possible so that the riders are most clearly tested against each other. At the very top, MotoGP is notionally a competition based on prototypes. It is theoretically possible for anyone to race in a local enduro, motocross, or club circuit event with a hand-built prototype, but this would entail costs and developmental resources out of all proportion to any financial reward or corporate return. Most racing regulations dictate how far one can modify a standard road or off-road bike, or of what kind of bike is allowable in competition.

There are two championships in MotoGP (as there are in F1): one for the riders and one for the constructors, with both running simultaneously in each race.[30] The machines, though subject to many rules to slow them down, are supposed to be true prototypes, the fastest of the fast and the absolute pinnacle of automotive development.

There are other tensions in the duality of the MotoGP contest. Suspicion, like some kinds of sponsorship, can follow a rider from childhood. The MotoGP rider steps onto the grid both alone and with a huge team behind him (no women have ever competed in MotoGP, although a very few have raced in other classes).[31] His reputation is in his own hands on the track, in a sense, but he also represents a team comprising mechanics and manufacturers' high-ranking representatives and engineers. He is connected to public relations teams and is responsible to sponsors and their media concerns.

Controversy over team orders can stem from the clash of interests that can arise between the individual and his team. Sometimes, a faster rider is told to allow a slower one on the same team to overtake him, to gain more points for the team constructor championship, or to enhance a previous advantage the slower rider had in the rider championship.[32]

Contributions to the Rebirth of Prototype Motorcycle Racing

Within an unusual minority sport, glamorous, global, and rich as it may be, Valentino Rossi has enjoyed a unique position in both the development of MotoGP (a very recent formula for prototype motorcycle racing[33]) and its continued success. The same could be said of many athletes, of course, who have come to define moments of change or new understanding in their respective fields and gone on to lustre (or tarnish) their reputations by their contributions to broader social concerns.

When athletes become famous, they come to represent their sports in a public imagination broader than that of the fans of that sport. Particular sports themselves may become closely associated with their heroes. For example, Muhammad Ali redefined boxing, while Martina Navratilova changed tennis, particularly on the women's side of the ledger. There are certainly many other examples.

Valentino Rossi's role in the making of MotoGP, itself a remaking of elite motorcycle racing, secures his continuing global reputation. His four poor seasons (2010, 2011, 2012, and 2013[34]) are of a lesser historical importance. However, his reputation is still unfinished. As will be made clear below, Rossi has the potential to extend the remit of his fame, to broaden its influence within MotoGP, and motorsport in general, well beyond his racing career. This sets

Rossi apart from his contemporaries. But to fully flesh this idea out, we must first consider what all the other elite-class motorcycle racers do when they race, and the machines on which they race.

So for example, look at your own palm and enlarge it or reduce it so it can accommodate a man's extra-large glove. The elongated oval area described is a very approximate guide to the size and shape of a MotoGP bike's rear tyre contact patch with the track, under ideal conditions, when the bike is not leant over toward its maximum cornering angle of roughly 63 degrees. As the bike leans over to corner, this contact patch gets a bit smaller. There is a smaller contact patch on the front.

A MotoGP bike weighs around 170 kilos wet,[35] and when the rider sits on it, he adds up to about 65–75 kilos (although Repsol Honda rider Dani Pedrosa weighs only about 55 kilos). The front-running engines in MotoGP currently make more than 250 brake horsepower from 999 cubic centimetres. To put it another way, MotoGP bikes have approximately twice the power-to-weight ratio of a competitive NASCAR machine,[36] and just one rounded-profile tyre to drive and steer with against any car's two fat, flat-and-low-profile tyres. An F1 or IndyCar machine is an upside-down airplane that is sucked to the ground on corners by its "wings," the bodywork surrounding the machine that channels air to create downward force at high speeds. A MotoGP bike is aerodynamically unstable, not least because the rider must climb all over it to make it lean around a circuit.

Above eighteen to twenty miles per hour, all motorcycles steer with the handlebars pointing in the opposite direction of travel to the direction intended; this is called counter-steering.[37] On a very fast racing motorbike in a corner, the back wheel is rotating faster than the front wheel by about eight kilometres per hour (roughly five miles per hour), making it steer even more acutely and helping to bring the bike upright at the apex of the corner for the next straight.[38]

Electronic aids now help keep these beasts on the track, a fact that Rossi has often bemoaned. He supports safety measures but believes that the competition between riders is becoming too dependent on technical conveniences such as anti-wheelie controls, anti-lock braking, slipper clutches,[39] and electronic fuel injection mapping that can be adjusted even for different parts of the same track.

Even with these aids, the business of steering a bike at such high speeds, cornering with the rider's inside elbow scraping the ground while he supports the bike's stability with his inside knee, all while managing to prevent the back wheel from overtaking the front, is not for ordinary mortals. In track parlance, braking points and lines must be almost centimetre-perfect, while the forces under braking and acceleration are well over a gravity, even either side of a relatively slow corner. The riders must endure these forces without the aid of a bucket seat or restraints. They often race with severe injuries sustained from previous crashes.

The prototype machine, for the constructors and their sponsors, is the most important and costly component of the team. Riders may bring their own sponsorship and the skill needed to pilot the machines successfully, but they are transitory labour secondary to the fixed and increasing costs of the bikes. Perhaps someone somewhere knows how much a MotoGP bike actually costs, but the answer may make less sense than the question assumes.

As prototypes have been consistently employed in the sport for decades, developed technologies are sold at discounted rates to satellite teams. These machines use the same base bikes as the factory prototypes, but satellite teams develop them themselves with limited assistance from the manufacturer. Because of this, the latest prototype machines can hardly be described as commodities, despite the sale of some bikes to non-factory teams. The metal of the bikes—their physical machinery—is also only a part of the machine package whose purpose is to win a MotoGP race. The factory machine has extremely complicated engine management systems, suspension performance sensor systems, and other electronic gadgetry, and it requires very, very expensive software support.

Essentially, prototype race bikes are handmade, high-technology artefacts created for commercial purposes but not for direct sale. It costs many millions of pounds to run a bike at the back of the grid, but this cost is certainly dwarfed by the ongoing financial and resource-related commitments needed to be competitive for decades in a contest between prototypes. There were only six prototypes on the 2014 grid, from Ducati, Honda, and Yamaha. This leaves just six seats for the best emerging young riders, and only four of them have a chance of winning the title. These young riders will have spent their lives racing for those seats.

The Racer as Personification of Our Times

There was a transition in the late seventies and eighties in the nature of the two elite motorsports, from a relatively haphazard strategic alliance between teams, manufacturers, sponsors, and the media toward a much more professionalised and total activity.[40] The days of Barry Sheene having a post-race cigarette or James Hunt swigging bottles of champagne were long over by the mid-eighties, when, by common reckoning, the suits started taking over.

The great international car and bike racers of the late eighties and nineties, whether North American, Australian, Brazilian, or European, were mainly seen as steely-eyed professionals with total focus and ruthless efficiency, their humanity subjugated to the needs of their unbelievably expensive machines.

Their hearts beat to the metronome of precisely controlled aggression, their strategies complete and wide ranging, no efforts spared in the need to gain advantage over competitors. Before they shut their visors, you could see their "race face," a next-corner stare that encapsulated exactly all the glamorised, resurgent capitalist ideology of their times. They embodied Margaret Thatcher's maxim, "There is no alternative," alongside Gordon Gekko's "Greed is good."[41]

The riders and drivers exemplified contrary trends in society as well. Fame seems to reflect only a single personality when society holds up a mirror to some aspect of itself, particularly in international sport. It is reasonable to assume that the personality who embodies positive values or ideals is created by the cultural needs of the moment. It can be adjusted with the fortunes of the actual person. This actual person, after some time and particularly after death, becomes preserved in an historical amber, such that society would have to radically change before the reputation of the person could be remodelled, destroyed, or rehabilitated.

An F1 driver who exemplified these trends is Ayrton Senna. He was the most competitive and focussed of racers, but he was also a spiritual person and a devout Christian who did not in the flesh embody the values ordinarily associated with world-famous racing drivers. His competitiveness and focus are still admired now as are his historic contributions to motorsport, both as a great driver and as his sport's diplomat to the emerging markets of South America. He fatally crashed his Williams Renault while racing in the San Marino Grand Prix in 1994, preserving his reputation just as such tragic circumstances freeze virtually all celebrities who die young in a state of perpetual youthful vitality.

Great characters and rivalries have always run through motorcycle sport, but the golden age of the American, Australian, and European riders on 500 cc two-strokes of the nineties was surpassed by the arrival of a fast Italian youngster who already had his own fan club and supporters before even winning a national championship. Rossi won both the 125 cc and 250 cc world titles over a period of four years and nearly won in his rookie year on the furious 500 cc bikes. He won the 500 cc in his second year and then six more titles in the elite classes.[42]

Winning many races and championships alone does not, as we have seen with the examples above, ensure that a personality makes its mark on perceptions of a sport. The particular and personal appeal of Rossi to the British is set within the appreciation of motorcycle racers in general, but it also owes much to cultural developments. These cultural developments express themselves in different ways around the world, but the peculiar form they took in Britain, at the same time Valentino Rossi was becoming famous, are instructive.

Rossi, Authenticity, and His Appeal to the British

The elite motor racer was not typically a media-friendly beast in the late 1990s. Cue Valentino Rossi: he indulged in madcap, egomaniacal trackside celebrations when he won; he talked both passionately and modestly about his worries and fears of his competitors and of his strengths and weaknesses; he took a seemingly blasé attitude to competing vigorously and entertaining the crowd; and he was able to step up to the technical challenge of being the figurehead of an international team and the personal challenge of revamping his sport wholesale. Motorcycle racing was, like so many other elements of contemporary life, coming under attack from the increasingly risk-averse societies that hosted it.

Rossi kept his finger squarely on the pulse of race fans around the world. It is tempting to locate him in tandem with the rise of reality TV at the turn of the twenty-first century, embodying the newly mainstream concern with emotional intelligence—like a sort of 200 mph Princess Diana—but his is a peculiar appeal to British fans that perhaps relates to reality TV in a different way. *Big Brother*, a show in which people are locked in a house and surveiled, was first shown in Britain in 2000 and prompted the first British instance of a new kind of celebrity.

Jade Goody, an uneducated working-class loudmouth with an ample bosom and long bottle-blonde hair, did not win *Big Brother*, but she might have been Britain's first ordinary working-class person to gain spectacular fame without accomplishing any conspicuous achievement. By her own admission she was ignorant, foolish, and shallow, but she was brash enough to put herself on display regardless of consequence. Goody seemed to have no ability to self-edit and was a marked contrast to her calculating, scheming competitors.[43] She also had a back story that was tabloid gold: her mum was a one-armed lesbian, and her estranged dad was characterised as a black drug addict and dealer. She became the first person in Britain to become truly famous for being nothing but herself.

On becoming a celebrity, Goody competed in *Celebrity Big Brother* with, among others, Bollywood film star Shilpa Shetty. Goody faced an astonishing media witch hunt that branded her a low-class racist after, in an argument on the set, she referred to Shetty by the derogatory term "poppadom."[44] It is difficult to communicate the level of abuse Goody received without resorting to unedifying examples, but I can only compare her character assassination to that of Kate McCann in 2008, wrongly and bizarrely accused by the Portuguese police of killing her missing daughter Madeleine.

Goody retreated from the public gaze until invited to appear in the Indian version of *Celebrity Big Brother*,[45] along with her supposed race-hate victim, Shilpa Shetty. While in the *Big Brother* house, Goody received the news that she had terminal cancer, and she movingly shared that news with viewers shortly afterward, in a typically unguarded and uncalculated way. She returned home, and her reputation was rehabilitated into a kind of folk worship. Stephen Fry, a British TV pundit,[46] dubbed her the People's Princess[47] "from the wrong side of the tracks," and after she died, thousands attended her televised, rolling-news funeral. To summarise: she was the first person to be the kind of person she was; her reputation was restored after an apocalyptic British tabloid witch hunt; and she died young in public, as those who had persecuted her were transformed into disciples now eager to canonise her as a national treasure.

Valentino Rossi, in contrast, is a calculating and self-editing person with focus and considerable intellectual resources in his field. As one might imagine, a bike race is a reality rather than a simulation or an idealisation. A heart-breaking back story will not make anyone even one-hundredth of a second faster. The central aspect of Goody's appeal (and infamy) to the British public was her authenticity. Despite his great difference from Goody in personality and context, a great part of Rossi's appeal to the British race fan is likewise his authenticity, which he displays in several different ways. There are parallels between the development of Goody's unique form of fame and that of Rossi, which began a few years earlier in Italy and then more broadly in Europe, and roughly simultaneously in Britain.

The madcap Rossi celebrations, in homage to the more elaborate football goal-scorer celebrations of the period, spoke to the British about his sheer joy in what he had the privilege to do for a living. He also created his own designs for his helmet and riding gear, as well as some of the non-sponsor stickers and decals on his bikes. One memorable helmet design was especially visible when he tucked himself down for the straights; it featured his own face frozen in a comedic rictus of fear.[48] He said that he added the stickers he designed to his bike by his own hand. In his autobiography, he wrote that he liked going into the garage where he kept his bike, alone, so that he could spend time with it and decorate it himself.

Cynics may say that these unusual aspects of Rossi's projected personality were marketing ploys designed to sell gear and helmets and sticker sets and other VR46-branded commodities. They are indeed that, but these factors all add up, at least in the British perception, to a kind of authenticity, a desire to communicate a sense of the ordinary bloke doing the same things with his motorbike that other ordinary blokes do in their garages with their machines. Rossi is a lower-middle-class hero in an elite sport supported by the global working classes. He is far from ordinary, but the projection of an enthusiast's personality onto a sport that had become a little soulless was a winning and popular move.

Rossi's fame was encouraged by the powers that be within the sport, and, importantly, it was TV coverage gold. MotoGP *was* Rossi diving under his rivals, staging theatrics, and engaging with the cameras as if his best friends were pointing them at him. At the time, F1 was a bunch of automatons marching in a procession followed by the disappointing and stilted results of their media training. The switch to four-strokes at the launch of MotoGP was initially derided by purists. But Rossi's personal contribution to the development of MotoGP is hugely significant because his spanning of eras allowed the purists to accept a new form of racing that maintained continuity with the past, through himself.

Rossi could have quit while he was ahead, already a strong candidate for the GOAT, but he did not. His defection from the winning Honda to the unsuccessful Yamaha for the 2005 season showed his willingness to accept new challenges and become the underdog again. And again, he won. This behaviour is irresistible to many British fans, and it seems to translate to others around the world.

When Rossi went to Ducati with high hopes of turning the factory's fortunes around, he was again taking on another huge challenge. His failures during the two seasons he raced the Ducati prompted many to assume he would retire, but he returned to Yamaha, eager to try again. His fourth position in the 2013 season is another failure by his own standards, but he is even more admired for trying, for adding new layers to his legend. Of course, to actually preserve his reputation as it stood at that point, he would have to die.

Death, Conclusions, and Speculations

According to the oracular international measure of such matters, Twitter, Rossi is by far the world's most popular bike racer, despite being no longer the fastest.[49] He was closely followed on the track before he was followed on social media. He is not a new media star, his fame predating Web 2.0. His pre-existing fame transmuted into whatever new media became available over the course of his career, and it is likely to continue to do so.

Death confers a different status on a person's reputation in the public eye. He (or she) cannot further his career, so therefore he (or she) can't mess it up. But post-death fame is out of the hands of its subject, passing into a broad and complicated set of interactions that combine sports fans' perceptions with an ongoing metanarrative, one that follows the contours of the requirements of a far broader section of society than those who follow the sport.

Should Rossi be killed on any Sunday, it would become more difficult to consider his career objectively. The backwash of a cultural reaction to his death would distort the legacy of the sportsman, as his shade would become the collective property of a wider consideration. An attempt to appropriate the living reputation of a person can be made through discussion among those who study it. The death of anyone prominent will provoke a contest among a wide set of commentators for the definitive "last word" on that person, and of course on what his or her historical significance actually is. Obituaries, editorially rustled up against the possibility of sudden death, might almost be carved in stone. It takes a lot to dislodge an opinion gleaned by almost everyone, everywhere at once, regardless of its accuracy, and a dead person's obituary is usually the first result in a Google search for that person. This is not to say that all obituaries are inaccurate, only that the living personality still has the potential to influence ongoing discussion, rather than being merely the object of discussion.

But reputation can be enhanced by an athlete's life outside of sport and also after the competitive years are over. Muhammad Ali, for example, is today famous for much more than boxing. "No Vietnamese ever called me nigger"[50] is my favourite of his quotations. His fame arguably expanded awareness of more than just his sport, and more than just his personal and political views. His combined sporting and political persona could be said to have simply expanded awareness generally.

When Rossi stops racing, there will be a convulsion as the sport's most bankable star will no longer be there to draw spectators, viewers, and sponsors. His VR46 company already represents other riders to the extent that he actually races his clients, including Cal Crutchlow, on a regular basis. In this way and several others more arcane to the sport's organisation, he will not go away when he retires from racing.

Rossi has enough wins and championships to statistically claim to be the GOAT, and enough fans to evolve his reputation into genuine organisational muscle within the establishment of the sport. Like Giacomo Agostini,[51] he can be an ambassador for two wheels. Beyond this, he is also unique in his spanning of the two forms of elite bike racing, in his attracting an international fan club, and in his longevity at the top level. If Marc Márquez, for example, goes on to become the indisputable GOAT,[52] that would not diminish Rossi's reputation. It might even enhance that reputation; because he is so closely associated with the sport, he is partially responsible for anything good that will ever happen in it, in a strangely English sense.

Because of the influence Rossi enjoys, he can potentially expand his contribution to the motorsport and automotive cultures more generally. For instance, we amateur athletes still play an assortment of sports invented in the nineteenth century or before, but only so-called petrol heads actually invest the time, money, and other resources to race at even the lowest levels. Why don't we do a lot more racing at a local level, an adolescent level? Why don't we catch up with the times and bring motorsport into schools?

A motor racing competition between schools would not even be limited to the sports department. Chemistry students can improve on fuels and batteries, budding biologists can grow ethanol, design and technology students can build the safest little bikes possible, art students can paint and market them, and new media and data students can integrate with the school's broader efforts to tie in with developments all over the world. The rivalry between schools or regions would introduce societal competition in a radically new, useful, and perhaps internationally significant way. To move forward with such an initiative would require a huge U-turn in our currently risk-averse societies.

Regardless, Valentino Rossi is an exemplar of risk taking who has enjoyed a popularity based upon his authenticity, a form of cultural capital that has become essential to celebrities of all kinds, not just musicians or reality TV stars. That authenticity, combined with a commitment to excellence, has not only enhanced Rossi's popularity but given him a platform from which to challenge prevailing cultural attitudes to risk. I have no idea whether he would agree with the idea of introducing motorsport in schools, nor would I expect him to mount some political campaign toward that end. The very fact of his exemplary existence makes challenges to risk aversion more possible for all people.

The risks of not embracing the benefits of our various automotive cultures are plain, as we witness the cultural and physical drawbacks of our post-industrial societies. Should we attempt to embrace the positives of motorsport in the future, we will need people exactly like Valentino Rossi, alive and kicking at the pricks of those who see only one side of a precautionary principle.

Notes

1. MotoGP bikes have had a number of engine sizes, from 999 cc down to 800 cc.

2. See "Marco Simoncelli Tribute 2011," at www.youtube.com/watch?v=R2tsxxWthoI, uploaded by lalaland. This YouTube clip is a recording of a BBC tribute to Marco Simoncelli, an Italian racer who died after crashing at the Sepang GP in 2011. In another tribute, Marco's father asked for a minute of noise, rather than of silence, in his son's memory.

3. As an example of risk aversion, in 2014 the Brighton and Hove City Council, led by the Green Party, sought to ban the Brighton Speed Trials, a seafront drag race and the oldest race meeting in Britain, after a competitor in the sidecar event was tragically killed in 2012. A petition signed by 12,500 people asking that the trials not be banned caused the council to reconsider. See Paul Hudson, "Brighton Speed Trials Saved," *Telegraph*, January 25, 2014, at www .telegraph.co.uk/motoring/motorsport/10595098/Brighton-Speed-Trials-saved.html.

4. Jürgen Habermas, *The Structural Transformation of the Public Sphere: An Inquiry into a Category of Bourgeois Society*, trans. Thomas Burger and Frederick Lawrence (Cambridge, MA: MIT Press, 1989), 1. This work traces the historical development of concepts of the public and highlights the difficulties of definition and coherence in the burgeoning era of mass communication. Since its translation into English, Habermas's work has been influential in many disciplines in Great Britain and the United States. Craig Calhoun writes: "Habermas's task in *Structural Transformation* is to develop a critique of this category of bourgeois society showing both (1) its internal tensions and the factors that led to its transformation and partial

degeneration and (2) the element of truth and emancipatory potential that it contained despite its ideological misrepresentation and contradictions." Craig Calhoun, ed., *Habermas and the Public Sphere* (Cambridge, MA: MIT Press, 1992), 2.

5. Viktor Mayer-Schönberger and Kenneth Cukier, *Big Data: A Revolution That Will Transform How We Live, Work and Think* (London: John Murray, 2013). This is a useful introduction to new techniques in the use and continued repurposing of all kinds of data—not just electronically gathered data.

6. Rossi also kept a flat in London, where he could also go about without attracting reporters. This seems astonishing when one considers the deserved reputation of British tabloid reporters, but for reasons touched on below in this chapter, he would not become a target for the London press. Rossi writes in his autobiography that London was the only city where he could relax and go about like a normal person. See Valentino Rossi and Enrico Borghi, *What If I Had Never Tried It* (London: Arrow Books, 2006).

7. See, for example, "Brad Pitt on the Greatest Love of His Life: MotoGP," *ShortList*, August 2015, at http://www.shortlist.com/entertainment/sport/brad-pitt-on-the-greatest-love-of-his-life-motogp.

8. The American Motorcyclist Association did not make road racing a separate part of its championship season until 1978, and riders competed in dirt-track, motocross, and other events in different classes. For a complete history of the AMA, see www.americanmotorcyclist.com/about/history.

9. Short-track racing is also known as dirt-track, flat-track, and oval-track racing.

10. The supermoto has an interesting vintage. In the United States, ABC TV created *Superbikers* in the late 1970s featuring riders from different racing disciplines competing on a twisty, combined dirt-and-asphalt track. They raced on lightweight off-road racers equipped with on-road duel-sport wheels, tires, and brakes. *Superbikers* was sold around the world; when the series finished in the mid-1980s, European riders, especially the French, continued to race and ride dirt bikes with road wheels. The "superbiker" became the "supermotard," while the bikes were called supermotos. They enjoyed a resurgence in the late 1990s and now are part of many top riders' training programmes, because they can be slid around asphalt corners at lower speeds. Most manufacturers now sell some version of a supermoto in their ranges. Thus, a section of the market evolved from an American TV show that garnered a French cult following and developed into a new subculture of machine and rider skills. See "Danny 'Magoo' Chandler SuperBikers 1982," at www.youtube.com/watch?v=V1LLP6QKCWA, uploaded by Endo Payne TV.

11. For a report of Márquez's Superprestigio short-track event, see Gary Inman, "Farm Boys v. Marquez," *Motor Cycle News Sport*, May 2014, 92–97.

12. Another form of drag racing in Britain is the "hill climb," which is typically staged up a steep, winding, narrow hill, either on dirt or tarmac. The oldest British drag race is the Brighton Speed Trials, held on an asphalted beach esplanade. A hill climb in Iceland or Finland might involve going almost straight up the side of a volcanic mountain on a bike with a really long swingarm and huge bolts, or ice spikes, stuck in the rear tire. See "Motorbike Hill Climb Crashes," at www.youtube.com/watch?v=ovsqeyM4ZXs, uploaded by fletchmaddog in 2010, for a selection of clips.

13. Lord's is an ancient cricket pitch now surrounded by North London. Thomas Lord's field was the venue for the Marylebone Cricket Club (MCC), which did much to shape the modern

game; it is still the Middlesex County Cricket Club's home ground as well as the spiritual headquarters of the sport.

14. Henman received actual honours, as from the queen. Multiple Olympic gold-medal winners usually get a knighthood, becoming a Sir or Dame, while winning the Ashes after a long wait bagged England's cricket players Member of the British Empire (MBE) gongs in 2005 and captain Michael Vaughan an Order of the British Empire (OBE).

15. A sports bike is now usually defined as a road-legal lightweight 600 cc–plus four-stroke designed to go well around a track. It has a sports fairing and bodywork, hard suspension, a highly tuned, fast-revving engine, and an uncomfortable "bum in the air" riding posture. These bikes go as fast as thought in the context of road use but resemble their distant MotoGP prototype cousins in appearance only. Why Britain is disproportionately fond of sports bikes is a good question. Strangely, more convertible cars are bought in England than in any other European country, despite, or perhaps because of, the rainy climate. British motoring in general has many peculiarities. No similarities whatsoever with an equally peculiar American automotive culture should be assumed.

16. TT races, involving cars and motorcycles, have taken place on the Isle of Man's public road circuit for more than a hundred years.

17. Barry Sheene wisely refused to race the TT because of the greater danger when crashing on street circuits. He was known as Meccano Man because so much metal was required by surgeons to hold the bones of his legs together after a major smash.

18. WSB and BSB are international and national, respectively, production machine–based race series, essentially contests between heavily modified versions of the bikes you can buy on the open market, as in the US SuperSport category.

19. John Surtees, OBE, has never received the recognition his unique achievements deserve. There is a petition to have him knighted, and you can sign here: www.petitionbuzz.com/petitions/sirjohnsurtees.

20. Rossi's iconic, trademarked, and copyrighted race number is 46. Riders have long been associated with particular numbers, but Rossi has transformed these digits into several brands for marketing purposes. See the company's homepage at www.valentinorossi.com/en/.

21. See Mat Oxley, *Valentino Rossi: MotoGenius* (London: Haynes Publishing, 2006), 41.

22. No other rider has ever tamed the Ducati as Stoner did.

23. Quoted in "Casey Stoner," *Motor Cycle News*, October 23, 2013, 14, 16; published in Casey Stoner and Matthew Roberts, *Pushing the Limits* (London: Orion Publishing, 2013).

24. I recommend Mat Oxley's work, *Valentino Rossi: MotoGenius*, for those wishing to pursue the details of Rossi's career. Oxley is a long-time authority on elite motorcycle racing and contributor to the British magazines *Motor Cycle News*, *Motor Cycle News Sport*, and *Bike*, as well as many documentaries on various aspects of motorcycling.

25. *Rush*, starring Chris Hemsworth and Daniel Brühl, is a simple story beautifully told, requiring no particular interest in motorsport to enjoy. Ron Howard, dir., *Rush*, Studio Canal, 2013.

26. For a selection of Rossi celebrations, see "Best Valentino Rossi Winning Celebration," at www.youtube.com/watch?v=T3eS6vvZsLo, uploaded by alfabesmart, 2013.

27. Oscar Pistorius competed in the 2012 London Olympics for South Africa, but had his team won, it would have been considered very controversial. Where would athletics be, some

said, if athletes had to surgically alter their bodies to compete against the "disabled"? See "Oscar Pistorius Makes Olympic History in 400m at London 2012," BBC Sport, August 4, 2012, at www.bbc.co.uk/sport/0/olympics/18911479.

28. In late September 1771, Mr. "Shock" White, of "Ryegate," played with a bat wider than the stumps. The Hambledon Committee's 1744 set of rules had neglected to specify a maximum bat width but speedily met to amend the rules just two days later. See Michael Rundell, *The Dictionary of Cricket* (Oxford: George Allen and Unwin, 1985), 15.

29. The development of equipment in cricket since the mid-nineteenth century has largely benefitted the batter in terms of protection and offensive capability. Lady cricketer Christina Willes, whose brother John played for Kent, invented roundarm bowling to replace the underarm standard of the early nineteenth century (Rundell, *The Dictionary of Cricket*, 154–55). She found that her voluminous skirt got in the way using the older technique, so she raised her action to great effect. Male bowlers copied her and soon developed higher actions that evolved, despite attempts to outlaw it, into the current overarm standard, greatly increasing the speed and accuracy of the ball. Players now wear armour and helmets frequently.

30. The rules are under constant revision. The tensions between testing the technique of the riders and the technology of the bikes often swing regulation in different directions. Currently, the set of rules that governs satellite machines and a lower class of competitor sharing the MotoGP grid is being rewritten yet again, the use of shared software being a big bone of contention.

31. Only one women ever has competed in the elite class Grand Prix, American Gina Bovaird, at 500 cc GPs in the early 1980s. She deserves more recognition than she's thus far been granted. See Sandra Hinson, "Art Is Long, and So Are the Odds against Painter Gina Bovaird in Macho Motorcycle Racing," *People*, May 12, 1980, at www.people.com/people/article/0,,20076462,00.html. The biggest barrier to female motorcycle racing is perhaps not that men are stronger, although strength is an advantage, but that the women racers start very late in life compared with their male counterparts. Rossi and others began to develop their skills from four or five years old. Ana Carrasco, seventeen, races in the lightweight support class of MotoGP on a 250 cc Moto3 bike. She was the first woman to score a point in the class and the first in twelve years to score a point in any Grand Prix race, in September 2013. Her best position so far is eighth. See "Ana Carrasco Makes History at Sepang," MotoGP.com, at www.motogp.com/en/news/2013/Ana+Carrasco+makes+history+at+Sepang. Pioneering stories of women racers abound from the earliest times; start with the scandalous treatment of Beryl Swain, the first woman to complete the Tourist Trophy solo in 1962 and the first to have her international racing licence revoked for being a woman. See Ariane Barua, "The TT Goddess of the Gas Pedals," BBC, November 16, 2014, at http://news.bbc.co.uk/local/isleofman/hi/people_and_places/history/newsid_8331000/8331928.stm; see also a feature on Beryl Swain by the BBC programme *Woman's Hour*, linked at www.bbc.co.uk/isleofman/content/articles/2008/01/17/swain_feature.shtml.

32. Riders are not in contact with their pits when they race in MotoGP. Team orders are given before a race, if at all.

33. MotoGP was invented to make the racing prototypes more similar to machines that could be ridden on the road. The elite class had been dominated by 500 cc two-strokes for decades and now bore little relation to the four-stroke machines that consumers could actually buy. Larger capacity two-strokes were no longer manufactured, as their exhaust emissions

would have violated European and American regulations. Now, the 125 cc two-strokes have also been replaced by 250 cc four-strokes in Moto3.

34. Rossi's 2010 campaign was blighted by injury, and his 2011 and 2012 seasons were write-offs on an uncompetitive Ducati.

35. All figures given on these secret prototypes are conservative approximations used by commentators on the sport. Usually, when the actual specifications of historic racers become public knowledge years or decades later, estimations such as these have proven to be very close to measured weights and power outputs.

36. NASCAR machines make about a thousand brake horsepower and weigh about two thousand kilos.

37. If you look at a still picture or super slow motion recording of a motorbike cornering, you will see that this is the case. Watch for the front wheel steering in the wrong direction and look for the back wheel going faster than the front in the compilation "Moto GP Slow Motion," at www.youtube.com/watch?v=N4CmopXiyZM, uploaded by FKRmovies, 2012. It is not clear if anyone has really satisfactorily explained the counter-steering phenomenon in terms of physical laws of motion, or whether a layperson would understand it if they did.

38. Rear wheel steer is one way to describe this. The back wheel is nearly always in a controlled state of speed disparity with the front wheel when approaching and exiting a corner. It seems impossible that this disparity can make the bike go faster than it would otherwise. Watch super slow motion replays and you will see the controlled slide effectively sharpening the steering. When you park a car on the street, you reverse into a space because the wheels steering from the back, in relation the direction of travel, make it easier to turn in a tighter circle. The back wheel of a racing bike needs to point out of the corner and be brought upright, making the rear contact patch bigger so that the utmost power can be used to fire the bike toward the entry point of the next corner. The controlled rear slide allows an orientation out of the corner sooner than the wheels-in-line technique. With preternaturally skilled riders, the technique has an effect analogous to steering from the rear when reversing into a parking space.

39. A slipper clutch is a device that prevents the rear wheel from locking up when changing down through the sequential gearbox.

40. I say "total" in the sense of "total war."

41. Gekko is Michael Douglas's character in Oliver Stone, dir., *Wall Street*, 20th Century Fox, 1987.

42. For a list of Rossi's achievements, see the Yamaha MotoGP website at www.yamahamotogp.com/valentino-rossi/career.php.

43. For a commentary on Goody's witch hunt, see Brendan O'Neill, "Jade and the Tyranny of Anti-Racism," *Spiked*, March 23, 2009, at www.spiked-online.com/newsite/article/6383#.U424BPldX4I.

44. For the flavour of the programme, see "Celebrity Big Brother: Shilpa Shetty Bullying Compilation," at www.youtube.com/watch?v=u7sqAIPR5oc, uploaded by desihitstv, 2007.

45. The show was called *Big Boss* in India.

46. Fry is the former comedy partner of British actor and comedian Hugh Laurie, star of the hit American medical drama *House*. The atmosphere at Jade Goody's funeral can be sampled in "Jade Goody's Funeral," at www.youtube.com/watch?v=zaHNL1GMRWM, uploaded by Cliff Harris, 2009.

47. "People's Princess" alludes to the title Princess Diana once famously said she wanted to achieve, that of a princess of people's hearts.

48. See Vali Mihaescu, "AGV Launches Rossi Helmet Replica," *Autoevolution*, November 22, 2010, at www.autoevolution.com/news/agv-launches-rossi-helmet-replica-2563.html.

49. *Motor Cycle News* claims that Rossi has about 500,000 Twitter followers, or some 51.5 million behind Justin Bieber.

50. "Muhammad Ali: Wit and Wisdom of The Greatest," *Telegraph*, January 7, 2012, at http://www.telegraph.co.uk/sport/othersports/boxing/9000451/Muhammad-Ali-wit-and-wisdom-of-The-Greatest.html.

51. "Ago," as Agostini is known, still races at classic events and makes guest appearances all over the world.

52. As this chapter goes to press, Márquez has won the first seven races of the 2014 season, so his elevation is by no means unlikely.

Andy Murray
Savior from Outside the Margins

—Lisa Doris Alexander and Dan Travis

Introduction

Depending upon whom one asks, men's professional tennis in the first two decades of the twenty-first century of can best be summed up in Charles Dickens's classic opening line from *A Tale of Two Cities*: "It was the best of times, it was the worst of times."[1] As for plusses, fans have witnessed what many believe to have been a seismic shift on the men's side of the ledger as far as the quality of play is concerned. On the other hand, the period has been dominated, for the most part, by three players: Roger Federer, Rafael Nadal, and Novak Djokovic. Since 2004, these three men have won the men's singles title in thirty-nine of the last forty-seven Grand Slam tournaments, which takes a bit of the fun if not the uncertainty out of the competitions.[2]

But in 2012, the Big Three suddenly took on a fourth when Great Britain's Andy Murray finally met expectations by first winning Olympic gold at the London Games, and then later that summer taking home the US Open men's singles title. The metaphoric pièce de résistance, however, occurred in the summer of 2013 when Murray bested Djokovic to win the Wimbledon men's singles championship. What made Murray's victory there so special was that upon winning Wimbledon, he became the first British man in nearly eight decades to win that vaunted men's title, and the first British Wimbledon champion of either sex since Virginia Wade, who kept the women's singles crown at home in 1977.[3] At that point, Murray became the toast of the United Kingdom[4]—at least for a brief while. As much jubilation from this victory, there was nearly an equal portion of trepidation, or at least some level of consternation. One excited fan declared, "Finally British tennis is back on the map,"[5] while Jackie MacMullan of America's influential Entertainment and Sports Programming Network (ESPN) declared, "Finally, Charlie Brown kicked the ball. For once, Lucy didn't humiliate him yet again by snatching it away at the last moment."[6] Keith McLeod of Great Britain's *Daily Record* took it even a step further when he noted that Murray's win was an "epic achievement which sealed Murray's place among the greatest of the greats in our nation's sporting history."[7] But while presumably the whole of the United Kingdom seemed to bask in the glow of this triumphant breakthrough, all this basking belies what was and remains a decidedly rocky relationship between Murray and the British fan base, the national tennis authority, and, perhaps most problematic, the British press, making this victory all the more challenging but certainly intriguing.

When Murray turned professional in 2005, many were already touting the eighteen-year-old as the savior-in-waiting of British tennis. Over time, however, the shine seemed to wear off his seemingly endless potential for two apparent reasons. The first stems from the fact that Murray did not deliver the United Kingdom to the Grand Slam "promised land" quickly enough to satisfy the legions of victory-starved and restless British fans and followers of the sport. Indeed, although Murray came close to winning a Grand Slam several times in the earlier stages of his career, it took seven years before he finally broke through. Second and perhaps even more complicated, as a Scot, Murray seems caught in the middle of the often thorny relationship between Scotland and the English-dominated United Kingdom, which accounts at least in part for how Murray and his place in British tennis circles are typically framed by the media and received by the fans. He is both regarded as one of their own while at the same time often pilloried as being not quite British enough. Such is the nature of trying to understand Murray's place within the larger British sporting culture.

This chapter seeks to analyze these phenomena by examining the roles that citizenship, history, and national pride have played in how Murray's career is perceived thus far. Of primary concern is the extent to which Murray has become part of a category of celebrity athletes who, while admired, are otherwise held at bay by a local and even regional fandom that claims him as their champion while ultimately questioning his commitment to them. Thus, while his Wimbledon win nudged him toward respectability if not outright stardom, his reputation within larger circles of athletic celebrity remains as of yet ill defined and even up for grabs.

British Tennis and the Henman Conundrum

Before discussing the particulars of Andy Murray's place in the eyes of British tennis fans, it is necessary to provide a little background information on the state of tennis culture in the United Kingdom writ large. It is no stretch to conclude that the story of men's tennis in Great Britain up until the moment of Murray's Wimbledon success had been one of disappointment and even despair for quite some time. As one Murray biographer couched it, during the seventy-seven-year drought in British men's Wimbledon singles titles that preceded Murray's victory, "the Empire disappeared, the Berlin Wall went up, the Berlin Wall came down, man walked on the moon, [and] the world entered the digital age."[8] That is not to suggest that British tennis fans have not had anything or anyone for whom to cheer since Fred Perry's back-to-back-to-back Wimbledon victories from 1934 to 1936; however, the heartbreak that fans have had to endure in the intervening seventy plus years has been daunting and tough to shake.

Prior to Murray, the most recent men's tennis player to capture the nation's attention, if not its collective imagination, was Tim "The Tiger" Henman. Born and raised in middle-class comfort in Oxford, Henman had a strong tennis pedigree to go along with the opportunities afforded by his upbringing. His grandfather, Henry Billington, reached the third round at Wimbledon in 1948, 1950, and 1951, and his great-grandmother, Ellen Stawell-Brown, the first woman on the tennis circuit to serve in the now ubiquitous overhead fashion, played her final match in 1905.[9] Although Henman never made it to a Grand Slam final, fans adored him and hung on his every loss. They even unofficially renamed the grassy area at the All England Lawn Tennis and Croquet Club where Wimbledon is played "Henman Hill." Such was the reputation Henman garnered. He had grown to be, in the eyes of the British public, a symbol of tenacity and grace in the face of recurring disappointment.

And yet, whereas the fans loved Henman despite his never having quite delivered, Murray would not be afforded anything close to that level of adoration even in victory. To be sure, in the first years of Murray's career, the British public never seemed to warm to their Scottish wunderkind in the same way they warmed to his English predecessor. As opposed to the driven and at times demonstrative Murray, Henman fit the much more time-honored stereotype of the stiff-lipped Briton fighting the good fight against all odds and with aplomb. Henman came close to winning so many times only to lose, but always with a palpable degree of graciousness. Through such displays, the English public grew accustomed to Henman's losing and grew comfortable with his smoothed edges; quite candidly, this persona simply fit the English cultural stereotype far better than anything Murray could provide, especially given his Scottishness and all that might imply—not least of which was his propensity for emotional displays and candor both on the court and off.

Another matter for Murray to overcome relative to the specter of Henman, which seems to overhang his legacy, is that the Scot demonstrated an appetite for success and desire that Henman, who at times seemed happy just to be on the court, quite simply lacked. While Henman often appeared resigned to losing, Murray was visibly angered by it. There is little doubt that the British public knew that, unlike his predecessor, Murray had the necessary physical qualities required to win major titles, and these qualities became more and more apparent as Murray climbed his way up the men's singles rankings. Still, British tennis fans seemed to have grown comfortable with their more likeable underdogs losing benignly; they seemed content to hang their collective hat on a lineage of graceful defeat. Murray, on the other hand, who lacked or perhaps even disdained the polish and on-court politesse of his forerunner, seemed much more comfortable snuffing out what was left of the "losing with dignity" leitmotif. In this regard, Murray's unwillingness to submit to defeat left him vulnerable to charges that he was far less gracious than Henman, and he was thus perceived as being uniquely *un*-British, a stigma that attached itself to his public persona.

Scottish Upstart in the Lawn Tennis Association

Murray's personal history, while modest in comparison to Henman's, still reads as typically British. He was born in Dunblane, Scotland, on May 15, 1987, to William and Judy Murray. Judy Murray was an accomplished tennis player in her own right, gaining national recognition as a tennis coach by the time her younger son was born. And she would continue to serve in a public role in British tennis well after her two sons had made it to the tour.

A dominant presence in her boys' lives and in particular their athletic development, Judy Murray taught Andy and his older brother James (often Jamie) to play the game as emergent professionals while encouraging and nurturing a competitive spirit between them. Of her boys' upbringing in the sport, she once noted:

> When Andy and Jamie were growing up, we didn't have a lot of space or money and, let's face it, the weather in Scotland is terrible. So we were always looking for things to do indoors to occupy these two active young children. I've always loved sport and just wanted the boys to share that passion and I knew that if they had good co-ordination, it wouldn't matter what sport they tried, because they'd be able to do it pretty well.[10]

She would later be recognized, fairly or otherwise, as the dominant force behind her boys' early success, particularly in the case of Andy, a phenomenon that is true for many tennis players whose careers were aided in part by a strong parental presence, bringing to mind other renowned or even infamous figures as Charles "Papa" Lenglen and Richard Williams, although as a player in her own right she need not apologize to anyone for her role in her boys' successes despite the enduring whispers that she had become the quintessential if not ubiquitous "tennis mom."

What is unmistakable is the extent to which tennis marked the younger Murray's entry into the world. Practicing laboriously from a young age, and with his mother's urging, Murray's rise in the ranks of youth tennis before his game went global happened quite swiftly.¹¹ A good deal of that success can be linked to Murray's controversial decision to leave the United Kingdom at age fifteen in order to train in the much more acclaimed Spanish academies. It is alleged that his contemporary and later circuit rival Rafael Nadal first put the idea in Murray's head during a conversation they had at a tournament in Pamplona. Nadal is said to have told Murray that if he really had aspirations to become a top-ranked tennis player, he would need to leave Great Britain and attend a training facility in Spain as Nadal had.¹² Within months, Judy Murray, who obviously agreed with Nadal's opinion, sought private sponsorship and secured some private investment in order to pay the £25,000 that training in Spain would cost.¹³

But there is much more to this story than simply that of a talented boy seeking out options elsewhere. By acting on this opportunity, Murray, for all intents and purposes a working-class Scot, was perceived to be rejecting the British system run by the elite (and decidedly English-dominated) Lawn Tennis Association (LTA), as enigmatic an organization as exists in the often colorful world of high-profile tennis. It is estimated that the United Kingdom has more tennis courts per capita than any other country in the world. Consequently, the price of hiring a tennis court or joining a club is significantly cheaper in the United Kingdom than almost anywhere else. The LTA also has around £25 million at its disposal to encourage more people to play the game and to support elite tennis players.¹⁴ But, while it might appear that opportunities to learn and even excel at tennis in the UK are abundant, the state of the sport nationwide, despite the LTA's resources, is anything but healthy.

Participation levels in tennis around the nation are estimated to be half of what is found in neighboring France. And the numbers have continued to fall and are close to dropping below the four hundred thousand benchmark figure.¹⁵ Many observers have concluded that, despite its resources, the LTA has been the single biggest failure in all of British sport and has become something of a national laughingstock. Moreover, the organization has long since lost the support of the tennis-playing public, who tend now to view it with disdain.

Added to the tenuous support the LTA provides for young tennis players, Murray's decision seemed quite straightforward. As the above quotation from Judy Murray explains, the weather, alongside the questionable condition of the facilities in Scotland, added extra hurdles to Murray's tennis development. So, when weighed against the disarray of the LTA and other factors, the decision to transfer to Spain made perfect sense. And yet many viewed the decision as nothing less than a betrayal. That feeling of abandonment resurfaced in 2007 when Murray declined an offer to represent the British at a Davis Cup tournament; two years earlier, he had accepted the same offer, and although he didn't appear in match play he was nevertheless the youngest player ever to be picked for the side.¹⁶

Although the more favorable conditions were the main impetus behind Murray's decision to make the move to Spain, there was an additional reason. He felt that he would be freer to work on his game without the distractions that have come to mark the dysfunctional British tennis system. Of course, this has served to cost him dearly in terms of the way he is today received in British tennis circles. Mark Hodgkinson, one of Murray's biographers, noted that as Murray continued to play well in international youth tournaments during this period, often against overmatched British opponents, he also grew to become a symbol of the systemic failure of the LTA, a matter not lost on local authorities and supporters. Certainly, by removing himself from that environment plagued by systemic failures, he was able to flourish, but as long as he continued to improve while others so obviously were not, Murray would become the target of hostility, which seems to have followed him into his professional days on the tour, always with the ghost of Tim Henman hovering in the background.[17] Hodgkinson explains:

> Andy Murray had often felt unloved at this garden party. There was the occasion at the All England Club one summer when he had walked past a woman and heard her hissing into her mobile phone, "there goes that Scottish w*****." Of the times he had read the letters sent to his locker telling him, "I hope you lost [sic] every match for the rest of your life." Those were extreme examples, yet for years a mutual unease had existed between many of the Wimbledon crowd and Britain's only contender for the golden trophy. When he was on court, he had regularly been reminded of the public's affection for a retired player, and how he compared (not so well).[18]

Murray typically recalled this period with incendiary terms, claiming that he found his cohorts to be generally unmotivated, that his coaches lacked fundamental teaching skills, and that the sport's governing body was as a whole turning a blind eye to the untenable state of the British training regimen. What's more, he claimed that no one seemed willing to take any responsibility for the sorry state of affairs.[19] Adding to Murray's displeasure with the LTA as a whole was the fact that his older brother and first on-court rival, Jamie, had similar experiences when he attended an LTA training school in Cambridge. As the younger Murray acknowledged, "[Jamie] used to enjoy himself on court but all that had changed,"[20] a bad experience that took the professional doubles player several years to shake.

How much of the criticism directed at Murray is directly attributable to his growing up on the margins of the British tennis establishment—as a working-class Scot trained in a Spanish facility—is up for debate. What we do know is that Murray was not and continues not to be shy about what he sees as structural problems in the British tennis establishment, even as he was becoming the face of British tennis. As an athlete whose allegiances have continuously come under scrutiny and whose move to the center of the sport comes only after his controversial decision to forsake the British tennis establishment and train abroad, he seems to routinely be required to pass something of loyalty test at nearly every juncture. On several occasions, particularly earlier in his career, Murray had to remind reporters that despite the controversies he took pride in his heritage, although as a Scotsman, the notion of heritage is a sticky matter.[21] While the subtleties of the distinction between Scottish and British may be lost on those outside the UK, ESPN's Ian Whittell summed up the matter quite succinctly when he noted that "those historical differences are felt keenly by sports fans for whom games of football or rugby between the English and Scots are played and watched with an enmity that makes Duke-UNC basketball or Michigan–Ohio State football look like little league."[22]

A far less historically fraught example of fans misplacing and/or recalibrating an athlete's allegiances whose loyalties were open to interpretation can be seen in the case of National Basketball Association (NBA) superstar LeBron James after the basketball phenom signed with the Miami Heat in 2010 instead of renewing his contract with the hometown Cleveland Cavaliers. Cleveland fans were outraged that James would flee their region, a situation that quickly turned the area's most favored son from folk hero to villain virtually overnight. Cavaliers franchise owner Dan Gilbert summed up much of the fan outrage when he published a scathing open letter that called James's decision to leave the franchise a "cowardly betrayal" and a "shocking act of disloyalty from our homegrown 'chosen one,'" while personally guaranteeing that "the Cleveland Cavaliers will win an NBA championship before the self-anointed 'king' wins one." Although James managed to win two NBA championships with the Heat before the Cavaliers ever made it back to the playoffs again, a feat the team only accomplished after James returned to the Cavaliers following the 2013–2014 season, what was lost in the discussion of James's perceived betrayal was the fact that he did not grow up in Cleveland but rather in Akron, America's erstwhile tire capital located some forty miles south of Cleveland, which has a decidedly different economic, social, and political history than its larger neighbor to the north. In hindsight, James was correct in his assessment that if he wanted to win a championship, he had to leave "home," as it were, just as Murray had done: to become an elite tennis player, he had to leave the UK and its declining LTA and train elsewhere. But the vindication both athletes experienced by winning is often swept aside in favor of the long-standing vitriol that has seemingly cemented their reputations as outsiders, while fans and detractors remain on near-constant vigil for potential signs of disloyalty often parsed in the most innocuous act or comment. In this regard, despite the remarkable athleticism they bring to their respective sports, both Murray and James have continued to face severe if not arbitrary challenges to their fidelities long after they returned home and demonstrated the soundness of their original decision to leave as well as their willingness to move on after returning.

Professional Development

Murray's status as an outsider trained abroad and symbolic of a loss of authority within British tennis notwithstanding, his appearance on the international tennis scene marked the evolution of an exceptionally gifted player who provided British tennis with a genuine threat to crack the upper reaches of the tour. In 2004, Murray won the US Open junior title[23] and was named the 2004 recipient of the BBC's Young Sports Personality of the Year.[24] In 2006, with new coach Brad Gilbert continuing to shape his game, Murray defeated the indefatigable Roger Federer in Round 2 of the Cincinnati Masters tournament. Also that year, he beat American Andy Roddick in the semifinals of the SAP Open as part of the Pacific Coast Championships. By 2007, Murray had won three Association of Tennis Professionals (ATP) titles, winning both the 2006 and 2007 SAP Opens as well Russia's St. Petersburg Open. He would go on to win more than twenty ATP titles by 2012.[25]

As mentioned at the beginning of this chapter, Murray had the misfortune of coming of age at a time when three game-changing talents had come to dominate the men's circuit. Although it was obvious that Murray was an extremely talented player, he continued to run into barriers that resulted in his having to adopt a newer, more assertive strategy that would allow him to initially challenge and ultimately join the likes of Federer, Djokovic, and his old friend Rafael Nadal as an equal. But while so much of this story can be viewed through the prism of Murray's own tenacity and will to win, a good deal of his success can also be attributed to his two-year association with eight-time Grand Slam champion Ivan Lendl, another recognized outsider as far as the tennis establishment is concerned.[26]

Himself a former world number one, Lendl, who was Murray's coach from early 2012 until mid-2014,[27] encouraged his new charge to become more aggressive as he helped bring Murray closer to the more combative style that led to Lendl's own successes throughout his active days on the tour. Under Lendl's tutelage, Murray moved from primarily assuming a defensive posture to one that sought to attack on each individual shot. According to ESPN's Lindsay Berra, "To stoke Murray's killer instinct, [Lendl] adjusted the Scot's position on the court, moving Murray closer to the baseline and forcing him to take the ball earlier. Doing so allows Murray to dictate points—he returns the ball quicker, forcing his opponents to make faster decisions and shots, which often leads to mistakes."[28]

Although no one could argue with Lendl's tennis credentials, the former champion had his own uneasy relationship with fans and the tennis world broadly conceived, and part of that baggage landed at Murray's already suspect feet. It also did not pass unnoticed that through this successful yet short-lived partnership with Lendl, Murray adopted some of his coach's more vexing personality traits—at least in terms of the standards set forth in the stylized world of professional tennis. Chief among these supposed deficiencies was a perceived lack of animation or youthful exuberance, interpreted by the public via the media to mean that each was sullen and unapproachable. Lendl in the past had been called more machine than man, an impression that continues to mark his public persona even all these years beyond his playing days.

Lendl's reticence lay in stark contrast to Murray's previous coach, the affable and quite approachable Brad Gilbert, author of the famous tennis manual *Winning Ugly*, who showed characteristic candor when he claimed in his preface to the book that he was never as talented as other players on the circuit but used guile to beat them.[29] Given Gilbert's propensity for creating drama of this sort alongside Murray's own well-chronicled reticence, it is hardly a surprise that the Gilbert-Murray partnership was not built to last. In contrast, the pairing up of Murray and Lendl, short lived though it was, is interesting on several levels, not least of which was what Lendl once represented in men's tennis. Lendl's ascension into the upper echelons of the sport marked a break with the game's recent past—namely the ubiquity of the enduring image of the jet-setting, celebrity tennis pro. Lendl approached tennis in a vastly different way from his contemporaries or even his predecessors. He professionalized his approach to tennis through a training regimen typically foreign to tennis that included weight training, something his contemporaries—especially the two biggest names of the era, John McEnroe and Björn Borg—would have never embraced. In addition to bringing strength and remarkable discipline to the courts, Lendl, who garnered such tongue-in-cheek nicknames as "Ivan the Terrible" and "the Teminator," was also stoic and much less animated than his contemporaries, a trait that continues to mark his persona to this day. As Murray joked shortly after his win at Wimbledon, he claims to have looked for Lendl's reaction and remarked: "What's that . . . is he . . . but he's almost . . . he's almost smiling!"[30] That internalization of emotion is a trait that Murray, once regarded as irrepressibly demonstrative bordering on perpetually surly, ultimately adopted. As Berra noted, "Murray historically has been emotional on the court, whereas Lendl was once described by John McEnroe as a 'scary robot.' Some of that iciness seems to have transferred to Murray, who showed incredible fortitude and discipline recently at the French Open."[31] When Murray was too expressive, he was vilified once again for being *un*-British, a not so thinly veiled reminder of the place that Tim Henman continues to occupy in British tennis; so, seeking to move past that tag, he embraced Lendl's more reserved court presence, which oddly, though not surprisingly, elicited backlash as well.

Indeed, caught somewhere between Lendl's icy glare and John McEnroe's well-chronicled explosiveness, Andy Murray's personality seems destined to keep him similarly caught in the crosshairs of public scrutiny, though often for reasons well beyond the playing surfaces. As he began his rise through the tennis ranks, it was clear that he was not quite used to dealing with professional reporters, the vagaries of social media, or even rabid fans who hang on a person's every comment, which exposed another flaw in his professional development, with two notable examples occurring in 2006.

The most innocuous public gaffe occurred when, after winning a sloppy match in New Zealand, a match that saw seven breaks of serve during the first set, Murray told the crowd, "We were both playing like women."[32] Although it is hard for anyone to know for sure, this was less a sexist remark, as typically interpreted, as much as it was a reference to the fact that, traditionally, women's games have more service breaks than men's. According to many reports, the comment, however, was said to have elicited loud boos from the crowd, although Murray disagrees, maintaining instead that "the crowd had been laughing with me, and they certainly clapped me off."[33] And while this incident was ultimately swept aside, it did give rise to this sense that Murray stood typically one syllable away from hot water, something that the media as well as his detractors seemed happy to exploit routinely. To be sure, a far more volatile moment, born of genuine silliness though no less controversial, was just over the horizon, courtesy of the traditional tensions between Scotland and England.

Later that summer during the World Cup, as England was preparing to play Germany, Murray joked to a reporter who had been taunting him playfully about Scotland's own football troubles that he would be wearing a Paraguay shirt during the tournament because "he was a typical Scot and was following the lead set by First Minister Jack McConnell, who also said he would be supporting England's opponents."[34] The implication here was that Murray was prepared to root for anyone but England. For Murray, who continued to struggle with questions about his loyalties, as chronicled above, this set off an even fresher firestorm of mayhem. Although he quickly responded that the comment was indeed a joke that had been blown out of proportion,[35] and while Tim Henman, who was present at the time, ultimately spoke out on Murray's behalf,[36] Murray later admitted that since that time, the backlash from this incident has influenced how he deals with the media:

> When I first came on the scene I could joke and laugh around and everyone saying it's great it was a breath of fresh air, something different and then you know as soon as you make that first mistake and say that one thing that everybody picks up

on you know whether it's a joke or not you know you start to become a lot more guarded.³⁷

Apologizing did little to stop fans from chiming in on the matter. The comments on Murray's blog ranged from typical pabulum encouraging Murray to move to Paraguay to fans swearing that from that point forward they would "be supporting anyone who is not Andy Murray." Some of the comments were deemed so vile they had to be immediately removed from the site. This kind of response was certainly to be expected, given the controversy that followed him throughout the earlier stages of his career and the seriousness with which England watches football.

The most contemptible remark, however, was written by a commentator who struck very close to home. Using the pseudonym Fred West, someone posted:

Can you tell us about DUNBLANE, Andy?³⁸

To those of us who live elsewhere, the name "Fred West" may not mean anything, while the reference to Murray's hometown of Dunblane might also seem innocuous enough. Unfortunately, that name and that comment were anything but. As it happens, Fred West was a serial predator who tortured and killed as many as twelve women in England in the 1960s and 1970s,³⁹ while the reference to Dunblane in all capital letters is less about the town and more about a highly publicized tragedy that occurred in March 1996 that involved Murray directly.

As an eight-year-old Andy Murray sat in his classroom at Dunblane Primary School, an armed man named Thomas Hamilton entered the facility and shot and killed seventeen people—sixteen students and one teacher—before turning the gun on himself. During this horrific event, Murray managed to escape and hide in his headmaster's office.⁴⁰ Certainly using such a horrific event to jab at Murray is beyond the pale, but it is not all that atypical either. Celebrities are constantly finding their personal foibles and even tragedies used as fodder for cranks, although it seems unlikely that Tim Henman receives such vitriol from fans. In Murray's case, however, it might just be indicative of the level of disdain that some continue to hold for him despite his on-court triumphs, including his historic win at the All England Lawn Tennis and Croquet Club in 2013.

Victory at Last

In his early years, Murray disappointed fans by not winning Grand Slam tournaments fast enough while being castigated by the British tennis establishment for airing their dirty laundry, as it were. At the same time, however, he was in fact creating a national profile within the larger tennis world. The same year he turned pro, Murray was a finalist at an ATP tournament in Bangkok and won his first ATP singles title in San Jose, California, that next year.[41] Strictly in terms of the UK's sport scene, Murray's victories marked a moment's celebration for a public that was not used to this level of success. Great Britain has been burdened by the malaise of sporting underperformance for several decades, and not just where tennis was concerned. This was felt as well in cricket and most acutely in football, with the English national team's inability to win anything of note on the international stage for several decades. Indeed, since winning the World Cup in 1966, the English football team's record in World Cup and European Cup finals was mediocre, to put it mildly. This single victory in 1966 nearly half a century ago was the source of pride for English sports fans and the nation as a whole. It was also a source of national shame.

This shame seemed to compound due to the fact that even though Murray was quite successful on the ATP tour, that success was not translating into Grand Slam wins, the benchmark for success in the sport. After finishing second at the 2008 US Open, the 2010 and 2011 Australian Opens, and the 2012 Wimbledon final, Murray seemed destined to fall into the trap of perpetual runner-up. Criticism of Murray ranged from those who wondered about his training or inner drive to those who questioned his emotional fitness, despite the fact that his arrival on the scene coincided with the primes of each of the vaunted Big Three. Obviously, there was a great deal of work yet to be done to prepare him to take that next colossal step up the ladder.

In 2009, Greg Garber of ESPN noted of Murray:

> Even as he has steadily lifted his game and his place in the world, there has been something missing from Murray's game. In a word: aggression. If you saw him lose to Andy Roddick in that taut, four-set semifinal match at Wimbledon, you know that when facing a top opponent Murray has a maddening tendency to go passive, to play the ball to the middle of the court.[42]

Peter Bodo would similarly query:

> How come this guy can take the measure of Federer on hard courts at Masters events? Murray is 5–1 against Federer in Masters events. The only time Federer beat him at a Masters event was Cincinnati in 2009. Either Federer brings a different game to the majors, or Murray has trouble coping with the Grand Slam challenge.[43]

And six-time Grand Slam champion Boris Becker argued that "in the respect of mental strength in such situations, [Murray] is a long way behind the top three guys in the world."[44] Despite the questions about his game and mental toughness, however, fans in the United Kingdom reluctantly stood by Murray if for no other reason than he was ultimately the nation's best hope for tennis glory irrespective of any perceived holes in his game or temperament.

All of the waiting paid off when in 2012, Murray won Olympic gold and then the US Open men's singles title. It seemed as though the entire United Kingdom cheered him on as "British leaders, tennis chiefs and former players have hailed Andy Murray after the Scot became the first British man to win a Grand Slam in 76 years."[45] As the celebrations continued, and as Murray forced his way into the Big Three, making it a Big Four, the question on everyone's mind remained Wimbledon. Namely, could he actually win it?

Winning a Grand Slam—or several Grand Slams—is wonderful, but winning a Grand Slam on one's own territory where no one has succeeded since the 1930s would be particularly special. Switzerland, Spain, and Serbia do not host Grand Slams, so there would be no chance for Federer, Nadal, or Djokovic to enjoy that honor and therefore there would be no pressure on them to do so. Indeed, the last men's champion anywhere to hoist a Grand Slam trophy at home was American Andy Roddick at the 2003 US Open,[46] so by all accounts, after near misses and a great deal of speculation and tension, the stage was set for something special.

As if to presage this, the BBC aired a documentary on Murray's life just prior to the start of the tournament. If nothing else, the piece reminded the nation of its investment in the game and what was riding on Murray's contested shoulders. It also offered commentary regarding many of the controversies surrounding, for example, Murray's decision to go to Spain, the tragedy at Dunblane, and his steady climb up the ranks to viable contender status against the backdrop of the omnipresent questions about his loyalties and fitness for the task. So in this regard, the documentary served to reconnect Murray to his more natural fan base. Thus, when Murray bested Djokovic 6–4, 7–5, 6–4 in the men's singles final, the British public and press seemed, at least initially, more at ease with their new champion despite all the false starts and faux pas over the years. And for at least that one moment, Andy Murray, seemingly perpetually on the outside, was hailed as the UK's undisputed sporting champion, while the cheers and resulting adulation poured in from what looked to be everywhere around the country.

For instance, writing for the *Guardian*'s online edition, Roy Greenslade observed: "Yesterday it was ball-by-ball coverage. Today it was wall-to-wall coverage. At a rough count, the papers between them devoted something like 125 full pages to his tennis triumph."[47] Oliver Hold of the *Daily Mirror*, writing in a much more tabloid vein, thought that he was witnessing nothing short of an exorcism of the nation's sporting demons:

> Farewell to those agonised cries of "C'mon Tim" that were the shrill accompaniment to Tim Henman's quartet of near misses. Farewell to the doomed annual lionisation

of also-rans such as Jeremy Bates, Buster Mottram and John Lloyd. Farewell to the memories of Roger Taylor's three semi-final defeats in the late 60s and early 70s and Mike Sangster's in 1961. Farewell to the sensation of hearing the name of Perry, who won the men's title three times between 1934 and 1936, and feeling its stinging reproach. And, best of all, farewell to the idea that British tennis is for losers and spoiled little rich kids.[48]

Newspapers from across the political and social divide carried the play-by-play of the entire match, with most of the headlines celebrating Murray's victory in all capital letters. Prime Minister David Cameron was in the Royal Box for the occasion and tweeted his congratulations. It was also reported that Queen Elizabeth II herself delivered a message of congratulations.[49] There were even calls for Murray to be knighted, while former boxing champion David Haye tweeted: "So buzzing @andy_murray for prime minister!!!"[50] The frenzy grew to such a fever pitch that, as one columnist put it, "Murray-mania has swept the UK, with songs, supermarkets and even sausages being created in his honour [and] DoubleTree by Hilton Dunblane Hydro have created their very own Murray Mocktail."[51] Of course, no victory would be complete without conspiracy theories, but even these were congratulatory in tone and lighthearted in nature.[52]

Even as the entire United Kingdom seemed to bask in the glow of Murray's triumph, no group of people was more excited about Murray's Wimbledon win than the residents of Dunblane. When Murray won Olympic gold and the US Open the previous year, the diminutive city, with its narrow streets and typically inclement weather, threw their favorite son a parade that fetched an estimated fifteen thousand celebrants.[53] This time around, however, with the Wimbledon match being screened at multiple locations throughout the city, when it was finally over, the town exploded as "strangers hugged one another in celebration, as champagne was sprayed over everyone," and while "stereo speakers outside the [Dunblane] Centre were blasting out Daft Punk's 'Get Lucky,' as if to chase away the bad luck of the previous year."[54] As one local journalist observed, "Dunblane has been so long wreathed in shadows, but yesterday it basked in the sun and the historic achievement of the man who first picked up a racquet as a boy at the local courts."[55] Many residents expressed relief that now when people hear the word "Dunblane," they can think about Andy Murray and not the tragic events that rocked the city almost two decades ago.

Short-Lived Regard

Given that it took seventy-seven years for a male tennis player from Great Britain to reclaim a Wimbledon singles title, one would assume that the citizenry would look to milk this victory for quite some time. But the initial gratification over Murray's history-making triumph only lasted about a year due in no small part to the political maneuvering brought about by the 2014 Scottish referendum on the question of independence. Although the intricacies of the referendum, which ultimately failed, are too complicated to hash out in this chapter, what is relevant to the Murray story and the rather abrupt departure from the celebratory tones around Wimbledon was the extent to which Murray's Scottish heritage came once more to the fore.

Although he initially refrained from weighing in on the measure, on referendum day Murray tweeted:

> Huge day for Scotland today! no campaign negativity last few days totally swayed my view on it. excited to see the outcome. lets do this![56]

When asked earlier to voice his opinion on the referendum, Murray had consistently offered none. Perhaps he genuinely had no opinion,[57] or perhaps because he was finally enjoying the spoils of his celebrity, he chose a more politically expedient route. But, as we have seen on other occasions, the backlash against Murray's last-minute foray into the political arena was swift, decisive, and eerily reminiscent of 2006.

Once again, the more vile comments were speedily excised from their respective websites, although most, in an age of instantaneous social media, were quickly forwarded on prior to their removal. As one might expect, they were often quite personal in nature, ranging from "Wish U had been killed at Dunblane you miserable anti-British hypocritical little git. Your life will be a misery from now on" to "You f****** c***. All the support you got at Wimbledon from the British people, and then you turn round a spew this s***. F*** You."[58]

Of course, many others voiced concern and were suitably appalled at the contempt hurled at Murray for simply expressing an opinion, but once again it is telling that the default incident in such rhetoric aimed at him was the primary school massacre, a matter that typically Murray does not discuss. Interestingly, this topic was broached by the producers of the aforementioned BBC documentary, which made for an emotional and indeed compelling moment and may in fact be his first public remarks on record concerning the incident. Sue Barker, herself a former Wimbledon champion turned television personality who conducted the interview, appeared uncomfortable raising the subject at all. Initially, Murray struggled with his composure, but after taking a moment to hug one of his dogs who was sitting on his lap, he acknowledged that he had found solace within the sport and recognized that he was consciously trying to move himself and, by extension, his hometown forward in the healing process by virtue of the hard work he put into his game.[59]

Picking up on such emotionally moving content, particularly from a man who had spent a great deal of time learning to hold his emotions in check,[60] has long been the purview of anonymous malcontents and what are today referred to as "Internet trolls," so it really is not all that surprising that this would be a scab at which they might pick when feeling threatened by a celebrity's words or actions. Of course, with such a controversial issue as Scottish independence, an added layer of nationalistic vitriol would certainly serve to ratchet up the tone of such condemnation. And indeed, Murray did show himself to be vulnerable here, which again was something that the British public had rarely, if ever, seen from him. It certainly left him open to such a predictable albeit contemptible backlash.

Parting Shots

Completely counter to tennis players from the United Kingdom who came before him, who were happy with winning a single round at a major event, Murray would not rest until he had lifted the trophies. After winning Olympic gold at the 2012 London Olympics, Murray became the (perhaps reluctant) leader of a British sporting renaissance, a resurgence that began in 2012 when countryman Bradley Wiggins won cycling's Tour de France. It was soon followed by a gold fest at the London Olympics that elevated the UK squad to an unprecedented third place at the medals table. Murray's subsequent win at the US Open put paid to, at least temporarily, the notion of Britain as a nation of sporting losers.

Strictly in terms of tennis, and following years of mediocrity, disappointment, and failure, the British tennis establishment could finally lay claim to a homegrown champion, albeit one whose motives remain suspect. And this fundamental contradiction that lies at the heart of the Murray narrative has all the signs of becoming a permanent question. It marks a tension between Murray being a champion tennis player whom the United Kingdom had sought for decades, and the troubling fact that Great Britain's tennis hopes continue to rest on the shoulders of a Scot at a time when tensions between the Scottish and the British state are at their most fractious. Thus, while fans continue to support Murray when he wins, he remains even in triumph a mere step away from a public relations disaster: an offhand joke, an ill-timed comment, an image taken just slightly out of context all stand to remind observers that his is the face of continued disenchantment—the face of a champion who just never really seemed to fit in as he should.

The continued invocation of a mass shooting, while not at the center of the Murray-related discord, nevertheless overhangs his legacy and to some extent illustrates the pettiness and petulance that marks the fragility of his relationship with not just British tennis fans but the nation as a whole. To be sure, as a player, Murray has done nothing but deliver what tennis fans in the United Kingdom have been missing since the 1930s. Steadfastly proud of his heritage, Murray is nonetheless forced to endure the vitriol of those who constantly challenge his loyalty to the kingdom. What has become abundantly clear, thus, is that no matter how many Grand Slam titles Murray wins over the course of his career, and no matter how much legitimacy he returns to British tennis, it is quite likely that he will continue to be framed as an outsider whose place within the larger British culture seems now set to remain mired in disdain.

Notes

1. Charles Dickens, *A Tale of Two Cities* (New York: Dover Publications, 1999), 1.
2. The only other players to win a Grand Slam since 2004 were Gastón Gaudio at the French Open in that year; Marat Safin at the Australian Open in 2005; Juan Martín del Potro at the US Open in 2009; Stan Wawrinka at the Australian Open in 2014 and the French Open in 2015; and Marin Čilić at the US Open in 2014.
3. Mark Hodgkinson, *Andy Murray, Wimbledon Champion: The Full Extraordinary Story* (New York: New Chapter Press, 2012).
4. [This chapter uses the names "United Kingdom" and "Great Britain" interchangeably, although the latter typically does not include Northern Ireland. Researching whether tennis fans in Northern Ireland side with the English or the Scottish where their thoughts of Andy Murray are concerned was outside the scope of this chapter, although such a study may indeed offer intriguing possibilities—*eds.*]
5. "Britain Unites to Hail US Open 'Legend' Andy Murray," Sport 360°, December 4, 2013, at http://sport360.com/article/tennis/8286/britain-unites-hail-us-open-legend-andy-murray.
6. Jackie MacMullan, "Murray the Bridesmaid No More," ESPN, August 5, 2012, at http://espn.go.com/olympics/summer/2012/tennis/story/_/id/8236089/tennis-andy-murray-bridesmaid-no-more.
7. Keith McLeod, "Pandy Monium: Tears and Triumph as Andy Lays Ghosts of 74 Years," *Daily Record*, July 7, 2012, 2, 3.
8. Hodgkinson, *Andy Murray, Wimbledon Champion*.
9. George Gross, "England Goes Crazy for Henman," *Financial Post*, July 2, 1996.
10. Judy Murray, "Games That Helped Make Murray a Champion," BBC Sport, July 24, 2013, at http://www.bbc.com/sport/0/get-inspired/23342076.
11. In 1999, Murray entered and won his first international tournament—the Junior Orange Bowl in Coral Gables, Florida—at the age of twelve. See "Andy Murray Biography," Biography, at http://www.biography.com/people/andy-murray-20875203.
12. Josephine McCusker, "Andy Murray: The Man behind the Racquet" (documentary), BBC, June 25, 2013.
13. Andy Murray, *Coming of Age: The Autobiography* (London: Cornerstone Digital, 2009), location 700.

14. Simon Hart, "Football and Tennis Face Funding Cuts as a Result of Sport England's 'Active People Survey,'" *Telegraph*, December 12, 2013, at http://www.telegraph.co.uk/sport/tennis/10514984/Football-and-tennis-face-funding-cuts-as-a-result-of-Sport-Englands-Active-People-Survey.html.

15. Ibid.

16. Sandra Harwitt, "Independent-Minded Jamie Murray Faring Just Fine," ESPN, February 25, 2008, at http://sports.espn.go.com/sports/tennis/news/story?id=3262577; and "Andy Murray Biography."

17. Hodgkinson, *Andy Murray, Wimbledon Champion*.

18. Ibid.

19. "Murray Slams British Players' Work Ethic, Mentality," ESPN, June 19, 2008, at http://sports.espn.go.com/sports/tennis/wimbledon08/news/story?id=3452746.

20. Murray, *Coming of Age*, location 667.

21. Ian Whittell, "Love Him or Hate Him, Murray's Profile Skyrocketed," ESPN, September 9, 2008, at http://sports.espn.go.com/sports/tennis/usopen08/columns/story?id=3576713.

22. Ibid. [These pairings refer to American collegiate sport rivalries—eds.]

23. "Andy Murray Biography."

24. Ibid.

25. Ibid.

26. Lendl won the Australian Open in 1989 and 1990; the French Open in 1984, 1986, and 1987; and the US Open in 1985, 1986, and 1987. He reached the Wimbledon finals in 1986 and 1987 but did not win. See Lendl's ATP summary page, at http://www.atpworldtour.com/Tennis/Players/Le/I/Ivan-Lendl.aspx.

27. Simon Briggs, "Andy Murray Admits Splitting Up with His Coach Ivan Lendl Left Him 'Gutted,'" *Telegraph*, March 20, 2014, at http://www.telegraph.co.uk/sport/tennis/10713034/Andy-Murray-admits-splitting-up-with-his-coach-Ivan-Lendl-left-him-gutted.html.

28. Lindsay Berra, "London Calling," ESPN, June 19, 2012, at http://espn.go.com/tennis/story/_/id/8041704/andy-murray-looks-primed-wimbledon-win-espn-magazine.

29. Brad Gilbert and Steve Jamison, *Winning Ugly: Mental Warfare in Tennis; Lessons from a Master* (New York: Simon & Schuster, 1993).

30. Brian Phillips, "Easy Lies the Head: Andy Murray, Who Carried the Dreams of a Nation, Is Finally a Wimbledon Champion," Grantland, July 10, 2013, at http://grantland.com/features/andy-murray-wins-wimbledon/.

31. Berra, "London Calling."

32. "Murray's First-Round Win Marred by Sexist Remark," ESPN, January 9, 2006, at http://sports.espn.go.com/sports/tennis/news/story?id=2285214.

33. Murray, *Coming of Age*, location 1583. Perhaps to reinforce his nonsexist nature, Murray, a vocal supporter of women's tennis, hired former Australian Open and Wimbledon champion Amélie Mauresmo as his coach in 2014; see Louisa Thomas, "Ladies and Gentleman: Andy Murray, Amélie Mauresmo, and Sexism at Wimbledon," Grantland, at http://grantland.com/features/andy-murray-wimbledon-2014-amelie-mauresmo-judy-murray/.

34. Ruairi O'Kane, "Fans' Volley of Abuse at 'Anti-English' Murray," *Daily Express*, June 29, 2006, 3.

35. Matheus Sanchez and Shekhar Bhatia, "Murray U-Turn; So, Braveheart Likes England

After All... But He Would Say That, His Girlfriend's a Sassenach," *Evening Standard* (London), June 29, 2006, 7.

36. McCusker, "Andy Murray: The Man Behind the Racquet."

37. Ibid. This passage is taken verbatim from the original text.

38. O'Kane, "Fans' Volley of Abuse."

39. For more on Fred West, see "Fred West Biography," Biography, at http://www.biography.com/people/fred-west-17169706.

40. O'Kane, "Fans' Volley of Abuse."

41. See Murray's ATP summary page, at http://www.atpworldtour.com/Tennis/Players/Top-Players/Andy-Murray.aspx?t=tf.

42. Greg Garber, "Murray Missing Aggression from Game," ESPN, August 30, 2009, at http://sports.espn.go.com/sports/tennis/usopen09/columns/story?columnist=garber_greg&id=4429182.

43. Peter Bodo, "Why Is Andy So Raggedy in the Slams?," ESPN, October 18, 2010, at http://espn.go.com/blog/peter-bodo/post/_/id/218/why-andy-murray-raggedy-slams.

44. Barry Flatman, "'Murray Is More Fragile between the Ears Than the Big Three'—Boris Becker; Winning Grand Slam Is All in the Mind for Despondent Scot," *Sunday Times* (London), July 3, 2011, 7. Becker won the Australian Open in 1991 and 1996; Wimbledon in 1985, 1986, and 1989; and the US Open in 1989. Becker also joined Novak Djokovic's coaching team in 2013. See Becker's ATP summary page, at: http://www.atpworldtour.com/Tennis/Players/Be/B/Boris-Becker.aspx.

45. "Britain Unites to Hail US Open 'Legend' Andy Murray."

46. This has been less of an issue in women's tennis, as Serena Williams won the US Open in 2014 and Mary Pierce won the French Open in 2000. Wimbledon and the Australian Open have not had hometown women's champions since the 1970s.

47. Roy Greenslade, "Andy Murray: How the National Papers Marked His 'Magical' Victory," *Guardian*, July 8, 2013, at http://www.theguardian.com/media/greenslade/2013/jul/08/andymurray-national-newspapers.

48. Oliver Holt, "How Andy Murray Finally Carried Us Home from Never-Never Land," *Daily Mirror*, July 8, 2013, at http://www.mirror.co.uk/sport/tennis/wimbledon-2013-andy-murrays-victory-2037411.

49. "Andy Murray Ends British Drought," ESPN, July 8, 2013, at http://espn.go.com/tennis/wimbledon13/story/_/id/9456682/andy-murray-tops-novak-djokovic-first-wimbledon-title.

50. Dan King, "Brit of History," *Sun*, July 8, 2013, 54, 55.

51. Marie Sharp, "Murray-Mania Sweeps Nation; Food, Drink and Songs Tribute to Tennis Hero," *Stirling Observer*, July 5, 2013, 5.

52. Hodgkinson, *Andy Murray, Wimbledon Champion*. Hodgkinson reports a frenzy over the number of times the number seven factored into the victory, making it the subject of many of the conspiracy theories that emerged.

53. Paul Newman, "We Are All So Proud of Andy Murray: Now You Hear Dunblane and Think of Tennis," *Independent*, September 17, 2012, 12, at http://www.independent.co.uk/news/uk/this-britain/we-are-all-so-proud-of-andy-murray-now-you-hear-dunblane-and-think-of-tennis-8143331.html.

54. Stephen McGinty, "Andy Murray Wimbledon: Dunblane Celebrates Hero," *Scotsman*, July 8, 2013, at http://www.scotsman.com/news/andy-murray-wimbledon-dunblane-celebrates-hero-1-2992718.

55. Ibid.

56. "Andy Murray: Don't Regret Opinion," ESPN, September 23, 2014, at http://espn.go.com/tennis/story/_/id/11573617/andy-murray-avoid-controversy-scotland-tweet.

57. "Andy Murray Unsure of Allegiance Post-Independence," *Scotsman*, June 8, 2014.

58. Gordon Robertson, "Britain's Sickest Troll," *Daily Record*, September 19, 2014, 6, 7.

59. McCusker, "Andy Murray: The Man Behind the Racquet."

60. Following Murray's loss to Roger Federer in the 2012 Wimbledon men's singles final, an emotional Murray was both chided for and given a pass for his public display. Tim Henman himself noted in the BBC documentary, "I thought it was sad on a number of levels obviously because he was incredibly disappointed but I find it slightly sad that it took him to cry in his acceptance speech for people to suddenly take a step back and go wow you know, he has got a heart, he is a sensitive soul." See ibid.

The Interaction of Personal, Local, and Global Forces
Yao Ming's Rise and Sustained Influence in Chinese Sport

—Dong Jinxia, Zhong Yijing, and Li Luyang

Introduction

Often referred to by such amusing epithets as "the Ming Dynasty" and "the Moving Great Wall," Yao Ming, the former National Basketball Association (NBA) player from China and 2016 inductee to the American Basketball Hall of Fame, remains one of the most popular sportsmen in both his home country and abroad. The embodiment of the humble albeit gentle giant, Yao established himself among the NBA's elite in a relatively brief career cut short by injury while turning himself into nothing less than a global sport phenomenon.

Yao initially caught the sporting world's attention with his enormous size of over seven feet, five inches tall (roughly 2.28 meters) and remarkable athletic talent, but size and talent have long been hallmarks of basketball players. What makes Yao's emergence on the sporting scene—and even beyond sport—such an engaging narrative is that for the first time in recent memory, one of the world's most recognizable celebrity icons hails from neither Europe nor the Americas but is, rather, Asian, and is one of the newer faces of China's emergence as a dominant player on the contemporary world stage.

Yao, who played for the NBA's Houston Rockets from 2002 to 2011, remains one of the most—if not the most—recognizable Chinese athletes in the world. His height coupled with his extraordinary athletic gifts, which took him to eight NBA All-Star game appearances and saw him honored as a five-time selection to the distinguished All-NBA team, thrust him into the global limelight and sparked considerable interest around the world. But, like so many other successful athletes, he did not turn into a star overnight. His teenage years were spent in focused, systematic training that prepared him physically and mentally, while his later years in the NBA helped fine-tune him into a mature, international basketball phenom. Many factors, including family dynamics, commercial considerations, and political concerns, played an integral role in determining his career path. Given that basketball has been dominated primarily by Americans, with a small percentage of Europeans and a handful of sub-Saharan Africans, and given that Chinese basketball has typically existed along the margins of world sport, it is indeed remarkable that Yao Ming could emerge as he did on the twenty-first-century world stage.

The multiple forces that catapulted Yao to world celebrity, and his various postathletic efforts to maintain both his national and international image while he expands his influence from sport to business to education to public affairs, offers a particularly expansive vantage point from which to assess his unique place among international sport celebrities. That he was able to ostensibly dodge the trappings of celebrity while nevertheless maintaining his worldwide appeal shines further light on his individual legacy, while it widens the vantage point from which we can view celebrity as it exists on a much broader scale. But questions remain, namely:

- How was Yao able to overcome the barriers in order to achieve supremacy in sport?
- And how was he able to retain his visibility long after he stopped playing in 2011?

As a means to explore these and other questions further, this chapter will trace Yao's professional path and analyze the relevant factors that had an obvious impact on his ascendance to international athletic stardom both at home and abroad.

Journey toward Stardom

Born in Shanghai on September 12, 1980, Yao Ming is his family's only child, a common phenomenon in China since the introduction of the "one child" policy in 1979. As a consequence of the mandated birth-control practice, Chinese parents, especially those in the cities, routinely focus all their energies and aspirations on their sole offspring. Moreover, they hope that they can furnish their progeny with those things that were unavailable to them during the challenging years before the more opulent 1980s. And Yao's parents were no exception. They expected Yao to achieve in all aspects of his life including basketball, even if it meant long hours of training each day. Yao certainly would not disappoint them.

It is widely recognized that Yao's height is a key contributor to his successful basketball career. His unusual albeit proportional physique, inherited from his similarly proportioned parents, themselves both former professional basketball players playing in Chinese circuits, in part underscores the familial support and encouragement that helped socialize him into the Chinese sporting environment at a very young age. When he was just four years old, he was given his first basketball as a gift from his parents. At age nine, his parents took him to watch an American basketball exhibition, which was reportedly when he first heard of the NBA. That same year, he began playing basketball at a local youth sport academy, typically the most common path toward playing professionally in China. At first his parents balked at the idea of his following in their athletic footsteps, as they wished him go to university to study, but they later gave him their full support after he demonstrated a genuine talent for the game.[1] Referencing typically Western norms, sport sociologist Jay Coakley contends that family is a crucial supporting factor in an individual's athletic success,[2] and this appears to have been the case with Yao as well. Indeed, more than the typical Chinese family, and perhaps owing to some underlying Western ideals, Yao's parents were able to demonstrate a firsthand knowledge of what it takes to participate in professional sport, given their insider experiences with the Chinese sport system and its subculture. This certainly influenced Yao in many aspects, from his attitude toward basketball to his way of dealing with people in and outside the sporting community. As Coakley concludes, such familial influence was invaluable in ensuring his smooth progression from young Chinese boy to international superstar.[3]

Yao's developmental path is reflective of most elite Chinese athletes in that they routinely experience a three-stage developmental process. Initially, they emerge as school-age athletes at what are referred to locally and regionally as sports schools, where a majority of successful Chinese athletes begin their athletic careers.[4] Success in the sport schools can lead to admission to the professional ranks with selection to a provincial team, which represents the defining moment of most athletes' careers. Most of these provincial or municipal teams consist of junior and senior teams, with the national team being, of course, the pinnacle of elite sport in China and for which the absolute top-tier talents from across the country are selected. Those who successfully make the transition are then said to "undertake 'specialized' training and lead a monotonous and militarized life in a 'semi-sealed' sports community."[5]

At age thirteen, following four years of extensive training, Yao was offered a tryout—his first of what would be many such opportunities—for his hometown Shanghai Sharks, a junior team in the prestigious Chinese Basketball Association (CBA). There, he practiced ten hours a day while competing against players who were two and three years older than he. By age fifteen he began to participate in national competitions and soon attracted attention from other professionals, the media, and the public. Two years after that, he was selected to be a member of the national team, further suggesting that he was indeed on a fast track toward elite athletic status, a great honor for any select athlete. Yao recalls:

As long as I can join the national team, it does not matter if I am not paid, have no fans, and even play as a substitute. To play for the nation is an honor. I was seventeen when I wore the national team vest for the first time. The first day I took the vest to the mirror and posed like a model with different postures. Though the vest was a little bit too big for me, to have my name on it is a great honor.[6]

As Yao would later explain, ascending through the exclusive level of the Chinese athletic system, as he had done from a relatively young age, afforded him many more opportunities than most other Chinese athletes. Further, we can conclude that the entire elite sport system worked to his advantage and helped him mature quickly as an athlete and presumably as one who was growing more and more accustomed to the glare of the spotlight.

Yao's family influence from throughout this period can certainly be viewed from a broader perspective. As many sport scholars have concluded, sport does not occur in a social vacuum but rather is an integral part of social life.[7] It reflects and is affected by the dominant social structures and values of the society in which it exists,[8] which is particularly evident in Yao's developmental trajectory and his many experiences both in China and in his travels around the global sporting world.

The Role of National Reform

Since 1979, China's move toward reestablishing international relations through overarching economic reforms has had a profound impact on, among other things, the country's sporting climate in general and on athletes such as Yao Ming in particular. One signature moment, for example, was that same year's reentry of China as a member of the International Olympic Committee (IOC) after more than two decades of isolation from the international sporting community.[9] In the ensuing era of marketization, privatization, and globalization in the early 1990s, the CBA began to experience commercialization. This brought with it more of a focus on bilateral exchanges, the migration of coaches and athletes, and the eventual employment of foreign players, which served to strengthen the competitiveness of league games.

Yao benefited enormously from the changing environment, and rather quickly too. After joining the national team at age seventeen, he was soon representing the country at both the Asian and Olympic Games as well as at other international tournaments. It was also in that year that Yao attended a six-day Nike camp in Paris where he learned, as he articulated it, "not just about basketball, but maybe about [myself] and [my] place in the world of basketball."[10] The following year he played for two months in the United States, which helped fuel his desire to play in the NBA.[11] But the momentum that had carried him this far was suddenly halted when disputes arising from a general lack of familiarity on the part of all parties with the signing of foreign nationals to both NBA contracts and representation deals made things quite difficult.[12] As *USA Today*'s Steve Friess explained, Yao's circumstances required that he have nine separate entities sign off on all contractual arrangements, which accounts in large part for why an original deal with the American agency Evergreen Sports fell through.[13] Later attempts to blend Evergreen and Chinese representation were also unsuccessful and further delayed the process, a matter that caught the attention of the NBA players' union. As then union spokesperson Dan Wasserman was to remark:

> [The challenge of getting Yao signed] certainly throws up some red flags that the clubs have to evaluate, and very carefully so.... Some clubs may not have as much expertise in dealing with foreign players and foreign entities, and they better get up on the curve quick if they're interested in Yao Ming.[14]

By the time Yao finally had the requisite representation in the United States, necessarily meeting with the approval of both his parents and Chinese officials, three years had lapsed.[15]

While awaiting his chance to play in America, Yao played for the Chinese team in the 2000 Olympics. A year later he was the star of the Asian Basketball Championships, in which the Chinese national team won a gold medal, a feat they repeated from 2003 to 2005. Thus, over a span of ten years, Yao not only entered the national stage, and quite abruptly at that, but was increasingly exposed to it as he grew more comfortable with the international sport scene.

Following Beijing's successful Olympic bid for the 2008 Summer Games and China's entry into the World Trade Organization in 2001, globalization accelerated in China, and Shanghai, Yao's hometown, was transforming into a global metropolis. Sport, in the meantime, became a strong component of China's global power, and its rise was likely driven as much by commercial forces as by political engagement. This is clearly reflected in the staging of a number of high-profile international events, including the 2000 Shanghai Masters tennis tournament, the 2004 Chinese Grand Prix Formula One World Championship, the 2010 German Touring Car Masters, and in 2011 both the BMW Masters and WGC-HSBC Champions golf tournaments. In addition to helping expand China's commitment to world sport, all this activity further paved the way for international sporting concerns, including the NBA, to make inroads into Chinese markets, which in turn helped facilitate Yao's signing with the NBA's Houston Rockets in 2002.[16]

Transition to the NBA

When the Houston Rockets selected Yao with the first pick of the 2002 draft, he became the first Asian player ever to be selected first, and he had never played college basketball in the United States. Still, his rise to stardom in the NBA, though quite rapid, was never a foregone conclusion, particularly given his relative unfamiliarity with the American game and continued questions regarding his physique in terms of the ruggedness of the NBA, some of which was steeped in traditional anti-Asian assumptions among Westerners. Indeed, Yao's early days in the NBA were marked by a range of physical and even cultural difficulties. He was held scoreless and registered only two rebounds in his first NBA game. His more passive playing style and thin body were exploited initially by opponents, and he routinely fell to the ground, which led to charges of flopping,[17] which is illegal and often results in other players challenging one's skill set and aptitude for the sport. This of course led to more widespread doubts about Yao's ability, as both fans and the American media continued to question the Rockets' decision to draft him at all, especially as the vaunted first pick. Hall of Famer Charles Barkley (among others) took to turning Yao's appearance on the NBA stage into something of a running punch line; Barkley joked that he would kiss his broadcast partner's *derrière* "if Yao Ming scores 20 points in a game,"[18] a promise he reiterated quite often. That it was assumed that Yao would be incapable of adjusting to the league's more physical style of play suggests how deeply the North American image of the "Oriental" outsider was ingrained.

Sensing this all around him, Yao grew worried that the team would release him and send him home. Through his first seven games with the Houston side, he was averaging only fourteen minutes of playing time while registering very meager outputs in terms of points and rebounds. Commentators continued their onslaught, expressing deep pessimism about his future in the NBA. Struggling with his disappointing performances in these early days, Yao sought refuge by reminding himself of the refrain, "This is a battle. I need time to get used to it."[19] And indeed, in the face of all the doubts and criticism, Yao slowly began to establish himself on the court, steadily increasing his contributions in performances that all culminated in a twenty-point output in Los Angeles on November 17, 2002, against the vaunted Lakers. This performance against one of the NBA's most storied franchises, before its celebrity fan base and in front of a nationally televised audience, seems to have been Yao's watershed moment, taking him from the ranks of an American sport spectacle to a genuine competitor on the national (and later international) sporting stage.[20]

After this breakthrough, Yao was able to adapt to the NBA tempo fairly quickly. Over the next two years, Yao progressed steadily and reached career marks in several statistical categories, becoming one of the league's elite centers while gradually assimilating the more physical demands of NBA play. And these changes—subtle or otherwise—were certainly garnering him notice in league circles.

Indeed, for some time, David Stern, then the NBA commissioner, had been on a quest to find an international star who could rival even the globally iconic Michael Jordan. In Yao, Stern seemed to have found not only the person who could rise to the occasion but one who could also offer the league a direct link to the enormous and certainly lucrative Chinese market. Even before Yao came to the United States for his first preseason training camp with the Rockets, the NBA promoted him extensively through radio, television, and Internet campaigns, creating a buzz and heightening anticipation about his arrival.

Following the draft, the Rockets made Yao the focal point of the franchise's marketing schemes, hitching their commercial wagons to his making a successful transition to the NBA. It was evident that both the franchise and the league had placed Yao at the forefront of their respective brands when Stern declared that this transition marked what was to be "a great and marvelous moment for the Rockets, for the NBA and for the whole world, and especially for China." He continued to proclaim that "Yao Ming is a skilled player, and he becomes the first international to be picked up with the overall first pick, but he will not be the last Chinese player to join in the NBA."[21] That Yao Ming had yet to do anything substantive as a basketball player seemed relatively immaterial at this juncture, as these campaigns continued to generate interest in him primarily as an attraction, which, while not uncommon in American commercial culture, must have seemed quite odd to Chinese audiences and to Yao in particular.

Moreover, the pressure on him to excel was extraordinary. The expectation that he would transition immediately and perhaps even seamlessly into superstardom combined with the belief that he would become the Chinese equivalent of the inimitable Air Jordan himself seems upon reflection an impossible task, essentially putting Yao in a position whereby nothing he accomplished would ever be good enough to meet, let alone exceed, expectations. The string of criticisms aimed at his early play certainly speaks to such claims. Nevertheless, from the start of his NBA career, Yao's presence was in fact paying dividends in terms of the interest he sparked throughout basketball circles and the resulting financial boon his presence offered the league, although it came long before he would blossom into the type of player he was assumed to be all along.

His effect on Chinese popular culture, however, was perhaps even more significant. The number of Yao supporters among both Chinese and Chinese Americans rose significantly to the extent that Mandarin captions began to appear on the digital screens at Houston home games. The NBA's official website showed a 40 percent increase in Chinese hits, which in turn exposed Chinese fans to other NBA players, furthering Stern's stated desire to expand into the

Chinese market. Yao had indeed grown to become Stern's Asian Jordan, endorsing products at home while continuing to generate interest in the league with remarkable consistency.

The Marketing of a Chinese Icon

Right from the outset of Yao's NBA career, a group of advisers, including his negotiator Erik Zhang, his Chinese agent Lu Hao, noted University of Chicago economics professor John Huizinga, and Bill Sanders and Bill Duffy, his representatives from the American sport management agency BDA, worked together to maximize his market value. The group, often referred to simply as "Yao's team," made concerted efforts to promote him through a range of methods. Among their many achievements that spoke to the marketing phenomenon they were stoking were creating a fan-friendly website, arranging for Yao to visit selected kindergarten classes to tell stories to children, playing songs composed by Yao's fans in the Rockets' arena during games, and posting Yao-related memorabilia, including a pair of his shoes and a life-sized portrait of him, in of all places the Basketball Hall of Fame in Springfield, Massachusetts. Yao also began to migrate toward multimedia appearances such as providing the voiceover for the Chinese animated film *The Magic Aster*, which was released on June 19, 2009. In general, they were working to tailor a Yao-related brand that was characterized by his unique image and Asian character while massaging his persona in such a way to make him appear earthy and humble and playful. In one instance, Yao, wearing a Rockets uniform while performing Taiji (usually written in English transliteration as *tai chi*), appeared in a promotional program with a group of people, including Rockets players, referees, and fans, learning the forms. Then, at the end of the sequence, Yao concludes: "I love the game."[22] These promotional packages were shown on local Houston television stations during time outs at Rockets games, again demonstrating the extent to which the team continued to play a crucial role in helping to ensure his success. These efforts ranged from signing him to the then-largest contract in NBA history to helping him secure dozens of product endorsements to building up his positive personal image and social status.

As a rare Chinese fixture in the American market, and certainly as the most celebrated Asian on the NBA courts, Yao also benefited from enormous support from his fans at home and around the world. Through the NBA's remarkable reach, it is estimated that Yao Ming's "Ming Dynasty" led to some three hundred million NBA fans emerging seemingly overnight in China.[23] The already large and growing Chinese community in the United States connected with him quite readily, as his presence underscored the immense pride they took in being represented by him in a cultural sense. This was particularly true in Houston, which boasts the fourth-largest concentration of Chinese living in the country, numbering about twenty-four thousand.[24] Nor was it surprising that Houston's mayor at that time, Lee P. Brown, went so far as to proclaim December 11, 2002, Yao Ming Day,[25] an honor not many athletes experience especially so early in their career.

With this flurry of activity surrounding Yao's initial appearances and subsequent accomplishments in Houston, he was voted by fans as a starter for the Western Conference in the 2003 NBA All-Star Game, making him the first rookie to start in that contest since Detroit Pistons star Grant Hill did it in 1995. This rapid turnabout can best be attributed to the growth of a strong multiethnic fan base due in large part to the introduction of a third language, namely Mandarin, alongside English and Spanish among the local and regional populace. With such a broad base of support, Yao easily outpaced established NBA megastar center Shaquille O'Neal by nearly a quarter of a million votes despite the fact that O'Neal was coming off three consecutive NBA Finals MVP awards. That same coalition of fans similarly voted him as a starter in the 2005 All-Star Game with over 2.5 million votes, breaking Michael Jordan's record for votes while reaffirming that Yao was indeed in rare company.[26]

Despite missing twenty-one games due to various injuries the following season, Yao was once again voted to start in the 2006 NBA All-Star Game and again with the highest vote total of anyone else in the league. In response to this, the seven-foot, one-inch (2.16 meters), 320-pound O'Neal, regarded as something of a beast on the court but often quite pensive off it, pointed out: "He [Yao] is writing history for his people, and his people is [sic] honored of him. He has over one billion people behind him. To block him down is too difficult."[27] Moreover, these soaring vote totals are typically viewed as proof positive that Yao was in the process of transcending the game before he had actually figured out how to navigate the many challenges of life on the NBA courts.

Yao's ascent in the American sporting scene certainly furthered David Stern's objective to make the NBA an even bigger player than it already was on the world sporting stage, but it also served to make Yao quite wealthy quite quickly. Throughout Yao's nine years in the league, he earned somewhere in the range $93 million in salary alone. He earned an additional $25 million in endorsement deals for local Chinese products as well as increasingly global American brands such as Apple, McDonald's, and Visa.[28] His inevitable advance into the massive and potentially lucrative Chinese market was also part of a carefully crafted approach that was as benign as it was successful. As Clifford Coonan remarked in the London *Times*, "[Yao's] team-first attitude, allied to an easygoing, affable personality and an ability to appeal to a Far East market, which the NBA is keen to exploit, guaranteed him superstar status."[29]

By October 2004, the NBA had encroached even further into the Chinese market by first hosting a series of exhibition games in Yao's home city of Shanghai as well as in Beijing before opening offices in the Chinese capital later that year. There, the league set up its own Mandarin website, signing contracts with twelve provincial TV stations to broadcast 168 NBA games and sending a number of players to China to display their skills and promote the products they endorsed. As a result, NBA shops and restaurants popped up throughout China seemingly one after another. The NBA then continued to make inroads into Yao's home country when it launched NBA China in 2008 with a $253 million investment from ESPN/Walt Disney Company and several Chinese partners, although the NBA owns a majority stake in its Chinese subsidiary that is divided evenly among its thirty teams. Bankers estimated that the venture, still very much alive long after Yao's playing career ended after the 2011 season, is worth somewhere in the area of $1.5 billion to $1.7 billion. NBA revenues in China are expected to approach $200 million by 2015 with significant growth potential to continue unabated into the future,[30] demonstrating, among other things, that from the start Stern had a firm handle on Yao's marketability and worked his aims carefully if not persistently.

Individually, Yao's appeal to the Chinese market was further reflected by the increased contacts between Chinese companies and the NBA. Yao-endorsed Yanjing Beer was among the first Chinese products to become an NBA sponsor. And in late 2002, the NBA's website reported the renewal of TV agreements with a range of international networks, including CCTV in China and ESPN Star Sports, broadcasting throughout much of Asia, adding further that "a record 12 telecasters from China will provide unprecedented NBA coverage to their region."[31] The 2007 game in which Yao squared off for the first time against his fellow countryman Yi Jianlian of the Milwaukee Bucks was broadcast on nineteen networks in China and watched by over two hundred million people in China alone, making it one of the most-watched NBA games in history. Thus, by every financial measure, Yao Ming was the first Asian superstar in the NBA, and he grew to become such an important cultural figure that he materially altered the league's business landscape even before he blossomed into one of the game's better players.

A Bridge between Worlds

Yao's success on and off the court indeed made him a global phenomenon. But first and foremost, he was a man trying to ply his trade far from his home while crafting the image of a national and cultural icon who would ultimately be embraced by both the East and the West.

To be sure, foreign players in the NBA can at times face a host of conflicting demands and expectations as they learn to span the social, economic, and political divides of global stardom. In Yao's case, the conflict was particularly acute given the historical tensions between China and the United States. This existing tension was often exacerbated by the cultural expectation that Chinese athletes were to place national interests above personal ones; while this same expectation is often preached in American sport, in America it ends up more a platitude than actual practice. As veteran American journalist Michael Wilbon acknowledged, "Yao had to carry a country all the time, during his NBA season and the Olympics or the World Championships,"[32] leading to a palpable sense that, given his place in the sporting spotlight, Yao was in one way or another inextricably bound to China's place in the world. Still, as the West came to equate Yao with China, it also appeared that China was intent on riding Yao's successes as a springboard to a more enviable position in terms of world commerce and politics.

Part of the justification for these expectations lay in the fact that top Chinese athletes grew and benefited from the state-financed sports system, which allocates national resources to a few talented elites. Given that international sport competition is "an effective platform for the assertion of national identity because competitions are grounded in the nation-state system,"[33] and that to become a global sports power had been part of China's persistent strategy as it sought to become a world power following a century's worth of humiliation from Western invasions and interventions from the mid-nineteenth century until the Maoist victory, Chinese athletes are in essence asked to champion China's emerging global position. In the face of such lofty expectations, an athlete's personal interests simply had to take a back seat to the greater good.

This tension between self-interest and subordination to the collective was clearly on display in the case of Wang Zhizhi, the first Chinese national to join the NBA. In 1999, Wang refused to return to China to play for the national team, and thus he was subsequently banned from the team altogether, which also had the effect of thrusting upon him an exceedingly negative image among the Chinese public. Wang's example most assuredly did not go unnoticed among those in Yao's inner circle.

Indeed, Yao was fortunate in the sense that he could learn from Wang's missteps. Unlike Wang, Yao would eagerly accept the CBA's expectation that he would make himself available to play for the Chinese national team whenever asked, and he kept his promise, often at a tremendous personal and professional price. For instance, he missed significant portions of the Rockets' preseason in 2002 in order to play for the Chinese side in that year's FIBA World Championship. But his links to the team went beyond his mere presence, which further differentiated him from Wang. So when Yao vowed not to shave his beard for half a year if the Chinese national team failed to qualify for the quarterfinals in the 2004 Olympics, he was actually accomplishing two very real things for his country and for his image insomuch as it further established his unique blend of self-awareness bordering on self-deprecation coupled with a strong degree of national pride that enabled him to maintain his lofty standing at home.[34] Moreover, as the Chinese team showed that it could indeed live up to its potential,[35] Yao continued to swing back and forth between his responsibilities to Chinese sport and to those with whom he was contractually aligned in the United States. And yet it was playing for a Rockets team that was consistently in contention and hence playing deep into the playoffs every season, alongside routinely leading the Chinese team into international competition including the 2006 FIBA World Championship as well as the 2008 Summer Olympics at home in Beijing, that forced him to play through a range of painful injuries that threatened his health and ultimately led to the premature end of his career.

Despite the physical toll, Yao stood resolute through his myriad responsibilities to the delight of fans and administrators across the sporting landscape. In the 2008 Olympic Games, Yao scored the first basket of China's opening game against the eventual gold medalist US team, noting with pride, "I was just really happy to make that shot. It was the first score in our Olympic campaign here at home.... It represents that we can keep our heads up in the face of really tough odds."[36] He also carried the Chinese flag during the opening ceremonies in both the 2004 and 2008 Olympic Games, an honor that recognized his outstanding athletic performance and his image as the nation's representative athletic figure. This optimistic image so carefully crafted was also on display in a 2010 Chinese promotional film shown on a giant outdoor screen in New York's Times Square, whose predominant theme was that after many years on the periphery, China had reemerged on the world stage in a big way. For these contributions, Yao's position as China's sporting ambassador was indisputable, and by 2011 he would be awarded two of China's most coveted athletic honors: the vaunted Trophy of Physical Education and Sport by the State Sports Administration and the award for Outstanding Contribution to Chinese Basketball.[37] And as if to reinforce his position in his home country, in 2012 Yao was voted one of the top ten figures to have made great contributions to spreading Chinese culture across the world.[38]

But his presence was more than a matter of cultural diffusion. As one of the NBA's top players, Yao was also quietly yet effectively defying widely held Western stereotypes about Chinese men. In the often highly masculinized world of professional basketball, where the media conflates talent with brute strength and more than a perceptible hint of aggression in a game whose on-court presence continues to be dominated by African Americans and, more recently, central and eastern Europeans, Yao's continued rise among basketball's elite presented a discernible challenge to the conventional image of the

Chinese male as somehow weak if not effeminate. As biographer Ric Bucher commented, "Yao's everything, from his square chin, flat top hairstyle to his giant body and basketball skills, overthrew our previous knowledge about China."[39] Bucher goes on to suggest that while Yao brought his own personal elements of gentleness and grace from his private life to his professional one, he was also confirming that despite the smile, speech, and reverential conduct, he was not what anyone expected. Quite the contrary, he was by all accounts the inverse. Tall, strong, valiant, and aggressive when necessary, Yao came to represent a wholesale revision of the mythology behind the lasting image of the "Oriental" other. He challenged the assumptions behind the stereotypes, dispelling many of those stereotypes regarding his body type and demeanor long before the basketball public actually got to know him. In this regard, Yao came to be viewed as a Chinese man who had successfully adapted to Western expectations of virility and machismo while at the same time softening deeply held Western suspicions about Chinese culture writ large. And it is perhaps this dichotomy that allowed him to be embraced by the West while at the same time remaining as revered a figure as there is in China as well as one of his home country's most prized cultural exports. As Commissioner Stern would observe in the *Houston Chronicle*, Yao had become an integral "bridge between Chinese and American fans."[40]

How did Yao Ming, who had no American cultural background at all, survive and adapt to NBA life? His own response to this question was to acknowledge: "Chinese culture has taught me to be inclusive, understanding, and easy to communicate with."[41] Of course, Yao took significant steps to overcome a range of barriers, not the least of which were language, custom, and, in general, the different pace of everyday life in America. So, for example, while Yao strongly preferred to eat traditional Chinese cuisine, he nevertheless taught himself to eat some Western foods even if they held very little appeal for him. In what is today a common practice in China, modern parents who have only a single child follow their successful child to his place of work, which in Yao's case led them to travel to Houston to help him transition into what was undoubtedly a strange new existence, particularly helping with his dietary situation so obviously vital to any young athlete's success.

Many of these matters went beyond the mundane landscape of ordinary life, forcing Yao to overcome a host of difficult sociocultural challenges. In order to communicate with coaches, teammates, and journalists, for example, Yao had to master English as quickly as possible, which he did at an extraordinary pace. When he first came to Houston, he had to rely on a translator to answer questions at press conferences, but by the end of his first full year with the team, he no longer required translation, which, considering that he suffers from significant hearing loss in his left ear, is quite a remarkable achievement indeed.[42]

Yao similarly worked hard to integrate many expected Western cultural patterns, although he also continued to exhibit some customary behaviors from his homeland. For example, during press conferences, Yao would often wear track suits and other comfortable styles of athletic wear instead of the expected Western-style suits that were never to his liking, although he would eventually have to acquiesce once business wear became codified in the NBA player rules in a controversial 2005 edict from the commissioner's office.[43] And even his choice of jersey number suggested how much thoughts of home informed his time in the United States, when he chose to wear number 11 with the Rockets because Ye Li, his then-girlfriend who played for a Shanghai women's basketball team as well as the Chinese national team, wore that number too.[44]

Just as telling is Yao's role in holding open the doors of opportunity to his colleagues and peers. As discussed above, Yao helped pave the way for the NBA to enter the world's most populous market with more than 1.3 billion people. Throughout Yao's NBA career, every single Rockets game was televised in China, while coverage of Yao and his teammates dominated local and regional media. As a result, Chinese fans became very knowledgeable about the NBA and many of the league's dominant players, particularly celebrating Yao's own Rockets teammates. In fact, Yao's presence helped some of the other Rockets, a diverse compendium of players that included Americans Shane Battier and the irascible Ron Artest (aka Metta World Peace) as well as Argentina's Luis Scola and the Congolese defensive specialist Dikembe Mutombo, acquire lucrative endorsement deals with the Chinese shoe brands Peak and Anta.[45]

But playing in the NBA also left its mark on Yao. Two years after his entry into the league, Yao once again led China's national team at the 2004 Olympics in Athens, and the extent of his transition into Western athletic behavior was apparent. Following the team's first game against Spain, Yao grew visibly angry at his Chinese teammates, publicly criticizing them for not playing their best. Such open criticism was rare in Chinese sporting circles and sparked a public debate. Likely associated with his experiences playing among the best and perhaps most vocal players in the world, this uncharacteristic public display is often viewed in hindsight as having spurred the Chinese team to reclaim their collective identity and fight their way back into contention, beating the defending European champion Serbia and Montenegro and becoming one of the world's top eight national teams.[46]

But it is off the court where most of Yao's impact was first felt and where it remains both in China and in the United States. As David Stern once said: "Through Yao, the Chinese were going to know a lot more about the USA and Houston, and through Yao we were going to get to know a lot more about China."[47] For all his global visibility and influence, Yao had indeed become a sort of cultural emissary between China and the United States as well as representative of each nation's interests. Pursued by local, regional, and national figures, Yao has been honored at and attended state functions in both countries, a partial list of which reads:

- April 2006: Attended a highly anticipated luncheon for visiting Chinese president Jiang Zemin at the White House, where Yao was given a chance to offer remarks.
- December 2009: Awarded the Special Contribution Reward of Sino-USA Relations.
- December 2011: Appointed as the Vice Chairman of the Shanghai Public Diplomacy Association.
- February 2013: Named Goodwill Ambassador of Houston.[48]

These and the many other off-court honors Yao has received are remarkable for an athlete, let alone one whose career lies between two very different cultures with very different sets of expectations, which at times appear to be in competition with one another. And yet it does offer a moment's pause if only to consider how far relations between the two countries progressed during Yao's ascent into prominence. Certainly, such conclusions lend themselves to a degree of overstatement; in 1992, the *Guardian* claimed that Yao's entering the NBA could be compared to President Nixon's heralded visit to China in 1972:

> Arguably, Yao is also transforming the global prospects for his sport and, on the most hyper-optimistic expectations, changing the relationship between the US and China in a manner not seen since the days of Ping-Pong diplomacy 30 years ago.[49]

Despite such lofty pronouncements, it is not necessarily hyperbolic to consider that initially Yao's presence and ultimately his success in American sporting circles did in fact mark, if only in bits, a transformative moment of sorts in US-Sino relations. As Thomas Oates and Judy Polumbaum note in their oft-cited work on what they term Yao's "elasticity" in the larger marketplace: "The bridge-building role he has created between the West and the East, the celebrity economic effects he has generated as a global sports icon, and the far-reaching influence in a historical period he has brought to the development of Sino-American relations"[50] make him a unique player all around. Or, as Wu Zhifei put it, Yao is "a symbolic icon that other Chinese in the 21st century can hardly surpass.[51]

Life after Basketball

Yao's basketball career was cut short due to a series of well-chronicled and quite debilitating injuries to his legs and, in particular, to his feet that ultimately required six surgeries from 2005 to 2011, when he decided to retire just shy of his thirtieth birthday. His announcement "My basketball career has ended" drew over 1.2 million comments on the Chinese social networking site Sina Weibo.[52] The statement was also widely circulated in Western media and in ways that suggested that it was more than simply a basketball story or even a sport story.[53]

And yet, regardless of its political or even cultural implications, Yao's athletic success both at home and abroad generated enormous economic as well as social capital for him and for those around him. He showed quite quickly, if not emphatically, that he was aware of his value almost from the start, as exemplified by his successful pursuit of legal action against soft drink giant Coca-Cola for using his image on their bottles while promoting China's national team in 2003. Characteristically, he would turn around and sign a lucrative endorsement deal with them in time for the 2008 Olympics, demonstrating above all that he had a firm grasp of his worth in the broader market.[54] This conscious embrace of his market value became particularly vital to his post-basketball life, and he worked to coalesce his brand in the commercial and even political arenas.[55]

To be sure, athletes are a unique group of individuals in the labor force if for no other reason than their careers are understood to be finite and quite often fleeting. While some athletes choose to ignore this reality and react slowly if at all to the inevitability of their changing economic circumstances, as a group, it remains essential that they find ways to reinvent themselves beyond their athletic reputation if they wish to attain anything close to a fully formed and meaningful post-sport life. Those who wield the type of star power that affords them fame and resources are better primed for such transitions, and many ease from bodily driven fame to commercial and even political clout, for example baseball's revered Jackie Robinson, who rose through the business ranks to become a vice president at Chock Full o' Nuts, and Gerald R. Ford, who ultimately parlayed his status as a recognizable collegiate athlete into first a vice presidency and ultimately a half term as America's thirty-eighth president. For Yao, the end of his playing career meant that like other athletes he would certainly have to reinvent himself, but being at ease with his environment and already having forayed into the economic sphere, he has made his transition a relatively smooth one.

In China, Yao has made several plays in the national economy from venture capitalism to the nonprofit sector. For instance, he pumped nearly $6 million into Top100.cn, an ad-supported digital music partnership between Beijing-based Orca Digital and Google. In the United States, he launched Yao Family Wines, a Napa Valley winery that sources grapes from nearby vineyards.[56] As an established businessman with the backing of a solid group of advisers, he has been fully cognizant of the vast business opportunities that underscore his personal brand. To protect the exclusive rights of this image, Yao has registered more than thirty commercial trademarks in China involving sports equipment, clothing lines, beverage concerns, and computer games and other high-tech products.[57]

In 2011, Yao began dipping his toes more deeply into the financial investment sector, becoming a board member overseeing the Huang Shen Fund initiated by his Chinese agent, Lu Hao. The following year, he extended his reach even further by taking over the Chongqing Fu Yuan equity investment fund, which, when combined with Huang Shen, placed his holdings in the area of a whopping 6.6 billion yuan.[58] Because of such efforts, he led *Forbes*'s Chinese Celebrity 100 list for income and popularity for eight straight years, earning a staggering $51 million (CN¥357 million) in 2008 alone.[59]

A major part of Yao's income also came from sponsorship deals. At one point, Yao held product endorsement agreements with twenty major companies, including Nike, Reebok, PepsiCo, Visa, Apple, Garmin, and McDonald's.[60] According to *Bloomberg Businessweek*, by 2010, Yao's net worth was estimated to be in the neighborhood of $150 million,[61] most of which is viewed as a carryover from his enormously successful playing career.

But the economic sphere was not Yao's only focus. In 2013 he began carving out a niche for himself in Chinese politics when he was elected as a member of the Twelfth National Committee of the Chinese People's Political Consultative Conference (NCCPPCC). Taking a mediating position in this important national assembly, Yao thrust himself into the emergent national physical fitness debate while acknowledging that he had a great deal to learn about the more practical applications of high-profile politics, once again demonstrating that unique blend of collective purpose and personal humility. There, he voiced his concerns about what some had deemed an inadequate measure of proper exercise being taken up by the coming generation, observing: "Chinese teenagers are not daring to practice long-distance running and strenuous exercise out of safety concerns, but the fears will inevitably bring about weakening physiques."[62] The gist of his remarks fell to the role that his beloved game of basketball could play in such debates. Reaching out on what must be a quite familiar level, Yao worked to encourage more people to play the game as a means toward the holistic development of body, mind, and spirit. Toward that end, and in partnership with the NBA, he would set up the first Yao Ming School in the WKS Hi-Park in Beijing in 2014.[63]

Yao's Legacy

For all the many roles he has played in Chinese life that date back to his rise within the ranks of national sport, Yao Ming has been able to generate and maintain a remarkably high level of public appeal and attention in an age that is not all that conducive to positive media coverage. His story—or at least aspects of it—has been chronicled in newspapers and tabloids both in China and in the

United States; it continues to be told and retold in such heralded pages as the *New York Times*, *Sports Illustrated*, *Sporting News*, *ESPN the Magazine*, *SLAM*, *Inside Stuff*, and *Basketball Digest*. His aforementioned endorsement arrangements with such high-profile entities as Visa, Apple Computer, and Gatorade also kept him both visible and sought after in print and electronic mediums. His English-language autobiography *Yao: A Life in Two Worlds* (2004; coauthored with Ric Bucher), which appeared in Chinese translation the following year,[64] and the documentary film *The Year of the Yao* (also 2004), which chronicles his rookie season in the NBA,[65] also furthered his positive image.[66] But home is where Yao's influence continues to soar. For example, beginning in 2005, the Chinese magazine *Newsweek*, whose editors once declared that Yao's confidence on the court encouraged the greater Chinese quest for a national identity,[67] increased its coverage of Yao, and the magazine continues to treat him as a top-tier celebrity.

Throughout this media blitz, Yao Ming has been presented not just as a basketball player but also as a flesh-and-blood human being, as suggested, for instance, by the timbre of the coverage of his 2007 marriage to Ye Li and the subsequent birth of their daughter, Yao Qinlei, in Houston in 2010. In an age of tabloid sensationalism, and at a time when the tabloid press has deemed sport in general and basketball in particular fodder for the most contemptuous headlines, that Yao was able to establish and later maintain an image of wholesomeness and earthiness is remarkable, helping him sustain his popularity long after the end of his basketball career. He is by every conceivable measure a genuine twenty-first-century media darling.

Ultimately, however, Yao Ming's legacy exists largely beyond sport, particularly in his home country. A predominant source of motivation for many Chinese at home and abroad, he is regarded as having brought genuinely positive international acclaim to a nation whose population totals are staggering, numbers that have translated back to the NBA in ways that have materially affected the game. Strictly in terms of the athletic arena, since 2002, about 75 percent of urban Chinese aged fifteen to twenty-four have been basketball fans, half of whom watch the game at least once a week on average.[68] As Michael Wilbon observed just prior to Yao's retirement: "Almost certainly, Yao Ming has introduced more people to professional basketball, surely the NBA brand, than any one man in the history of the sport.... Approximately 200 million have frequently watched [CCTV broadcasts] when the Rockets play, which is about one-third of the time."[69] This has had an extraordinary impact on the nation's overall attitude toward sport, sports participation, and sport-related consumption in China. Clearly, Yao Ming helped accelerate commercial interest in sport, expanding the business in particular and the sport industry more generally[70] while at the same time projecting "an image of youth, vigor and greatness to a Western world that had long viewed the Chinese as 'inscrutable.'"[71] But again, this is where we can also see him transitioning away from the one-dimensional designation of celebrity athlete toward a more fully formed cultural icon.

Indeed, Yao's impact both during and after his playing career can be felt far beyond the basketball court. In addition to his ever-expanding business portfolio, Yao allied himself with a number of charitable organizations such as the NBA's Basketball without Borders program, demonstrating a commitment to humanitarianism through positive action.[72] A partial list of his charitable endeavors reinforces this aspect of his legacy:

- Summer 2003: Yao hosted a series of telethons, which raised hundreds of thousands to combat the spread of SARS in China as well as in the United States to help stop the spread of the virus, which was epidemic in China at the time.[73]
- September 2007: Yao, along with fellow NBA stars including Steve Nash, Carmelo Anthony, and Baron Davis as well as movie star Jackie Chan, held an auction and competed in a charity basketball game that raised US$965,000 (CN¥6.75 million) for underprivileged children in China.[74]
- May 2008: Following the Sichuan earthquake, Yao donated $2 million to relief work and created a foundation to help rebuild schools.[75]
- August 2012: Yao inspected the corpse of a poached elephant in Namunyak, northern Kenya, and filmed a documentary about the northern white rhinoceros.[76]

In all, Yao's story sums up the complicated, demanding, and multifaceted aspects of life for a modern Chinese national in a globalized context. His unique physical qualities led him to unprecedented international acclaim in basketball, which he was then able to parlay into a broader global platform for national and personal interests in the new century. His ability to overcome the challenges of having to traverse so many sociopolitical and cultural barriers as he adjusted to an alien environment added to his legacy, which accounts in part for why his postathletic career might actually be more impressive than his unique athletic accomplishments.

There is little doubt that Yao has inspired, and will likely further inspire, young Chinese men and women and perhaps a more broadly conceived base of Asian youth to pursue their athletic dreams in the West and elsewhere. His continued presence in various influential circles suggests that he will continue to exert his impact through multiple means that will be felt for generations while helping to maintain, if not enhance, his own globally iconic status in the decades to follow.

Notes

1. Wu Zhifei, "Yao Ming: qianhe yu jiqing zhujiu chenggong" [Yao Ming: modesty and passion make success], *Zhi Ye* [Profession], August 15, 2007, 4–6.
2. Jay J. Coakley, "Sport and Socialisation," *Exercise and Sport Sciences Reviews* 21 (1993): 169–200.
3. Wang Jingyu, Shan Lei, Xu Jicheng, Liang Xiyi, Liang Jinxiong, and Luo Zhengguang, "Yao Ming cheng zhang zhi lu: bu bao de linjia nanhai cheng juxing" [The road of Yao Ming's growth: the hungry boy in the neighborhood turned into a superstar], *Shenyang wanbao* [Shenyang evening daily], July 20, 2011.
4. Between 1992 and 1996, China produced 361 world champions in various sports, of whom 90 percent had received training in various sports schools. All the gold medalists at the 1996 Atlanta games experienced sports school training. See Nan Mu, "Quanguo yeyu tiyu xunlian gongzuo yantao hui zongshu" [Review of the national seminar on the coaching of amateur sport], *Tiyu gongzuo qingkuang* [The situation of sports affairs] 655, no. 23 (1997): 8–11.
5. Dong Jinxia, *Women, Sport and Society in Modern China: Holding Up More Than Half the Sky* (London: Cass, 2003).
6. Xin Bianyuan Ren, "Yao Ming: aiguo bushi juti de mou jian shi" [Yao Ming: patriotism is not a concrete issue"], www.163.com, September 30, 2006.
7. Peter Hain, "The Politics of Sport Apartheid," in *Sport, Culture and Ideology*, ed. Jennifer Hargreaves (London: Routledge and Kegan Paul, 1982), 233.
8. Gunther Lushen, "The Interdependence of Sport and Culture," *International Review of Sport Sociology* 2 (1967): 127–41.
9. Taiwan has been considered by the People's Republic of China as merely one province of China. The island was ruled by the Nationalist Party led by Jiang Jieshi (Chiang Kai-shek), who withdrew from mainland China to Taiwan in 1949. Mainland China has since been ruled by the Communist Party of China. Nationalists in Taiwan loudly proclaimed their right to rule the mainland and occupied China's seat at the United Nations and other major international organizations such as the IOC until the 1970s. However, Taiwan did not qualify according to the IOC's own political criteria for membership, by which a National Olympic Committee could only represent the territory and people controlled by its sponsoring regime. Nevertheless, teams from Taiwan competed in Olympics games in the 1950s and 1960s under different names. As for mainland China, even though the IOC invited the PRC to participate separately in the 1956 Melbourne Games, Beijing withdrew from the IOC and eight other international sport federations in 1958 in protest at the IOC's acceptance of "two Chinas."
10. Yao Ming with Ric Bucher, *Yao: A Life in Two Worlds* (New York: Miramax, 2004). The Chinese version is titled *Yao Ming: wo de shijie, wo de meng* [Yao Ming: my world, my dream].
11. Ibid.
12. Brook Larmer, "The Center of the World," *Foreign Policy*, no. 150 (September–October 2005): 66–74.
13. Steve Friess, "Signing Yao Will Take Plenty of Paperwork," *USA Today*, May 15, 2002, at http://usatoday30.usatoday.com/sports/nba/stories/2002-05-14-yaocontract.htm.
14. Ibid.

15. Yang Yi, *Yao Ming Zhuano* [Yao Ming biography] (Beijing: Xinxing Press, 2011); see also Friess, "Signing Yao Will Take Plenty of Paperwork."

16. Douglas Choi, *The Tao of Yao: Wit and Wisdom from the "Moving Great Wall" Yao Ming* (Seattle: Almond Tree Books, 2003).

17. Flopping refers to an act of purposely falling down in order to draw a foul on an opponent, a tactic that the league has deemed illegal and that is enforced by referees. In Yao's case, however, there is evidence to suggest that the speed of the game coupled with his size, rather than an intention to draw fouls illegally, often forced him to the ground. Moreover, as his play improved, evidence suggests that opposing players themselves resorted to flopping as a means to draw fouls on him. See, for example, David Hartnett, "Flopping Epidemic Strikes Cleveland, Rockets Lose," Clutch Fans: The BBS, December 24, 2008, at http://bbs.clutchfans.net/showthread.php?t=159721.

18. Joe Lago, "Smith Scores against Charles with the *Kiss*," ESPN, November 20, 2002, at http://static.espn.go.com/nba/columns/misc/1463585.html; and Fran Blinebury, "Nostalgia Runs Deep in Yao's Bittersweet Return to Houston," NBA.com, March 21, 2012, at http://www.nba.com/2012/news/features/fran_blinebury/03/21/yao-returns/.

19. Tian Jun, "Huiwei Yao Ming" [Second look at Yao Ming], *Shenzhou Xueren* [CHISA], August 15, 2003, 48–49.

20. "Yao Effective in First Meeting with Shaq," ESPN, January 19, 2003, at http://scores.espn.go.com/nba/recap/_/id/230117010/gameId/230117010/la-lakers-lakers-vs-houston-rockets.

21. "Yao Ming Makes NBA History in 2002 Draft," Eastday.com, June 27, 2002, at http://www.china.org.cn/english/NM-e/35721.htm. [Stern was erroneous about Yao being the first international player to be picked first in the draft, given that Mychal Thompson of the Bahamas (1978) and Nigerians Hakeem Olajuwon (1984) and Michael Olowokandi (1998) all preceded Yao as the top NBA picks in their draft years—*eds*.]

22. "Yao Ming Tai Chi Commercial: ClutchFans," ClutchFans: The BBS, January 6, 2003.

23. Frank Langfitt, "China's Basketball Fans Drawn to NBA Stars," NPR, August 11, 2008, at www.npr.org/templates/story/story.php?storyId=93490130.

24. "Demographic Statistics: Houston, Texas," Infoplease, at http://www.infoplease.com/us/census/data/texas/houston/demographic.html.

25. "Reception Welcoming Yao Ming," Asia Houston Network, December 11, 2002, at www.asiahouston.org/pages/events2002.html.

26. "2005 All-Star Game Recap," NBA.com, February 27, 2003, at http://www.nba.com/history/allstar/2005-all-star-game-recap/index.html.

27. "Yao Has Billions on His Side in Awaited Battle of Superpowers," *Times* (London), August 9, 2008. [O'Neal was fond of referring to himself as "the Big Aristotle," among other things—*eds*.]

28. Steven Jiang, "Yao Ming Retirement Marks End of an Era," CNN, July 21, 2011, at http://edition.cnn.com/2011/SPORT/07/20/yao.ming.retire/.

29. Clifford Coonan, "Once China's National Heroes Dug for Coal, Now They Play Basketball," *Times* (London), April 29, 2005, at http://www.thetimes.co.uk/tto/news/world/article1974411.ece.

30. Kurt Badenhausen, "As Stern Says Goodbye, Knicks, Lakers Set Records as NBA's Most Valuable Teams," *Forbes*, January 22, 2014, at http://www.forbes.com/sites/kurtbadenhausen/

2014/01/22/as-stern-says-goodbye-knicks-lakers-set-records-as-nbas-most-valuable-teams/ #740ea316b88b.

31. "NBA Renews International TV Deals," NBA.com, November 12, 2002, at http://www.nba.com/news/international_tv_deals_renewed_021112.html.

32. Michael Wilbon, "Can't Overestimate Yao Ming's Impact," ESPN, December 20, 2010, at http://espn.go.com/espn/commentary/news/story?page=wilbon/101220.

33. Dong Jinxia, "National Identity, Olympic Victory, and Chinese Sportswomen in the Global Era," in *The Olympics in East Asia: Nationalism, Regionalism, and Globalism on the Center Stage of World Sports*, ed. William W. Kelly and Susan Brownell (New Haven, CT: Yale University Council on East Asian Studies, 2010), 161–84.

34. "Olympic Briefs," *Guardian*, August 14, 2004.

35. After Yao scored 39 points in a win against New Zealand, China lost 58–83, 57–82, and 52–89 against Spain, Argentina, and Italy, respectively. In the final group game, however, a 67–66 win over the reigning 2002 FIBA world champions Serbia and Montenegro moved them into the quarterfinals.

36. Brian Mahoney, "On Basketball: Yao Did Much in Little Time," Boston.com, July 11, 2011, at http://archive.boston.com/sports/basketball/articles/2011/07/11/on_basketball_yao_did_much_in_little_time/.

37. Yang Shen, "Yao Ming jili nianqing guoshou nuli yuan meng" [Yao Ming inspires young national players to make effort to realize their dreams], *China Youth Daily*, July 26, 2011.

38. "Zhonghua wenhua niandu renwu pingxuan yu yangshi xin taizhi juxing" [Selection of annual figures of Chinese culture took place in the new building of CCTV], SINA.com, January 12, 2013, at http://ent.sina.com.cn/v/m/2013-01-12/20423833549shtml.

39. Yao and Bucher, *Yao: A Life in Two Worlds*.

40. Jonathan Feigen, "Rockets' Yao Makes It Official, Retires from Basketball; Rockets Center Announces Decision at News Conference in Shanghai," *Houston Chronicle*, July 21, 2011, at http://www.chron.com/disp/story.mpl/sports/bk/bkn/7660932.html.

41. "Yao Ming: 'To Be Respected, You Better Grow Stronger,'" Pro Basketball Alumni, March 12, 2013, at http://www.china.org.cn/opinion/2013-03/12/content_28217767.htm.

42. Wu, "Yao Ming: qianhe yu jiqing zhujiu chenggong."

43. Eric Marmon, "How David Stern's Dress Code Transformed the Modern NBA Star," *Huffington Post*, April 19, 2015, at http://www.huffingtonpost.com/eric-marmon/how-david-sterns-dress-co_b_6687904.html. The controversy concerning this decision stemmed from the presumption that players not in traditional suits were thought to be fronting US street gangs. The decision was criticized for being racially based and for being a blatant attempt to make the league more appealing to white, middle-class consumers.

44. Wu Zhifei, "Yao Ming: zhengfu meiguo de 'di ba da shijie qiji'" [Yao Ming: the 'eighth world wonder' who won over the USA], *Zhiye jishu* [Vocational technology], August 15, 2007, 22–28.

45. Fran Blinebury, "Fran Session: Teammates Bask in Limelight of Yao Effect," NBA.com, February 5, 2009, at http://www.nba.com/2009/allstar2009/01/23/fran.yao.012309/.

46. Liu Yingyu, "Yao Ming de si bu wuqu meiyou ren keyi suisui bianbian chenggong, Yao Ming ye bu liwai" [No one can succeed easily and Yao Ming is no exception], *Dandai laomo* [Modern model], September 1, 2010.

47. Sid Ventura, "NBA Commissioner David Stern Talks about Globalization, Stepping Down, and His Legacy," Yahoo! Sports, October 10, 2013, at https://sg.sports.yahoo.com/news/nba--nba-commissioner-david-stern-talks-about-globalization--stepping-down--and-his-legacy-085215209.html.

48. "Mayor Annise Parker Honors Yao Ming with 'Good Will Ambassador' Title and Key to the City," City of Houston Official Site, at www.houstontx.gov/intltrade/yao.html.

49. Matthew Engel, "Yao Leads Cultural Revolution," *Guardian*, December 19, 2002, at http://www.theguardian.com/sport/2002/dec/19/ussport.comment.

50. Thomas Oates and Judy Polumbaum, "Agile Big Man: The Flexible Marketing of Yao Ming," *Pacific Affairs* 77, no. 2 (Summer 2004): 187–210.

51. Wu, "Yao Ming: qianhe yu jiqing zhujiu chenggong."

52. "Yao Ming tuiyi fabu hui yin wangluo guanzhu—yi xiaoshi nei fa shu baiwang weibo" [Press conference of Yao Ming's retirement caught attention, several million microblogs were written within one hour], SINA.com, July 21, 2011, at http://sports.sina.com.cn/k/2011-07-21/02215667953.shtml.

53. Li Ge, "Yao Ming tuiyi zhibo! Yige meijia shijian de goujian yu zhanyan" [Live broadcast of Yao Ming retirement! Construction and display of a media event], *Shengping shijie* [Voice screen world], January 15, 2012, 16–18.

54. "Yao Ming, Coke's China Subsidiary Settle Lawsuit," ESPN, October 17, 2003, at http://sports.espn.go.com/espn/wire?id=1640181.

55. Eddie Pells, "Injury Doesn't Diminish Yao's Ability to Sell Products," *Houston Chronicle*, March 11, 2008, at http://www.chron.com/disp/story.mpl/sports/5610303.html.

56. J. P. Mangalindan, "Yao Ming's Second Act," *Fortune*, July 12, 2012, at http://archive.fortune.com/2012/06/21/technology/yao-ming-businessman.fortune/index.htm.

57. Li Guangdou, "Cong yundong dao shangye, Yao Ming de xia ban chang rensheng" [From sport to business: the second half life of Yao Ming], *Shangwu pinglun* [Business review], September 15, 2011, 136.

58. Ibid.

59. "Yao Tops Forbes List Again, But Ziyi Catches Up," *China Daily*, March 18, 2009, at http://www.chinadaily.com.cn/showbiz/2009-03/18/content_7591787.htm.

60. Ken Hoffman, "Yao Stands Tall for McDonald's," *Houston Chronicle*, March 11, 2008, at http://www.chron.com/CDA/archives/archive.mpl?id=2004_3743308.

61. "Yao Ming Retires from NBA after Leg Injuries Cut Short Career," *Bloomberg Businessweek*, July 20, 2011.

62. Wen Jia, "Zhengxie weiyuan Yao Ming: wo de 'zhongguo meng' shi rang tiyu huigui jiaoyu" [NCCPPCC member Yao Ming: my "China's dream" is to return sport to education], Xinhua, March 3, 2013, at http://news.xinhuanet.com/politics/2013-03/03/c_114867446.htm.

63. "NBA Yao Ming xuexiao shouqi kecheng wanmei luomu" [The first course of NBA Yao School came to an end successfully], May 24, 2014, at http://sports.sohu.com/20140525/n400000235.shtml.

64. Yao and Bucher, *Yao: A Life in Two Worlds*.

65. Bruce Westbrook, "The Year of the Yao," *Houston Chronicle*, April 15, 2005, at http://www.chron.com/disp/story.mpl/ae/movies/reviews/3134692.html.

66. Tong Lin, "Mei jie de kua wenhua gou tong neng li he mei jie xingtai guan xi fen xi: yi tai wu shi bao de yao ming bao dao wei li" [Analysis of the relationship between the communication power of the media and its state: the example of *Times*' coverage of Yao Ming], People, July 5, 2011, at http://media.people.com.cn/GB/22114/49489/225937/15077778.html. Tong reports that, between June 2002 and June 2010, the *Times* of London published roughly forty-five articles about him.

67. Zheng Lei and Liu Bo, "Meiti guanyu Yao Ming xingxiang de jiangou, yi zhongguo xinwen zhoukan wei li" [Construction of Yao Ming's image by media, by illustration of China Media Week], *Xinwen shijie* [News world], July 2010, 153–54.

68. Chen Aimin, "'Ming wang chao' de 'qian' tu: 'Yao Ming zao xing yundong' zhi caifu jiedu" [Money making of "Ming Dynasty": analysis of "star making campaign of Yao Ming"], *Tebie guangzhu* [Special concern], February 15, 2003, 8–14.

69. Wilbon, "Can't Overestimate Yao Ming's Impact."

70. "NBA: Yao Ming Info Page," NBA.com, at http://www.nba.com/playerfile/yao_ming/bio.html.

71. "Shooting High, Bouncing Back: Yao Ming," CNN, August 6, 2008, at http://edition.cnn.com/2008/WORLD/asiapcf/07/23/talkasia.yaoming/index.html?iref=mpstoryview.

72. "Basketball without Borders: Asia," NBA.com, June 16, 2005, at http://www.nba.com/bwb/asia2005_report.html.

73. "Yao Implores Everyone to Join in Battling SARS," ESPN, May 8, 2003, at http://assets.espn.go.com/nba/news/2003/0508/1550841.html.

74. "Yao Scores 21 Points in Charity Game" Xinhua, September 14, 2007, at http://news.xinhuanet.com/english/2007-09/15/content_6724598.htm. See also "Basketball Stars Raise 7 Million Yuan at Charity Auction," Xinhua, September 14, 2007, at http://news.xinhuanet.com/english/2007-09/14/content_6720883.htm.

75. "Yao Ming Announces Major Initiative to Help Rebuild Schools in China," NBA.com, June 10, 2008, at http://www.nba.com/rockets/news/yao_foundation_080610.html.

76. Rhishja Cota-Larson, "Rhino Crisis Round Up: Yao Ming in Kenya and More," Planetsave, August 17, 2012, at http://planetsave.com/2012/08/17/rhino-crisis-round-up-yao-ming-in-kenya-more.

Duke Kahanamoku
Racialized Colonization and the Exoticization of Aquatic Royalty
—Joel S. Franks

Introduction

During the early twentieth century, Duke Paoa Kahanamoku was sport's most famous aquatic athlete and, for much of the twentieth century, the most famous Hawaiian in the world. Unmatched in his time as a competitive swimmer, Kahanamoku served in the vanguard among those Hawaiians spreading the gospel of surfing to the US mainland and Australia. He mastered the outrigger canoe and excelled in water polo. Legally, he was a US citizen. But substantially, because he was born in colonized Hawaii and racialized and exoticized by the press, Kahanamoku was perceived as a foreign presence in American sport. At the same time, that presence was not necessarily unwelcomed. Many not only marveled at Kahanamoku's splendid athletic achievements but frequently acclaimed his personal charm and warmth as well as his physical courage. The tension between these two images of the same celebrity athlete resembles in many respects the circumstances of two more-renowned twentieth-century athletes—Jim Thorpe, who, like Kahanamoku, possessed indigenous ancestry, and Roberto Clemente, who, like Kahanamoku, was a nonwhite, colonized resident of the US empire. Significantly, therefore, it is important to see that tension as emblematic of the problematic nature of race and colonization and any ensuing commentary that emerges from these phenomena.[1]

Scholar Jim Nendel can help us frame the way Kahanamoku was depicted on the mainland and in his native Hawaii. Nendel points out that Kahanamoku served as "the popular face of a new Hawaiian identity." On one hand, he was identified with what Nendel calls a "vanquished race" overwhelmed by the forces of modernity. On the other, he was represented as "an image of twentieth century Hawaii," bursting to join the world of modern capitalism. Therefore, as Nendel writes, "Kahanamoku became the link between the old and new images of a Hawaiian culture, a role for which he was perfectly suited." From the perspective of elite, white cultural authorities on the mainland and in Hawaii,

Kahanamoku should appear civilized by white society's standards without actually becoming white.[2]

Yet it is important to keep in mind the very real person who set the swimming records and personified surfing to the world in the twentieth century. Born in what had once been an independent nation, he became a racialized, colonized subject of another, more powerful one. In the process, he seemed to assert a sense of cultural citizenship in an empire and a nation-state that managed to simultaneously marginalize and embrace him. The concept of cultural citizenship seems appropriate in pondering the experiences of people like Kahanamoku, pulled, with predictably mixed results, into the orbit of the United States as a nation-state. As advanced by Latino scholars Renato Rosaldo, William Flores, and Rina Benmayor, the concept of cultural citizenship argues that cultural groups, identified along racial and ethnic lines, do not need to assimilate in a dominant, national culture. They have a right to preserve their distinctiveness without surrendering their claims on equal citizenship. For Kahanamoku, this apparently meant that he was fine with being American, but he was finer still with being Hawaiian.[3]

This chapter will serve as an excursion into Kahanamoku's Hawaiian roots, recounting a brief biography of this great athlete to further clarify many important aspects of his life and legacy. Throughout, I will examine exoticism as a cultural construction that helped inspire popular perceptions of Kahanamoku. I will then take a look at the complicated ways in which the mainland and Hawaiian presses viewed and shaped Kahanamoku's image. Finally, I will consider Kahanamoku's posthumous image as generated both on the mainland and in the islands.

To Be Hawaiian

Duke Kahanamoku always claimed pride in his indigenous Hawaiian roots. It is important to note that when white sailors, commanded by English sea captain James Cook, first saw the islands in 1778, there were about 750,000 Hawaiians. Centuries earlier, people from southern Asia had migrated eastward by boat, populating the various islands of the western Pacific. The Hawaiian archipelago was the last to be populated.

For centuries Hawaiians fostered their own varied political-economic systems. Politically and physically divided, the various islands in the Hawaiian chain were not united under one state until Kamehameha I, with the aid of the British navy, imposed unity on the islands in the early 1790s, setting up a capital on the island of Oahu in what is now Honolulu.

For nearly a century, Hawaii was an independent, mixed monarchy. The Hawaiian monarch was, indeed, a native Hawaiian. And to be sure, native

Hawaiians learned to share the islands with a vast, not always happy, assortment of European and European American merchants, sailors, and missionaries. But European and European American diseases proved fiendishly effective in cutting down the indigenous population—nobles and commoners alike. Likewise, land, the source of economic wealth on the islands, was disproportionately controlled by white elites. Called haoles by indigenous Hawaiians, these white elites sought to recruit thousands of Asian laborers for the sugar plantations that largely dominated the Hawaiian economy.

Thus, native Hawaiian rulers and representatives constantly had to deal with the growing haole economic power and political influence, while their people were losing their struggle to hold on to land as they battled the deadly scourge of poverty and disease. When Kahanamoku was born in 1890, Hawaii's then-ruler, King Kalakaua, had fought a losing war to maintain the monarchy as an effective institution of the Hawaiian people. He had signed an agreement allowing the United States to install a naval station at Pearl Harbor so that the Americans would not impose onerous tariffs on Hawaiian sugar. Then, the king grudgingly conceded to haole demands to alter the Hawaiian constitution. These concessions diminished not only the power of the monarch but the suffrage rights of the Hawaiian people as well.

Kalakaua died in 1891 and was succeeded by his remarkable sister, Liliuokalani, a determined nationalist who sought to restore the old constitution. Rather than let this happen, however, pro-American haoles, with the backing of the US ambassador and military, staged a coup. A republic was set up, and the haoles awaited US annexation. As it turned out, they would have to wait a bit. The US government at that time was headed by Democrat Grover Cleveland's administration, which doubted the legitimacy of the coup and the support of the Hawaiian people for the new republic. However, Cleveland's successor, William McKinley, embraced Hawaiian annexation more warmly, and much of his Republican Party was absolutely enraptured with the idea. Fired up by cries of the white man's burden and global manifest destiny, the United States waged war on Spain and Filipino revolutionaries and annexed Hawaii in 1898.[4]

The Life of a Champion

Duke Kahanamoku was born in Hawaii in 1890, at which time the islands formed an independent nation ruled by a constitutional monarchy. While some mainlanders believed that Kahanamoku's first name signified membership in a Hawaiian aristocracy, he was actually named after his father, who, as it turns out, was named Duke to honor the Duke of Edinburgh, who had visited the islands in 1869.

In 1911, Kahanamoku attracted the attention of the sports world by swimming to a world sprint record. However, since this was accomplished by a nonwhite competitor at a meet at Honolulu Harbor and not in a pool in, say, Philadelphia, Boston, or New York, and because Kahanamoku did not have to perform any turns but rather just swim straightaway, officials of the mainland Amateur Athletic Union (AAU) doubted the Hawaiian's achievement. Island athletic authorities, hoping to gain positive publicity for the islands on the mainland and not only persuade the AAU of Kahanamoku's credibility as a world-class swimmer but land him a spot on the 1912 US Olympic team, sponsored a journey to the mainland by Kahanamoku and Vincent Genovese, another Hawaiian swimmer but not as skilled. On the mainland, the two aquatic athletes would square off in the spring of 1912 against mainlanders and compete for the favor of the AAU.

While Genovese's performance on the mainland was respectable though not stellar, Kahanamoku's was a sensation. Mainland experts in competitive swimming conceded that he could swim a straight line through ocean water with perhaps unmatched swiftness, although some, if not most, doubted his ability to negotiate the turns in an Olympic-style freshwater pool. Yet Kahanamoku's sheer speed now on display persuaded AAU officials that he could in fact claim the title of the world's fastest swimmer with some legitimacy. However, in the minds of mainlanders, Kahanamoku was not just a Hawaiian but a native Hawaiian, and some raised voices that indigenous people within the US empire—people like Kahanamoku and the great Jim Thorpe—should not compete in the 1912 Olympiad because they were insufficiently American.[5]

Moved by a willingness to overlook vicious racism when it might pose an obstacle to US Olympic hopes, American Olympic officials eventually relented and allowed Kahanamoku and, of course, Native Americans such as Thorpe to compete for Uncle Sam. And they made the right move in both cases. For his part, Kahanamoku came from behind after a slow start to win the Olympic trials before winning gold in the 100-meter freestyle, in addition to collecting a silver in the 4 x 200-meter freestyle relay.[6]

Kahanamoku emerged from the 1912 Olympiad as a representative hero to Hawaiians and as a global celebrity. From the East Coast of the United States to Australia, Kahanamoku would reveal his marvelously diverse mastery of aquatic athletics. At various meets and exhibitions, sports fans marveled at his swift and powerful strokes through the water. They saw, as well, his exciting exhibitions of the Hawaiian sport of surfboarding. Kahanamoku not only was a charismatic ambassador of surfboarding but helped popularize water polo and outrigger canoe racing, and he demonstrated invaluable techniques designed to preserve the lives of potential drowning victims.

Because of World War I, Kahanamoku could not match his 1912 Olympic triumphs in 1916. However, in 1920, he won two more gold medals—one in the

100-meter freestyle and the other in the 4 x 200-meter freestyle relay. Well into his thirties by then, Kahanamoku copped a silver medal in the 1924 Olympics in the 100-meter freestyle, finishing behind future Tarzan star Johnny Weissmuller. Eight years later, the forty-plus-year-old Kahanamoku made the US Olympic team as an alternate on the water polo team. As such, he won a bronze medal in the Los Angeles Olympiad.

Kahanamoku spent much of the 1920s in Los Angeles, where he demonstrated an amazing and diverse arsenal of talent. He appeared in a variety of movies—generally in decidedly "exotic" roles. While hobnobbing with Hollywood celebrities, he also continued to reinforce southern California's growing image as an aquatic sport capital of sorts. And as if that were not enough, while on a surfboard, he saved the lives of eight Japanese American fishermen off the Orange County coast.

Kahanamoku returned to Hawaii in the 1930s. There, he coached water polo at the University of Hawaii, ran a gasoline station in Honolulu, served as county sheriff, and was generally regarded as a roving Hawaiian ambassador to tourists and would-be tourists. Furthermore, as surfing gained a fervent following in the United States in the 1960s, Kahanamoku became something of a revered father figure to California's youthful surfers. A picture of health until well into his seventies, Kahanamoku died of a heart attack at age seventy-seven in 1968. And yet, in spite of his impressive array of accomplishments, his legacy is also tied to the various and often predictable ways he was depicted.

Exoticism

Exoticism helped justify the colonization of Hawaii. The curious mixture of denigration and admiration that greeted Kahanamoku on his journeys to the US mainland can at least partly be attributed to his exotic appeal. Exoticism is a complicated cultural invention. On the one hand, it surely worked to reinforce and even justify colonialism and a racial hierarchy inside and outside of the United States. On the other, it spoke to a sincere concern with the human costs of modernity and the hope that a socially constructed premodern people could, by example, breathe fresh air into the factory, office, department store, and train station. Whether ill intended or not, exoticism could fashion people perceived as premodern into people foreign to modernizing America.

Often represented as a child of nature, Kahanamoku and the image fashioned around him could be seen as a critique of modernity. However, blurring that image was another purporting that American modernity had transformed him through training into a world champion as well as into someone more "American." Perhaps most important of all, exoticism could abet modernity and, in particular, modern capitalism. That is, exoticism could sell. It could sell Harlem nightclubs, Tarzan books and movies, ukuleles, pineapples, vacation packages, and artworks that were influenced by supposedly exotic people or that depicted supposedly exotic settings. It served well the consumer culture developing in the more advanced capitalist countries in the late nineteenth and early twentieth centuries—a consumer culture that advocated the beneficial effects of "going native" as long as it was temporary and reinvigorated people's ability to perform effectively their various roles serving the market economy and the modern nation-state.

More particularly, exoticism could sell Hawaii. In the early twentieth century, Hawaiian economic leaders sought to attract US capital to the islands. This westward movement of capital represented mainland investment in Hawaiian economic enterprises, tourism, and the consumption of Hawaiian or pseudo-Hawaiian commodities such as pineapples, ukuleles, and music. Hawaiian athletes played a role in all this. The same year that Kahanamoku and Genovese were dispatched to the mainland, a baseball team of Chinese Hawaiians barnstormed from California to New England, even venturing briefly into Canada. One of their primary tasks was to promote Hawaii and Hawaiian products. The 1910s and 1920s would see not only troupes of Hawaiian athletes venturing to the mainland but troupes of Hawaiian musicians and dancers.[7]

The cultural traveling of Hawaiian performers, along with the merchandising of Hawaiian pineapples, promoted a comforting exoticism to prospective investors, tourists, and consumers. Native Hawaiians, in others words, might appear as a nonwhite, relatively primitive people. But unlike others similarly labeled, Hawaiians' racialized foreignness, rather than exuding hostility to the supposedly more civilized white society, offered a desire to genially please their racial superiors with exotic fruits, hula dancing, and water sports. We can see the effects of exoticism on the narrative of Kahanamoku's career.[8]

View from the Mainland

The mainland did not become aware of Duke Kahanamoku until he broke the sprint record at Honolulu Harbor in 1911. Amateur athletic authorities on the mainland expressed misgivings about Kahanamoku's record-shattering performance. In part, they may have considered the conditions too primitive. After all, Kahanamoku's feat was accomplished not in a freshwater pool but, rather, swimming in a straight line through Pacific Ocean waters. However, the fact that Kahanamoku was by every measure a racially colonized foreigner correspondingly factored into how official society ultimately viewed his accomplishments. As Susan Brownell and others have demonstrated, early twentieth-century mainlanders entertained serious doubts that indigenous people were capable of the intelligence and discipline necessary to compete effectively in organized, modern sports. Accordingly, in 1913, the *Washington Post* reported that the AAU doubted that an athlete from far-off Hawaii could have broken a world record. One AAU official was skeptical, but, according to the Honolulu-based *Pacific Commercial Advertiser*, he advised that the Hawaiian be "sent to the United States" to find out how fast he really was. If he proved capable of beating the speediest Americans, then the AAU would most likely accept the record of a hitherto unknown swimmer.[9]

The mainland press seemed largely receptive to Kahanamoku upon his arrival, but they often seemed readily determined to exoticize him whenever possible. Nendel maintains that the mainland press was bent on representing Kahanamoku and even the European Hawaiian, Genovese, as "primitive natives from a distant tropical land in order to draw spectators to . . . meet[s]." In doing so, the mainland press often pointed out that the Hawaiian swimmers had never competed in a pool, "which would create problems for them in having to turn thereby showing their lack of sophistication as modern athletes." Moreover, according to Nendel, the press seemed reluctant to call Kahanamoku an American even after he wound up on the US Olympic team.[10]

There were real consequences to all this. Nendel reports that during Kahanamoku's 1912 tour of the mainland, his "ebony skin," which seemed so fascinating to some in the press, meant that he was sometimes denied basic services, including a particular incident at a Pittsburgh restaurant that highlights the Jim Crow landscape of the era. Kahanamoku himself observed that, during his first stay on the mainland, "friendliness was scarce."[11]

Prior to the 1912 Olympics, the mainland press frequently racialized Kahanamoku's achievements. In 1912, the *New York Times* seemed somewhat fixated on Kahanamoku's body. It noted remarks from Jamison Hardy of the Chicago Athletic Association, who described Kahanamoku as "a giant ebony-skinned native" as well as a "magnificent specimen of manhood." After an early performance on the mainland, the *New York Times* noted that Kahanamoku "did well in straight ways but lost distance in turns." He still won the 100-yard contest, remaining, according to the *Times*, a prospect for the Olympics.[12]

In May 1912, the *New York Telegram* called Kahanamoku "a native of Honolulu and twenty-one years old. He is a tall, handsome, dark skinned athlete." Calling attention to a sport as yet fairly unknown outside of the islands, the *Telegram* added that Kahanamoku excelled in all branches of aquatic sport, but "it is [in] surf riding that he stands in a class by himself." In terms of competitive swimming, the *Telegram* appeared fairly unimpressed, declaring that the "dusky champion" had not done much in the way of serious preparation. The *New York Herald* seemed to agree with the *Telegram* that Kahanamoku was not mentally ready for elite, competitive swimming. A daily newspaper published out of Chicago, *Day Book*, after depicting Kahanamoku as a "full blooded Hawaiian," offered that Kahanamoku's success was largely a product of nature: "The warm waters [in Hawaii] make it possible to spend the whole day in the surf without being chilled and from childhood the Hawaiians swim more than they walk, that is the younger ones do."[13]

While criticism of Kahanamoku's training and technique was persistent in the mainland press, generally mainland journalists did not seem to condemn the idea of the Hawaiian making the US Olympic team. Indeed, the *Washington Post* defended Kahanamoku from those who believed that he should not represent Uncle Sam at the Olympics because he was a colonized subject. The *Post* writer asserted that "he is in exactly the same position as the Indian Ranji, who for years represented England in cricket."[14]

Kahanamoku may have been seen as eligible for the US Olympic team. Still, at least a portion of the mainland press remained reluctant to concede that he deserved to perform for Uncle Sam. Nendel points out that after a meet in Pittsburgh in the spring of 1912, sportswriter Ralph Davis contended: "Kahanamoku, the Hawaiian, has discovered that there's all the difference in the world between surf riding and a 75-foot tank." In other words, as Nendel puts it, "the swimmer was introduced to real competition in Pittsburgh and had been found wanting."[15]

The sporting press widely agreed that prior to the 1912 Olympiad, and even after that, Kahanamoku needed to upgrade his competitive swimming technique. According to a *Washington Post* article in the spring of 1912, Kahanamoku was "being instructed in starting from 'go' in the dash by George Kistler, coach of the University of Pennsylvania." Subsequent to the Olympics, another *Post* piece depicted Kahanamoku as a great natural athlete, but one smart enough to understand the need for improvement. In this article, sportswriter Leonard Connes asserted that Kahanamoku learned on the mainland to effectively make turns in swimming pools as well as adjust to swimming in fresh water.[16]

A few years after his Olympic triumph, Kahanamoku spent a great deal of time in southern California engaging in competitive swimming but also helping spread the gospel of surfing. During the Hawaiian's visit to the region, William Henry of the *Los Angeles Times* emphasized Kahanamoku's primitiveness. To Henry, Kahanamoku was the world's greatest swimmer. Yet he also asserted that the Hawaiian was "a child of the Pacific" in that he was visibly easygoing, good natured, and free of worries. Henry conceded that Kahanamoku had worked on improving his starts, adding that at the Los Angeles Athletic Club, he fell under the influence of Irish Hawaiian George Freeth, in whom Kahanamoku preserved a "childlike confidence."[17]

Through his early years on the public stage, Kahanamoku remained a major sporting figure capable of evoking racialization and rapturous forms of exoticization from the press. In February 1913, a Philadelphia daily stressed Kahanamoku's natural ability to swim swiftly. The paper claimed that Kahanamoku and other native Hawaiians retained such an affinity for water that they could actually play tag with sharks. Indeed, they supposedly even had trouble walking on land. In late October 1913, a *Washington Post* piece identified Kahanamoku as the "dusky paddler." Five years later, the *New York Tribune* described the athlete as "dark as a stove pipe lid with flashing white teeth." This latter description might have also been used to identify his contemporary Jack Johnson, the former and controversial African American heavyweight prizefighting champion. However, the *Tribune* went so far as to connect Kahanamoku with, of all things, Hawaiian musical culture, which was by then on the verge of being co-opted by Tin Pan Alley songwriters. As one writer quipped, Kahanamoku had a "great ability to perform either upon the water or the Hawaiian guitar. He can play ragtime upon the harmonious instrument[,] and he can swim ragtime."[18]

As late as 1922, some mainland journalists remained reluctant to credit Kahanamoku's success to hard work. One wire story attributed his many triumphs to his physique, although it did concede that the Hawaiian was generally "a clean liver." At the same time, it pointed out that Kahanamoku did not train systematically but happily lingered in the water whenever possible.[19]

The mainland press proved at least occasionally capable of cheering for Kahanamoku without resorting to exoticizing him. In 1913, for example, a New York–based sportswriter, obviously ignoring those who considered the swimmer a foreigner, simply named Kahanamoku as America's fourth-best athlete behind Jim Thorpe, pitcher Joe Wood, and boxer Willie Ritchie. A 1916 piece in Louisiana's *Bogalusa Enterprise* praised the Hawaiian as "a good sport in defeat." Situating Kahanamoku alongside idealized sports heroes of the early twentieth century, including the very real Christy Mathewson and the very unreal Frank Merriwell, the article had Kahanamoku maintaining that a "man's got to be cheerful to be a victor."[20]

Despite the discussion about Kahanamoku representing the United States in the Olympics, and despite the rhetoric of the time, he was in fact a US citizen, although a portion of the mainland press continued to cast doubts on his citizenship while racializing his achievements as being based in nature. *Day Book* reported in 1914 that mainland swimmer Bud Small said: "The Duke talks of making another trip to this country." In 1915, the *Washington Herald* contended that Kahanamoku's swimming technique was "instinctive" but added that "Americans" had refined that technique effectively. In April 1916, the *Duluth News Tribune* depicted Kahanamoku as a magnificent natural swimmer, which, the paper added, was to be expected from a Hawaiian. Upon his initial arrival on the mainland, Kahanamoku was thought to have evinced little in the way of technique. Nevertheless, the much more common refrain became that "Duke" was "made" into a world-class swimmer "in America by Americans." In the process, thus, the supposedly non-American Hawaiian was deftly being transformed, if not rebranded, as an attentive and earnest student.[21]

One could catch a glimmer of the process of exoticization in a wire story about Kahanamoku's 1918 triumph in Chicago. And yet one could also sense considerable respect for the Hawaiian's skills in the same piece: "Kahanamoku's swimming was a revelation to the large crowd ... who saw the contests. Duke uses the least effort of any swimmer ever seen in the local tank. He did not fight the water, as local boys do, while his long, powerful strokes, combined with perfect turns, enabled him to gain an early lead which he never was in danger of losing." But if there was a problem with Kahanamoku and the other Hawaiians competing at the Chicago meet, it was not their exoticism but their firm embrace of American sporting competitiveness. The Hawaiians, the piece informed readers, "know every trick of swimming." They warmed up in the pool, while the non-Hawaiian competitors rested outside the pool in order to not expend their energies prematurely. The Hawaiians even jumped the gun in order to unnerve the opposition. While the writer seemed to admire the Hawaiians' clever competitive strategies, their behavior—more specifically, the depictions of their behavior—at the same time suggested evidence of primitive treachery.[22]

Mainlanders also knew Kahanamoku as a leading missionary of surfing. A 1914 article published in the monthly magazine *Outing* racialized the exploits of "Duke Paoa" and another Hawaiian. Author George Marvin purported:

> No race in the world is so beautifully developed as the Polynesian, and these two men are the pick of their race. Without changing a line you could put them into a Greek frieze, but you would have to animate or electrify the frieze to keep it in key with their poised grace supreme in this immemorial pastime of their people. Both are as much at home on the streaming mane of a breaker as a Pawnee brave on the bare back of a galloping bronco.[23]

Sportswriter Robert Edgren, who told readers that the thirty-year-old Kahanamoku was preparing for the 1920 Olympiad, struck a similar theme. Kahanamoku appeared to Edgren as a racialized, physical marvel. He wrote: "Like many other Hawaiians, he clearly shows his breeding. His head is very well shaped, his hair thick and black. I never saw a man with a finer torso." Edgren furthermore likened Kahanamoku to classical renderings of ancient Greek male athletes, gods, and warriors.[24]

Throughout Kahanamoku's early amateur career, rumors persisted on the mainland, as well as in Hawaii, that he was set to cash in on his aquatic skills by going professional. Apparently, at least some promoters believed that Kahanamoku could (and should) profitably display his swimming and surfing skills for pay, although the press railed against such a possibility. For example, *Sporting Life*, a weekly published in Philadelphia, expressed regret that the amateur world might lose Kahanamoku. In the summer of 1916, it reported that the same manager who ran professional pool player Willie Hoppe's career had also signed Kahanamoku. Despite the rumors, Kahanamoku remained an amateur, but in 1922 he was accused of turning professional when he reportedly received payment for endorsing a surfboard varnish. Around the same time, San Jose sportswriter William Unmack condemned the Hawaiian AAU for casting a suspicious eye on Kahanamoku because he had supposedly inked a movie contract. Unmack said that until the Hawaiian actually made money from a Hollywood career, Hawaiian amateur authorities should back off. Unmack protested that Kahanamoku "has been nothing but a pure amateur, he has represented Hawaii well, and has done more for tourism than anyone or anything else in Hawaii. Hawaii should support him."[25]

Indeed, Kahanamoku did go Hollywood. He moved to southern California and appeared in several movies, usually in supporting roles portraying primitive indigenous people. That Kahanamoku did not appear in these movies as a competitive swimmer perhaps kept him an amateur in the eyes of AAU officials. And by all accounts Kahanamoku's adventures in Hollywood failed to free him from the shadows of exoticization. Indeed, one movie project with which he was supposedly identified cast him as a character inspired by King Kamehameha. The legendary Hawaiian monarch was said to have performed the feat of surfing while catching seven spears thrown at him by seven warriors. A 1922 article in the *Duluth News Tribune* claimed that Kahanamoku had repeated that feat for the movie cameras. Among the "warriors" tossing spears at the athlete-turned-actor were his brothers.[26]

Interestingly, even though he sought a movie career, Kahanamoku was still protective of his amateur status—at least according to the mainland press. A report circulated in 1926 that the Hawaiian was interested in swimming in a Los Angeles to Catalina Island race. However, Kahanamoku insisted that, if he won, he would not collect the $35,000 prize money because he wanted to remain eligible for the 1928 Olympiad.[27]

As Kahanamoku edged toward the age of forty, the mainland press continued to exoticize him or at least allow the Hawaiian to exoticize himself. In 1926, Thomas Curran asserted in a syndicated article that Kahanamoku was hoping to make the 1928 Olympic team. Curran reported that Kahanamoku grinned as he admitted that he had never truly been devoted to methodical training intervals. While one presumes that Curran accurately reported Kahanamoku's sentiments, it is not clear why Kahanamoku would have said that. Perhaps he told Curran what the journalist expected to hear, or perhaps he bought into the prevailing racial ideology concerning Pacific Islanders. According to Curran, Kahanamoku further emphasized that regular training burned out athletes because it "is boring and artificial." Kahanamoku, however, admitted that he did in fact train, saying: "I do it naturally and, according to my inclination, not according to a mechanical schedule."[28]

Curran asked Kahanamoku if he would have done better with a coach. He responded that if a coach had been available to him as a youth, that would have been fine, though he went on to add: "At the time I went to my first Olympic games in 1912, American teachers tried to instruct me, but it was too late. It cramped me all up to do the way they said."[29] His use of the term "American" is curious given that he was a former and, he hoped, future US Olympic champion who could boast of US citizenship. Again, perhaps, Kahanamoku bought into the exoticism that estranged native Hawaiians from American civic culture. Perhaps, as well, his remarks prefigured the arguments later made by advocates of Hawaiian sovereignty; that is, that native Hawaiians should *not* regard themselves as Americans.

Several years after Kahanamoku won his first Olympic gold, he could still excite the literary passions of mainland sportswriters. A case in point was Olympian sprinter-turned-syndicated sportswriter Charley Paddock. In 1929, mainlanders could read Paddock's perhaps well-meaning but exoticized declaration that Kahanamoku had fulfilled the prophecy of the legendary Hawaiian monarch, Kamehameha:

> Someday my people will lose their freedom and their nationality. Someday they will be supplanted in their own islands and sickness will spread among them and their strength will pass away. But before they are entirely gone there will come one in my image who shall have within himself all the glorious strength of a dying race, and he shall be honored throughout the world, and he shall bring fame to my people.[30]

Hawaii

As Duke Kahanamoku rose to prominence as an international sport celebrity, it is important, Nendel points out, to realize that the Hawaiian press was controlled by haoles. The haole press, Nendel writes, "represented Kahanamoku as a proud symbol of their polyglot Hawaiian society while at the same time underscoring the image of the inferior savage throughout their papers." To Hawaii's haole leadership, Kahanamoku's achievement of global fame proved usefully marketable because he "symbolized Hawai'i and the romantic allure of the islands."[31]

If the *Hawaiian Gazette* is any indicator, the Hawaiian sports world was surprised but not stunned by Kahanamoku's record-breaking performances in Honolulu. The *Gazette* opined that Kahanamoku was known as a fast sprinter but no world beater. In any event, Honolulu officials, recognizing that something very special had happened, ordered the course measured and consulted five different timekeepers to document how swiftly Kahanamoku had moved through the Pacific waters.[32]

The project of sending Kahanamoku to the mainland to try out for the US Olympic team found support with the Honolulu press. E. S. Kopke, describing himself as an "Island Boy" and a swimming expert, asserted in the *Pacific Commercial Advertiser* that Kahanamoku should travel to the mainland. Kopke guaranteed Honoluluans that the Hawaiian was superior to mainland competition. But, he complained, Hawaiian residents seemed to take Kahanamoku's skills for granted, concluding that too few applauded Kahanamoku's recent record-breaking performances because they believed that good swimming was commonplace on the islands. To fears that Kahanamoku would not respond well to the novel swimming conditions of the mainland, Kopke declared that other, unnamed "island boys" had already shown that they could compete on the mainland. So why not Kahanamoku? In addition, dispatching Kahanamoku eastward was good business for Hawaii because his performances would be "a great novelty and serve to attract the attention of people there to Hawaii which could not be done in any other way."[33]

These themes were taken up in the Honolulu press in late 1911 and early 1912. Of Kahanamoku's impending journey eastward, the *Hawaiian Star* assured readers that "win or lose he will give a credible performance." Moreover, Kahanamoku's trek would reap economic benefits to the islands because he would "provide good publicity for Hawaii." Despite the apparent interest in Kahanamoku's expedition shown by the Hawaii Promotions Committee and the "Honolulu public," the *Pacific Commercial Advertiser* worried that the swimmer's planned trip was not receiving enough financial support. It urged readers to consider the benefits to local business and advertising if Hawaiian commercial interests supported Duke Kahanamoku. Tellingly, moreover, the *Advertiser* suggested that a haole should accompany Kahanamoku to help him win his likely battles against perhaps reticent amateur authorities on the mainland.[34]

To perhaps ease the minds of well-heeled haoles reluctant to financially support a "native," the *Pacific Commercial Advertiser* assured readers that Kahanamoku was readying himself earnestly for mainland competition. The newspaper declared, "Duke has been in constant training of late—in fact he is in the water for hours each day." Further, he was behaving himself in that "[h]e has no bad habits and is always in perfect condition."³⁵

Hawaiian sports fans were aware of Kahanamoku's initial problems adjusting to competitive swimming on the mainland. The *Hawaiian Gazette* pointed out that in March 1912, while swimming in Pittsburgh, Kahanamoku and Genovese started fast. But there was bad news. The two athletes faded before the finish. The problem was that, "[a]ccustomed only to salt water and straightway courses[,] the confinement of an indoor pool worried the swimmers from Hawaii." Moreover, the *Pacific Commercial Advertiser* informed readers that Kahanamoku was expected to conform to the racial conventions of the mainland. That is, the swimmer and members of his entourage had been asked by mainlanders to perform the hula on at least one of their stops.³⁶

Apparently, there was talk of George Freeth, a marvelous aquatic athlete of indigenous Hawaiian and European descent, helping Kahanamoku during his 1912 mainland ventures. The *Advertiser* scoffed at the idea. It claimed that the visiting swimmer was being treated with respect by mainlanders and would not need a personal "Hawaiian manager."³⁷

Kahanamoku did a great deal of training for the Olympics in Philadelphia, where he worked with a University of Pennsylvania swim coach. While Kahanamoku was staying in the City of Brotherly Love, the *Advertiser* told readers that he and a companion went on a canoe excursion on the Schuylkill River. In the midst of enjoying themselves, they chanced upon two drowning men, whom they pulled out of the river. Kahanamoku's "usual modesty" prevented him from relating the event to his haole chaperone, Lew Henderson. Rendering Kahanamoku even more impressive, the *Advertiser* added that but a few weeks earlier he had saved a man from drowning in an Atlantic City swim tank.³⁸

Within months of Kahanamoku's departure for the mainland, the *Pacific Commercial Advertiser* advocated continued financial support in the islands for the swimmer. It dubbed Kahanamoku as "Hawaii's Greatest Publicity Agent" on the mainland. Thus far, Kahanamoku had largely depended monetarily on the Hui Nalu Club, an aquatic organization largely made up of native Hawaiians. However, the *Advertiser* said that the club was too small to provide sufficient funding and hinted that it was too indigenous to be of much monetary use. Thus, a greater swath of presumably white Hawaiian residents would have to dig into their pockets and help Kahanamoku out.³⁹

While Kahanamoku journeyed to Sweden and Olympic glory, the *Honolulu Star-Bulletin* assured readers that he was doing credit to Hawaii. In an editorial, the daily reported that Kahanamoku had made many friends on board the *Finland*, the ship that was transporting him and other American athletes to Sweden. Kahanamoku even performed an impromptu vaudeville show for the passengers, which only served to reinforce his growing popularity. Confused about the origins of Kahanamoku's given name, the *Star-Bulletin* added: "'The Duke,' as they call him, won friends by his modesty, his quiet determination to win, his fine personal habits, and his happy temperament[,] and such qualities as these are worth a thousand times more than his wonderful arm and leg muscles that drive him through the water at a rate never before equaled by a human being."[40]

The *Pacific Commercial Advertiser* celebrated Kahanamoku as the "swimming wonder of the world" after he won Olympic gold in 1912. But the Honolulu daily also editorialized in a fashion seemingly casting doubt either on Kahanamoku's personal background or on the cultural habits of the Hawaiian people: "All praise to Duke Kahanamoku, a credit to his race, to his native islands, and to those who started him upon the road of sobriety, without which his name would not today be blazoned upon the athletic honor roll."[41]

Back on the islands, Kahanamoku was greeted as a hero after the 1912 Olympiad. *Thrum's Hawaiian Annual of 1913* pointed out that thanks in part to Duke Kahanamoku, "much beneficial promotion has accrued to Hawaii." Influential Honoluluans set up a fund intended to finance the purchase of a home for the Olympic champion "within," according to *Thrum's Annual*, "the sound of the famed surf of his beloved Waikiki." In late August, the *Maui News* boasted that $210 had been raised for the "Duke Kahanamoku Fund." Subsequently, Kahanamoku toured the other islands to thank non-Oahu Hawaiians for donating to the fund. Indeed, Kahanamoku got his home on Waikiki Beach. The *Honolulu Star-Bulletin* said that the gift of a house and lot was for Kahanamoku's "feats and for the modest and trustworthy manner in which he bore himself on the mainland and in Europe." The *Star-Bulletin*'s focus on Kahanamoku's modesty and trustworthiness could have been a commentary on his youth, his athletic celebrity, or perhaps even his racial affiliation.[42]

Meanwhile, however, a collage of cartoons and illustrations dispensed mixed racial signals, portraying Kahanamoku as a figure to be pitied because unscrupulous haoles were allegedly taking advantage of him. One illustration, published in early October 1912 in the *Star-Bulletin*, realistically rendered Kahanamoku's features. More troubling was a panel of cartoons displaying the swimmer with the physical features that American iconography commonly used to demean the African American man. The work was signed by an artist calling himself Randall.[43]

Nevertheless, publications in Hawaii were sensitive to how well Kahanamoku represented the islands. They celebrated his achievements but were predictably downcast when he did not meet expectations. In October 1912, the *Maui News* hailed him as "the lad who made Hawaii famous." But when Kahanamoku fell short of victory at various meets, the *Pacific Commercial Advertiser* wondered in late 1913 if the twenty-three-year-old star was losing it. The daily lamented that Kahanamoku had grown lazy with victory; that "success has turned the head of the young Hawaiian[,] and he is embodied with the idea that he is invincible." Interestingly, the *Advertiser* likened Kahanamoku's shortcomings to those of other prominent athletes who had emerged from similarly plebian backgrounds—Native American Jim Thorpe and Irish American prizefighting hero John L. Sullivan, to name but two. Meanwhile, however, the *Star-Bulletin* fretted that San Francisco's Olympic Club would steal Kahanamoku away and that the athlete, despite what he presumably owed island supporters, was giving Hawaii a "cold shoulder."[44]

In 1915, the *Pacific Commercial Advertiser* wondered about Kahanamoku's journey to Australia, where, it insisted, his competitive performances had been less than stellar. The daily sensed that there was something racial behind Kahanamoku's lack of success. It complained that he would have done better had he trained more, declaring: "But your island native will not work more than he can help. Besides he looks upon swimming as a pleasure not a labor and takes it in that spirit."[45]

A few months later, however, the *Advertiser* changed its tune. It reported that "Kahanamoku's Kick," similar to the kick accompanying the butterfly stroke, inspired enthusiasm in Australia. Indeed, the daily even seemed to predict that the Hawaiian's technique would eventually eclipse the Australian crawl. All in all, the *Advertiser* surmised, "[g]eneral interest in swimming has received a big impetus in Australasia as a result of the tour of Duke Paka [sic] Kahanamoku."[46]

In April 1915, the *Advertiser* reinforced its positive coverage of Kahanamoku's trek to Australia, while still showing a racist slant. According to Fred Williams, whom the *Advertiser* described as "the father of sun bathing in Australia," Kahanamoku had ingratiated himself to Australians. Williams insisted, however, that while "one would not be surprised at seeing that in one of our own origin, ... it was an eye-opener to find it so through an island native, even though we know Hawaiians were a cut above most of the aborigines of the Pacific."[47]

In June 1915, the *Honolulu Star-Bulletin* boasted not that Kahanamoku was the best swimmer in the world but the "best advertised swimmer in the world." The *Star-Bulletin* observed that his excursions to the Pacific Coast had produced "a great stimulus to surf board riding." Kahanamoku, according to the daily, carried his board on his journeys so that he could surf while away from the pool. Consequently, great crowds gathered at the beaches "to marvel at the ease with which he stood upright and rode the bucking waves as skillfully as a cowboy rides a bronco." Consequently, beach-loving Californians sought to become "his surfing pupils."[48]

The Hawaiian press sought to bolster Kahanamoku's image as an expert in all things aquatic. Early in 1913, the *Hawaiian Gazette* dutifully added to Kahanamoku's legendary prowess in the water by reporting that he had lost a middle finger while battling a "four-foot man-eating eel." Some years later, the California Feed Company discovered that one of its cases of bacon had fallen off a boat harbored at Honolulu. According to an issue of the *Honolulu Star-Bulletin* of January 1917, Kahanamoku was dispatched to salvage the case because he presumably possessed as great an affinity for deep-sea diving as for surfing. When Kahanamoku proved successful in recovering the case, the Hawaiian was offered a side of bacon. Nevertheless, the *Star-Bulletin* worried that perhaps Kahanamoku would be breaking AAU etiquette by accepting the gift, and the daily did not clarify whether Kahanamoku had extra bacon at breakfast or not![49]

The *Star-Bulletin* also reported that, because Kahanamoku had largely generated positive publicity for Hawaii, the islands' professional publicists sought to hire the athlete to work in promoting the islands. Kahanamoku, according to the daily, supposedly turned down the offer because "it was not promising enough." Sensitive to the possibility that such job offers compromised Kahanamoku's amateur status, one of the recruiters, A. P. Taylor, insisted that Kahanamoku was offered the job not because he was an athlete but because "we need a Hawaiian on our staff."[50]

In Retirement

Even after his active career as an aquatic athlete ended, Kahanamoku continued to symbolize Hawaii in a positive way. In 1939, Sam Otis of the Cleveland *Plain Dealer* reported that Kahanamoku had become an official greeter of visitors to Honolulu. Syndicated columnist Robert McShane called Kahanamoku "the most popular man on the islands" as well as "the most interesting man of his race." In 1941, Harry Grayson, a mainland syndicated writer, penned a gushing account of Hawaiian sports and the ability of middle-aged and older Hawaiians to display "youthful vigor." Grayson advised: "Get a load of Duke Kahanamoku. At 51 his speed in swimming 50 yard would surprise you." Late in 1950, readers of the *Reno Evening Gazette* were treated to a photo distributed by the Hawaii Visitors Bureau showing Kahanamoku greeting the Reno's Rotary Club's president with "the traditional Hawaiian lei of friendship." In 1956, he accompanied a Hawaiian baseball team to the Global World Series in Milwaukee. Referring to his appearance, The *Official Baseball Annual* called Kahanamoku "Hawaii's goodwill ambassador."[51]

Heading into his seventh decade of life, Kahanamoku remained a popular figure in Hawaii. Apparently, his popularity crossed political party lines. In 1961, famed political gossip columnist Andrew Russell "Drew" Pearson revealed that Hawaii's Republican senator Hiram Fong wanted Kahanamoku to run against

Democrat Daniel Inouye for the state's other Senate seat to avoid the possibility of running against the Olympian himself.[52]

Meanwhile, surfing had grown to become quite a popular pastime on the mainland, and Duke Kahanamoku, owing to his significant contributions to the sport, became an honored senior figure. While too old to compete, Kahanamoku paid regular visits to surfing events in California. Long Beach sportswriter Hank Hollingsworth noted Kahanamoku's attendance at a local meet in 1966, observing: "Having Duke Paoa Kahanamoku attend one of your events would be akin to the presence of Babe Ruth at a function. In fact, the Duke is considered the Babe Ruth of the swimming and surfing world. His feats are legendary and still recalled the world over."[53]

Hollingsworth also recognized Kahanamoku as a potent Hawaiian ambassador. To the sportswriter, Kahanamoku "has done more for Hawaii than all the hula girls and Hawaii Visitors' Bureau [sic] combined." Even though Kahanamoku was by this time well into his seventies, still, "the Duke stands as the symbol of Hawaii to millions the world over," a status that would indeed continue years after his death.[54]

Indeed, Duke Kahanamoku was named surfer of the century by *Surfer Magazine* late in the 1990s. Momi Kealana, the mother of famed Hawaiian surfer Rusty Kealana, responded that Kahanamoku deserved the honor but not just because of his talent as a surfer. In other words, Kahanamoku "exemplifies what being a Hawaiian is: generous and humble." Rabbit Kehai, a magnificent Hawaiian surfer, declared: "No matter what he did, he spread aloha, and everybody absorbed that." Writer Greg Ambrose added that Kahanamoku was "a really true Hawaiian ambassador.... He had that aloha spirit that we want to see, but he was the epitome of it."[55]

Another Hawaiian-based journalist acclaimed Kahanamoku's memory in 2000. "Duke Kahanamoku," Bobby Command wrote, "is the best athlete Hawaii ever produced. Period. No one has come close, and no one probably will. He is the once-in-a-generation athlete so strong, so precise—Ruth, Chamberlain, Laver, and now Woods immediately come to mind—that he forced everyone to play by his rules or face extinction."[56]

Upon the issuance of a US postage stamp bearing Kahanamoku's likeness, journalist Jeff Stage exoticized Kahanamoku, writing in 2002 that readers should "[f]orget those California golden-haired musicians from the 1960s. Kahanamoku was literally born next to the ocean and was never too far from his environment. A high school drop-out, he and his colleagues, who spent their days swimming, surfing, canoeing, and singing, were known as 'beach boys.'"[57]

Stage's reading of the stamp seems consistent with a scholarly piece by Gary Osmond published in 2008 in *Journal of Pacific History*. Osmond claims that the "stamp's iconic meaning" renders Kahanamoku "a key representation of

Hawaii, with Diamond Head and surfing minor metaphors for the islands and their culture." Osmond notes that "a touristy, mock-Hawaiian font style is used to spell" the athlete's name to more readily associate him with Hawaii. Interestingly, the photograph of Kahanamoku on which the stamp's representation was based shows him in the pose of an early twentieth-century swimmer. However, identifying Kahanamoku as a world-class swimmer seemed to be insufficiently Hawaiian, insufficiently exotic. Thus, surfing imagery pervades the stamp. Figures surf in the background, and looming further behind is Diamond Head, a constant in many visual representations of Hawaiian surfing.[58]

Meanwhile, in 1990, Kahanamoku's life was commemorated with a statue erected at the entrance to Waikiki's Kuhio Beach. With a long board sculpted behind the bare-chested figure of Kahanamoku, the statue has become a favorite haunt for tourists. Visitors often queue up to have a "Kodak moment" with the figure and place leis on his extended, welcoming arms.

One could properly look at this statue and understand how Duke Kahanamoku's image has served Hawaii in complicated ways. To be sure, his career has been depicted in a manner that seemingly delegitimates the Hawaiian sovereignty movement embraced by a good number of indigenous Hawaiians and fiercely articulated in Haunani-Kay Trask's classic *From a Native Daughter*. While varying in objectives, movement activists have decried what they understandably consider an illegitimate overthrow of a sovereign state in order to transform Hawaii into a colonial possession of the United States. Kahanamoku's fame as a US Olympic medal winner and his postathletic career as a gracious greeter to US tourists seem to suggest that he was one very illustrious native Hawaiian who could abide contently under American rule. On the other hand, the exoticized image of a racially demeaned, colonized Kahanamoku appears to sustain the movement's argument that the US empire has historically regarded native Hawaiians as economically exploitable, as well as politically and culturally *othered*.[59]

In Retrospect

Michael Nevin Willard has offered an alternative interpretation of Kahanamoku's significance. The scholar claims that Kahanamoku's image actually countered efforts to racialize Hawaiians while helping to spur the development of Hawaiian local culture. While tensions have existed between the Hawaiian sovereignty movement and the largely multiethnic Hawaiian local culture, the two sides have posed themselves together in opposition to haole domination. Yet while the former has been largely sustained by Hawaiians with indigenous ancestry, the latter, crafted on an edifice built by creole Hawaiian or pidgin

English speakers who are relatively tolerant of interracial, interethnic marriage and supportive of labor organization on the plantations and docks, has transcended race and ethnicity to a notable degree. In this view, local culture is a vibrant, historically dynamic blend of working- and lower-middle-class, racially and culturally mixed Hawaiians, with ancestors not only from precolonial Hawaii but from Asia, South America, and southern Europe.[60]

To Willard, it is important to stress that the Hawaiian haole-dominated hierarchy was not moved by Kahanamoku's accomplishments to rid the islands of racialized colonialism. Rather, they promoted Kahanamoku to the top of the nonwhite pecking order in order to promote tourism. On the mainland, Willard maintained, Kahanamoku was originally represented and perceived as a racialized primitive. Once he made the US Olympic team, he was increasingly seen as symbolic of a "unified America." In other words, according to Willard, "[t]he exotic primitive proved the civilized status and rank of white civilization, and the assimilation of nonwhite athletes proved sport's civilizing and elevating influence."[61]

However, some of the more important points Willard makes concern not just how Kahanamoku was represented but how he sought to represent himself. Willard is convinced that Kahanamoku preferred seeing himself as a contributor to the Hawaiian local culture, often despised and feared by the haole hierarchy. For one thing, he helped organize and remained a member of the Hui Nalu Club. Aimed at encouraging competition and recreation in various water sports, the Hui Nalu Club was multiethnic and even had female members. The club stood in contradiction to the predominantly haole, male Outriggers' Club, which unsuccessfully sought to recruit Kahanamoku. Kahanamoku's insistence, Willard stresses, that the club hold meetings under a tree reveals his strong sense of place so vital to Hawaiian local culture. Second, Kahanamoku pointedly admonished rude white tourists who thought that their race privileged them to order him and other native Hawaiians about. Third, Kahanamoku struck Willard as proud that his powerful stroke and kick possessed Pacific Islander origins. And fourth, Kahanamoku protested against the racism expressed by many of his haole contemporaries—the notion that native Hawaiians could "go so far and then stop."[62]

Willard further argues that the famous (and posthumous) Waikiki statue would have distressed Kahanamoku. To Willard, it turns "both the landscape and [Kahanamoku's] body into a commodity" for the tourist eager to soak up a bit of the spirit of aloha. The statue faces away from the Pacific so that tourists can position both the front of the figure and a view of the ocean into their photographs. While convenient for photographers, the direction of the statue's gaze provokes ridicule from modern-day Hawaiian "beach boys," who count Kahanamoku as their founding father. Kahanamoku, Willard writes (perhaps unfortunately attempting to duplicate the beach boys' pidgin) would "nevah, nevah turn his back on the ocean."[63]

Scholars such as Willard and Osmond remind us that while Hawaii has been, as a colony and then as a state, American since the dawn of the twentieth century, Hawaiians, and especially nonwhite Hawaiians, are automatically perceived in the United States as racialized foreigners. Because he was a victorious Olympian, Kahanamoku could be embraced intermittently as one of America's own. But accepting Kahanamoku's cultural citizenship in the United States with excessive enthusiasm would have undermined the racial hierarchy constructed over decades of American history, as well as the Hawaiian haole elite's efforts to promote Hawaii, even after statehood, as exotic.

Citing Stuart Hall, Osmond asserts that cultural forms like stamps, statues, and newspaper articles can dispatch multiple and contradictory messages. The words and images used to describe and evoke Duke Kahanamoku have not always helped us figure out, "Who is Duke? ... Who is this man and how did he get on my stamp?" Seen through lenses crafted by racialized colonization, Kahanamoku's substantial athletic achievements and his complicated relationship to the American empire, let alone his humanity, flicker in and out of focus.[64]

Notes

1. Robert W. Reising, "Remaking of an Overlooked Icon: The Reconstruction of Jim Thorpe," in *Reconstructing Fame: Sport, Race, and Evolving Reputation*, ed. David C. Ogden and Joel Nathan Rosen (Jackson: University Press of Mississippi, 2011); and David C. Ogden, "Roberto Clemente: From Ignominy to Icon," in *Reconstructing Fame: Sport, Race, and Evolving Reputation*, ed. David C. Ogden and Joel Nathan Rosen (Jackson: University Press of Mississippi, 2011).

2. Jim Nendel, "New Hawaiian Monarchy: The Media Representations of Duke Kahanamoku, 1911–1912," *Journal of Sport History* 31, no. 1 (Spring 2004): 34, 36.

3. Renato V. Rosaldo and William V. Flores, "Ideology, Conflict, and Evolving Latino Communities: Cultural Citizenship in San Jose, California," in *Latino Cultural Citizenship: Claiming Identity, Space, and Rights*, ed. William V. Flores and Rina Benmayor (Boston: Beacon Press, 1997), 57.

4. Elizabeth Buck, *Paradise Remade: The Politics of Culture and History in Hawai'i* (Philadelphia: Temple University Press, 2000); Davianna Pōmaika'i McGregor, *Nā Kua'āina: Living Hawaiian Culture* (Honolulu: University of Hawaii Press, 2007); Sally Engle Merry, *Colonizing Hawai'i: The Cultural Power of Law* (Princeton, NJ: Princeton University Press, 2000); Gary Okihiro, *Island World: A History of Hawai'i and the United States* (Berkeley: University of California Press, 2009); Noenoe K. Silva, *Aloha Betrayed: Native Hawaiian Resistance to American Colonialism* (Durham, NC: Duke University Press, 2004); and Michael Kioni Dudley and Keoni Kealoha Agard, "A History of Dispossession," in *Pacific Diaspora: Island Peoples in the*

United States and across the Pacific, ed. Paul Spickard, Joanne L. Rondilla, and Debbie Hippolite Wright (Honolulu: University of Hawaii Press, 2002).

5. Sandra Kimberley Hall and Greg Ambrose, *Memories of Duke: The Legend Comes to Life* (Honolulu: Bess Press, 1996), 4.

6. *New York Times*, June 12, 1912, 11.

7. Buck, *Paradise Remade*; Gary Okihiro, *Pineapple Culture: A History of the Tropical and Temperate Zones* (Berkeley: University of California Press, 2010); and Joel S. Franks, *The Barnstorming Hawaiian Travelers: A Multiethnic Baseball Team Tours the Mainland, 1912–1916* (Jefferson, NC: McFarland, 2012).

8. Franks, *The Barnstorming Hawaiian Travelers*; and James Clifford, *Routes: Travel and Translation in the Late Twentieth Century* (Cambridge, MA: Harvard University Press, 1997).

9. Susan Brownell, ed., *The 1904 Anthropology Days and Olympic Games: Sport, Race, and American Imperialism* (Lincoln: University of Nebraska Press, 2008); *Washington Post*, June 13, 1913, 48; and *Pacific Commercial Advertiser*, November 10, 1911, 3.

10. Nendel, "New Hawaiian Monarchy," 38, 40.

11. Ibid, 40.

12. *New York Times*, January 14, 1912, C7; and *New York Times*, March 3, 1912, C7.

13. Cited in *Pacific Commercial Advertiser*, May 15, 1912, 3; and *Day Book* (Chicago), July 3, 1912, 29.

14. *Washington Post*, July 10, 1912, 12. [Kumar Shri Ranjitsinhji, known as Ranji, was the prince of the Indian state of Nawanagar and a test cricketer who played for the English side in the early years of the twentieth century. He is widely regarded as one of the greatest batsmen of all time. See Board of Control for Cricket in India, "History," at http://www.bcci.tv/about/2016/history—*eds.*]

15. Nendel, "New Hawaiian Monarchy," 42.

16. *Washington Post*, April 7, 1912, 43; and Leonard Connes, "Americans Were Skeptical of Kahanamoku's Prowess," *Washington Post*, June 22, 1913, 48.

17. *Los Angeles Times*, December 10, 1914, pt.3, 3.

18. Cited in *Honolulu Star-Bulletin*, February 18, 1913, 9; *Washington Post*, October 26, 1913, 53; Louis Lee Arms, "Title of Duke Merely Wished on Kahanamoku," *New York Tribune*, August 11, 1918, 4; Buck, *Paradise Remade*; and Okihiro, *Island World*.

19. *Duluth News Tribune*, June 18, 1922, sec. 4, 4.

20. Cited in *Honolulu Star-Bulletin*, January 21, 1913, 9; and *Bogalusa (LA) Enterprise*, February 17, 1916, 4.

21. *Day Book* (Chicago), March 19, 1914, 23; *Washington Post*, April 18, 1915; *Duluth News Tribune*, April 9, 1916, sports sec., 2; and Nendel, "New Hawaiian Monarchy," 38.

22. *Kokomo (IN) Tribune*, July 13, 1918, 7.

23. George Marvin, "Riding the Wild Surf," *Outing*, April 1914, 33.

24. Robert Edgren, "Edgren Expects Hawaiian to Help the United States Swimming Career," *Duluth News Tribune*, August 1, 1920, sec. 3, 8.

25. *Sporting Life*, July 1, 1916, 3; *Washington Post*, May 18, 1922, 12; and *San Jose News*, February 4, 1922, 7.

26. *Duluth News Tribune*, June 18, 1922, section, 4, 4. The movie casting Kahanamoku as Kamehameha was shot but, due to lack of funding and lack of interest in Hollywood, never

finished; see David Davis, *Waterman: The Life and Times of Duke Kahanamoku* (Lincoln: University of Nebraska Press, 2015).

27. *Elyria (OH) Chronicle Telegram*, September 3, 1926, 22.

28. *Lake County (IN) Times*, June 24, 1926, 16.

29. Ibid.

30. Charley Paddock, "The Duke Again Is King," *Charleston (WV) Daily Mail*, June 9, 1929, 6.

31. Nendel, "New Hawaiian Monarchy," 334.

32. *Hawaiian Gazette*, August 5, 1911, 3.

33. *Pacific Commercial Advertiser*, November 20, 1911, 3.

34. *Pacific Commercial Advertiser*, January 8, 1912, 3; *Pacific Commercial Advertiser*, January 13, 1912, 3; and *Hawaiian Star*, January 4, 1912, 3.

35. *Pacific Commercial Advertiser*, January 14, 1932, 3.

36. *Pacific Commercial Advertiser*, March 31, 1912, 3; *Hawaiian Gazette*, March 5, 1912, 3.

37. *Pacific Commercial Advertiser*, April 11, 1912, 3.

38. *Pacific Commercial Advertiser*, May 17, 1912, 3.

39. *Pacific Commercial Advertiser*, May 25, 1912, 3.

40. *Honolulu Star-Bulletin*, July 20, 1912, 4.

41. *Pacific Commercial Advertiser*, July 11, 1912, 4.

42. *Pacific Commercial Advertiser*, October 3, 1912, 3; *Thrum's Hawaiian Annual of 1913* (Honolulu: Thomas G. Thrum, 1912), 179–81; *Maui News*, August 31, 1912, 5; and *Honolulu Star-Bulletin*, May 31, 1913, 1.

43. *Honolulu Star-Bulletin*, October 2, 1912, 9.

44. *Honolulu Star-Bulletin*, August 9, 1913, 9; *Maui News*, October 26, 1912, 5; and *Pacific Commercial Advertiser*, November 8, 1913, 8.

45. *Pacific Commercial Advertiser*, January 29, 1915, 12.

46. *Pacific Commercial Advertiser*, March 3, 1915, 8.

47. *Pacific Commercial Advertiser*, April 2, 1915, 11.

48. *Honolulu Star-Bulletin*, June 19, 1915, 10; and *Honolulu Star-Bulletin*, August 14, 1915, 10.

49. *Hawaiian Gazette*, January 28, 1913, 1; and *Honolulu Star-Bulletin*, January 25, 1917, 12.

50. *Honolulu Star-Bulletin*, January 20, 1917, 15.

51. *Plain Dealer*, February 9, 1939, 17; *Cambridge (MA) Tribune*, March 9, 1939, 3; *Helena Independent*, January 26, 1941, 13; *Reno Evening Gazette*, December 18, 1950, 5; and *Official Baseball Annual 1956: Rules, Teams, Photos* (Wichita, KS: National Baseball Congress, 1956), 14–15.

52. *Chillicothe (MO) Constitution*, October 14, 1961, 4.

53. *Long Beach Press-Telegram*, September 23, 1966, D1.

54. Ibid.

55. Greg Ambrose, "The Greatest Ever: Duke Kahanamoku Is Selected by Surfer Magazine as the Surfer of the Century," *Honolulu Star-Bulletin*, July 29, 1999, at http://archives.starbulletin.com/1999/07/29/sports/index.html.

56. Bobby Command, "Duke Kahanamoku Simply Hawaii's Greatest Athlete," *West Hawaii Today*, January 21, 2000.

57. Jeff Stage, "Postal Service Honors Duke Kahanamoku," *Syracuse Post-Standard*, August 11, 2002, 29.

58. Gary Osmond, "Modest Monuments? Postage Stamps, Duke Kahanamoku, and Hierarchies of Social Memory," *Journal of Pacific History* 43, no. 3 (December 2008): 324.

59. Haunani-Kay Trask, *From a Native Daughter: Colonialism and Sovereignty in Hawaii* (Honolulu: University of Hawaii Press, 1999).

60. Michael Nevin Willard, "Duke Kahanamoku's Body: Biography of Hawaii," in *Sports Matters: Race, Recreation, and Culture*, ed. John Bloom and Michael Nevin Willard (New York: New York University Press, 2002).

61. Ibid, 17, 23, 25.

62. Ibid, 30–32.

63. Ibid, 32.

64. Osmond, "Modest Monuments?," 325.

Chad Rowan
Ritual, Religion, and One American's Pitch-Perfect
Performance inside Japan's Hall of National Sport

—Mark Panek

In the end, the meaning and beauty of sumo reside in this characteristically Japanese aesthetic: a comparatively simple image represents great underlying complexities. After all of the discussion on cultural significance, and after the countless hours of training, it came down to this moment. How did Chad Rowan from Hawai'i wind up as Japan's most important cultural symbol, only one of sixty-four over the course of more than two hundred years of contemporary sumo, and the first foreigner? An extremely complex question—one with a simple answer.
—**MARK PANEK**, *Gaijin Yokozuna*

Introduction

The 2006 University of Hawai'i Press book where I explore the above question—at once complex, thanks to professional sumo's position as a cultural touchstone in a country not known for its acceptance of foreigners, and simple, once the public performance of Chad Rowan as the sport's first non-Japanese top-ranker is unpacked—carries what I had hoped to be an ironic title: *Gaijin Yokozuna*, with *gaijin* meaning "foreigner" and *yokozuna* the title conferred on the top-ranker, the public upholder of every stoic samurai-related forge-on-with-honor-in-the-face-of-tremendous-adversity ideal that folks in the Land of the Rising Sun like to consider uniquely "Japanese."

At the time it didn't make sense that a non-Japanese could ever hold such a national ethos-defining position, and to bring the oxymoronic title point home, the book centers upon two salient images. In the first, when Japan presented itself to the world during the 1998 Nagano Winter Olympic opening ceremonies, to capture "Japanese" in a single face, they improbably choose Rowan. The second occurred on *senshuraku*, "the final day of the performance," of the 1993 New Year's sumo tournament, and even more than two decades later, Rowan's individual performance on that day stands out in all its vivid detail as the image that gave birth to the book in the first place. Back in 1993, the whole of Japan, all 120 million–plus on those famously crowded islands, or so it seemed, stopped whatever they were doing to gather around the nearest television, car radio, or storefront window to catch the broadcast streaming live from inside Tokyo's Hall of National Sport, where a crowd of ten thousand strong sat impatiently through the day's penultimate bout. That audience included Takahanada, a twenty-year-old son of sumo royalty with a teen-idol following, and a man with the ring name of Akebono—Rowan—his unlikely rival ever since the pair began at the sport's lowest rank some five years earlier. The two sat stoically on either side of the raised clay ring waiting to square off in the tournament's last fight. And while everything was on the line, much more than just the gleaming silver Emperor's Cup presented to the champion, through protocol and ritual stretching back centuries, one couldn't tell by looking at either of them. No spotlights. No blaring ring music. No trash talk or taunting. No self-branded shoes or shoulders covered in tattoos. Just two mirror images: rippled arms folded over thick bare stomachs, faces staring ahead in Zen-like concentration.[1]

Above them, a Shinto shrine's wooden roof hung down from the arena's rafters, evoking the spiritual roots of a sport dating back to the age when bouts were held outdoors on temple grounds to coincide with planting and harvest ceremonies. The referee scampering around the ring was dressed like a Shinto priest. Five aging black-robed judges sat one at a side of the square ring (two on the south side), all of them long-retired elders who had once triumphed in this very arena. The ring itself had been blessed in an elaborate pretournament ceremony before ten thousand empty seats.[2] The arena: built not for basketball and tennis and music concerts and whatever else but exclusively for battles such as this one. Standing in it when empty felt like being in church. And even now, the two waiting fighters looked as though what they were about to do connected them to the ancient gods.[3]

Not so, the crowd: all ten thousand let out a deafening roar the moment Takahanada and Akebono finally stood, the preceding fighters having finished their business. Although noise wasn't unusual for a tournament's final bout, when these two men bowed to one another, the feudal-era announcer at ring's center had to work to audibly sing out their names. When each man raised a leg high off to the side and then stomped it into the hard clay to frighten off the evil spirits, it got louder still. When each spread his arms wide and twisted his palms forward to indicate that he carried no weapons and would fight honorably: thunderous applause. By the time Akebono brought his hands together to awaken the gods, his clap was eaten by deafening sound. Long and sustained, pierced with a few thousand Beatlemania-type squeals aimed at Takahanada, the cheering smothered even the more contemporary-style introduction amplified out over the public address system that followed each man back to his corner.[4]

More than just loud, the roar understood the full implications of what was at stake way back in 1993. Listening back now on a YouTube clip of the event, one can actually hear it: the collectively shouted memory of the president of the United States, George H. W. Bush, who only a year earlier had traveled all the way to Tokyo on a diplomatic mission to sell American cars—cars far too bulky for Tokyo's narrow side streets, let alone its bed-sized parking spaces that leased for the price of a small apartment—only to fly home empty-handed after puking on the prime minister.[5]

One could also hear echoes of Tokyo governor Shintaro Ishihara's ultra-nationalist bestseller *The Japan That Can Say No*,[6] which had just appeared in English, along with an American-penned bestselling novel called *Rising Sun* that depicted a chilling Japanese economic world takeover. That roar: it screamed out that just as the spectacular speculative bubble that had fueled Japan's 1980s rise to *we're-going-to-buy-up-everything-from-Rockefeller-Center-to-Pebble-Beach* international dominance was beginning to hemorrhage yen at mortally rapid rates, an entire nation—even the hordes of young people attracted by Takahanada to a sport that for years had been nothing but supremely dorky, kept alive only so that retirees and taxi drivers could pass away boring afternoons—had begun to clutch at the notion of sumo as something *purely Japanese*.[7]

When Takahanada and Akebono each squatted down to accept the traditional ladleful of purifying water, and each wiped his mouth with a ceremonial sheet of paper (*kami*, a homonym for "god"), those words—*purely Japanese*—were underscored, capturing completely what in fact was on the line. It wasn't just that envelope of cash, tens of thousands of dollars thick, filled by the corporate sponsors whose elaborate Edo-era-looking banners circled the ring, each held aloft by a flag bearer straight out of some seventeenth-century woodblock print. Or the Emperor's Cup—that Lord Stanley–esque silver chalice handed off to the champion. Or even the spoils that went along with the cup: a ton of rice, a cask of exotic mushrooms, a barrel of top-shelf sake, various other sponsor-donated gifts, a million-dollar cash award, along with the piles of under-the-table sponsor money that would flow in the weeks to follow, courtesy of an ancient Japanese patronage system whereby a champion was paid a five-figure sum to simply appear at some corporate dinner.[8] No, more than any trophy or wad of brown-tinted ten-thousand-yen notes, was this: if Akebono were to come out on top, in convincing enough fashion, with the proper amount of a certain kind of *I-know-it-when-I-see-it*, purely Japanese dignity, the chances were good that he would then be promoted to *yokozuna*—holder of the sport's highest rank.

Yokozuna. The translation "Grand Champion" doesn't even come close. And if there were any doubts when Takahanada and Akebono each began to towel off the sweat that had already begun to accumulate that this entire spectacle had long since transcended "sport" to become cultural performance or even religion, all anyone had to do was translate yokozuna literally: the "rope." The concrete image, blinding white, of the sacred thick belt-like rope that a man bearing the title yokozuna wears whenever he purifies the ring with time-honored steps before each day's schedule of fights. Modeled after those hanging from the gates of Shinto shrines across Japan, adorned with the same five zigzag strips of white paper that mark those shrines as sacred places, the rope is ritualistically constructed by a dozen or more men, so symbolically heavy it takes eight of them to wrap it around the waist of the yokozuna they serve.[9] The rope: meaning little until that day when promotion is made real before the gods in yet another ceremony following those reaching back centuries at Tokyo's Meiji Shrine. The rope: sometimes even worn outside the ring, when yokozuna are called upon to consecrate the grounds of a new building, or bless a harvest ceremony, or open the Olympics when that contest visits the homeland. The Shinto rope: purely Japanese at a glance.[10]

Another nod to Shinto ("the way of the gods") is the water in those two ringside wooden buckets. The water is so pure that the loser of any bout is thought to contaminate it and is thus prohibited from the little ceremony where the winner of the prior bout offers up the ladle in one corner, the winner of an earlier contest in the other. It is pure like the salt spread across the ring even in daily practice after someone is hurt, because it truly will change the luck that must have caused the injury in the first place.

Caked now in hand-sized ringside wooden boxes in each corner, the salt chases evil spirits away.[11] And when Takahanada and Akebono each grabbed a handful and sent it skyward, the ritual renewed the roar, which only rose as they reached the ring's center and crouched down like opposing linemen in the final stare-down before the charge. Takahanada himself: purely Japanese. Son of one of the sport's all-time beloved stars, nephew of a legendary yokozuna, he had been raised in a house that contained its own practice ring, watching his father and uncle train daily with a whole stable of eager fighters, and training with his older brother Wakahanada, the two of them picked since birth to carry on the family's legacy.[12]

Yes, an entire nation had come to a standstill, whether they had ever much cared about what went on inside their Hall of National Sport before or not, because nothing like this particular standoff had ever happened in well over two centuries of sumo in its current form, let alone the millennia reaching all the way back to Japanese creation myths in which the gods Takemikazuchi and Takeminakata battled for control of Japan, and whose progeny are said to extend all the way down to the current emperor.[13] And it wasn't as though anyone necessarily disliked the humble and soft-spoken Akebono ... except that ... well, in 1993 anyway, in Japan, one could say it right out loud. One could, as we will see, argue one's point in a newspaper. One could talk about it on TV without coming off as a bigoted xenophobe straight out of a World War II propaganda video: Akebono was gaijin. To the Japanese, not even "American"—and certainly not "Chad Rowan from Hawai'i"—just gaijin. Foreigner. Outside Person.

The Way of Sumo

"We Don't Need Gaijin Yokozuna" is a benignly translated headline whose verb construction often falls more toward *they are useless* than *we don't need*. It appeared in a magazine called *Bungeishunju*, according Velisarios Kattoulas, et al., not quite a year before the historic New Year's bout between Akebono and Takahanada.[14] An attempt to spell out the culture-defining role of a yokozuna, the article was written by novelist Noboru Kojima, whose available ammunition included the structural nature of sumo familiar to many Japanese: a rigid ranking system based on majority-win performances over time in the sport's six annual bimonthly tournaments where, unlike with tennis-type elimination, the man who piles up the most wins in each division across the full fifteen days is named a tournament's champion.

But at the very top, a mere winning record won't win anyone yokozuna promotion—not any more than defeating a sitting yokozuna in an individual bout will. Only after two consecutive top-division major championships or an "equivalent record" is promotion even considered, and then it is voted on by the Yokozuna Promotions Council, of which Kojima was a member when he wrote his article. And what does the committee consider? Kojima summed it up like this: "What makes sumo different is its own particular characteristics of civility, which is the basis of Japanese morals and values." And then, like a foregone conclusion, he added, "I cannot agree with a school of thought that would make a gaijin yokozuna a part of internationalization."[15]

Not some rogue nationalist manifesto, Kojima's article was simply one more voice in a chorus that had formed a decade earlier when a Samoan from Hawai'i walked into Japan and plowed over his first twenty opponents before losing. His name was Saleva'a Atisanoe, and from the get-go his athletic prowess in a sport he had never even tried was a polar opposite from his understanding of sumo—or more accurately, *sumōdo*, "the way" of sumo, the very cultural root of the sport that most reflected how the Japanese like to think of themselves, as austere, humble, and technically superior warriors who persevere in the face of tremendous odds and never deviate from the correct tradition-dictated steps. For starters, Atisanoe had arrived weighing more than four hundred pounds— a weight most of the top-division *sumotori* never reach in a sport that has no weight classes—which turned his bouts against the mostly scrawny dues-paying teenagers who populate the lower divisions into embarrassing one-sided affairs. It didn't help that the gaijin had been given the century-old ring name of one of sumo's ancient legends, Konishiki—especially when it emerged that he intended to return to Hawai'i as soon as he'd plundered enough prize money to start his own business.[16]

Nor did it help when, not long after reaching sumo's second-highest division in a then-record seven tournaments, Konishiki began to attract relentless media attention, long before his proficiency in the Japanese language had reached the point where he could express himself with any level of nuance. At one point when the cameras caught him on the street, an unseen interviewer goaded him by saying, "If you get better, you may have to take on ōzeki"— sumo's second-highest rank—"and yokozuna." Instead of bowing his head according to the sumo script and saying "I will try my best" with great humility—or with Noboru Kojima's brand of civility—the American answered with this: "Ataru-yo!"[17] Roughly translated: "It's on target," or, in this case, "That's right: bring 'em on." After he did face those top-rankers, taking out two yokozuna in just his second upper-division tournament, he allegedly let loose with another disastrous pronouncement comparing the sacred national sport to a street brawl.[18] Calls of "meat bomb" and "dump truck" and "elephant" rained down on him—even death threats and an effigy nailed to a Shinto shrine.[19] A more measured response, though no less pointed, came from Yokozuna Promotions Council chair Yoshitaka Takahashi. Journalist William Wetherall quotes Takahashi defining a *sumotori*'s humble cultural obligations before concluding with this: "But now this strong guy barges in with the idea that winning is all he needs to do."[20]

To make matters even worse, the young American was being compared not only to his Japanese colleagues—an idealized image of them at that—but also to the only other gaijin ever to impact the national sport: a Hawaiian named Jesse Kuhaulua, who had helped recruit him. Competing under the name Takamiyama, Kuhaulua first arrived amid Japan's postwar recovery way back in 1964, long before such terms as "internationalization" had ever even crossed the mind of a Yokozuna Promotions Council member. Significantly, it took Takamiyama more than six years to reach sumo's salaried divisions, allowing him both to become fluent in Japanese before attracting much attention, and to craft the humble persona of an underdog enduring against tremendous odds—or, better put, to *come off* as "being Japanese" in an idealized cultural sense by eliciting the well-worn word for such endurance: *gaman*.[21] Takamiyama became the first gaijin to win a major tournament, going on to compile an iron-man record of 1,231 consecutive upper-division bouts, competing, astoundingly, past the age of forty. It has been speculated that those milestones resulted from holding back in the ring, a tactic that kept the gaijin injury free but also safely distant from the sacred white rope then worn by Takahanada's uncle.²² So it was with little controversy that Kuhaulua adopted Japanese citizenship, became the first foreign-born elder in sumo's long history, and opened his own training facility upon retiring in 1986.²³

Thanks to the unforgiving sport's violent nature, the hard reality of practicing daily on a rock-hard clay surface, and a weight increase to over six hundred pounds that robbed him of much of his early agility, Konishiki was eventually able to begin crafting his own narrative of *gaman*. Humbled by a knee injury that could have ended his career and astute enough to have learned from his earlier cultural missteps, Konishiki, now the lone American in sumo's top division after Takamiyama's retirement, had come a long way from likening the Shinto-rooted sport to a brawl. In a more thoughtful interview done by a far more linguistically capable sumo veteran, he explained that years earlier he had been trying to use the offending term *kenka* to mean "fight" in its positive sense. "My comment was misinterpreted," he said. "I have the feeling of a fighter inside. Whenever I face a match, I give it all I've got. It's the fighting spirit in me. Even my coaches tell me, 'Put up a good fight.' They mean, 'Do the best you can.' The media thought I was talking about *kenka*. You shouldn't do *kenka* with anyone." His use of the term, he admitted, "was wrong."²⁴ And as if to top things off with a tangible reversal of his earlier goal to simply make money and return to Hawai'i, ten years into what was looking more and more like a permanent stay and with fanfare fit for a prince, the big man married a Japanese model.

Nevertheless, according to Shintaro Ishihara,²⁵ none of this would be enough. Weeks before the fiftieth anniversary of the bombing of Pearl Harbor, Konishiki did march through the November tournament to take his second Emperor's Cup. In January, he did finish strong with twelve wins. And in March, he may have celebrated his wedding with yet another championship, his three-tournament record of thirty-eight wins exceeding those of each of the two previously promoted yokozuna by two wins. But a yokozuna? This was the most prominent visible living symbol of national purity in a country that fingerprinted foreign residents long before 9/11, that refused to grant permanent visas even to tenured foreign professors, that required foreigners to contribute to the pension fund but never allowed them to collect, that singled out as potential troublemakers anyone not one hundred percent ethnically Japanese,²⁶ including even legendary home run king Sadaharu Oh, born in Japan of a Japanese mother and a Chinese father, raised within walking distance of sumo's Hall of National Sport, denied a Japanese passport, and barred as a high school student from the 1957 National Amateur Athletic Competition baseball tournament.²⁷ As late as the year 2000, Ishihara, then governor of Tokyo, would publicly finger descendants of foreigners as the cause of a rise in the city's crime rate, emphasizing his point with the term *san-goku-jin*, "third-country people," well aware, no doubt, that it was an offensive racial slur even to many of his own compatriots.[28] Yokozuna? A gaijin? In 1992?

The Yokozuna Promotions Council met as usual following Konishiki's March championship. Their chairman, according to sumo historian Chris Gould, emerged with this announcement: "We wanted to make doubly sure that Konishiki is worthy to be a yokozuna. Therefore we decided to wait for another tournament"—the May tournament, two months away.[29] A transpacific political ... *kenka* ... ensued, with Noburo Kojima introducing the world to the concept of *hinkaku*—a culturally specific kind of dignity he claimed only an ethnic Japanese could possibly possess, and a requirement for yokozuna promotion as important as the requisite wins—and, on the other side, the *New York Times*, which phoned Konishiki's training facility and extracted the money quote of the year by asking if race had played a role in the nonpromotion. Konishiki reportedly said it had, unloading with this: "I cannot contain my feeling any longer. I hope this makes a point to [the Japan Sumo Association] so they just don't leave me hanging."[30] Konishiki later denied everything, saying that one of his underlings had impersonated him on the phone—an assertion confirmed by the underling years later.[31] Either way, irreparable damage had been done, and the American was forced to apologize for having lacked the civility to restrain himself from stating the obvious.

If nothing else, the whole fiasco forced the Japan Sumo Association to clarify its admittedly subjective yokozuna promotion standards. For one, had Konishiki won the New Year's tournament sandwiched by his two championships instead of finishing third, his objective results would have moved him out of the "or equal worth" gray area onto what Sumo Association chair Dewanoumi Rijichō described, during a 1992 Foreign Correspondents' Club lecture translated by sumo journalist Mark Schilling, as solid ground for promotion. "As for Konishiki," Rijichō said flatly, "we didn't feel he had the necessary record" of two consecutive championships. "In other areas of his character," the chairman went on, "it would be ill-mannered of me to mention here these personal things that we would like to see him change. It involves his own personality and is something we discuss directly with him. There are a variety of points that we considered, but it's just that this is not the forum to discuss those points. There is also the idea of personal opinion. For example, someone might say that he might be too heavy as far as health is concerned."[32]

So by the time he stepped into the ring in May 1992, Konishiki had become an ambassador for an America enraged at a country whose leader, Kiichi Miyazawa, had branded Americans "lazy," during an election year in which campaign speeches were peppered with such transpacific trade terms as "level playing field." In the middle of all of this, Konishiki was expected to uphold the side that was whining loudly about America's "Japan bashing." "Win," he was being reminded from home. But from Japan, he was advised: do so with that ever-elusive form of Japanese dignity, *hinkaku*.

In a Hollywood version, the American would have gone undefeated in the crucial tournament, left his precious yokozuna rope in the middle of the ring, and walked off into the sunset back to an adoring American public. Instead Konishiki, understandably, failed to come through. He opened the tournament with four consecutive wins but followed with a disastrous four-loss plunge that took him out of contention early. "I was trying to find myself," he later told *Sumo World* magazine, "but everything just fell apart after that.... I was just lost."[33]

If the Japan Sumo Association's intention had been to set Konishiki up to crumble under the weight of such previously unheard-of international political pressure and thus prevent any gaijin from ever wearing the sacred white rope, it worked. (The big man finished far out of the running with only nine wins in what would turn out to be his last championship run.) The only problem was this: with the Emperor's Cup up for grabs that May, Takahanada's older brother Wakahanada was sent airborne by ... another gaijin ... a towering young Hawaiian who competed under the name Akebono, which means "dawn."

A Hawaiian Son . . .

"Look how tall he is!" was all anyone could say when they first saw eighteen-year-old Chad Rowan, newly arrived from Hawai'i, because back at the little ceremony, where sumo's incoming members of the Class of February 1988 were being weighed and measured and formally registered into the Japan Sumo Association, the bank of blinding flashing cameras was mostly aimed ... elsewhere.[34] Sure, there was this brand-new gaijin with that great ring name to match his gangly height, Taikai, Rowan's sumo name before someone thought to call him the more majestic Akebono. Taikai meant "Big Sea," but everyone caught the pun on *takai*—tall!—and, well, you know, that easily tippable six-foot, eight-inch frame is going to hurt him in the ring ... nothing like Konishiki (and what an aberration *he* was) ... this gaijin isn't going to last the year, and anyway ...

Look! Here come the Hanada brothers! Takahanada and Wakahanada! Now those are *names*! Listen to the echoes of the names made into legends by their father, Tahanohana, and their uncle, the great Yokozuna Wakanohana. They'll pass the Emperor's Cup back and forth for years to come! And did somebody say something about another gaijin? Get a good shot of the brothers![35]

Right then it started to sink into Chad Rowan's head that maybe all the buttering up the recruiter had done back in Hawai'i—*Everything will be taken care of*, and *You have everything within you to become a yokozuna!*—maybe the words had been little more than a sales pitch. Maybe Boss, the elder Azumazeki

Oyakata and former Takamiyama—maybe he hadn't been joking back at their brief meeting in Hawai'i when he'd laughed at Rowan and swayed him back and forth like a palm tree in the wind for the TV cameras, finally agreeing to sign him up only as a way to try to entice his younger brother to come join once he finished high school, knowing all along that Rowan couldn't even say *hinkaku* let alone explain it, and that he would likely never even be worthy to set foot in a yokozuna's practice ring, let alone compete with one.[36]

And if all the attention on induction day heaped . . . elsewhere, upon the Hanadas . . . if the pointing and stares and laughter and the *Takai! Takai! Takai!*—the *Look how tall he is!*—if that hadn't convinced Rowan that things would be more involved than the recruiter had let on, then his immediate introduction to Azumazeki Oyakata's training facility, his new home, drove the point home like an open-handed slap to the head. The daily routine of getting kicked awake in the predawn darkness and thrown around a rock-hard sumo ring for hours on end in biting winter cold, slaving away the rest of the day for those ranked above him—meaning *everyone*, including the fifteen-year-old punks who'd entered the training stable before he had—and enduring the worst kind of hazing coming from all angles in the incomprehensible babble that was the Japanese language—as Rowan recalled many years later, it all added up to two words. "See, I thought when I first came to sumo, you join some kind of club, you practice for a little while, and then you get to be on TV," he said, not realizing at the time that there was "a whole ranking system, almost nine hundred wrestlers. And when you come into sumo, you start at the *ass bottom!*"[37]

Those two words may as well have amounted to a literal translation for the place the sumo ranking sheet's archaic little black-painted Japanese squiggles had defined for the gaijin, for Takahanada and Wakahanada, for every other bottom-ranker scattered around Tokyo's fifty-odd sumo stables, each of their names scrawled in the width of a single brush hair you could hardly make out without a magnifying glass. *Ass bottom*, Rowan began his daily training long before the yokozuna, whose own squiggled names thickened all the way up to headline bold atop the ranking sheet, were even awake, and well ahead of many of his own stablemates, too, who would file into the practice ring hours into the day, according to rank, just before Rowan, covered in sand and sweat and salt, headed not to the bath but straight to the kitchen to fix the day's main meal for his seniors, unable to quiet his own grumbling stomach until everyone else was through sating theirs. Later, as they all napped, the ass-bottom new guy would drag his exhausted body around for the rest of the day running errands for Boss. And for all this he was paid nothing but room (shared with more than ten other slaves), board (whatever wasn't vacuumed up before his turn came to eat), and the little monthly stipend he poured straight into the international payphone around the corner just to hear his mother's voice. This, in total, amounted to the *everything* in *Everything will be taken care of.* And as far as *You have everything within you to become a yokozuna!* was concerned, well ... it went without saying that that little career goal was going to be a bit more complicated than what the recruiter had laid out.³⁸

Still, rather than quit in the face of tremendous tear-jerking homesickness, confusion with the language, anger with the constant hazing, and frustration with the technical aspects of what was really more of a martial art than a football charge at the line; rather than retreat from the lack of faith that Boss showed in him in front of everybody, and most of all from the challenge of fitting into this monastic stone-age world straight out of some old samurai movie, Rowan took a look around and boiled everything down to its simplest form—even that ranking sheet, indecipherable up close in its detailed characters but oh-so-clear from a couple of steps back, its names, yes, microscopic and worthless at the bottom but thick, prominent, and important once they reached the top.

"It's the most basic thing," Akebono would later say. "It's easy: you win, you move up, you lose, you go down. All you do is win, and you move up."³⁹ So for now, forget about yokozuna. Grab the newspaper, cut out the pictures of the Hanada brothers getting weighed and measured and anointed. Tape them to the wall next to ... not his bed but that little space on the floor where he rolled out his futon, just to make sure that was the last thing he saw before crying himself to sleep every night, all sick missing Hawai'i, his mom, his "boyz," sick for something to eat and not this "Japanese stew shit" they were making him eat every day—this bowl of *fish* and frikken *cabbage* floating in dead-gray broth. Nobody would believe it when he told them what sumo wrestlers ate to get so big.⁴⁰

Basic. Sure, maybe sumo was based on this complicated ranking system, these complex seniority codes, these precise ritualistic steps for pretty much everything you had to do. Maybe all the moves were parsed into over seventy types of winning techniques. But in the end, the whole thing boiled down to this: two guys charge at each other, and the first one who touches the ring with any part of his body other than the soles of his feet, or who steps outside the circle, loses. The whole thing could be over in seconds. No closed fist punching. No hair pulling. No eye gouging. Finish with more wins than losses and move up. Finish with the most wins and become the division's champion. All one has to do is hit the target straight ahead.

That, and keep quiet, which Akebono was able to do with ease even when he improbably managed to hit the most important targets right in front of him: the Hanada brothers. He kept quiet, even a few months later when somehow he managed to launch his tall frame across the ring in front of ten thousand empty seats in one of those early-morning bottom-division bouts nobody bothers to watch, and managed to send Takahanada himself, all at once a terrified and shocked fifteen-year-old prodigy, flying somewhere deep into the second row.

Even then Akebono kept quiet, holding in a need to celebrate right there on the spot—a need only revealed when he recalled the moment many years later, long after accumulating an endless memory reel of far more important wins: "Ho, you seen the video of that? No one thought I could beat him, but I came up fast at the *tachi-ai*," the initial charge. "You shoulda seen when I got back to the stable—everybody seen me; they started cheering!"[41]

. . . Rising

When the rest of the world dismissed the unsightly win as a fluke, Akebono continued to keep quiet, as hard as it may be to imagine for anyone who knows Chad Rowan, a man for whom talking seems as important as breathing. Even in the stifling humidity of a Tokyo summer, aching from another bone-jarring practice session as he dragged his lifeless body up the stairs, aiming for a few moments of a precious afternoon nap before getting back to the grind—even upon hearing his boss, Azumazeki Oyakata, a man whom he had come to look up to as a second father, the very first gaijin to make it in this ancient sport—even upon overhearing Boss on the phone, with the man who had recruited him: "You'd better come and take this boy home"—*home!*—he kept quiet.[42]

Not that any of it was easy, but that was what he had promised his father the night before getting on the plane in the first place. His father, who had overheard him promising his younger brother that "the Japanese [are] all going be looking up to me!" and that he wouldn't come home until he became a yokozuna, had told him this: "Be humble—never brag or speak big-headed." The words had been running through his brain when the news crew had come to interview Boss that very first day at the stable, when Rowan had told them again and again that he'd come to Japan to work hard, follow instructions, and try his best.[43] And Boss, after all, was Boss. To a Hawaiian like Chad Rowan, raised in a world where his first priority as a kid upon arriving at a family party of hundreds of people was to seek out and respectfully kiss grandma and then kiss all the aunties and shake hands with all the uncles before being allowed to go play with his cousins, respect for his boss, no matter what, came as naturally as sleeping.

So instead of calling out a man who had only recently completed his own two-decade sumo career, Akebono took up an invitation to work with a quirky personal trainer in Boss's small expat-in-Tokyo circle—a military doctor named Bob Beveridge—and he began dragging himself not just downstairs to his own stable's practice ring in the predawn darkness but all the way across Tokyo to spar with . . . the Hanadas. Nearly every morning. From Beveridge, an expert in body mechanics, he learned to charge with his knees bent and his weight lower to the ground to compensate for his height, just as he strengthened his arms to take full advantage of his devastating reach.[44]

From the Hanadas, he learned to win.

"They were *good* you know," Akebono recalled years later. "Even back then. Waka, when we were in *sandanme*," sumo's lowly third division, "he was already beating Akinoshima," a top-division *sumotori*. "We used to practice more than a hundred bouts at a time. Was mean. The Oyakata had to make us stop, 'cause we all just wanted to keep wrestling, nobody wanting to be the last man to lose."[45]

Least of all Akebono himself, born with a streak of competitor's arrogance as wide as Michael Jordan's, as Tiger's, as a young Mike Tyson's—although no one would ever know it. Listen to him privately look back on an injury sustained right after his May 1992 championship: "My foot? Fuck—I was wrestling with one broken foot, and I was still kicking everybody's ass. That's how bad I was, you know."[46] Listen to Percy Kipapa, who joined Akebono's stable a few months prior to that championship and trained with his fellow Hawaiian for seven years: "When I met Chad, he wasn't that nice of a person," Kipapa recalled. "I guess 'cause of all the stress and stuff, but when I got to know him, he was one nice guy. Real humble. But mean personalities. After practice, he go back to the shower, nobody bother him. Come back from the shower, eat, nobody bother him. After he eat, then you can talk story with him. You gotta catch him on perfect time. You don't catch him on perfect time, he's a bitch. Nobody can talk to him at all."[47]

So Taka, Waka, Akebono—they didn't just *push* each other up the ranks; they *raced*. Six two-week tournaments a year, seven bouts per tournament in the lower four divisions, fifteen in the top two, and soon they were fighting for their lives, because that's what happens when one reaches the upper *makushita* division, sumo's fourth division, and aims for the next level: *jūryō*, literally "ten ryō," an ancient form of Japanese currency. *Money*. "The number-one guy in *makushita*, and the number thirteen guy in *jūryō*—the difference is night and day," Akebono later explained. "The upper-*makushita* guy lives in a big room with all the rest of the other younger wrestlers. He gets not a salary but, like, a bonus every tournament depending on his win-loss situation, and that's it. Now if you move half a rank up into *jūryō*, you get a salary, you get your own room, you get the guys that serve under you, you get to look beautiful when you go in the ring, you start wearing expensive kimonos." Promotion also thickened a *sumotori*'s wallet with ten-thousand-yen notes courtesy of the sport's ancient patronage system, chances for more contemporary forms of sponsorship, and a rock-star status ... especially with women—that wasn't at all limited to a heart-throb like Takahanada. It's no wonder that the five-odd-percent who manage to cross this, the most important line of any man's career, are then referred to as *sekitori*—takers of the barrier. "When you speak about *jūryō*," Rowan went on, "it's not even breaking into the top hundred—it's breaking into like the top sixty-five guys out of almost nine hundred wrestlers."[48]

Right around the time of the television interview that saw Konishiki backpedaling on his earlier equation of sumo with street brawling, Takahanada won the race to *jūryō*. Two tournaments later, Wakahanada and Akebono both joined him there. At the time, the tall Hawaiian had nothing to say of taking on yokozuna. What he told the *Asahi Shimbun* was, "I thought that if I make it to the *jūryō* division in five or six years, that would be fast . . . that would be good enough for me."[49]

By year's end all three had blown through *jūryō* to the top division—sumo's big leagues. Some two years after that, Takahanada won the next race, igniting a national debate in the process: should the nineteen-year-old top-division champion substitute oolong tea for the sake a winner traditionally drinks from the Emperor's Cup? Because the prodigy had at last fulfilled all expectations, walking away with the 1992 New Year's tournament that everyone thought was Konishiki's for the taking. And while Akebono had kept the pace, finishing runner-up ahead of his fellow gaijin, it was hard to even notice. The lines snaking out from the Hall of National Sport in those days all the way to Ryōgoku Station two football fields away, the front-page news, this sumo renaissance—sumo really *was* the national sport again—it all came courtesy of two historic happenings: Can Konishiki do it? And, Here come the Hanadas!

And the tall gangly gaijin, the one they'd simply wanted to name Taikai as if to make his height a running joke? The one with that lucky win against Takahanada years earlier in an empty arena? The one Boss had wanted to send back to Hawai'i? While all the excitement was being directed . . . elsewhere . . . Akebono had been turning his height disadvantage into one of the more devastating weapons his centuries-old sport had ever seen.

"Fear, brah—fear," is how another gaijin top-division competitor from Hawai'i, George Kalima, explained what it was like to face Akebono in the ring:

> 'Cause you gotta face one fuckin' mountain comin' at you. His arms are so long, you get *scared*, brah, because the guy hits you before you even step over that line. He's hitting you in the chest or in the shoulders, and because he's got five hundred pounds, you're not gonna *move* him. If he comes off with his chest or his shoulder, then that's another thing—you can work with it. But when he comes with the hands, the only way to go is [to] try to go around him. You know, get on the side and try and throw him off balance. But you move forward and try and do the initial hit, and these two giant hands come up and stop you in your tracks. Then all of a sudden your mind is wondering, "What the fuck do I do now?" And because Akebono was

so tall, when you're hitting him, your head is hitting his chest. That five hundred pounds coming across the ring right into your head—it could pretty much break your fuckin' neck.⁵⁰

Such were the thoughts, it is safe to say—the Japanese version of *What the fuck do I do now?*—that ran through the head of Wakahanada in May 1992. The answer, as it turned out, was to pick himself up out of the third row, step up into the ring, bow to Akebono, and retreat to the changing room as the gaijin accepted his first Emperor's Cup with this thought in mind: "I tried my best." Perfect, according to the script, and filled with . . . civility . . . as were the words Akebono delivered moments later, captured by the Associated Press: "I am extremely happy. I take training hard because without it I cannot be promoted."⁵¹ As were those he spoke even to the *Honolulu Advertiser*'s Ferd Lewis, even in English, when he became only the second gaijin in sumo history to reach the sport's second-highest rank, one step away from a word he knew enough not to utter—yokozuna. "I am at a loss for words," he told Lewis. "But I feel great."⁵² Taken together—the incredible arc from his unlikely beginnings to the Emperor's Cup, the devastating final win over the anointed future star, to say nothing of the symbolic gaijin torch-passing from the fading Konishiki, all of it punctuated by such an incredibly humble, purely Japanese reaction—it all suggested that Akebono had been working as hard at mastering *hinkaku* as he had at breaking somebody's fucking neck.

Except he hadn't.

"Look around," is how he once summed up this incredible cultural performance. "Don't be ignorant. Look at the situation before you say anything."⁵³

But surely there had been some kind of interview-coaching version of Bob Beveridge to tutor him, some slick corporate sports agency that groomed its stars to deal with the media. Boss? Surely it was more than just a word of advice from dad before he got on the plane to Japan, right?

Ask, and he shakes his head.

Or Konishiki? Did Rowan learn from his mistakes?

"Nah," he counters. Another shake of the head, because it's simpler than that. "You can't pay attention to that kind of stuff," Akebono recalls. "When you start thinking stuff like that, that's when you start getting scared. To me, I feel when you mess up is when you start to think. If you just say what you feel and say it in a nice way, you should be all right."

But Konishiki was his *senpai*—his senior—didn't he explain it all?

"Because of him, I'm at where I am today," Akebono replies. "He gave me advice in the ring; off the ring; he used to practice with me; he made me get strong. And it's real important to have somebody like that because, like I said, we're only human, and you get tired from doing this every day. Some days, you just want to run and hide, and he would come look for me, watch, and you need somebody to push you like that."54

So then Konishiki taught him to bow his head and speak humbly, how to handle the relentless crush of media, the Japanese paparazzi hiding out in the bushes around the corner from your stable just dying to catch another gaijin committing another horrific cultural misstep.

Another shake of the head: "Konishiki, he tends to speak his mind," Akebono explains. "And sometimes I envy him for that, but not all the time. And like for me, the way I was brought up being the oldest, my parents, they didn't give me the *chance* to speak my mind." A pause. "When I was about three, four years old, I used to tell my mother all the time, she would tell me 'Shut up! Shut up!' I used to tell her, 'One day I going be one supa star, I going be on TV, everybody going be looking up at me!' Ever since I was small, she used to say, 'Ah, you just talking bubbles!'"55

Mom. Dad. Uncle Sam. His big cousin Nate—Akebono always pointed to Nate, a state champ in basketball who lived down the street he grew up on, as one of the three most important influences in his life. Play golf with Nate, hit a spectacular shot and start to celebrate, and he'll say it under his breath: "Eh! Make like you hit it that way all the time!" Or Uncle Haywood, his best friend George Kalima's dad—even after George had reached sumo's top division—home on vacation Uncle Haywood had him up on the roof cleaning out the gutters. These people who raised Akebono—they must have known all about *hinkaku*.

To those who gathered around the TV in a carport in the mainly native Hawaiian neighborhood of Waimānalo, where Chad Rowan had grown up, the way he carried himself, the dignity he showed when he was *representing his family*, was as important as the wins he kept putting up, even after overcoming that July foot injury, especially after flying out to a 14-1 championship in the same November tournament that would have catapulted Takahanada to yokozuna had the prodigy won it. Instead, there was Akebono, samurai-stoic and surrounded by a table of news personalities, talking about *doing his best*, dressed in his kimono and his samurai topknot, looking more purely Japanese than anyone else in the room. And acting that way too, especially when they got his mother on the phone, who said something so endearingly *un-Japanese* in a country packed with *ma-za-com* sons (a Japanization of "mother complex"), all so culturally bound from expressing any real affection that everyone just had to melt in envy when they heard her voice: "We love you Chad!"

Even then, Akebono could only bow his head and say, "I'll call you folks later."56

So two months later, could there be any doubt about what would happen inside the Hall of National Sport on *senshuraku*—the final day of the performance—when the last handful of salt rained down, and the two rivals who had been pushing each other for the past five years—Akebono, the gaijin, and Takahanada, the ancient institution's legacy—at last squatted down and stared into each other's eyes before the final charge?

That *roar*! It renewed itself, much louder now, like someone had hit a walk-off home run in the World Series. It filled the cavernous hall, shaking the rafters. It reached out into the streets of one of the world's most crowded cities and across a nation.

Seconds later, when it was all over, just by looking at the two men returning to ring's center to bow to one another, there was no way to tell which of them had won what had been one of sumo's more convincing hand-to-the-throat throwdown victories in recent memory.[57]

Which, of course, was the whole point.

Gaijin Yokozuna

Five years later, the Japan once feared to have embarked on a global economic takeover opened its doors to the world for the eighteenth Olympic Winter Games. The opening ceremonies that year were marked by the usual host-culture-defining performances—in this case, each contingent of athletes in the parade of an Olympic-record seventy-two nations was led into the stadium by a kimono-clad, topknotted *sumotori*. The Olympic flame was handed from marathoner Hiromi Suzuki to figure skater and silver medalist Midori Ito to light the stadium's torch. But since this was Japan, the proceedings could not be officially declared open until the gods had been summoned and the evil spirits frightened away in a ritual whose measured steps dated back centuries.[58]

Naturally, the task of performing this solemn ceremony fell to the giant man now entering the hushed stadium to the familiar Shinto ring of two polished wooden sticks rhythmically struck together. His mighty chest and thick legs were bare to the thirty-four-degree winter chill, his breath visible as he approached the raised platform at the very center of a cherry-blossom-shaped infield, his hair sculpted into a samurai topknot evoking, at a glance, the most familiar image the world has ever known to mean Japanese. When he mounted the platform, those familiar zigzag strips of white paper hanging from his waist—*paper*, in Japanese a homonym for *god*—and they swayed, drawing the attention of a worldwide television audience numbering in the hundreds of millions to the brilliant white belt-like rope worn by Yokozuna Akebono.

A somber, powerful look on his face—oblivious to the crowd, the television cameras, the collection of world-renowned athletes—the big man raised his arms above his head before bringing them down into a powerful clap that echoed through the highest reaches of the stadium and beyond. He clapped again, then lifted his right leg in the air and brought it crashing down. The stomp brought him into a low crouch, his left hand to his side, his right arm extended to its full length, his massive body compacted and bent forward, eyes facing straight ahead so all could see the whites of them below their upturned pupils. With a dancer's grace he slowly rose to his towering height, slightly twisting his feet from side to side until his legs came together and he was standing again. He repeated the powerful leg stomp, completing the steps that would purify the grounds in the most culturally, spiritually, and visually purely Japanese way for the world's most important sporting competition. And in so doing, gaijin or not, Chad Rowan from Hawai'i became the very embodiment of one of the most proudly ethnocentric nations on earth.

How?

Stretching back to the moment he had so convincingly sent Takahanada tumbling into the crowd five years earlier and then *not* reacted, Akebono had left the Japanese with little choice when the time came for them to choose their Nagano ambassador. Although the Konishiki fiasco had forced the Japan Sumo Association to apply the objective two-consecutive-championships criteria for yokozuna promotion, in the changing room that day after his big win Akebono had had nothing to say of *deserving*, or of being *left hanging*. Instead, he told a crush of reporters including *Sumo World*'s David Shapiro: "All I can do is work hard.... What happens after that is up to other people."[59] The perfect line—and yet, it wasn't a line at all. In a phone call home later than night, he said, "I did all I can, Ma. The rest is up to them."[60]

When news came that he would become the very first gaijin yokozuna—and despite a three-tournament total two wins shy of what had failed to win Konishiki promotion—Chad Rowan, brought up on the sports images of boxers raising their arms in triumph, of basketball players strutting up the court with a "number one" finger raised, of football players making fools of themselves in end zone dances, greeted it as his mother, his dad, as Uncle Haywood Kalima, as his cousin Nate ("Make like you hit it that way all the time!") had all raised him to greet it: with the same stoic humility.

"I guess after all the years, you learn," he recalled years later. "I did my jumping, when nobody was watching. Just me and my boys and the people who count,"[61] which was what continued to happen, in and out of the ring, right up to Nagano—an accomplishment, in its full context, at least as impressive as the promotion itself given what is known as the Burden of the Tsuna. Yokozuna promotion is the equivalent of being inducted into Major League Baseball's Hall of Fame, except that while Cooperstown has already admitted nearly three hundred legends in its relatively short lifespan since opening in 1936, Akebono was, by 1998, one of only sixty-five yokozuna reaching back well past the seventeenth century. In this regard, the numbers are little short of staggering. Furthermore, a yokozuna is expected to *maintain* his hall-of-fame dominance, winning or at least positioning himself in the running of every single tournament he competes in for the rest of his career. Failing that, he is expected to retire immediately, regardless of his age. Further still, Cooperstown has nothing to say of *hinkaku*. Above all, from the moment Akebono donned the white rope, he was expected to continue to act at all times as a model of *hinkaku* for an entire nation.

By the time he was picked to bless the Olympic opening ceremonies, Akebono had done so almost flawlessly. Sure, thick crowds of celebrity-crazed Japanese would indeed swarm to paw at him wherever he went, and the relentless crush of paparazzi had increased at least tenfold. But the best they could do in those five years was misconstrue an event at which a frustrated Akebono had accidentally upended a tableful of glassware at an Osaka bar—a mishap that had in fact allowed him to recover with a humble public apology that underscored his respect for his public role.[62] Inside the ring, he had gone on to pass the Emperor's Cup back and forth with Takahanada, who eventually joined him at yokozuna and adopted his father's ring name, and Wakahanada, who would adopt his uncle's name and reach the top rank just after the Olympics. On his way to an additional six championships (he would wind up with eleven in all), Akebono's heroic recoveries from two debilitating knee injuries allowed him to perform one of the more powerful examples of *gaman* sumo had ever seen. So when a fellow gaijin named Fiamalu Penitani, who competed as Musashimaru, won his second consecutive tournament just over a year after Akebono had introduced a worldwide television audience to the white rope, his promotion as the sixty-seventh yokozuna was taken as a matter of course.

As was the subsequent promotion of Akebono's Mongolian protégé, Asashōryū. And the next yokozuna, another Mongolian, Hakuhō. And the next: a third Mongolian, Harumafuji. In fact, now, more than fifteen years after Akebono's retirement, sumo's top division has become so clogged with foreigners from Mongolia and eastern Europe that when Japan-born Kotoshogiku finally managed to outpace the Mongolians in the 2016 New Year's tournament, he became the first non-gaijin to hoist the Emperor's Cup in a decade. As for the sacred white rope, no Japanese has come close since the Hanada brothers stepped down for good years ago.[63]

Fully a third of current top-division *sumotori* now hail from *outside*, led by the continuing dominance of the Mongolians, who have followed in Akebono's footsteps both athletically and culturally—with the notable exception of Asashōryū, who dominated in the ring but left the sport in disgrace after a long string of behavioral missteps ranging from simply failing to follow correct protocol, to getting filmed playing soccer after having withdrawn from a mandatory exhibition tour due to injury,[64] to an alleged public assault that finally led to his retirement.[65] That fellow Mongolian Harumafuji could be promoted without incident less than two years later suggests that Asashōryū's transgressions were widely viewed as of his own making rather than some kind of symptom of barbaric foreignness—a perception that must have made Konishiki, who had watched a couple of simple slips of the tongue form an impenetrable barrier between his more-than-worthy record and the white rope less than twenty years earlier, just shake his head in wonder.

Back then, of course, a gaijin's approach to sumo's sacred top rank had made international news. These days, the term *gaijin yokozuna* has lost its power to surprise or to offend even the sumo purist, who continues to display his devotion to what goes on in the Hall of National Sport. If in fact it ever happens again, the term that will raise eyebrows is the no-longer-redundant *Japanese yokozuna*, because the Japanese man who comes along to stand aside Hakuhō and Harumafuji will have his work cut out for him not just in hoping to match their athletic mastery of what is one of the more complicated martial arts, but more importantly, in measuring up to their spot-on public behavior—performances rooted in the example of Akebono, the man who paved their way to understanding, in every step they take, what it means to act in a way that will be viewed as purely Japanese.

Notes

1. Mark Panek, *Gaijin Yokozuna* (Honolulu: University of Hawai'i Press, 2006), 193.
2. Lora Sharnoff, *Grand Sumo: The Living Sport and Tradition* (Tokyo: Weatherhill, 1993), 71.
3. Panek, *Gaijin Yokozuna*, 2, 78, 190–91.
4. Chad Rowan, interview by the author, October 17, 1998.
5. Panek, *Gaijin Yokozuna*, 113, 181.
6. Shintaro Ishihara, *The Japan That Can Say No: Why Japan Will Be First among Equals* (New York: Simon & Schuster, 1991).
7. Ibid, 118–23.
8. Chad Rowan, interview by the author, August 7, 1998.
9. Panek, *Gaijin Yokozuna*, 145–46.
10. P[atricia] L. Cuyler, *Sumo: From Rite to Sport* (Tokyo: Weatherhill, 1991), 78, 162.
11. Sharnoff, *Grand Sumo*, 82–85.
12. Panek, *Gaijin Yokozuna*, 122–23.
13. Sharnoff, *Grand Sumo*, 38.
14. Velisarios Kattoulas, George Wehrfritz, Kay Itoi, and Hideko Takayama, "Selling Sumo," *Newsweek*, June 21, 1999.
15. Ibid.
16. Lora Sharnoff, "Foreigners Making Their Mark in Sumo," *Japan Quarterly* 37 (April–June 1990): 164–70.

17. Joanne Ninomiya, Robert Furukawa, and Jim Leahy, *Konishiki's Contribution to Sumo*, videocassette, JN Productions, 1989.
18. Ibid.
19. Kattoulas et al., "Selling Sumo."
20. William Wetherall, "Striking Sensitivities in Sumo's Inner Sanctum," *Far Eastern Economic Review*, November 8, 1984, 50–52.
21. Jesse Kuhaulua, interview by the author, June 17, 1998.
22. Larry Aweau, interview by the author, October 28, 1998.
23. Jesse Kuhaulua and John Wheeler, *Takamiyama: The World of Sumo* (Tokyo: Kodansha, 1973).
24. Ninomiya et al., *Konishiki's Contribution to Sumo*.
25. Ishihara, *The Japan That Can Say No*.
26. Patrick Smith, *Japan: A Reinterpretation* (New York: Vintage, 1998).
27. Sadaharu Oh and David Falkner, *Sadaharu Oh: A Zen Way of Baseball* (New York: Times Books, 1984).
28. Panek, *Gaijin Yokozuna*, 111.
29. Chris Gould, "Konishiki," *Sumo Fan Magazine*, no. 12 (August 2007).
30. David E. Sanger, "Sumo Star Charges Racism in Japan," *New York Times*, April 22, 1992, A3; and David E. Sanger, "American Sumo Star Denies Accusing Japanese of Racism," *New York Times*, April 24, 1992, A11.
31. Eric "Fatabull" Gaspar, interview by the author, May 23, 1999.
32. Rijichō Dewanoumi, "Dewanoumi Speaks Out," trans. Mark Shilling, *Sumo World*, July 1992, 5–6; and Rijichō Dewanoumi, "Dewanoumi Speaks Out: 2," trans. Mark Schilling, *Sumo World*, September 1992, 7–8.
33. Andy Adams, "Konishiki Eyes Future," *Sumo World*, November 1994, 6.
34. Chad Rowan, interview by the author, October 17, 1998.
35. Chad Rowan, interview by the author, October 21, 1998.
36. Chad Rowan, unpublished autobiographical notes, September 1997.
37. Chad Rowan, interview by the author, May 28, 1999.
38. Ibid.
39. Ibid.
40. Janice Rowan, interview by the author, December 2, 1993.
41. Chad Rowan, interview by the author, May 5, 1999.
42. Larry Aweau, interview by the author, October 28, 1998.
43. Chad Rowan, unpublished autobiographical notes, September 1997.
44. William Henry Beveridge, interview by the author, June 18, 1999.
45. Chad Rowan, interview by the author, May 5, 1999.
46. Chad Rowan, interview by the author, August 7, 1998.
47. Percy Kipapa, interview by the author, November 18, 1998.
48. Chad Rowan, interview by the author, May 28, 2009.
49. "Hawai'i's Rowan Earns Sumo Promotion," *Honolulu Star-Bulletin*, January 24, 1990.
50. George Kalima, interview by the author, September 7, 2007.
51. "Rising Son," *Honolulu Star-Bulletin*, May 25, 1992.
52. Ferd Lewis, "Akebono Earns Promotion to Ozeki," *Honolulu Advertiser*, May 27, 1992.

53. Chad Rowan, interview by the author, June 17, 1998; the entire exchange comes from this interview.

54. Ibid.

55. Ibid.

56. Janice Rowan, interview by the author, November 19, 1998.

57. For video footage of the moment, see "Akebono vs. Takahanada: Hatsu 1993," at http://www.youtube.com/watch?v=2leR-n-WqyE, uploaded by SumoParis, October 13, 2007.

58. Chad Rowan, interview by the author, October 17, 1998.

59. David Shapiro, "Akebono: First Foreign Yokozuna!," *Sumo World*, March 1993, 3–4, 7.

60. Janice Rowan, interview by the author, August 22, 2000.

61. Chad Rowan, interview by the author, June 17, 1998.

62. Percy Kipapa, interview by the author, November 18, 1998. See also Clyde Newton, "Akebono Fights His Frustrations," *Sumo World*, May 1996, 2–4.

63. Daniel Krieger, "In Japan, Sumo Is Dominated by Foreigners," *New York Times*, January 24, 2013; and Mark Buckton, "Fortune Smiled on Kotoshogiku during Surprise Run to Emperor's Cup," *Japan Times*, January 27, 2016.

64. "Soccer Match Draws JSA's Ire," *Japan Times*, July 27, 2007.

65. "Asashoryu Ends Stormy Career," *Japan Times*, February 5, 2010.

From Out of the Shadows of Invisibility
Brazilian Women's Football and the Pioneering Figure of Marta
—Cláudia Samuel Kessler and Silvana Vilodre Goellner

Introduction

Football is a sport that has the ability to unite a nation. Particularly here in Brazil, where it's called *futebol*, the sport is considered to be representative of our national identity, as it serves to unify the various cultures throughout the many regions of a vast and diverse country. In terms of gender, however, football is less representative of a changing national or even international landscape.

A sport of distinctly English origins, football was appropriated by Brazilian culture and has grown to become a predominant force in terms of analysis and opinion in several public and private spheres, including events, academic works, informal discussions, party politics, and a broadly conceived media agenda. The extent to which football in Brazil has taken on this loftier role can best be seen in the response to Brazil's hosting of the 2014 FIFA World Cup, an event of great international distinction that has brought global attention to the country to the delight of some and to the chagrin of others. And yet, despite the wealth of attention heaped upon the sport via the tournament, it is important to point out that when Brazilians talk about football, it's almost always men's football. Specifically, the sport is thought of as comprising a spectacular array of physicality defined almost exclusively by its male version.[1]

Certainly in terms of athletes, money, league management, and media coverage, it is a small group of high-profile men who almost exclusively occupy this particular space. However, despite the historically and culturally male-oriented status of football in Brazil, Brazilian women have continued to make inroads into this milieu, with some even finding a measure of celebrity all their own. Predictably, though, most Brazilians are unaware of the pull of the national game that lies beyond the margins played in the virtually unheralded female dimension. Once Marta Vieira da Silva, or simply Marta, found her way into the mix, however, the continued suppression of the women's game was harder to maintain.

One of a handful of female athletes known only by her first name, Marta has helped raise Brazilian women's football to both national and international prominence. Her success in the sport challenges, however subtly, the gendered history of Brazilian football and perhaps even football globally. Marta's personal and professional narratives serve as examples of individual achievement in the face of seemingly insurmountable odds that has inspired others, paving the way for more women to take an interest in the Brazilian game. Unlike a generation ago, when women had no credible entryways into the upper echelons of the sport, twenty-first-century Brazilian women have expectations to play football for its social as well as cultural and even professional opportunities. In this regard, while Marta may not have been the first woman to play football in Brazil, she is certainly the most dominant and influential Brazilian woman to have played the game, making her something of a pioneering figure in ways that extend beyond the game.

Marta realized her dreams of becoming a recognized footballer initially in Brazil and eventually on the international football stage by overcoming economic, ethnic, cultural, and certainly sporting obstacles with the same tenacity and drive to success that in a male context would have garnered her the praise and admiration of millions of fans. But as a woman in a traditionally male domain, she did so often under a cloak of invisibility and without the acknowledgment and rewards that have followed her male counterparts. And it is perhaps this image above all else, of an athlete whose excellence is virtually unmatched yet who often toiled in obscurity, that defines Marta and her legacy even to the present day.

The Brazilian Women's Game

In order to fully engage Marta's legacy, it is imperative that we begin with an overview of the Brazilian women's game itself. While women's football may indeed lie along the fringes of discussions concerning national sport, its existence is no less real than the men's game, and its popularity is growing in the early decades of the twenty-first century.[2]

Even though the rules that apply to the sport as practiced by Brazilian women on the field are the same as those practiced in the men's game, only in 2013 did the Brazilian government begin to sponsor a national championship for women. Indeed, there is not even an official calendar to organize the few existing competitions or circuits that have emerged around the women's game. The uncertainty is such that organizers of these events simply don't know if they will be able to count on future opportunities. In fact, most Brazilian clubs don't even keep a women's team, because they are considered a financial burden rather than an asset. Among the clubs that do have women's teams, only a few have sponsors, given that Brazilian sponsors prefer to support men's football with its expectation of feverish public support and the resulting potential to generate outsize profits.

Another glaring matter that plagues the women's game is its continuous marginalization within Brazilian media circles. National sports journalism still offers little coverage of women's football, and when reports do appear, they amount to just a few lines of content conveying only the most basic information about a particular match and its score without the sort of commentary or analysis one regularly finds in coverage of the men's game.[3] Such scant coverage led Kleiton Lima, who coached the Brazilian women's team from 2008 to 2011, to refer to the women's sport as *ghost football* given its relative invisibility in spite of the women's national team having built an admirable history of achievements and international recognition.[4]

Still, the starkness of the Brazilian sporting landscape did not prevent women from crossing into this decidedly male-dominated sport[5] and leaving their indelible footprints. It is noteworthy that since the late nineteenth century, Brazilian women have indeed been present in sporting arenas: first as spectators and then only later as participants. But the legacies of these sportswomen barely register on the Brazilian scene regardless of the numbers of women who participate, which is what makes Marta's story all the more remarkable.

Challenging Upbringing

Marta was born on February 19, 1986, in the town of Dois Riachos (population approximately eleven thousand), 189 kilometers from Maceió, capital of the state of Alagoas in northeastern Brazil. The regional economy is based entirely on small agriculture, local commerce, and resources allocated from social programs for poverty alleviation. Marta is one of the few people, men or women alike, who has managed to successfully make her way out of such a remote and troubled place so noted for its deprivations.[6] That she emerged at all is a story in its own right. That she did so as an athlete—a female athlete and a celebrated one at that in an overwhelmingly male-driven environment—gives her narrative even more heft.

The youngest daughter of Audalio, a barber who deserted his family when she was just fourteen months old, Marta came from decidedly humble origins. Her father's abandonment left her mother, Tereza, to fend for the whole family, forcing her to work outside the home while also caring for her four children—Ângela, Valdir, and José in addition to the youngest, Marta—virtually unaided, an experience that seems to have left its mark on Tereza's youngest child.

Throughout her life, Marta has often mentioned her mother with a mix of pride and reverence for the many things she did for her and her siblings throughout their young lives. Without question, Tereza's dedication was certainly very important during Marta's formative years; Marta attributes her fighting spirit to the example set by her mother. And, like her mother, Marta had the odds stacked against her, but she made every effort to persevere in all aspects of her life, including her athletic career.

Throughout much of Marta's childhood, Tereza was only able to see her children at night due to her often oppressive work schedule. Yet they remained as close-knit a family as possible, and Tereza came to count on her children to help supplement the family's meager income through any odd jobs or opportunities they could find. Marta's grandmother also helped, particularly with keeping basic food on the table. Marta says that although they never starved, they struggled to afford subsistence meals, making such child-friendly luxuries as sweets and sodas rare treats that typically only appeared at the largess of friends or relatives. All the children helped earn money for the house; for her part, Marta sold homemade popsicles made of juice, called *geladinho*, at the nearby street market.[7]

The family's difficulties making ends meet also affected Marta's ability to attend school. Although education was offered free to the public, Tereza rarely had the disposable income to purchase necessary school supplies, making schooling beyond the very basics quite challenging. With all the distractions and deprivations, it's not hard to see why Marta was frequently absent from school. In fact, when she did attend, she would often skip classes to play football or even ride horses,[8] before she finally gave up altogether and dropped out when she was just eleven.[9]

Given Tereza's frequent absences, Marta's older brother José essentially served as head of household, assuming the expected male role. Following the examples of the many fathers he knew in the neighborhood, he would beat Marta, claiming, among other things, that as a girl she should remain subservient to the family unit, stay at home, and steer clear of the streets and especially the football fields that had captivated her from a young age, although the record suggests that she ignored most of his directives.[10]

Such a demanding environment led Marta to seek refuge from the vagaries of her home life elsewhere, which in her case led her to the dry riverbed at one of the town's entrances, she hoped far from her brother's disapproving eye but apparently not far enough. There, on a sandy field just under the bridge along the course of the river, with goalposts made of bamboo, Marta, much to the chagrin of both her family and her neighbors, learned to play football.[11]

True to form, José went to great lengths to keep his resolute and relentless sister off the sandy fields where she played pickup games with the boys. Tereza too, perhaps bowing to tradition, would often advise her daughter not to spend so much time in the company of young boys, telling her that such company was not proper for young girls regardless of their class. However, Marta was not to be dissuaded.[12]

Despite her family's misgivings and the prevailing social norms regarding females and sport, Marta continued to play, sometimes dominating the boys. Regardless, Marta's family remained convinced that nothing good would ever come of her continuing to play football, given that no female football players of any significance had ever emerged from Brazil. Yet Marta continued to demonstrate her passion for the game, which was set in stone from the first time she watched her beloved favorite team, the Corinthians,[13] play a match on television when she was ten. That day, ostensibly joking, she proclaimed: "One day, I will be there,"[14] although as yet there were no proper women's teams in Brazil.

From a young age, Marta also routinely followed and observed her cousins, who played for a venerable local team. From the time she started to show an ability to play well, she enjoyed playing even more. She didn't like playing with dolls like the other girls. Rather, her passion was playing football, but to do so, she had to learn to ignore the taunts and barbs of neighbors and townspeople, including the most obvious: "How can your mom and brothers let you play?"[15] She used to sneak out to play, although whenever one of her brothers found her on a field, she sought protection from them by appealing to her mother. But in the end, whatever fear she may have had over further beatings was overridden by her drive to play.[16]

Marta's talents were first acknowledged by a local coach named José Júlio de Freitas, known as Tota, who invited her to play with a local boys' side in 1995. Amazed that this poor child could play so well barefoot, Tota arranged as a gift a pair of cleats to help her develop. And while they turned out to be three sizes too large, they were in fact her first actual football shoes, which she made work by stuffing pieces of paper in them. More importantly, she was moved by the gesture and used this act of kindness as motivation.[17]

The confluence of these events—her absent father, her hardworking albeit overburdened mother, her restrictive brothers, and Tota's charitable tutelage—acted as a springboard for Marta to become the single-name phenom she would later be known as. Her background also underscores the heralded aspects of her personality, which in turn inform the way she approaches her craft: fiercely, resolutely, and with little regard for how her life plays out off the pitch.

Futebol Phenom

Ironically, the biblical meaning of the name Marta is "housewife," a direction in which the young phenom most certainly would not venture. Rather, Marta chose to rush beyond the limited expectations of the domestic sphere and enter the male-dominated world of Brazil's beautiful game despite the sociocultural implications of doing so. Always daring, Marta would not be bowed by adversaries or reprimands. She was feisty and cantankerous and preferred to kick at rather than suffer those who chafed at her nerves. Irrespective of personality, however, what stands out is the way in which she grew to approach the game, something she learned while far removed from the expectations of the urban and male-centered football schools, astonishing thousands of spectators who watched her brilliant strikes cross one goal line after the next.

Marta's physical development was remarkably ordinary for someone so gifted. A left-footed playmaker, she grew to be only five feet, four inches tall (1.62 meters) and 126 pounds (57 kilos). In her teen years, she did not undergo any specific muscle strengthening program; however, she showed on the field a burst of speed that was far superior to that of the other women players and a desire to engage with others that was decidedly more aggressive than most, which would certainly make up for any significant size difference.[18]

At age twelve, Marta joined an all-boys team called Centro Sportivo Alagoano (Alagoa's sport center), the hometown club for which her cousin Roberto served as both a player and an administrator. Throughout these earliest developmental years, Marta typically played with boys her own age, but once she turned thirteen, especially after one local coach refused to play against her team if Marta was on the field, she was forced into playing competitively in circuits designed solely for girls and women. This caused her to look for another place where she could play competitively and have access to more opportunities, given the dearth of competitive all-girls teams in her home region. Her search ultimately led her to the big city of Rio de Janeiro, some two thousand kilometers from home, a three-day bus journey made possible only through the financial aid of friends and family.[19]

In 2000, age fourteen, Marta started her professional career with Club de Regatas Vasco da Gama, for whom she played two years, a period that marked her ascension toward fame. At that time, she didn't earn a salary, receiving what in Brazil is called *ajuda de custos*, shorthand for a small allowance that covers only minor expenses. Players commonly did not have contracts with their clubs, although they did receive housing and meals as part of their aid package, which took some of the edge off the sense of their being so indentured.

Although the beginning of her career mimicked her life so far with its trials and obstacles, Marta was fortunate enough to be able to rely on her immense though still embryonic arsenal of talent to help see her through these bleaker times. As a young woman on an established, veteran club like the Gama team, she found herself struggling to overcome interpersonal issues including the often glaring age disparities that won her few friends among the older players on the side, several of whom who had played for the Brazilian national team and were already known and valued. Partly because of her brazenness (and perhaps jealousy over the talent that others saw in her), her older teammates routinely bullied her, leveling personal assaults on everything from her bucolic accent and smallish physique to her humble origins. These unfortunate interactions exacerbated Marta's already combative demeanor, making her even more reluctant to relate with her teammates—who had taken to calling her by the taunting (and far from flattering) nickname "bicho do mato."[20] But while these interpersonal hardships may have quieted her off the pitch, her play spoke volumes.

Indeed, it would not take long for young Marta to be recognized as a future star in the Brazilian women's game. By 2002, she was no longer simply raw potential, having demonstrated her worth as she was selected to play for the national team. A few years after that, she was afforded one of the highest honors available to the women's circuit when she was chosen to wear the vaunted jersey number 10 for the Brazil national team, the number that previously belonged to the masterful Sissi, one of the pioneers of women's football in Brazil whose ranks Marta seemed destined to join.[21]

From 2002 to 2004, Marta played for Santa Cruz Futebol Clube in the town of Contagem, Minas Gerais. Still relatively young at age seventeen, she found herself in the spotlight during Brazil's matches in the Pan American Games held in Santo Domingo, the Dominican Republic, in 2003. The Brazilian side won the gold medal and Marta drew such international acclaim that she was compelled for the first time to look beyond the limitations of her homeland, signing on to play with the Swedish team Umeå IK at the end of the tournament.

From there her career took off even more dramatically, particularly as a result of the exposure she was getting from playing in so many international events and circuits. In 2004 and 2005, she finished third and second, respectively, in the voting for FIFA World Player of the Year.[22] In each year from 2006 to 2010, she was awarded FIFA's trophy as top player. And in 2007, she was awarded the famed Golden Boot[23] for her performance in the World Cup tournament in China, scoring seven goals to top all scorers, although the Brazilian team lost in the final to Germany.

As a result of such brilliant performances, in particular at the Pan American Games, which saw Marta as top scorer with a whopping twelve goals including five of the seven against the Canadians, she earned her place on the fabled Walk of Fame at Maracanã, Brazil's largest and most storied football stadium, making her the first female athlete ever to receive such an honor. Thrilled with the tribute, Marta, who was still only twenty-one, acknowledged:

> It was really heartwarming to play on Brazilian soil again, after so long. There is nothing more fair than to win this medal to finish our work with flourish. It is wonderful to be remembered alongside great players in the history of Brazilian football

[on Maracanã's Walk of Fame]. I hope it is an incentive for many other girls who want to play football in our country.[24]

Marta's recognition as a top-flight player gaining worldwide acclaim came about in no small part due to the great efforts she made to better her circumstances, including her decisions to leave her home for Rio de Janeiro and later to leave Brazil altogether. The struggles she faced and ultimately endured throughout her young life were indicative of her exceedingly strong personality and her determination, both of which later translated into her combative nature on and off the field and indeed became part of her trademark. To add to her growing reputation as an international sport icon, her time in Sweden was broken by a stint in the United States. Sweden has become something of a second home to Marta and has provided her with even more visibility, allowing her talent to be fully recognized—and, ironically, finally winning her acclaim back home in Brazilian football circles.

Swedish Home (and Elsewhere)

Marta's transition to international stardom was never a smooth one, a theme that has followed her both on and off the pitch throughout her earliest days in the public spotlight. And yet, as suggested by her meteoric rise in the game and the accompanying steadily rising salaries she has negotiated, she was at least being recognized and compensated for the brilliance of her play. This is particularly the case in Sweden, where she transitioned from regional to international stardom in a relatively brief time frame.

To be sure, the nature of Swedish football is quite different from that of Brazil. According to Staffan Stjernholm, spokesman for the Swedish Football Association, in contrast to Brazil, where Marta's presence challenged existing gender hierarchies, his country of nine million people has eighty thousand female football players who, from the age of fifteen, play in more than three thousand clubs around the country.[25] Sweden has six national youth teams that engage young people of ages fifteen, sixteen, seventeen, eighteen, nineteen, and twenty-three. In Brazil, according to data from FIFA (2012), there are 812 football clubs, of which 159 have male and female teams and 61 have female-only teams—so indeed, this must have been quite a different set of experiences for the young, emergent star who would come to dominate the game abroad.[26]

During the first six years that Marta lived and played in Sweden, her team won a Champions League title (2004), four Swedish Championship titles (2005, 2006, 2007, and 2008), and a Swedish Cup (2007). In her first year, she was the top scorer with twenty-two goals, and she repeated the feat in 2005 with twenty-one goals. She reclaimed her scoring title in 2008 when she tallied twenty-three times. But such success always seemed to come at a high price for her, given that alongside her success, she always had to be away from her family.

Marta's Swedish experience in many ways exemplifies the sorts of personal and professional challenges she had had to endure thus far in her career. When she first arrived in Sweden in preparation for the 2004 season, it was winter, a cold climate she'd never encountered. Accustomed to the Brazilian sun and balmy temperatures, Marta was startled by the bitter Scandinavian cold, which often dipped as low as minus fifteen degrees Celsius, by the voluminous snowfall, and by the shortened daylight hours during the winter months, all of which forced her to adapt quickly. To protect her from these unfamiliar elements, the team worked hard to outfit her with gloves, a warm hat, and ample protection for her arms and legs, which certainly made for a very different type of uniform than she had known back in Dois Riachos, where she usually played pickup games only wearing shorts and a shirt while barefoot.[27]

There were other factors to consider in those earliest days in Sweden. Marta knew no one, but being away from family and friends was a sacrifice she knew she had to make in order to achieve a successful professional career. The common path for people in her hometown was to get married, have kids, and work in the rural area. But Marta wanted more, acknowledging:

> I think the hardships, in a way, helped me in my career, because I had to be very strong. Every day, I'd wake up and think, I've got to overcome the fact that I come from a really poor region, that I don't have the finances to fund my own dream. I couldn't let those obstacles be stronger than me.[28]

Sweden, then, for all its challenges, became the place where she transcended the expectations of others and found her own way, playing at a peak performance level and captivating Swedish football supporters with her skill and colorful persona, starting with her stint at Umeå IK, with whom she played until 2008.

Money factored into these matters as well. Recalling the destitution of what were essentially subsistence wages that she earned in her earlier professional engagements in Brazil, what she was earning in Sweden (and certainly later in the United States) was little short of a windfall. Her starting monthly salary of R$20,000 (approximately US$8,695) helped smooth things considerably, but when she resigned with Umeå for between US$75,000 and $85,000 for ten months in 2007,[29] it was obvious that she had arrived as a genuine football star who could demand top money for her broadening skill set and get it. This too seemed to further motivate her in her desire to up her performance levels, which were certainly on full display as she successfully transitioned into her new environment.

By some measure, once she left the warm confines of Brazil, Marta was making the most of the opportunity, shutting out the negative aspects of her sojourn abroad in favor of creating and re-creating herself and her game into something much more than anyone might have imagined. This first of many foreign experiences certainly spotlighted her name and would ultimately serve to forge the sort of career she might have only imagined in her dreams back in the days playing in the riverbed in Dois Riachos. With so many new opportunities along with accolades and money coming her way, it is not at all surprising that the emergent world star had come to regard Sweden as her second home; it was certainly the place where she finally broke free from the pack and established herself as a force within the sport.

But even as she continued to find success, she also continued to demonstrate a certain restlessness. Thus, after six successful seasons in Sweden, in 2009 Marta sought even newer challenges when she accepted an invitation from the Los Angeles Sol to venture to the United States and play in the new Women's Professional Soccer (WPS) circuit there. But while most other players earned a customary salary of US$50,000 to $100,000 per season, Marta earned between $400,000 and $500,000.[30] To contextualize just how much money this was, consider that most WPS clubs generated less than a million dollars in annual revenues, so her asking for that astonishingly high amount—in essence half of the club's revenue—caused a great deal of uncertainty among most of the league's teams, who simply could not afford her high salary. This led to a frustrating situation for all concerned; Marta was the best player in the American league, but no one club could afford to meet her price tag for more than a year, forcing her to hop from team to team each season.

In 2010, Marta again changed teams, ending up this time with the hapless FC Gold Pride, whose base of operations was Santa Clara, California. Marta's participation enabled the team to surge from worst in the league to a first-place finish, and as the top scorer in the league, Marta reaped the benefits of fulfilling the expectations of those huge contracts. The following year, she once again was forced to start over, this time with the Western New York Flash, although she split part of that season (and the one before) on loan to the Brazilian team Santos FC. She was certainly not without suitors, but the on-field dominance she promised was tempered by her uniquely high salary requirements and the financial issues they raised for the teams.

Her career in the United States came to a sudden end when the WPS folded in 2012. She then returned to Sweden, where she secured a two-year contract with Tyresö, helping the team win a championship in 2012. In 2014, she played for Sweden's FC Rosengård. But despite all the team hopping and other irregularities surrounding her career, Marta had managed to meet or exceed expectations everywhere she went by winning titles and awards, including the prestigious

Michelle Akers Player of the Year Award as the best player in US women's soccer in 2009 and 2010.[31] By virtually every measure, she was considered in most football circles to be the preeminent women's player in the world.

Athletic Royalty

From her earliest days on the football scene, and despite any controversies in which she may have found herself, Marta's technical skills and athletic instincts had been constantly if not consistently praised by fellow players and sportscasters alike. As a Brazilian, it was predictable that she would find herself being compared to many of her compatriots who had also achieved greatness. Chief among this reserve of Brazilian greats is Pelé, the football legend known in Brazilian football circles as "the King of Football"[32] and to whom Marta has been favorably compared. In fact, she has been dubbed "Pelé in skirts,"[33] which suggests that while she is the logical heir to his athletic throne, her gender at the same time redraws attention to the gender divide and all that comes with such discussions relative to Brazilian sport. To be sure, it would be hard to imagine that in a climate that has produced Pelé and more recent male stars such as Neymar, Kaká, Ronaldo, and Ronaldinho, a woman could leap over them and occupy Pelé's legendary spot at the top of Brazilian sport. Kleiton Lima's earlier pronouncement that in Brazil, women's football is "ghost football," still held water.

To be sure, Marta's similarities to Pelé go further than their common nationality and the fact that they share the same jersey number. Like Marta, Pelé too came from humble origins and had to deal with prejudices related to class built on the expectations of color once he took to the larger stage. Even when they were treated like stars and national icons, both experienced challenges. For Pelé, as predominant a figure to have ever appeared in international football, his biggest challenge at home and abroad was skin color. But for Marta, her gender placed her in the crosshairs of criticism and at times unflattering supposition. The near-constant reminders of this pressure can be found in obvious slights as well as in less obvious comments that typically come wrapped in the cloak of compliment.

Take for example the significance of the epithet "Pelé in skirts." On the surface, there seems to be a general consensus that by comparing her to the international megastar who virtually single-handedly sold world football to North American audiences when he played for the New York side in the North American Soccer League (NASL) in the 1970s,[34] writers were paying favorable if not gracious recognition of her importance as an athletic celebrity. And Marta certainly agrees, noting:

That's a compliment that motivates me; I'm flattered by this comparison to the greatest icon of football—the football player of the century and king of this sport—but it also brings me a great responsibility, for Pelé's legacy is virtually unreachable.[35]

Strictly in terms of the athleticism involved in the comparison, the label is apt. Like Pelé, Marta is fast and aggressive, and her on-the-field skills are worthy of the highest praise wherever the sport is played. And like Pelé, she is aware of those aspects of her talent that set her apart from her teammates and opponents; both players are particularly able to combine technical abilities with creativity and strength. Marta is similarly known for being a warrior on the field: resolute, demanding, tough, and willing to do what is necessary, especially when it comes to goal scoring.

But there is also something disturbingly condescending in this comparison. Placing Marta alongside the legendary Pelé by pointing out their difference in attire ("Pelé in skirts") only delegitimizes Marta's place within the sport—suggesting that her greatness is limited by her sex. Indeed, Pelé himself made a punch line of the matter during an interview for the Brazilian newspaper *O Globo*. When he was asked who was responsible for Marta's nickname, Pelé claimed that it was his press adviser, Papito, although he was also quick to add a bit of levity to the moment by claiming that she had the athletic advantage over him because "her legs are prettier than mine."[36] This is a common refrain heard throughout sport and any other institution in which a previously un- or underrepresented group enters the fray and vies for legitimacy where none existed before. What is clear by implication is that such language serves to delegitimize Marta's place in Brazilian football alongside that of other women who play, by reminding fans that where it counts, football remains a man's sport with a very limited place for women regardless of their talent or dedication to the national culture. In this regard, talent may have taken Marta to the brink, but tradition, and in this case a tradition that continues to mark gender as a legitimate lever to reinforce social inequalities, is still too high an obstacle to climb.

One glaring indication of this persistent gender inequality is salary. Despite being a groundbreaker in football, Marta on average earns less in a year less than the male football player Kaká makes in a week. The difference in earning potential between male and female athletes has always been overwhelming, but strictly in terms of envisioning Marta's place alongside that of Pelé or any of the other men, it stands to reason that one cannot assume a position of dominance without the requisite compensation that suggests, in her case, an overall value, writ large. Marta has been throughout much of her career one of the highest-paid women in the sport, but she probably won't be seen playing football professionally, in the near future, for the clubs of her home country, considering the financial restraints and the instability of the women's competitions calendar.

Warrior for Women's Visibility

Despite leaving her home country for greater financial rewards and playing opportunities, Marta has used her global status in football to work for changes and improvements in women's football in Brazil. On January 9, 2012, Marta provided her opinion on the slow development of opportunities for female Brazilian players:

> I do what I can. For my part, I try to do everything in my power. But it's not up to me alone. We seek our space little by little, showing the world what we can do, but it has to come from all sides: from the press, TV networks, because they are the ones who attract sponsorship, but also from the government, the confederation.... There are lots of people who can do something. We have been demanding attention for a long time, but things haven't been as they should.[37]

Later that year, Marta further challenged her country's gendered traditions, explaining:

> Brazil needs to change how women's football is seen. You can only keep a good athlete motivated with a salary. You can't say that the girls are fat or out of shape if they don't earn enough for their work. It's hard to demand professionalism from players who work unpaid.[38]

The low salaries for women footballers in Brazil remain a barrier to the sport's growth. Brazilian elite female players generally cannot live off what they make playing football, requiring them to work other jobs to survive. Like in the United States, where there is similarly a difference in financial compensation between male and female players, many in the public rationalize these divides because of the greater media coverage received by the men, reaffirming the notion that women's football and sports in general have lower value. Usually it is argued that women earn less than men and that women's sports produce much less revenue than men's sports, although this "discourse of absences" should be challenged. To be fair, little money is invested in women's sports in Brazil, so to directly compare the two genders in terms of profits and salaries is misleading because they can be understood as vastly different worlds, with different structures and histories.

Moreover, in Brazil, women who play sports must conform to norms related to hegemonic femininity. These women suffer the paradox of having to show manly performances on the pitch and to look sexy off it. As a result, there are many cultural pressures placed upon women athletes, and machismo[39] is one of the arguments everyone drifts to when trying to explain the attention deficit—Brazilian men prefer their women to be feminine, and Brazilian women who might otherwise want to participate in athletics are just as likely to fear being labeled as too manly. Marta, tired of hearing the contempt of people who despise women's efforts to play, responded with a predictable level of frustration at both sides of this debate. On one hand, she decries the resiliency of the prejudice. On the other, she also insists that others rise up to pull their own weight. As she once proclaimed, "I can't carry, nor can the other female players, the weight of changing women's football in the country."[40]

Unfinished Business

In remarks following an award presentation, Marta asserted:

> From an early age, I've had the goal of becoming the best football player in the world. I have fought and worked hard for it. But I will never say I'm the best. I'm still ambitious, this title motivates me to work even harder."[41]

Among her goals yet to be reached, Marta reveals that winning the World Cup and the Olympic gold medal for the Brazilian national team are dreams she's still chasing.

To be sure, these two goals have long been among Marta's obsessions. In 2012, at a press conference, she affirmed the importance at least one of them:

> If you ask me whether I'd trade the five Golden Ball awards for a World Cup, I'd say yes. It is an important title. It is, no doubt, necessary for any athlete, for all of us to dream of winning a gold medal and the World Cup.[42]

After being eliminated by the Japanese team in the quarterfinals of the London 2012 Olympic Games following a performance that was well below her own expectations, Marta similarly declared:

> This time, we came with all the requirements to achieve good results, but that support should have started way back, and now we demand that it continues. Maybe I won't be able to live it. I don't know if, in four years, I'll be at the Olympic Games again. But maybe the girls who dream of one day playing for the national team will benefit from these efforts.[43]

In both of these quotations, Marta is paying notice that she has grown beyond the personal targets of her youth into a more obvious leadership role that takes a decided turn toward team orientation. The power of her image has certainly granted greater exposure to women's football, particularly in the media. What this newly discovered sense of team-first ideology has done for those around her, however, is that she has become not just a lone force in the game, scoring points and racking up personal glory, but has transcended her talent to the extent that she is making her teammates better in the process, which is the mark of a truly memorable champion.

But Marta is hardly a typical performer in that she remains both haunted and driven by her past. Her quest for victory is aided by her remembrance of hardships and challenges, and she continues to face challenges today. Through it all, her mother remains her beacon, and she lavishes her with whatever creature comforts she can now give to her while dedicating her every success and trophy in her mother's honor.[44]

In all, it is quite clear that Marta has ascended to the top tier of sport occupied by only a handful of internationally renowned sport celebrities. That she has at least in part added to a rather sketchily written history of Brazilian women's football is also quite clear. How both of these conditions play out in terms of helping to construct a more egalitarian future as a result remains to be seen. But what is unmistakable at this stage of Marta's career is that, as a woman who has always chosen to run toward the flames rather than away from them, she still has a great deal of the fight left in her and seeks to make the most of every challenge—on the pitch and off.

Notes

1. Arlei Sander Damo, *Do dom à profissão: a formação de futebolistas no Brasil e na França* (São Paulo: Hucitec, Anpocs, 2007).

2. In Brazil, the most common term for the sport, used by the government and media, is *futebol feminino* (female football). But in this text, in opposition to the former term, we use the expression *futebol de mulheres* (women's football); the adjective *feminino*, at least in Brazil, implies a hegemonic femininity and heteronormativity that reinforces an idea of women's fragility and sensuality, which are also related to the ideals of beauty and youth. The football players are often called *meninas* (girls), reflecting the implicit need for them to be cared for and supervised by someone more experienced. This discourse of *feminino* obscures the fact that spectacular male performance is constantly imposed as the ideal for achievement and constantly hides the deeds of these women as historical agents, something that can be called the "discourse of absences." This harms not only women but also men who don't measure up to the high parameters. See Cláudia Samuel Kessler, "More Than Barbies or Ogresses: An Ethnography of Women's Soccer in Brazil and the United States," PhD dissertation, University of Rio Grande do Sul, 2015.

3. This chapter relied on various written sources such as published books, news outlets, and websites. It's rare to have access to news related to women's football in Brazil or much media coverage about their lives, mostly because of the invisibility of their practices.

4. The Brazil national football team won the following titles: the America's Cup (from 1991 to 2014, excluding only 2006), the South American Women's Football Championship (2003), the Pan American Games (gold medals in 2003, 2007, and 2015), the Olympic Games (silver medals in 2004 and 2008), the South American Women's Football Championship (second place in 2006), and the Women's World Cup (second place in 2007).

5. Eric Dunning and Joseph Maguire, "As relações entre ossexos no esporte," *Estudos Feministas* 5, no. 2 (1997): 321–48.

6. Alagoas is a tropical region, hot and dry, with a semiarid climate. It is characterized by low rainfall and high average temperatures, with seasonal extremes ranging from 82.4°F (28°C) to 113°F (45°C). The people are poor and undereducated, and often neglected when it comes to government assistance.

7. Karla Monteiro, "Fenômeno," *Revista TPM*, July 2014, 22–31.

8. Redação Esportes, "Uma mulher obstinada," *Estadão*, February 5, 2011, at http://www.estadao.com.br/blogs/jt-esportes/uma-mulher-obstinada/.

9. Ibid.

10. Monteiro, "Fenômeno."

11. Redação Esportes, "Uma mulher obstinada."

12. Monteiro, "Fenômeno."

13. Sport Club Corinthians Paulista is a team from the state of São Paulo; it has one of the largest fan bases in Brazil.

14. Monteiro, "Fenômeno."

15. Ibid.

16. Ibid.

17. Diego Graciano, *Você é mulher, Marta!* (São Paulo: All Print, 2008).

18. Marta's first coach, José Júlio de Freitas, said: "When she missed a move, she used to pull her hair and weep with rage. She was always a very determined person and suffered a lot to get to where she is today" (authors' translation). See Redação Esportes, "Uma mulher obstinada."

19. Mauro Graeff Jr., "O berço da rainha Marta, a melhor jogadora do mundo," Lance!Net, February 9, 2011, at http://www.lancenet.com.br/minuto/berco-rainha-Marta-melhor-mundo_0_423557883.html.

20. The literal translation is "animal of the forest," a term that generally is used for someone who has not adapted to urban manners or who avoids close contact with others. See "Marta reencontra sua 1ª técnica no Vasco, Helena Pacheco, e se emociona," Netvasco, October 24, 2010, at http://www.netvasco.com.br/n/83963/marta-reencontra-sua-1-tecnica-no-vasco-helena-pacheco-e-se-emociona.

21. Sissi, or Sisleide do Amor Lima, is currently coach of Las Positas, a junior college team in Livermore, California. Before Marta's arrival on the scene, she was considered one of the best players to have performed on the Brazilian national team. She participated in the World Cup competitions of 1995 and 1999 and the Olympic Games of 1996 and 2000. Apart from its association with Sissi, in Brazil, the jersey number 10 is usually reserved for a team's most valuable player.

22. FIFA World Player of the Year is an award given to the player who is considered to have had the best performance that year. In 2010, the FIFA World Player of the Year award and the publication *France Football*'s Ballon d'Or award were merged.

23. The Golden Boot is an award given to the player who has scored the most goals in the World Cup.

24. Translation by the authors; the original is as follows: "Para mim foi uma emoção muito grande voltar a jogar pelo Brasil depois de tanto tempo. Nada mais justo do que essa medalha para terminar o trabalho com chave de ouro. Foi uma maravilha poder ser lembrada ao lado de grandes jogadores da história do futebol brasileiro (na Calçada da Fama do Maracanã). Espero que sirva de incentivo para muitas outras meninas que querem jogar futebol no nosso País." See Allen Chahad and Celso Paiva, "Após ouro, Marta deixa os pés na Calçada da Fama," Portal Terra, July 26, 2007, at http://esportes.terra.com.br/panamericano2007/interna/0,,OI1788332-EI8332,00.html.

25. Paula Adamo Idoeta, "Londres 2012: 'Casa' de Marta, suécia é modelo de organização no futebol feminine," BBC Brasil, July 25, 2012, at http://www.bbc.com/portuguese/noticias/2012/07/120724_olympics_suecia_futfeminino_pai.shtml.

26. Osmar Moreira Souza Jr., "Football as a Career Project for Women: Legitimacy Search Interpretation," PhD dissertation, University of Campinas, 2013.

27. Redação Esportes, "Uma mulher obstinada."

28. Bonnie D. Ford, "Marta's Quest for Soccer Glory," ESPNW, June 10, 2015, at http://espn.go.com/espnw/news-commentary/2015worldcup/article/13041656/women-world-cup-marta-quest-soccer-glory.

29. Timothy F. Grainey, *Beyond Bend It Like Beckham: The Global Phenomenon of Women's Soccer* (Lincoln: University of Nebraska Press, 2012).

30. "Marta's Agent in Talks with Four Swedish Clubs Tyresö FF, Malmö, Linköping and Umeå," Women's Soccer United, January 26, 2012, at http://www.womenssoccerunited.com/martas-agent-in-talks-with-four-swedish-clubs-tyreso-ff-malmo-linkoping-and-umea/.

31. "Two-Time WPS Michelle Akers Player of the Year Marta Is Joining the Expansion Western New York Flash," Women's Soccer United, January 26, 2011, at http://www.womenssoccerunited.com/two-time-wps-michelle-akers-player-of-the-year-marta-is-joining-the-expansion-western-new-york-flash/.

32. Pelé was Brazil's top scorer in the 1950s and 1960s.

33. In 2005, a Swedish documentary was made about her life called *Marta, Pelés Kusin* [Marta, Pele's cousin].

34. David Hirshey, "Pelé: When Soccer Ruled the USA," ESPN, July 5, 2006, at http://sports.espn.go.com/espn/eticket/story?page=cosmos.

35. Translation by the authors; the original is as follows: "Esse é um elogio que me deixa muito motivada, porque comparar-me ao ícone maior do futebol, o jogador do século e o rei desta modalidade, só pode deixar-me muito lisonjeada, mas também me traz responsabilidade porque o legado de Pelé é praticamente inatingível." See Catarina Morais, "Marta admira Ronaldo porque 'batalha muito e trabalha imenso,'" Zerozero.pt, February 8, 2013, at http://www.zerozero.pt/noticia.php?id=98916.

36. Translation by the authors; the original is as follows: "Quem fez a comparação foi o Papito, meu assessor. Estou plenamente de acordo e acrescento: ela tem uma vantagem, suas pernas são mais bonitas que as minhas." See "Pelé diz que Marta é Pelé de saias," *Globoesporte*, July 28, 2007, at http://globoesporte.globo.com/PAN/Noticias/0,,MUL78950-3873,00.html.

37. Translation by the authors; the original is as follows: "O que posso fazer, eu faço. Da minha parte, procuro fazer tudo o que está ao meu alcance. Mas não depende somente de mim. Vamos buscando espaço aos poucos, mostrando que temos condições, mas isso tem de partir de todos os lados: da imprensa, das TVs, porque com eles se atrai patrocínios, mas também o governo, a confederação... muitas pessoas que podem fazer algo. Há bastante tempo a gente vem cobrando, cobrando, mas as coisas não vem sendo da forma como tem que ser." See Rafael Maranhão, "Segurando o choro, Marta lamenta fim do time feminino do Santos," *Globoesporte*, January 9, 2012, at http://globoesporte.globo.com/futebol/futebol-internacional/noticia/2012 /01/segurando-o-choro-marta-lamenta-fim-do-time-feminino-do-santos.html.

38. Translation by the authors; the original is as follows: "O Brasil precisa mudar a forma como o futebol feminino é visto. Você só mantém uma atleta de nível motivada com um salário. Não adianta falar que as meninas estão gordas ou fora de forma se elas não recebem para isso. É difícil exigir profissionalismo de jogadoras que trabalham sem remuneração." See "Marta pede remuneração para atletas levarem Seleção ao ouro olímpico," Portal Terra, December 10, 2012, at http://esportes.terra.com.br/futebol/marta-pede-remuneracao-para -atletas-levarem-selecao-ao-ouro-olimpico,ce1d4ab0b7f7b310VgnCLD2000000dc6eb0aR CRD.html.

39. Machismo is a certain set of attitudes and ideas that puts males at a higher level in society, subjugating women.

40. Translation by the authors; the original is as follows: "Não posso carregar, e nem as outras jogadoras, o peso de mudar o futebol feminino no país." See Fábio de Mello Castanho, "Marta desabafa: 'não posso ter o peso de mudar o futebol feminine,'" Portal Terra, January 9, 2012, at http://esportes.terra.com.br/futebol/marta-desabafa-quotnao-posso-ter-o-peso-de -mudar-o-futebol-femininoquot,e07a1d81c499a310VgnCLD200000bbcceb0aRCRD.html.

41. Translation by the authors; the original is as follows: "Desde cedo eu tinha a meta de me tornar a melhor jogadora de futebol do mundo. Lutei e trabalhei duro para isso. Mas nunca direi que sou a melhor. Continuo ambiciosa, este título me motiva a trabalhar ainda mais duro." See "Marta: 'Muitas vezes choro depois de um gol,'" Swissinfo, January 17, 2009, at http://www .swissinfo.ch/por/esporte/Marta:_Muitas_vezes_choro_depois_de_um_gol.html?cid=7156474.

42. Translation by the authors; the original is as follows: "Se me pergunta se eu trocaria as cinco Bolas de Ouro por um Mundial, é claro que sim. O Mundial é um título fundamental. Sem nenhuma dúvida é necessário para qualquer atleta porque todo mundo sonha em ganhar a medalha de ouro e o Mundial." See "Marta diz que trocaria suas cinco Bolas de Ouro pelo título do Mundial," *Globoesporte*, January 7, 2013, at http://globoesporte.globo.com/futebol/ selecao-brasileira/noticia/2013/01/marta-diz-que-trocaria-suas-cinco-bolas-de-ouro-pelo -titulo-do-mundial.html.

43. Translation by the authors; the original is as follows: "Desta vez, chegamos com todos os requisitos para desenvolver um bom trabalho, mas isso deveria ter começado lá atrás e cobramos agora que continue. Talvez não para mim. Não sei se daqui a quatro anos vou jogar a Olimpíada de novo, mas para as meninas que sonham um dia em chegar a seleção." See "Emocionada, Marta coloca em dúvida presença nos Jogos de 2016," *Veja*, August 3, 2012, at http://veja.abril.com.br/noticia/esporte/emocionada-marta-coloca-em-duvida -presenca-nos-jogos-de-2017/.

44. Graeff, "O berço da rainha Marta."

The Many Faces of Samuel Eto'o Fils
(Re)Solving an Irascible Persona
—Benn L. Bongang

Introduction

For all his brilliance as a football prodigy, Cameroon's Samuel Eto'o Fils remains an enigma both at home and abroad. His professional career has brought him wealth and fame, much of which he has been able to leverage in various phases of his life. And yet, his wealth and fame have also come at a great personal cost with regard to his public persona, in particular his athletic legacy as he nears the end of his career and seeks recognition as a sort of elder statesman of Cameroonian sport and all that might entail.

Born in 1981 in Douala, Cameroon's largest city, Eto'o turned professional in Spain at the tender age of sixteen. From then on, he helped win globally coveted trophies for his teams in Europe and for the Cameroon national football team, the celebrated Indomitable Lions. Throughout, he entertained fans, gave generously of himself and his money, and even dabbled in diplomacy. But in his many encounters with fans, the media, and dignitaries, exchanges often filled with heavy-handed claims and a conspicuous dose of arrogance, he often leaves the impression of a man who shows both a touch of a superiority complex as well as the unmistakable signs of inherent insecurity. He has tangled with teammates, opposing players, the media, coaches, football officials, governmental agencies, ministers, and even crowds, altogether leaving few people indifferent to his game alongside his often domineering, at times erratic, persona.

To be sure, Samuel Eto'o is a man who can both fascinate and frustrate, given the multiple facets of his game and his multifaceted personality. To reconcile these often competing elements within Eto'o's persona requires peering into those aspects of his life and times that help explain this brilliant, engaging, complex, and certainly controversial character. Some clues can be found in aspects of his meteoric rise to stardom, in his wealth, in the adulation he enjoys at home and abroad, and in his public works. But these matters can also be viewed by looking into how he has learned to leverage these assets not only to challenge football and political authorities at home and throughout global football but also as he continues to carve a place for himself as an international icon of consequence beyond his storied football career.

Kicking Plastic-Wrapped Balls

Samuel Eto'o rose to such an exalted position in a relatively short span of time. He came of age at a promising time when the Cameroonian government and private business interests envisioned opportunity in advocating sport and invested in identifying and training young football talent. Rather small and gangly, Eto'o showed enormous potential very early on, weaving his way past the bigger boys to score goals with uncanny ease. According to John Carlin, like most kids in Cameroon, where fans revere football and the talented players who entertain them, a young Eto'o started out kicking balls or any spherical object "made out of plastic bags, wrapped tight and bound with tape."[1] Although Eto'o was too young to have watched the legendary Samuel Mbappé Leppé, the very first Cameroonian football star whose magical shots into opponents' goals won trophies for his team, Oryx of Douala, and for the Cameroon national team, he came of age as Cameroon was making significant advances in international football, a motivating factor for his entire generation.

Eto'o was nine years old when the beloved and uniquely talented Roger Milla captained the Cameroonian national side in the 1990 World Cup, the tournament that ultimately propelled the nation onto football's global stage. Milla's dance moves to celebrate Cameroon's goals delighted soccer fans around the world just as African football was securing a place for itself among the elite of the sport, which had been dominated by Europe and South America. For his role in bringing honor to the country, Milla was appointed a roving ambassador by the country's president, Paul Biya, and represented Cameroon at the International Federation of Association Football (FIFA) and at similar organizations that decide on global football rules. Milla remained the ideal player for rising footballers to emulate, and like many young Cameroonian boys, Eto'o hoped for the day he would celebrate a World Cup goal like Milla by similarly gyrating his waist to an imaginary *makossa* dance rhythm—the popular Cameroonian musical style. Later, however, these two stars would come to clash in a battle for national football supremacy.

Nevertheless, springboarded by the success of the legends who had preceded them, Eto'o and the other footballers of his generation would ultimately fare much better. The Cameroonian government as well as national business interests ramped up their investment in sports complexes and academies for training young children in football and other sports, which is how Eto'o was spotted very early in his ascent. Indeed, he was barely twelve, though already regarded as a genius ball handler, when he was recruited into the football academy funded by a Douala brewery company, Les Brasseries du Cameroun. He then found himself playing for the Kadji Sports Academy, financed by one of Cameroon's wealthiest investors, Kadji Diffousso. These structured training opportunities accelerated his transformation to the extent that by age fourteen he was playing for the junior national team. He displayed remarkable talent for a teenager on the world stage—so much so that a scout from Spain's powerful Real Madrid club spotted and tabbed him for the team when he was barely sixteen years old. He was certainly fortunate to have come of age at a time when facilities and resources were available to identify and train talent and when well-endowed football teams in Europe sought and recruited talent from around the world, often for colossal amounts of money.

Irascible Professional

Eto'o experienced a slow and bumpy start in Europe. He spent two years with Real Madrid without playing in major matches. The team started to lend him out, initially to a relatively unknown Madrid club team, Leganés, then to another, Mallorca. Rather than take him back, however, Real Madrid eventually sold Eto'o to Barcelona, its archrival in the Spanish La Liga. This decision, in hindsight, was a "spectacular misjudgment"[2] on the part of Real Madrid. With Barcelona, Eto'o experienced his first real professional success as the side won both the Spanish National League and the European Champions League, with Eto'o himself taking home the Spanish scoring title. In five seasons playing for Barcelona, Eto'o scored 152 goals. During this stretch, Barcelona also won the Spanish League title three times and the European Champions League twice.[3]

While these years of triumph with Barcelona on the field brought fame and fortune to Eto'o, they also revealed a darker side of his personality. At times he behaved like the child he still was, often displaying a degree of insensitivity unbecoming of an athlete of his stature. For example, after Barcelona beat Real Madrid to win the Spanish championship in 2005, Eto'o was heard chanting "Madrid, cabrón, saluda al campeón" (Madrid, bastards, hail the champions). In insulting the defeated team, Eto'o ignored the fact that it had been Real Madrid that brought him to fame in Spain in the first place. As Fermin Calero, president of the Federation of Real Madrid Fan Clubs, put it: "This character is a fantastic player, but he leaves a lot to be desired as a person. . . . He has forgotten that it was Real Madrid that first allowed him to escape hunger."[4] While Calero overstated his point in suggesting that his team had rescued Eto'o from hunger, he summed up the contradictions within Eto'o's emerging persona that the young man would continue to display throughout his career.

In a similar situation later in his career, in 2011, Eto'o lashed out at a reporter after Cameroon lost a match to Senegal when the reporter dared to suggest that age was catching up to the entire national side, including the star striker.[5] According to Mohamed Keita, a blogger and advocacy coordinator for the New York–based Committee to Protect Journalists (CPJ), this incident escalated as Eto'o's frustration over the loss mounted. Keita reported that during the post-match press conference, Moussa Tandian, a reporter for Cameroonian broadcaster Equinoxe, asked Eto'o to explain the Lion's disappointing performance. As cameras rolled, Eto'o lashed out: "I'm rather surprised, dear brother, because you are making yourself noticed negatively.... I think that you are not Cameroonian.... I will speak to your boss at Equinoxe because you don't deserve to work for this wonderful channel."[6] Eto'o would ultimately apologize to Tandian, but such attacks on journalists by a star player who should know better the important role of the media in trumpeting his successes showed him to be both tactless and mistrustful of media coverage. Oddly, such outbursts would reveal a good deal of the very public persona he seemed to be trying to protect.

Some three years earlier in June 2008, one of Eto'o's eruptions had turned violent. Still starring for Barcelona, Eto'o reacted violently when Cameroonian sports journalists, including his nemesis Philippe Boney of Radio Tiemeni Siantou, staged a walkout during a press conference held at the Hilton Yaoundé to demonstrate their frustrations with the Lion team members, who, they concluded, preferred to speak only to foreign reporters rather than the domestic Cameroonian media. According to Priscilla Moadougou, writing for the newspaper *Mutations*, Eto'o's reactions to what he deemed an affront baffled many. He began a rant in colloquial French that included calling the lot of disgruntled journalists "bastards" and telling them that he would not play any match if any of them were to cover it. But this was just for starters. Later, he approached Boney, seized him by the collar, and head-butted him on the mouth, cutting open his upper lip.[7]

Eto'o's reason for targeting Boney in particular seems to have stemmed from an earlier clash between the two in 2005, when Boney revealed that he had seen Eto'o and two of his teammates carousing well after curfew and just a few hours before a match between Cameroon and Benin. An obviously embarrassed Eto'o, apparently reluctant to forgive or forget, was angry to have been caught violating team regulations, and his anger spilled over into the renewed confrontation three years later. Although Eto'o apologized to Boney and agreed to pay his medical bills, it was crude and reckless behavior from a gifted athlete seeking to climb to even greater achievements.[8]

Twenty-First-Century Football Celebrity

Eto'o's career was marked all along by this split between brilliance on the field and intractable behavior off it, which may have ultimately led to Barcelona's decision to let him go, although this rationale has never been articulated. Nevertheless, the duality of his place in professional football was on display once he transferred to Italy, where, "with Eto'o playing like a warrior,"[9] Inter Milan, his new team, beat his old team, Barcelona, in the semifinals of the 2010 UEFA Champions League tournament. With such laurels in hand, Eto'o expunged memories of his slow and bumpy European debut (though certainly not his off-field demons), and by 2010 he would become the first player to win two European continental titles. He was only the second player to have scored in two separate UEFA Champions League finals and the fourth player to have won the UEFA Champions League two years in a row with different teams.[10]

Europe was not the only continent on which Eto'o's star power was on display. Back home on the African continent, he continued to display the on-field qualities of a twenty-first-century superstar as well. No other player in the history of the Africa Cup of Nations had scored as many international goals as Eto'o. Playing for the Cameroonian national team, Eto'o participated in three World Cups and six Africa Cup of Nations tournaments, winning the latter twice; he was voted African Player of the Year in 2003, 2004, 2005, and 2010. The successive laurels for Eto'o followed the year 2000, which by any measure was the best year to date for the Cameroonian national team and in particular for him, the squad's standard bearer and emergent star.

After winning the Africa Cup of Nations in 2000, the Lions descended upon Australia, where they systematically demolished a gauntlet of global football powers during the 2000 Summer Games. They beat Brazil 2–1 in the semifinals, and, in the finals, when Eto'o's goal for victory was denied as offside, the Lions won in a penalty shootout over, coincidentally, Spain. It was the first ever Olympic gold for Cameroon in any sport. With these victories, Eto'o, who was barely nineteen years old at the time, had through his contributions secured a place among the demigods of Cameroonian football and for which he would be worshipped accordingly.

Indeed, the victories of 2000 instantly propelled Eto'o to the top of the Cameroonian football hierarchy. He had not merely won trophies for his professional teams in Europe. Rather, in one year, he helped lead the Cameroonian national side to a standard of fame and glory comparable to that of Milla and even the great Leppé himself. So much was expected of him that he was perceived as the difference maker in all Cameroonian athletic challenges. For instance, as World Cup 2010 approached, interest in Eto'o grew to global proportions. A

Time magazine piece published just before the event titled "Samuel Eto'o Reigns as Uncrowned King" proclaimed him to be little short of Cameroonian royalty.[11] Carlin suggested that Eto'o was more than a football phenom. He implied, rather, that Eto'o's athletic presence, as well as his wealth and cultural influence, inspired generations of young people. Indeed, Carlin then predicted that because of such influence, alongside his growing salary and its accompanying benefits, Eto'o could wield extraordinary power throughout the country, conjecture that proved to be most prescient.

Besides his salary, which would ultimately peak at an unprecedented US$54 million per season by 2013 (not including endorsement deals from multiple businesses), Eto'o's fame and celebrity status were enhanced by various awards and recognitions from around the world. The only person to be named African Player of the Year for a fourth time, Eto'o also established a charitable foundation while championing the cause of antiracism in sport both inside and outside the lines. By virtually every measure, Eto'o represented a much different type of Cameroonian athletic icon—one who enjoyed global reach—although this would place a very public target on his back as well, which, given his often erratic personality, would make for some explosive exchanges.

A Clash of Generations

Earlier football stars from Cameroon were neither as wealthy nor as openly defiant as Eto'o. Most, such as Milla and Leppé, were much older when their stars shone. In addition, they did not enjoy the modern training facilities that breed young talents. They may have been household names in Cameroon, where artists wrote songs in their honor, but they did not enjoy the global reach that players of Eto'o's generation would. Rather, they were locally renowned, earned only modest stipends, and were grateful for any allowances the government offered for their performances on the field. But they also had little recourse when it came to addressing grievances large or small. They respected authority and would not dare to challenge institutions such as the Fédération Camerounaise de Football (FECAFOOT), the governing body of Cameroonian football. Nevertheless, it is this earlier generation of players who paved the way for Eto'o's generation, who usually emulated the performances of the older generation but not necessarily their modesty.

The earlier Cameroonian football stars relied on their passion for the game, their talent, and the relatively rudimentary structures available for their club teams and for the national team. Although they were regarded as celebrities countrywide, they lacked the power and influence that comes with international celebrity and all its trappings. Also, unlike their successors, they did not enjoy the same global adulation, nor did they champion and advocate for causes off the field. Thus, while the previous generation based its collective celebrity on significantly more modest foundations, the influx of wealth and the power garnered by media fascination made stars and, to some extent, monsters of Eto'o's generation, which would lead to a clash of icons from various generations as Eto'o continued to establish himself as the newest face of Cameroonian sport.

Such generational differences fueled by strong personalities came to light as two of the favorite sons, Eto'o and Roger Milla, began to feud over who was the country's undisputed star of stars. On the eve of the 2010 World Cup, Eto'o threatened to walk out of the tournament while Milla countered that even if Eto'o had triumphed in Europe, he had brought nothing to Cameroon, as this episode would suggest. In his angry retort, Eto'o stated, rather brazenly: "It's always just before the [major] tournaments that the old geezers wake up. What's Milla done? He hasn't won the World Cup, they played in the quarter finals."[12] To further diminish Milla, Eto'o suggested that Milla shone in 1990 only because "he had better players around him."[13] But by suggesting that Milla shone because he was supported by "better" players, Eto'o again revealed more about himself than about his target. It is fair to conclude from Eto'o's comment that he felt that the national squad that he captained did not advance as far as Milla's had in World Cup tournaments because he did not have "better" players to assist him. If he really implied that, then his statement confirms not only his arrogance but a surprising degree of narcissism from someone whose fame and fortune came from football, which is most decidedly a team sport. Eto'o omitted—deliberately or otherwise—to acknowledge that both he and Milla were prolific scorers because other players made that possible. Regardless, Eto'o and his fans may dismiss such conclusions based on remarks he might have made in anger and out of disappointment with Milla's barbs, but they do underscore the more cantankerous elements of Eto'o's overall demeanor that continue to plague his reputation. Moreover, it certainly could not have won him points with his Lion teammates either. Nevertheless, in terms of Cameroonian sport, the spotlight seems to shine brightest on Eto'o regardless of how he might be behaving at any given juncture.

Another interesting albeit pop-psychology take on this feud between national icons came from Atango, a noted Cameroonian football blogger. He suggested that within the Eto'o-Milla rivalry were hints of an Oedipal battle in which Eto'o, as heir to the Cameroonian football throne, felt the need to grapple with Milla, his symbolic father, before ascending to the throne himself. Writing about a social event in France organized by the sporting goods company Puma in May 2010, Atango observed the two men actively if not emphatically avoiding each other. He concluded that Milla focuses on what Eto'o has failed to do for Cameroon simply because he wants football fans to remember his own accomplishments from the 1990s.¹⁴ Furthermore, Eto'o bristles at Milla's continued focus on Eto'o's World Cup hiccups, namely what befell the Cameroonian side captained by Eto'o in both the 2010 World Cup in South Africa and the 2014 World Cup in Brazil. Nonetheless, Eto'o supposes that Milla deliberately ignores his other triumphs while exaggerating his failures in Europe and with the national side in African and other tournaments as a pretense toward reestablishing the grand order of celebrity in local football lore.

Their feud successfully divided Cameroonian football fans into raucous groups of pro-Eto'o and pro-Milla supporters, with each side tabulating the accomplishments of their respective heroes and diminishing the contributions of their rival. But, in 2010, Eto'o extended something of an olive branch in this interpersonal cold war when he offered the older star a Porsche (probably plucked from his fleet of expensive sports cars estimated to be valued at over $6 million) as a Christmas gift.¹⁵ Reports vary as to whether Milla saw this as a genuine peace offering or as another of Eto'o's passive reminders of the class division that remains at the center of their ongoing dispute.¹⁶ Regardless, as if to confirm the thaw in their relationship, Milla did step in to defend Eto'o's decision to retire from the Indomitable Lions in 2012. Milla was quoted as saying that Eto'o was rightly frustrated with the poor governing of football in Cameroon. Eto'o's choice, as he put it, "to quit the national team [was] not a haphazard move.... It was a strong signal [that] he is once again sending to the authorities."¹⁷ Milla's support of Eto'o was important to football fans—particularly older ones, who continue to respect Milla as a legend. It was also an acknowledgment that Eto'o's generation should continue to challenge the authorities while perhaps laying a foundation for better football organization in Cameroon. Moreover, Milla was also tacitly conceding that, unlike Eto'o's generation, his did not have the instruments of power, namely money and global media attention, to leverage and pursue the best interests of his teammates often under the thumb of Cameroon's football authorities at FECAFOOT.

Eto'o versus FECAFOOT

As the feud between Eto'o and Milla indicates, Eto'o has shown a propensity to react defensively and even uncompromisingly to perceived threats to his career and reputation. But while any alleged Oedipal squabble with Milla might have indeed been resolved through Eto'o's Christmas peace offerings, Eto'o's disputes with Cameroonian football's hierarchy showed the more aggressive side of his nature, particularly as it pertained to his penchant for responding harshly to frustration. To be sure, this ongoing clash took on a decidedly national character, bringing in government officials at the highest levels often in support of

Eto'o to appease fans, thereby undermining the relevance of FECAFOOT as a national institution. At almost every stage in this saga, Eto'o's strategy was to either threaten to sit out a match or, perhaps worse, retire from the national team altogether. Throughout, he has effectively harnessed fan support in his efforts, ultimately driving a wedge between the federal organization and national political leaders while revealing further the complexity of his own personality—namely, that when challenged, he can be both manipulative and combative, even to the point of risking his personal as well as the nation's reputation.

His rocky relations with FECAFOOT stemmed from what he perceived to be their mismanagement of resources and outright corruption at the top. On December 16, 2010, the football federation imposed a fifteen-match suspension against Eto'o as punishment for leading his teammates on the national team to boycott a friendly match against Algeria over late payment of player stipends. As the leader of the rebellious players, Eto'o certainly got FECAFOOT's attention, but the organization's strategy backfired as football fans, and especially Eto'o's fans, condemned their decision as too severe. President Paul Biya himself intervened on behalf of Eto'o, compelling FECAFOOT to reduce the suspension to only four competitive matches.[18]

Eto'o's self-worth grew as a result of this episode, as did his hold over the nation's sporting consciousness. He learned, among other things, that he was virtually an institution unto himself, pushing even the nation's highest office to reject decisions of a national institution in order to satisfy his agenda, making him for all intents and purposes an unassailable national fixture. Buoyed by the power he wielded, he once again tested FECAFOOT's resolve nearly two years later when he refused to play a match against Cape Verde because of what he called an "amateurish and poorly organized"[19] national team. According to Junior Binyam, a spokesman for the federation, regulations require a player called to the national team to play. Moreover, Binyam confirmed, sanctions levied against players who refuse to participate carry international repercussions. As Leocadia Bongben of BBC Sport explains, FECAFOOT's Article 28 clearly recognizes that a player who refuses to play for the national team faces sanctions that range from a warning to a suspension to an outright ban from football activities even at the international level.[20] However, Eto'o defied the rules again only to win—again—when this time Cameroon's prime minister, Philémon Yang, intervened and convinced Eto'o to play the second leg of the match despite the federation's statute. Cameroon failed to qualify for the Africa Cup of Nations that year, given that the team was unable to make up for the two-goal deficit of the first leg. Yet even if Eto'o's actions negatively affected the team while creating further tensions between the players and FECAFOOT, Cameroonians still clamored to have Eto'o captain the national side. Such was the sway Eto'o held over the nation.

With Eto'o back at the helm, the Indomitable Lions began the process of qualifying for the 2014 World Cup in Brazil. In March, Eto'o helped move Cameroon to the top of its qualifying group by scoring two goals against Togo. This victory did little to improve relations with FECAFOOT as he continued to tangle with officials including the federation's president, Iya Mohamed. As Moutakilou Mumuni of Africa Top Sports observed, the two men refused to shake hands on live television during ceremonies before the match when officials of both countries typically shake hands with their respective players. According to Mumuni, Eto'o claimed that he had received death threats and went so far as to refuse to eat or drink anything offered by the Cameroonian authority.[21] Nonetheless, the real damage seems to have been incurred by the football federation itself, as Eto'o's continuous "threaten-to-quit" strategies worked for him unabated, to the delight of his fans—and to the relief of high government officials, who were growing weary of the near-constant warfare. Such was the rocky road that took the Eto'o-led Indomitable Lions to Brazil in 2014.

Shame and Infamy in Brazil

Eto'o's lofty place in Cameroonian culture in what had been a storied narrative, erratic behavior notwithstanding, took a significant hit in the summer of 2014 in what has been referred to as nothing less than a debacle at that year's World Cup in Brazil. Eto'o continued to serve as team captain at thirty-three, an age when many top footballers begin to contemplate retirement. Regardless, the 2014 tournament began as yet another opportunity for Eto'o to bring glory to Cameroonian sport while once again serving to justify the enormous emotional investment in him by both the citizens of Cameroon and the country's political leaders. But in the end, Brazil 2014 turned out to be little short of disaster for both the country and its illustrious superstar.

Frankly, the team's showing at this tournament can be seen as something of a turning point not only in Eto'o's otherwise prodigious football career but also in the worldwide reputation that Cameroonian football had been developing since their remarkable showing in the 1990 World Cup. Eto'o was at the helm, and thus it is not surprising (although it's not particularly fair) that he is held accountable and has garnered the lion's share of criticism for the team's poor showing. His visibility during the tournament also may come to mark the beginning of his fall from the lofty heights to which he had once been elevated by Cameroonian fans, government officials, and football enthusiasts worldwide.

To be sure, the team's behavior prior to departure for Brazil did not forebode good fortune. As he had done several times in the past, Eto'o led a player revolt that might have scuttled Cameroon's participation in the tournament altogether. The team missed its scheduled flight out of Yaoundé as Eto'o refused to allow his team to board any aircraft until the federation agreed to pay the players triple the amount in stipends than had been originally promised. Eto'o argued that FIFA, the world football governing body, had provided more than enough money for the team to be paid exactly the amount the players requested. The standoff was eventually resolved and the players ultimately made it to Brazil but only after President Biya once again intervened by chartering a plane and granting the extra funding.[22] And while in hindsight Eto'o may be justifiably applauded by his teammates and others for standing up for fair compensation of players, the embarrassing standoff, widely reported in the global media, loomed large, especially after the team's dreadful performance in Brazil. Thus, what once again began as a display of civil disobedience turned into a public relations nightmare for the principals involved—and among the casualties was Eto'o himself, which is something of a shock considering that he was always able to hang onto his popular support in the face of official sanctions and criticism. But this episode was different in that whereas he had historically been able to deliver even in the darkest of times, his failure to meet expectations at the World Cup bypassed him personally and placed the entire national side squarely in the crosshairs of national and even international ridicule.

Indeed, the day after Cameroon was finally ousted from the tournament, the *Wall Street Journal*'s Jonathan Clegg summed it up best in his recap "Well, Cameroon, It Could Have Been Worse" when he noted that Joel Matip's lone goal saved the Lions from "being saddled with the dubious distinction of going down as one of the worst teams in World Cup history."[23] But the lone goal was hardly consolation. What many considered a distinct lack of discipline on the part of the Eto'o-led Lions eroded Cameroon's pride as a football-mad nation, and it was an especially far cry from the enthusiasm that swept the country and much of the African continent following the Lions' unprecedented runs in previous World Cups dating back to the celebrated 1990 performance. Rather, the conclusion was that in Brazil the Lions had not only dragged Cameroon's name through the scandal sheets of world football but actually managed to erase nearly a quarter century of memorable performances, sending the nation's reputation hurtling back to the lower rungs of the international game. Moreover, while historians will surely compare Milla's storied 1990 squad to Eto'o's 2014 side, the final verdict may not be based upon on-the-field performance alone but rather upon Eto'o's inability to lead whether on the field or off it, beyond his successful effort to secure larger stipends for the players.

But the team's lack of competitiveness was not even the biggest story to emerge from the 2014 experience. Eto'o's squad not only lost all its matches, but its collective casual misbehavior and apparent ignorance of professional conduct was crude and baffling. A few days prior to Cameroon's match against

Mexico, coach Volker Finke essentially quarantined his players. Perhaps predictably, Eto'o and teammate Alex Song ignored the policy outright when they snuck their wives into their rooms, an act that was ultimately caught on camera (and was reminiscent of the 2005 incident recounted above). Seemingly nonplussed by it, rather than attempt to conceal his transgression or even offer up a quick mea culpa, Eto'o, according to one published report, found the revelation humorous. The report noted that he "just waved his hand and said 'hi' to fans and photographers staring at him," although the same report also suggested that he looked uncomfortable if not downright embarrassed by it all.[24]

Another scandal that added to the collective shame for the Lions involved Song and occurred on the field with television cameras whirring. In full view of the world, Song chased a Croatian player who did not even have the ball, raised his elbow high in the air, and brutally clobbered him, a humiliating episode that quickly went viral. A photoshopped version of this video went so far as to replace the midfielder's elbow with a spear, which played to the deeply held stereotypes of "barbaric"[25] African athletes and ultimately racialized not only this incident but many of the discussions of the tournament itself.[26] The incident further ignited discussions about the team's shameful performance and whether the world was witnessing the beginning of Eto'o's long-awaited fall from grace, as his team continued to threaten and attack opponents and otherwise shove each other around in inexplicable displays of frustration and incivility on the pitch.

In all, this was a lamentable spectacle for which Eto'o was more often than not held responsible—both at home and abroad. Indeed, as soon as the team returned home, President Biya, who had only recently personally intervened on behalf of the team prior to their departure, asked Prime Minister Yang to investigate these circumstances. The prime minister was given a month to turn in his report,[27] and whatever details emerged from the investigation, Eto'o surely bore the brunt of the blame and any resulting backlash.[28] As David C. Ogden and Joel Nathan Rosen contend in the introduction to their edited book *Fame to Infamy*:

> The process by which an athlete's reputation erodes over time is of little interest when compared to the aftermath of that erosion. That aftermath, as portrayed by press and media, usually encompasses the athlete's betrayal of the public trust and the fan's emotional investments. Press and media not only convey public disapproval and disappointment but also in some cases such disappointments are often framed with the athlete's promising beginnings.[29]

For many observers, the display in Brazil was inevitable—a long time in the making and indicative of Eto'o's often infuriating lack of on- and off-the-field comportment. For others, it was an opportunity to figuratively stick a finger in the eye of a man who many believed was unworthy of the sort of international adulation he had received throughout his career. That the resulting condemnation came with at least a soupçon of racial animus adds yet another dimension to the affair.

A History of Petulance

As discussed above, and as on display in the Brazil debacle, Eto'o's reputation as a problematic superstar was a discussion long in the making. His tendency to infuriate both football officials and detractors alike was certainly nurtured in Europe and evolved as his reputation soared as one of the most talented players in the world. Before he could infuriate FECAFOOT officials and impel senior Cameroon government officials to do his bidding, Eto'o had honed his strategies, particularly his way of threatening to quit, during his meteoric rise on European teams. He often deployed this latter strategy when he perceived threats to his reputation and directly to his person, whether such threats were real or imagined.

Unquestionably, Eto'o's successes with his European teams inflated his already healthy ego. He genuinely believed that, as an indispensable feature of each team, he could dangle threats with impunity. For instance, while playing for Barcelona, Eto'o sparked a crisis when he refused to play as a late substitute in a match against Racing de Santander one week before an important Champions League match against Liverpool. Eto'o, who had returned to play after an injury, was slated to appear as a substitute toward the end of the match. However, after his warm-up drills, Eto'o returned to the bench without playing, furious that he had not been given enough time to prepare. It was obvious later on that Eto'o and his coach, Frank Rijkaard, had had prior disagreements long before the match, and that the fact that he was brought in as a substitute toward the end of the match was simply a trigger for the ensuing outburst. During the postmatch press conference, Eto'o could barely hold back his scorn for his coach, proclaiming: "Anyone who comes out in the press room and says that I refused to play is a bad person.... Rijkaard said what he said. It's up to him to explain that. I don't have to give any explanations to anyone except the club."[30] Eto'o also accused the former vice president of the team, Sandro Rosell, of "fostering a civil war at the club which has divided the dressing room. It is not my war, but I am the one taking all the hits."[31]

Eto'o's tangling with coaches and football officials will score poorly in evaluations of his career, and in his ultimate legacy. Even after Brazil 2014, when he played for Chelsea in the English Premier League, Eto'o again displayed a pattern of attacking his superiors and coaches and finding fault with all except himself. He also had some unflattering words for Chelsea coach José Mourinho, who dared to question Eto'o's age and fitness. As he explained, albeit graphically: "Contrary to what a puppet says about my age, I am still physically fit.... There are other players who went on until the age of 41."[32] Not long after this incident, however, Eto'o left Chelsea for Everton, and then Sampdoria in Italy, but the damage to his reputation was already set. Such brash talk quickly erodes fan confidence, especially if it is accompanied by less than stellar on-the-field performance.

Whatever the nature of his disagreements with coaches and team officials, that Eto'o displayed such infantile behavior and disrespected them at a press conferences is yet another indication of his complex, often petulant nature. He had certainly learned early in his life that so long as he performed, he could get away with almost anything. He also came to recognize that so long as he continued to perform at a superstar level, he could take his talent virtually anywhere and be paid accordingly. Talent was certainly his trump card, but talent begins to fade with age, something that he would come to learn as he moved into his thirties, especially with regard to his team's performance in the 2014 World Cup and the ensuing backlash.

Confronting Racism

However troublesome his behavior was to some, Eto'o certainly had some valid reasons to be angry, especially at some European football fans whose racist rants during matches could unhinge even the most stoic of players, let alone a volatile personality. Eto'o obviously assumed that his prodigious display of talent, which brought victory to his teams and entertained football fans, would generate nothing less than approval and applause. So when football fans made animal noises or threw food on the field directed at him, he must have taken it as a personal affront as well as an affront on all people of color. Such behavior provided Eto'o with a cause to champion, namely the uncivilized behavior of European football fans and the failure of European authorities to implement effective policies to police unruly crowds.

Eto'o was resolved to confront racism on the football field with the resources his star power could generate, and his defiance of authority can similarly be viewed as a challenge to the prevailing racialized attitudes he encountered in his travels through the European leagues. In a 2009 blog post titled "Samuel Eto'o: Heart of a Lion," journalist and football analyst Cord Nowell portrays Eto'o as one of the most feared and admired strikers in the world, who regularly quenched his goal-scoring thirst with "blazing pace, [an] array of moves, and [a] prolific ability at finding the back of the net."[33] But Nowell further notes that, more than any other player, Eto'o endured racial slurs "from monkey chants [to] nuts and other objects being tossed at him." Nowell adds that, as one of Africa's leading sports icons, Eto'o realized that he could effect change in racial perceptions given the platform that his celebrity afforded him, something that Eto'o himself confirmed as his deliberate mission beyond the pitch:

> It is something that has affected me personally. I think players, leaders, and the media have to join forces so that no one feels looked down upon because of the color of their skin."[34]

It was earlier in his career when he played in the Spanish La Liga that Eto'o endured the worst forms of racism directed at him personally and at African players in general. In November 2004, for example, Spain's national antiviolence commission issued a fine of $8,200 to two supporters of Spanish club Albacete for directing monkey-like chatter at Eto'o. According to the BBC, the two were also banned from sporting events for about five months.[35] The racial slurs were so outrageous at times that Eto'o decided against bringing his family to his games in order to shield them from the spectacle.

In another incident during a match at Zaragoza in 2006, Eto'o went to retrieve a ball for a corner kick awarded to his Barcelona team as "bottles were tossed in his direction and monkey noises erupted from the crowd."[36] A public address was made to appeal to the crowd to stop the racial chants, but Eto'o stormed off the field, and it took the efforts of coach Rijkaard and his equally talented teammate Ronaldinho to console and ultimately convince him to return. Predictably, when play resumed in a match that had been hotly contested until then, an Eto'o-led Barcelona erupted, scoring twice within a few minutes of his return, a reaction that the *New York Times* maintained "seemed fated to silence the boo boys of La Romareda."[37] According to Eto'o himself, "We can't wait until some crazy fan jumps from his seat and kills a black player before measures are taken."[38] Eto'o definitely had reasons to fear for the safety of black players performing before racist fans, and his quitting strategy in this instance serves to bring attention to the serious problem of racism in football. As a superstar, he seems to have mastered this strategy as an effective way to draw attention to himself and to his causes.

The inconsistent and paltry financial penalties levied against a few spectators and teams by the Spanish football federation justified Eto'o's anger. As Rob Hughes of the *New York Times* opined, "Whether fining the clubs, or indeed shutting them down for a number of home matches gets at the hard-core is a moot point. But if it is to be done at all, a financial penalty has surely to reflect the anger of the federation and the state."[39] Regardless, Eto'o believed that the racist attitudes he endured from crowds may, according to the *New York Times*, "reflect wider social attitudes which find expression amid the passion, emotion and anonymity of the football crowd."[40] In the specific case of Spain, Eto'o suggested that the Spanish media should have played a key role "not just by highlighting incidents of abuse but in creating an environment in which racism in the stands is no longer condoned."[41]

For all the interpersonal drama he ignites, Eto'o has indeed been applauded for his antiracism efforts. And on March 9, 2015, Eto'o was honored for his work fighting racism in football when he was awarded the European Medal of Tolerance and Reconciliation from the European Council on Tolerance and Reconciliation (ECTR), a nongovernmental organization. At an award ceremony in Kensington Palace in London, ECTR president Moshe Kantor said of Eto'o that he had "the courage and the will to stand against the racists, building awareness and inspiring fellow footballers and millions of football fans."[42]

Championing Goodwill

Besides confronting racism in Europe, Eto'o has also shown an even more charitable side to his character as well. Thanks to his talent and wealth, and the global megaphone the media has long provided him with, Eto'o has had opportunities to pursue various causes.

For instance, he funneled part of his wealth back to his home continent in 2006, establishing the Samuel Eto'o Private Foundation. Early beneficiaries of the foundation included the pediatric Hospital Laquiquinne in his hometown of Douala and a sports study center in the neighboring country of Gabon. In 2010, the foundation was honored with a Best Charitable Work award by the Cameroon Professional Society (CPS), an organization of Cameroonians in the United States. Eto'o stated that his charity had undertaken activities in Gabon "in a bid to extend its global activities of fostering social integration, education and youth training."[43]

Eto'o saw charitable work as an opportunity to give back, recalling: "I couldn't have made it this far if someone hadn't rendered the help I needed then. A certain rich man gave me the chance to play football, and you can see where I am today. So it's my turn to help those who need it to succeed in their career."[44] With additional financial support from fellow athletes, Eto'o said that his objective was to ensure that "our little brothers could have pleasure playing football and studying as well in their environment."[45] This generous side of Eto'o's personality suggests that he is keen to leave a personal (as opposed to a professional) legacy and to give back so that others may have opportunities to emerge in the future as he did thanks to the generosity of many. This may be a possible outlet for his wealth and energy after he hangs up his football cleats.

Besides his charitable work, Eto'o mined his status as a global celebrity to contribute to reconciliation efforts in the Middle East, particularly as it pertains to Israeli and Palestinian youth. In 2006, while traveling in Israel one week after his FC Barcelona team beat Arsenal of the English Premier League to win the European Champions League, he was the featured guest at the Shimon Peres Center for Peace to promote his message of tolerance.[46] He told reporters there that he had come to Israel to help both Israeli and Palestinian children through their common love of football, proclaiming: "It is very important to bring them together so they will know to live together." While there, he participated with both Palestinian and Israeli youth in a charity football match they dubbed a "mini world cup." Eto'o thrilled players and spectators alike while speaking out against discrimination in Israeli football. He told his audience above all else that the first stage of tackling discrimination was to recognize that the problem exists at all. As Jeremy Last reported in the *Jerusalem Post*, Eto'o stated: "We need to be together in the war against racism.... It is a long road that we have to take together." Later, in the presence of Israeli vice premier Shimon Peres and other dignitaries, Eto'o accepted a trophy from the Israeli sports minister, Ophir Pines, telling the crowd: "I have scored many goals in my life, but this, to promote peace here, is one of the most beautiful."[47]

Although the intractable problems between Israelis and Palestinians cannot be resolved by celebrities, the common love of football by youth from both sides of the divide brings them together for a brief moment on the field with a global superstar like Eto'o. It would be presumptuous of Eto'o or any other celebrity to assume that their fleeting flame of stardom can bridge deep-rooted political problems anywhere. Nonetheless, dignitaries, international organizations, and national populations continue to turn to such stars, whose global reach can bring attention to issues and bring unlikely parties together around a common, attractive personality. The stars for their part engage in such activities in the belief that by drawing attention to difficult problems, the publicity thus generated can garner positive reactions from those with the power to bring about real change.

Indeed, Eto'o, like most politically engaged celebrities and goodwill ambassadors, was aware of the impact that he could bring to off-the-field issues. But he also believed that his good works required large sums of liquid capital, a notion that he took to an entirely different level when in 2011 he surprised the football world by leaving Inter Milan and moving to Dagestan, a relatively unknown albeit volatile region of the Russian Caucasus, where he joined the Anzhi Makhachkala team for a contract valued at roughly $54 million a year. Right or wrong, this instantly elevated Eto'o to the rank of the highest-paid professional athlete of any sport, leading many analysts to quickly dismiss the move as the lure of an enticing check, which would certainly explain why he would transition from the relative stability of western Europe to a place that is not only impoverished but where people live in fear of daily attacks from Islamic separatists. The move also fueled Eto'o's detractors by demonstrating that, for all his talk of rights and equality, he could be so easily swayed by the lure of money as to essentially relocate his career to a war zone. As David Hytner writes in the *Guardian*, in 2011 alone more than 200 people were killed while another 149 were injured in regional attacks in Dagestan. Anzhi players lived and trained in Moscow, flying to Makhachkala, a city that Eto'o seemed to embrace, for home matches.[48]

But Eto'o framed his transfer to Dagestan in terms that were more political than perhaps he intended. As he put it:

> The club is not only a football club; it represents the whole region, and it represents the hope of everything. I am not a politician and I don't know how to do politics. I am a footballer, I know how to play football and manage projects in football. This is what I want to limit myself to.[49]

Whether deliberately or accidentally, Suleiman Kerimov, the team's billionaire owner, might have selected Eto'o to propel his team to compete on a par with the top European clubs, but in Eto'o he found more than just a player. He had found someone whose enormous talent could bring together fierce political partisans with a common love of football for brief celebratory moments in their otherwise war-torn region. In interviews, Eto'o steered away obvious questions about his salary to speak more about a loftier goal of inspiring a region at war to hope for better times. Some analysts agreed as well that Eto'o had found a mission "underpinned by social and philanthropic goals."[50]

Managing His Celebrity

Few talented athletes or celebrities in other fields are schooled in managing stardom, especially when it comes to engaging in issues they are not qualified to handle. Yet the world looks up to celebrities to lead and champion causes, to offer their larger-than-life images as magnets to publicize important global issues. In this regard, Eto'o represents the celebrity athletes of the twenty-first century who, as they train to perform in their sport, must also learn to grapple— successfully or not—with adulation and the responsibilities that come with living under the glare of an omnipresent media spotlight. Global celebrity status certainly confers wealth, reverence, and a mediated platform from which to embrace causes beyond sports. According to Siegwart Lindenberg, Janneke Joly, and Diederik Stapel, celebrities have a "norm-activating power" inasmuch as their actions are viewed as the norm, giving them enormous reach into the public sphere.[51] As Daniel Künzler and Raffaele Poli observe, young men who lionize star athletes by, for example, displaying their posters or otherwise mimicking their style, "appear to be ideal vectors through which to express their dreams and ambitions."[52] Such tendencies certainly expand the reach of high-profile celebrity athletes. Young people see in these players the leaders they believe they deserve. And political leaders see in the fan adulation of sports stars real opportunities to promote national unity.

This is quite apparent in a politically and ethnically diverse nation such as Cameroon, where the government is ready to bend to the wishes of athletic standouts such as Eto'o. As a result, rather than strictly adhering to FECAFOOT's disciplinary measures, political leaders even including the nation's president, under extraordinary pressure from fans, felt compelled to minimize Eto'o's instances of recalcitrance while offering him the opportunity to lead the national team. They believed in his ability to bring victory and honor to the country, but they also recognized that by hitching their collective wagon to his celebrity, they could be shielded from criticism as long as the team won and the people were united in celebration—at least for a time.

Political leaders also crave the rare and positive international press coverage that follows sporting success. As Kari Jaksa put it: "Through the sports medium, underserved nations across the world create for themselves an identity and a voice, enabling them to be heard on the international stage."[53] Indeed, since its first appearance at a World Cup tournament, Cameroon has carved a place of some distinction among football nations and memories for many football fans around the world, thanks to the surprising, excellent performances of the Indomitable Lions. This has served the Cameroonian government well, as it has diverted attention from the country's lackluster reputation as one of the most corrupt dictatorships on the African continent. At a time of political turbulence in Cameroon in the early 1990s, the Indomitable Lions found a way to proudly bring a nation together. Eto'o's celebrity, then, becomes a sort of shield by which political authority can at least temporarily protect itself from gathering sociopolitical forces.

Approaching Sunset

Samuel Eto'o Fils's career has resulted from a combination of natural talent and good luck. He emerged as a young prodigy at a promising time in the development of football in Cameroon, soared like a phoenix to the heights of global football success, and shone brilliantly amid the glitter of trophies on several continents. With stardom came enormous wealth, prestige, and generosity, but his stardom has also shown an arrogance and lurking narcissism that often informs his public persona as much as his extraordinary talent has. In challenging authorities around the world and espousing causes both on and off the football field, Eto'o viewed his activities as legitimate battles for justice and fairness. In time, however, those fans who were seduced and blinded by his brilliance on the football field and who worshipped him unconditionally have also begun to reevaluate their position on Eto'o, seeing him as less infallible and more the fragile and insecure personality that he was all along, shielded only by the aura of invincibility that often comes with fame.

As younger and more agile players emerge, Eto'o will certainly remain a football legend, although perhaps not the demigod fans and politicians mined for their own excitement and for their country's glory. Oddly, he will most likely end up standing with the likes of his erstwhile rival Roger Milla—honored but often miscast by oncoming generations of Cameroonian fans. And like Milla before him, he might be forced to debate the merits of a new star and what his (or perhaps her) presence on the national or even international stage suggests about his own legacy, and whose will prove to be more permanent.

As horrible for Cameroon's honor and for Eto'o's personal reputation as Brazil 2014 was, that single event, with time, could diminish to a blemish, a mere footnote to an otherwise exceptional career. And indeed, Eto'o has moved on. He has resigned from playing internationally for Cameroon altogether. What's more, he left his Russian side in favor of two stops in the English Premier League, with Chelsea and Everton, before transferring to Sampdoria in Italy in January 2015, and later that year to Turkey. In his first match for the Italian team, he even flashed some of that goal-scoring brilliance of his youth when he "collected a pass on his chest, turned, let the ball bounce and then rifled an unstoppable in the net."[54]

Ultimately, however, Eto'o's legacy may well be determined, at least in part, by when and how he quits football. In this regard, he will have to decide whether to walk away from the game at the height of his glory or to be booed into retirement by fans and the media, like so many other tragic figures who hung on just a little too long past their glory years, their talent no longer sufficient to enable them to get away with public displays of superiority or discourtesy. The combination of waning success and an engaged albeit fickle media often turns the tide against even the most beloved celebrity. And indeed, Eto'o's star may begin to dim along with whatever influence he may have enjoyed as an erstwhile god on the pitch.

Celebrity status is, after all, a manufactured process—and a mediated one at that. Thus, as Lindenberg, Joly, and Stapel contend, the "media can make or break the prestige (and thus the norm-activating ability) of celebrities just by the choice of words describing their doings."[55] Clearly, this story's ending is still to be written.

Notes

1. John Carlin, "The Global Game," *Time*, June 3, 2010.
2. Ibid.
3. "Legends: Samuel Eto'o," FC Barcelona Online, at http://www.fcbarcelona.com/club/history/detail/card/samuenl-eto-o.
4. "Eto'o Apologises for Outburst," BBC Sport, May 16, 2005, at http://news.bbc.co.uk/go/pr/fr/-/sport2/hi/football/africa/4553179.stm.
5. Mohamed Keita, "Cameroon Soccer Star Samuel Eto'o Lashes Out at Reporter," Committee to Protect Journalists, at http://cpj.org/x/4295.
6. Keita, "Cameroon Soccer Star Samuel Eto'o."
7. Priscilla G. Moadougou, "Philippe Boney: La cible de Samuel Eto'o," *Mutations*, June 2, 2008.
8. "Eto'o Apologises for Head Butt," BBC Sport, May 6, 2008, at http://news.bbc.co.uk/sport2/hi/football/africa/7438122.stm.
9. Carlin, "The Global Game."
10. Ibid.
11. Ibid.
12. "World Cup 2010: Cameroon Striker Samuel Eto'o Threatens to Walk Out," *Telegraph*, May 30, 2010, at http://www.telegraph.co.uk/sport/football/teams/cameroon/7785449/World-Cup-2010-Cameroon-striker-Samuel-Etoo-threatens-to-walk-out.html.
13. Ibid.
14. Atango, "Milla-Eto'o: les varies raisons du conflit," May 10, 2010, at atangofoot.over-blog.com.
15. John Drayton, "Eto'o's Auto Obsession: Chelsea Striker's £4m Fleet of Cars Roll into Cobham," *Daily Mail*, October 2, 2013, at http://www.dailymail.co.uk/sport/football/article-2441512/Samuel-Etoos-4million-fleet-cars.html.
16. Of his auto obsession, Eto'o said: "I like to have a few cars because it gives me choice and it doesn't hurt anybody. To give happiness, the first thing is to be happy oneself, and I am." See Drayton, "Eto'o's Auto Obsession." For someone with an estimated worth of over $75 million in 2013, it may not be excessive to own such a fleet of cars, especially given Eto'o's generous charitable activities. Still, it does beg the question of the wisdom of such a display from someone from a humble background in a relatively impoverished country.
17. "Milla: Eto'o Unhappy with Authorities," ESPN, September 10, 2013, at http://m.espn.go.com/soccer/story?storyId=1549085&wjb=.
18. Bisong Etahoben, "Cameroon's Biya Seeks Eto'o Suspension Lifted," *Africa Review*, January 3, 2012.
19. Leocadia Bongben, "Eto'o Risks Life Ban for Rejecting Cameroon-FECAFOOT," BBC Sport, August 28, 2012, at http://www.bbc.co.uk/sport/0/football/19399211.
20. Ibid.
21. Moutakilou Mumuni, "Cameroon: Eto'o Refuses the Handshake of the Federation President," Africa Top Sports, March 28, 2013, at http://en.africatopsports.com/2013/03/28/cameroon-etoo-refuses-the-handshake-of-the-federation-president/.

22. Nick Schwartz, "World Cup Team Refuses to Board Plane to Brazil," *USA Today*, June 8, 2014, at http://ftw.usatoday.com/2014/06/cameroon-world-cup-plane-brazil-bonus.

23. Jonathan Clegg, "Well, Cameroon, It Could Have Been Worse," *Wall Street Journal*, June 23, 2014, at http://www.wsj.com/articles/well-cameroon-it-could-have-been-worse-1403572894.

24. "Alex Song and Eto'o Get Visits against Directive," CameroonWeb, June 12, 2014, at http://www.cameroonweb.com/CameroonHomePage/SportsArchive/artikel.php?ID=303860.

25. Greg Price, "Alex Song's World Cup Punch and Elbow: Cameroon Player Receives a Red Card for Attack on a Croatian Player," *International Business Times*, June 9, 2014, at http://www.ibtimes.com/video-alex-songs-world-cup-punch-elbow-cameroon-player-receives-red-card-attack-croatian-1606572.

26. Mohamed Keita, "Did Cameroon's Police Interrogate Samuel Eto'o and Take Away His Passport over the World Cup? Who Knows," Africa Is a Country, July 11, 2014, at http://africasacountry.com/did-cameroons-police-interrogate-samuel-etoo-and-take-away-his-passport-over-the-teams-performance-at-the-world-cup-who-knows/.

27. By the time of publication, a public report had not been published.

28. "Biya Probes into Lions Abysmal Performance," CameroonWeb, June 26, 2014, at http://www.cameroonweb.com/CameroonHomePage/NewsArchive/artikel.php?ID=304409.

29. David C. Ogden and Joel Nathan Rosen, eds., *Fame to Infamy: Race, Sport, and the Fall from Grace* (Jackson: University Press of Mississippi, 2010), 3.

30. Sid Lowe, "Eto'o Outburst Opens Barca Wounds," *Irish Times*, February 14, 2007, at http://www.irishtimes.com/sport/eto-o-outburst-opens-barca-wounds-1.1195290.

31. Ibid.

32. Giuseppe Muro, "Chelsea's Samuel Eto'o Still Fuming with 'Puppet' Jose Murinho," *Evening Standard*, May 21, 2014, at http://www.standard.co.uk/sport/football/chelseas-samuel-etoo-still-fuming-with-puppet-jose-mourinho-9409586.html.

33. Cord Nowell, "Samuel Eto'o: Heart of a Lion," *Bleacher Report*, January 30, 2009, at http://bleacherreport.com/articles/117446-samuel-etoo-heart-of-a-lion.

34. Ibid.

35. "Two Fined for Eto'o Taunts," BBC Sport, December 17, 2004, at http://news.bbc.co.uk/sport2/hi/football/africa/4104067.stm.

36. Nowell, "Samuel Eto'o: Heart of a Lion."

37. Rob Hughes, "Soccer: Racist Spanish Fans Push Eto'o to Edge," *New York Times*, February 27, 2006, at http://www.nytimes.com/2006/02/26/sports/26iht-soccer.html.

38. Simon Hooper, "Eto'o: We Can't Wait until a Black Player Gets Killed," CNN, June 13, 2008, at http://edition.cnn.com/2008/SPORT/football/06/13/etoo.interview/index.html?iref=allsearch.

39. Hughes, "Soccer: Racist Spanish Fans Push Eto'o to Edge."

40. Ibid.

41. Hooper, "Eto'o: We Can't Wait."

42. Bob Harris, "Samuel Eto'o Honored for Work Fighting Racism in Football," Yahoo! News, March 9, 2015, at https://www.yahoo.com/news/samuel-etoo-honored-fighting-racism-football-021426650.html.

43. Kingsley Kobo, "Cameroon Star Samuel Eto'o to Launch Foundation in Gabon," *Goal*, August 15, 2011, at http://m.goal.com/s/en/news/2621671/.

44. Ibid.
45. Ibid.
46. Jeremy Last, "Eto'o Thrills Children and Players," *Jerusalem Post*, May 25, 2006, at http://www.jpost.com/Sports/Etoo-thrills-children-and-players.
47. Ibid.
48. David Hytner, "Samuel Eto'o: Anzhi Makhachkala Are Striving to Be Like Barcelona," *Guardian*, November 16, 2011, at http://www.theguardian.com/football/2011/nov/16/anzhi-makhachkala-samuel-etoo.
49. Ibid.
50. Ibid.
51. Siegwart Lindenberg, Janneke F. Joly, and Diederik A. Stapel, "The Norm-Activating Power of Celebrity: The Dynamics of Success and Influence," *Social Psychology Quarterly* 74, no. 1 (March 2011): 98–120.
52. Daniel Künzler and Raffaele Poli, "The African Footballer as Visual Object and Figure of Success: Didier Drogba and Social Meaning," *Soccer and Society* 13, no. 2 (2012): 207.
53. Kari L. Jaksa, "Sports and Collective Identity: The Effects of Athletics on National Unity," *SAIS Review of International Affairs* 31, no. 1 (Winter–Spring 2011): 39.
54. Brian Homewood, "Samuel Eto'o Scores First Goal Since Leaving Everton," *Daily Mail*, March 7, 2015, at http://www.dailymail.co.uk/sport/football/article-2984468/Samuel-Eto-0-scores-goal-leaving-Everton-Gianfranco-Zola-s-Calgiari-cut-adrift-Serie-relegation-zone.html.
55. Lindenberg et al., "The Norm-Activating Power of Celebrity," 115.

Murali and Sanga

Forging Identity and Pride through Cricket in a Small Island Nation

—Gamage Harsha Perera and Tim B. Swartz

Introduction

It was the seminal moment in Sri Lankan cricketing history. A nation's heart was aflutter. Nearly every eye was glued to the television. For those without means, every ear was tuned to the radio. It was Sri Lanka versus powerhouse Australia in the 1996 One-Day International (ODI) World Cup final, only the sixth ODI World Cup to be contested.

It was also a time of uncertainty in Sri Lanka. The Tamil Tigers had recently bombed the Central Bank in Colombo, killing 91 people and injuring 1,400 others. With India, Pakistan, and Sri Lanka jointly hosting the World Cup, there were security concerns over the Sri Lankan venues, and two of the Group Stage matches had been abandoned. Yet, in this troubling time, on the world stage, tiny Sri Lanka had made it to the final. They were a decisive underdog. In the openings innings of the match, Australia was held to 241 runs, largely due to the bowling expertise of Muttiah Muralitharan ("Murali"), then a twenty-three-year-old newcomer to international cricket. He was the most outstanding bowler of the finals, limiting Australia to 31 runs through ten overs.[1] In the second innings, Sri Lanka scored 245 runs, winning by seven wickets[2] with twenty-two balls remaining.

At the end of the match, wild celebrations erupted in Sri Lanka and among the Sri Lankan diaspora throughout the world, including in Australia. Murali had become a national icon. Hardly an imposing figure at five feet seven inches tall and of Tamil background, Murali was worshipped by Sri Lanka's Sinhalese majority. Meanwhile, back in the provincial capital of Kandy, a young schoolboy of eighteen years named Kumar Sangakkara ("Sanga"), who was climbing the ranks of great batsmen, had been watching the final and was duly inspired.

This chapter tells the story of Murali and Sanga, two Sri Lankan cricketers whose backgrounds could not be more different. Yet together they have made a deep impression on the game of cricket, forging identity and pride in the small island nation of Sri Lanka. Moreover, this chapter speaks to the excellence of these two cricketers in the face of challenging politics and ethnic turmoil in a country that is relatively new to the game of international cricket. Our chapter begins by examining the roots of cricket in Sri Lanka beginning from colonial times. We then describe the paths taken by Murali and Sanga from childhood to their prominence in world cricket, to their status today as ambassadors and icons for Sri Lanka.

Sri Lankan Cricket in Context

To understand the context of cricket in Sri Lanka, we first need to delve into the history of Sri Lanka in general and the history of cricket in Sri Lanka in particular. Sri Lanka is an island with a diverse population of nearly twenty-one million people in a land area of twenty-five thousand square miles—about the size of West Virginia. It is located just off the southeast coast of India, which is the second-most populous country in the world.

Originally, the island was inhabited by Veddah tribes who were the equivalent of Canada's First Nations, namely aboriginal people. Prince Vijaya and his followers migrated to the island circa 543 BC, arriving from what is now West Bengal in India, and originated the Sinhalese ethnicity. They were followed by Dravidians (of Tamil ethnicity) from South India.

Traders and sailors from Arab nations followed—the Moors in particular—who in turn were followed by colonists from Europe (Portuguese, Dutch, and British) lured by the rich trade in spices. In 1815, Ceylon, as the island was then called, became a British crown colony. During the British Raj, numerous ethnicities settled in Ceylon. A second wave of Tamils, brought by the British, worked as labourers in the tea plantations in the 1860s, including Murali's grandfather.

All of these groups had deep influences on aspects of Sri Lankan life in terms of politics, ethnicity, language, religion, art, architecture, music, food, dress, and other facets of life, all of which remain evident in the early twenty-first century. The Portuguese and the Dutch, many of whom intermarried with the local population (unlike the British) and whose descendants are called Burghers, left their mark in place names, family names, food, and religion. The island has been known by many names by many peoples, including the British Ceylon, the name that continued to be used after independence in 1948 until the island was officially renamed Sri Lanka in 1972.[3] With such a history, one can readily appreciate the current multi-ethnic and multicultural society in Sri Lanka, where religious practices include Buddhism, Hinduism, Islam, and Christianity.

Looking forward, it is difficult to imagine how a simple game (cricket) came to dominate the consciousness of this diverse country. Under British control of the maritime provinces in 1802 and the whole of the island in 1815, the British instituted many customs, including cricket, which was chief among the British recreational activities. The game itself dates back to England circa 1600. In Sri Lanka, however, the Colombo Cricket Club, the first such association, was set up in 1832, although club members did not play their first official match against a British regiment until the next calendar year.

The first international match between a Sri Lankan team and an English team was held in Colombo in 1882, facilitated by the opening of the Suez Canal thirteen years earlier, which eased travel considerably between the British Isles and South Asia. The match was a consequence of a travel break taken by the English team en route to Australia, when the ship stopped for fuel and provisions in Colombo. These matches were known as "limb-looseners" for the travelling cricketers. The matches provided an opportunity for local players to gain "first-class"[4] experience and were awaited with bated breath by the residents of Colombo. With the popularisation of air travel in the mid-1960s, ships carrying cricketers no longer called in at Colombo, and, as a result, by the second half of the twentieth century few international cricketers came to Sri Lanka.

Many of the founding Sri Lankan cricketing clubs have ethnically based names dating back to the 1890s, including the Sinhalese Sports Club (SSC), the Tamil Union, the Moors' Sports Club, and the Burgher Recreation Club (BRC). In the early twenty-first century, club teams are no longer ethnically based, although the club names have not changed.

Significantly, Murali and Sanga hail from the two main ethnic groups in Sri Lanka: Tamil and Sinhalese, respectively. Although these two communities have had a troubling relationship, cricket has been a unifying factor in Sri Lanka, and with respect to cricket, ethnicity has never been an issue. In fact, the current Sri Lankan cricket team includes almost all of the different ethnicities and religious persuasions prevalent on the island. This speaks volumes for the passions generated by the game, such that ethnic loyalties can be drowned under by an overriding national loyalty for the Sri Lankan cricket team.

Between 1953 and 1975, the only serious international matches involving Sri Lankan teams were between the Ceylon Cricket Association and the Madras team from India. These were first-class matches played for the Gopalan Trophy, with the venue alternating between Colombo and Madras (now Chennai). During this period, cricket was commonly played by boys in village fields, backyards, beaches, and even fallow rice paddies using discarded tennis balls and bats, when such were available, or with improvised equipment such as balls made of *kaduru*, a type of large, round hard seed, and bats made of *polpiti*, the leaf stalk of a coconut frond. In contrast, real cricket with proper equipment was reserved for boys at elite schools that had the necessary resources and cricket grounds. Youngsters at these venues had an opportunity to play for the local cricket clubs that held first-class tournaments.

To be sure, cricket is the most popular sport in Sri Lanka whether at the international, club, or school level. However, school cricket has the longest history and also perhaps the most partisan supporters. Some of the schools have played each other for well over a century. The "Big Matches" between schools get far more publicity and press coverage than any first-class club matches. The associated parades and carnivals create a festival atmosphere and are now embedded in the local culture. The original Big Match between Royal College and St Thomas's College, two elite boys' schools in Colombo, dates back to 1879. By the beginning of the First World War in 1914, there were three Big Matches on the island, one of which was played between the two elite schools in Kandy, St Anthony's College and Trinity College, the recognized crucibles for schoolboys. Since school cricket teams are age denoted, Murali, who was born in 1972, and Sanga, born in 1977, did not actually face each other on the field in any of the "Trinity-Anthonian" Big Matches.

Murali and Sanga began their cricketing careers at a time when international cricket in Sri Lanka was still in its infancy. Sri Lanka had not yet attained international Test status, and even opportunities to watch high-level cricket were limited.[5] Although future talent was being developed through the school system, the game was raw, coaching was undeveloped, and the odds of a player rising to international star status seemed insurmountable.

Sri Lanka attained Test status, the highest designation in international cricket, in 1981 after years of canvassing with the Marylebone Cricket Club (MCC). The MCC is England's original cricket club established in 1787, its home grounds being the hallowed Lord's Cricket Ground in St John's Wood, London. The MCC evolved over time to become the governing body for international cricket until the establishment of the International Cricket Council (ICC) in the early 1990s. Until 1981, the only countries enjoying Test status were England (1877), Australia (1877), South Africa (1889), the West Indies (1928), New Zealand (1930), India (1932), and Pakistan (1952). For a while, it seemed like only these seven countries would ever play Test cricket. However, after a hiatus of thirty years, Sri Lanka managed to gain entry as the eighth country by displaying skills in both cricket and diplomacy. Subsequent to Sri Lanka's ascension to Test status in 1981, two other countries have been admitted to the Test cricket club: Zimbabwe in 1992 and Bangladesh in 2000.[6]

Notably, all of the ICC's Test-playing nations were once part of the British Empire through varying degrees of colonization. Understandably, there has always been particular joy for Sri Lankans (and other former British colonies) when the English are defeated in cricket. Sri Lanka also revels when it defeats its neighbouring superpower, India.

The story of how Sri Lanka achieved Test status from its humble beginnings in cricket is a consequence of diplomacy, determination, and skill. Sri Lanka's inclusion as a Test country in 1981 can be mainly attributed to Gamini Dissanayake, a senior cabinet minister in the Sri who delivered a watershed speech to the MCC. Dissanayake was a lawyer by profession as well as a great orator with a dynamic personality. At the time, there was a feeling among MCC committee members that Sri Lanka should wait several more years before being admitted to the fold. However, Dissanayake was persuasive as he unleashed his charm, political savvy, oratorical skills, and legal mind with a promise to deliver on various infrastructure commitments to the MCC. In 2001, journalist David Hopps wrote: "The cricket world will be forever grateful that nearly 30 years ago the mission to grant Sri Lanka Test status was successful."[7]

The Sri Lankans played their first Test, fittingly against England, in Colombo in February 1982. After attaining Test status, the government established funding for proper cricket to be played all over the island. Consequently, as the selection pool of talent increased, Sri Lanka began to achieve greater success at the international level. By the time Sri Lanka achieved Test match status in 1981, Murali was nine years old and Sanga was four, which meant that they were coming of age at a time when opportunities were beginning to open.

Indeed, after those heady days of the 1980s, the popularity and excitement of cricket in Sir Lanka has grown dramatically in the last few decades, much of which can be attributed to the popularity of our two subjects. Another factor is that cricket officials had figured out ways to create shorter, though no less competitive, formats for the game, such as one-day cricket and Twenty-20 (or T20) cricket, a roughly three-hour game limited to twenty overs per side. In whatever format, the drama in the sport has historically been known as the "glorious uncertainty of cricket." In the *Wisden Cricket Almanack*, Rowland Ryder writes:

> Among the myriad delights of cricket, not least is the glorious uncertainty of the game. Nothing is certain in cricket except its uncertainty. It is not likely that a batsman will hit every ball of an over for six; that a last wicket stand will add three hundred runs to the score; that a wicket-keeper will take off his pads and do the hat trick: none of these things are anything more than remotely possible, yet all of them have happened; and improbable events, their duration in time varying from a split second to a long drawn out week, interesting, exhilarating, something unbearably exciting, are happening every year that cricket is played.[8]

Murali: Sport Triumphing over Ethnic Divisions

As mentioned earlier, Murali's grandfather emigrated from southern India and came to Ceylon, as the country was then called, to work in the tea plantations run by the British. Not much is known about Murali's grandfather, however, as he eventually went back to India, although his sons stayed on and established themselves in the central hill capital of Kandy, an area adjacent to the high mountains where the best tea plantations flourish.

Murali's opportunity to succeed at cricket from a young age shows how age-old antagonisms can be overcome by the egalitarian nature of sport, particularly spectator sports that engulf whole nations in fervent national pride. It is true to say that when important cricket matches involving the Sri Lankan team are being played, especially the shorter versions of ODI and T20, the nation comes to a halt, with most people watching the progress of play on TV in their homes or even their offices while very little work gets done. A palpable "cricket above all else" attitude is omnipresent, much to the detriment of office productivity, although on the positive side the obsession creates a socially sanctioned sense of national unity where it is sorely needed.

Murali was disadvantaged, both economically in terms of his family's vocation and socially as part of a minority ethnic group. Murali rarely gives interviews, but he discusses his ethnicity and childhood in an interview with Peter Roebuck in the Melbourne newspaper the *Age* in November 2010:

> PETER ROEBUCK (PR): Let's talk about your background. Tell me about your ancestors.
>
> MUTTIAH MURALITHARAN (MM): They come from India. I still have [the] right to live there. My grandfather came to Sri Lanka to work on a tea plantation. Afterwards he went back, but my father and his brothers stayed, and they built a biscuit factory in Kandy in the 1950s. All sorts of biscuits. Still we have that.
>
> PR: Growing up as a Tamil in Sri Lanka wasn't an easy thing in your early days?
>
> MM: There were riots, but after 1983, it was normal. Remember: I was staying at hostel in school for seven years and living with many Sinhalese and Tamils in the same dormitories, so it was not that difficult.
>
> PR: But in the early days a lot of harm was done to the Tamils. Do you have any memories of that?
>
> MM: Our factory and our house were burnt down in 1977, and that was painful for a time. We were saved by Sinhalese. They came and stopped the crazy people before they killed us. We never forgot that. We rebuilt them and moved on. That was our family way. We are businessmen not politicians. My father kept things as simple as possible.
>
> PR: Do you think that these troubles and growing up in a mixed community helped to give you strength of character? The Tamils had a hard time.
>
> MM: The Sinhalese as well. They had hard times when the Communist Party came. [T]hey were targeted and a lot of people were killed.

PR: You've never spoken up on political issues. You've been a unifying figure. Is that how you see yourself?

MM: Our lives in Kandy were mostly fine. I could not talk about problems I had not seen.[9]

The "hostel in school" to which Murali refers is the hostel of St Anthony's College in Kandy, a private school run by Benedictine monks. It is interesting to note that as opposed to the English system that, nevertheless, inspired such institutions during colonization, Sri Lanka's private schools foster a sense of egalitarian citizenship despite the challenges of a multicultural, multi-ethnic, and multi-religious society. Here was Murali, a Tamil follower of the Hindu religion, enrolled in a school run by Catholic Benedictine monks, some of whom came from Italy. Similarly, as we discuss later, Sanga, a Sinhalese and a follower of Buddhism, was placed at the city's other high-profile academy, Trinity College, run by the British Anglican Church through the Ceylon Missionary Society.

Murali grew up in a Sri Lanka where ethnic fissures were a by-product of many factors including land and hunger in an overpopulated island, "official language" issues, job shortages, and terrorism as a result of a conflict that was being fought between the majority Sinhalese and the minority Tamils. Although the origins of the conflict date back more than two thousand years when there were repeated invasions of the island from southern India, there were intervening centuries of peace due to various geographical and political factors, including 450 years of colonization by European powers.[10]

Murali began playing school cricket at eight years of age and went on to become a schoolboy cricketing prodigy with a haul of over a hundred wickets in a fourteen-game season in 1990–1991 and winning the coveted title of Bata Schoolboy Cricketer of the Year, an award that considers players from all schools in Sri Lanka.[11] Following his storied schoolboy career, Murali was recruited to play for the Tamil Union club while being included in the Sri Lanka "A" team that toured England in 1991. Although that tour was not very successful, by 1992, at the age of just twenty, he joined the Sri Lanka Test team and played his first Test match in August against the Australians. During this otherwise unremarkable match, however, Murali took one wicket that put his extraordinary skills on display and focused the spotlight on him with the promise of greatness to come. Murali pitched a ball to Tom Moody that had the most unusual movement in the sense that it bounced in a completely unanticipated direction. Moody recalled: "I can clearly remember the ball he got me out with. It almost pitched off the strip and spun back five feet to bowl me middle-and-off while I was padding up. We thought he was a leg-spinner; his action was that unusual."[12]

Murali's form continued to improve, and he played a pivotal role in most of Sri Lanka's matches, even though the team's wins were few and far between. Arjuna Ranatunga, the Sri Lanka captain and a Sinhalese Buddhist, had absolute faith in Murali despite the traditional ethnic divide, believing that Murali's presence would herald a new age for Sri Lanka's short, struggling Test history. Murali exceeded the high expectations and continued to mesmerise batsmen from opposing teams, both in Sri Lanka and overseas, even when Sri Lanka as a team failed miserably.

By the last quarter of 1995, Murali had played in twenty-two Tests against internationally renowned cricket powers such as Australia, England, New Zealand, South Africa, India, and Pakistan while taking eighty wickets, although his accompanying bowling average allowing 32.7 runs per 100 balls was not that flattering. In the midst of this remarkable run came the fateful Boxing Day Test against Australia in Melbourne in 1995, a match that was destined to change some fundamental rules in relation to bowling and umpiring.

Murali was bowling against Australia in the second Test in front of a huge crowd of fifty-five thousand spectators at the hallowed Melbourne Cricket Ground. Suddenly, Australian umpire Darrell Hair called Murali for "throwing," which in cricketing parlance means bending one's arm at the elbow and straightening it while making the delivery, the sort of action that is characteristic of a baseball throw. Throwing is illegal in cricket and is ruled as a "no-ball," which means that the batsman cannot be called out, a run is added to the batting side's total, and the bowler has to bowl an extra ball. Hair continued to no-ball Murali, making the call seven times in three overs. Murali had by then already bowled three overs in this Test and had also bowled in twenty-two Tests previously without incident, using the same action, and was therefore completely baffled by the repeated charges now.[13]

As the controversy continued, there was much discussion involving Sri Lankan captain Ranatunga and others in team management. After yet another no-ball ruling by Hair, the team decided to make Murali bowl from the other end of the pitch to avoid Hair's judgment, and he did so for another twelve overs that day without further no-balling. What was more puzzling was that Hair, being at the bowler's end, did not have the necessary square-on (90 degree) view of the bowling action, yet he assigned to himself the authority normally given to the square leg umpire, who is in a much better position to judge the action. To add to the controversy, Murali bowled many more overs during the Test with Hair as the square leg umpire without any more protests from either umpire. This led to various allegations including racism against the Australians. There was a sense that Murali was considered too talented for a Sri Lankan and, therefore, must have been cheating. The claims of racial discrimination were ironic, since such claims would be expected to come from the majority Sinhalese–dominated Sri Lanka Cricket Board and not from some other source. Murali would later address these events in his aforementioned interview with Peter Roebuck:

PR: You had a great time in Melbourne yesterday, but in 1995 it was not so good. On Boxing Day you were called for throwing from the bowler's end. What was your reaction?

MM: I was shocked. Darrell Hair had umpired me so many times before. Before the match I had bowled 10 overs in Sydney in a one-day game. So I was very surprised when he said I was illegal next match.

PR: What was it like to be called in front of 55,000 people on the first day of a series?

MM: I was so upset. The team was behind me, and I was able to change ends, but that's not real cricket. He had made up his mind what he wanted to do. That should not happen to another bowler. It's very embarrassing. A single umpire cannot decide on the career of a bowler. If you are narrow-minded, then you will see it that way.

PR: Don Bradman said it was the worst umpiring decision he had seen, and that you were obviously not throwing. Not every Australian was on your case. How did you feel that night?

MM: It was terrible because I didn't know what to do or what was going to happen to my career.

PR: Alone among modern bowlers, you put your arm in a splint, went live on television and bowled all your variations. You went to England with Michael Slater and Mark Nicholas in charge, both [sceptics] at the time, and bowled with your arm in the splint. Both changed their minds. What made you do that?

MM: Because I always thought I was not doing anything wrong—it's an illusion caused by my wrist and the way my joints and arm are built. To the naked eye it looks like throwing, but when you use technology, it shows I don't throw. I have gone through more tests than any other bowler since 1995 and passed them all. But I wanted to prove it. But still I was being booed in Australia, so a reporter gave me the idea and I thought it might end the talk.

PR: What material was used?

MM: Doctors said plaster of Paris can bend, so we put in steel rods. They weighed two pounds, which made it harder to bowl. But I bowled [the] same pace.

PR: Nicholas said there was no way a bowler could straighten his arm in that splint. It's a pity more Australians have not seen the footage. They say it's too expensive to buy. These things seem to crop up only in Australia. Why is that?

MM: Hard to say. Maybe the two umpires [were] premeditated. Maybe someone [was] behind it. I don't know.[14]

In 1996, Murali's action was subjected to scientific biomechanical analysis by researchers at both the University of Western Australia in Perth and the Hong Kong University of Science and Technology, who concluded that the action was legitimate.[15] To be sure, Darrell Hair was no stranger to controversy both before and after the Murali incident, for instance during the 1992 Adelaide Test between Australia and India where Hair was umpiring, and which Australia won. *Wisden Cricketers' Almanack* reported that the match was "marred ... by controversy on lbw [leg before wicket] decisions—eight times Indians were given out, while all but two of their own appeals were rejected."[16] Subsequently, Hair was involved in litigation with the ICC on other matters.

The Murali fiasco was one that, among others, acted as a catalyst for the ICC to eventually enact rules appointing umpires from non-participating countries for all international matches. It also led to the further development and refinement of biomechanical analysis of bowlers' actions and to the revision of the ICC rules governing throwing such that the permissible elbow extension or straightening was changed from a range of 5 to 10 degrees to the current 15 degrees, as it was found that 99 percent of bowlers examined exceeded the existing elbow flexion limits.[17] Moreover, this matter also brought Murali to international attention. The resolution concerning his arm action was critical, as it established that he was a truly great bowler rather than simply a cheater. Furthermore, he has impacted the game in terms of rule changes probably more than any other cricketer.

Murali went on to become the greatest Test bowler of all time, ending his Test cricket career in spectacular fashion by taking his eight hundredth and last Test wicket with the last ball of his last over in his last Test match in 2010.[18] There is no other bowler on the horizon who appears likely to match this phenomenal record, as Murali has amassed 534 wickets in ODI matches. He held the number one spot in the ICC's player rankings for Test bowlers for a record period of 1,711 days, which times out to roughly four and a half years.

Sanga: Pursuing Sport amid Familial Expectations

Unlike Murali, whose grandfather was an immigrant labourer brought by the British to work in the tea fields, Sanga was raised in Kandy by a privileged family with an aristocratic lineage dating back to the era of the Kandyan kings.

As with many of the Kandyan privileged classes, all of whom were Sinhalese Buddhists, the children were, paradoxically, sent to study at the elite Anglican school Trinity College by parents who saw the benefits of a Western liberal education emphasising all-round development and egalitarianism over privilege as a means to success in the wider world.

Sanga thrived at Trinity, playing the violin and participating in most of the sports that the school provided in the junior section (ages five to twelve), namely badminton, tennis, table tennis, swimming, and, of course, cricket. A natural at sports, he won junior national colours for badminton and tennis. However, the principal of the school wanted him to concentrate and excel in one activity and persuaded Sanga's mother that the boy should take up cricket. Thus began a career that was to take Sanga to the top of the cricket world.[19]

As he grew up, Sanga played for his school's cricket sides at all age levels beginning with teams in the under-thirteen circuit. In schoolboy cricket, Sanga was ultimately awarded the Trinity Lion, the most prestigious yearly sporting prize at Trinity College given to a member of the senior team. Sanga earned the award due to his remarkable batting and wicket-keeping performances in the 1996 school season.[20]

Trinity College has always tried to foster what the school refers to as "the complete man," one who is an all-rounder in academics, sport, and other extracurricular activities. Sanga was the definition of the complete man and was accordingly awarded the prestigious Ryde Gold Medal in 1996.[21] Presented each year to the "best all-round boy" at Trinity, the Ryde Gold Medal is the highest honour that the school can bestow, with the recipient being chosen via secret ballot conducted among the senior boys, the staff, and the school's principal. The prize has been awarded at least since 1894. All parents of Trinity students hope that their son will win this coveted award and, therefore, try to foster a balance between academics and sport.[22]

Sanga's father, Kshema Sangakkara, a well-known lawyer in Kandy, was no different. As Sanga remarked during an interview on ESPN's online cricket site Cricinfo, Kshema would "throw him balls and instruct him on technique in the backyard of their beautiful hillside home in Kandy." The article goes on to explain that "Sanga had designs to follow his father into the [legal] profession before cricket called him properly, part-way through law school, at 22." Maybe Kshema, while promoting Sanga's cricketing ambitions, also held out hope that his son would follow him as a lawyer. In any event, once Sanga achieved the rank of captain on the Sri Lanka Test team, he had the full support of his father, who continued to be his most ardent and perhaps critical supporter. To quote from the interview again, Sanga's father remarked: "Actually, he has never reached my expectations." He continued: "You see, now, for example, Don Bradman was one person whose every other match gave him a century.... According to Bradman, it is he who gets out—the bowler can't get him out. So Kumar must perfect first the art of not getting out, and the balance will work for itself."[23]

As mentioned earlier, upon leaving school, Sanga's first choice of career was to be a lawyer like his father, and he entered the Law Faculty of the University of Colombo. However, fate had other plans. While studying for his law degree, Sanga continued to play club cricket. Whereas Murali gravitated to the Tamil Union Club, Sanga played for the Nondescripts Cricket Club (NCC) in Colombo. As Sanga stated in a later interview, he really blossomed at age nineteen while playing at NCC and "seeing real competition . . . in a very competitive surrounding, amongst better known players."[24]

In 2000, Sanga made a dramatic entry into international matches, playing for the Sri Lanka "A" team and scoring an impressive 156 runs against Zimbabwe in only 140 balls, which ensured his selection to the Test team. But it also foretold doom to his university studies, of which he was very nearly on the verge of completion. The demands of Test cricket and the rigorous levels of training and travel precluded any opportunities to attend classes or sit for exams. Nevertheless, years later, Sanga was cited as the inspiration to continue his academic studies by Bangladesh captain Mushfiqur Rahim, who went on to receive a master's degree.[25] Perhaps if Sanga had envisioned beforehand the immense amount of time and effort, the endless hours of practice that were needed to make the national team, leave alone achieve success in the international arena, he might have had second thoughts about abandoning a university education for cricket. Fortunately for the game of cricket, Sanga persevered.

It is worth reflecting on the possibility that Sanga the cricketer could easily have been Sanga the lawyer. Giving up his university education was a risky decision at a young age, compounded by the fact that cricket is full of what are often referred to as "glorious uncertainties," which might more accurately be called "inglorious certainties." A lawyer with Sanga's oratorical skills can have a lucrative career and a comfortable life almost anywhere, whereas a cricketer who does not make it to the big leagues and is unable to have sustained success over a long period of time can end up in penury. Indeed, there are few if any active cricketers with a university-level formal education. And in a country like Sri Lanka, the level of adulation by fans is such that one rarely sees a press article that is critical of the star players. Young people often overlook the fact that there is more to life than cricket, much to the detriment of their studies. In that respect, Sanga is perhaps not the best example for everyone to follow, as few reach Test level success while tens of thousands fall by the wayside.

The MCC is aware of this problem and has initiated a program called "A degree in life, not just cricket" with the goal to prepare cricketers for "life after the game." As the journalist George Dobell so eloquently states on the subject:

Professional sport is a seductive beast. It sucks you in with whispered promises of glory and glamour and spits you out with broken dreams and an aching body. For every cricketing career that ends in a raised bat and warm ovation, there are a thousand that end on a physio's treatment table or in an uncomfortable meeting in a director of cricket's office. Many, many more stall well before that level.

And that's where the trouble starts. Young men trained for little other than sport can suddenly find themselves in a world for which they have little training and little preparation. Without status, salary or support, the world can seem an inhospitable place. It is relevant, surely, that the suicide rate of former cricketers is three times the national average.[26]

By the age of twenty-two, Sanga had graduated to Test cricket, debuting against South Africa in July 2000.[27] The following year he achieved his first Test century.[28] In his second Test match, he won his first Man of the Match award, giving further rise to the notion that a new star was on the horizon in Sri Lanka. Sanga became the captain of the Sri Lanka national team for two years beginning in 2009. He then decided that it was not for him, stating that "captaining Sri Lanka is a job that ages you very quickly.... It's rarely a job you will last long in.... I had a two-year stint, and I enjoyed it at times, certainly on the field where our results showed we were one of the top two sides in the world for one-and-a-half years, especially in the shorter form of the game."[29] What was left unsaid, but broadly hinted at, was the debilitating effect the politics of the game in Sri Lanka was having on him and the other players. A suave diplomat as always, he did not directly attack any politicians, but everyone got the message. But as S. R. Pathiravithana queried in the *Sunday Times*:

> One of the greatest cricketing mysteries of the twenty-first century would be as to why Sanga, after leading his side to a Cricket World Cup final, turned his back on the crown a few hours later and decided to abdicate. Yes, we have listened to reasons touted, but none of them are plausible. The truth is yet to arrive, but we at this end do not want to hear it.[30]

In the midst of his cricket career, Sanga delivered the vaunted 2011 MCC Spirit of Cricket Cowdrey Lecture at Lord's, becoming the youngest person and the first current international player to deliver the lecture, for which he was widely praised by the cricketing community. The hour-long speech appeared in the front pages of almost all of Britain's mainstream newspapers, a first for any speech of this nature.

In his remarks, Sanga spoke reverently of his father's heroism during perhaps the most defining week of Sri Lanka's post-colonial history. At that time, in late July 1983, Sinhalese mobs scoured parts of the nation hounding Tamils, killing them, and burning down houses in retaliation for a Liberation Tigers of Tamil

Eelam (LTTE) ambush on troops in the north. Sanga remembered watching his parents, Kshema and Kumari, rally together some thirty-five Tamil neighbours and friends, providing refuge at Engeltine Cottage, Sanga's family home, at great personal risk.[31]

Journalist Peter Roebuck referred to Sanga's Cowdrey Lecture in reverent terms, insisting that it was one of the most stirring speeches on cricket he'd ever heard in that it grounded the game in Sri Lanka's own troubled history while imploring administrators to safeguard cricket for, if nothing else, its immense social value. Sri Lankan Tamils have not forgotten what brave Sinhalese men and women like Kshema and Kumari did in those dark times. Their story certainly has not escaped the denizens of the once-embattled northern city of Jaffna, where Sanga is wildly, unreservedly popular—where he is every boy's idol and every coach's favourite exemplar. "What his father did for Tamils in 1983," Roebuck muses, "is rarely far from northerners' lips when Sanga comes up in discussion."[32]

Sanga's various records are too numerous to elaborate in detail, but a few are worth noting. Sanga has thirty-eight Test centuries including eleven double centuries (i.e., 200 runs and above) and one triple century with 319 against Bangladesh in February 2014. To put this in perspective, there have been a total of only twenty-eight triple centuries in Test cricket since the first one was recorded in 1930. Sanga's tally of eleven double centuries is second only to legendary Don Bradman's tally of twelve. He is also the first cricketer ever to amass more than 150 scores in four consecutive Test matches. Along with teammate Mahela Jayawardene, Sanga holds the world record for the highest-scoring partnership in Test cricket—624 runs against South Africa in 2006, when Sanga scored 287 runs and Mahela 374. And as a wicketkeeper, Sanga has the third-highest number of dismissals in ODIs, 382, which includes 81 stumpings, the highest ever for a wicketkeeper in one-day international cricket. Moreover, Sanga was the fastest batsman in terms of innings to reach 8,000, 9,000, and 11,000 runs in Test cricket.[33]

In 2012, Sanga had an unprecedented year with five notable distinctions. He was awarded the Sir Garfield Sobers Trophy for being the ICC Cricketer of the Year, the Test Cricketer of the Year award, and the People's Choice award. He was also selected to the World Test and World One-Day cricket squads. Sanga has collected many more awards throughout the course of his career.

Sanga retired from the T20 format soon after leading Sri Lanka to victory in the T20 World Cup in March 2014. He retired from ODI cricket after the 2015 Cricket World Cup, where he established an all-time tournament record of scoring four consecutive centuries. But in August 2015, at the age of thirty-seven, Sanga announced his retirement from Test cricket after the second Test match with India in Colombo. The tournament marked his farewell to international cricket in front of a partisan Sri Lankan crowd.

Beyond Cricket

We have made the case that through different and difficult paths, Murali and Sanga have risen to the pinnacles of world cricket. However, as icons and as ambassadors for Sri Lanka, their impact has been felt beyond cricket.

While both Murali and Sanga, whose faces adorn numerous advertising billboards around Colombo and other parts of Sri Lanka, have earned money by endorsing products, they also lend their names and make their presence felt for charities, each having established his own charitable trust. Murali partnered with his Sinhalese manager, Kushil Gunasekara, to establish the charity Foundation of Goodness. With the support of cricketers and administrators from England and Australia, this charity raises funds to support local needs in Seenigama, a coastal village in the Sinhalese-dominated south of the island. The foundation helps children, providing education and training, health care, sporting facilities, and other forms of assistance.

When the Boxing Day tsunami of 2004 devastated many parts of Sri Lanka, including Seenigama, Murali mobilised resources to bring aid to the affected people. Due in Seenigama twenty minutes after the tsunami hit for a prize distribution ceremony involving his charity, he himself was able to change plans at literally the last moment and narrowly escaped injury or worse. In the subsequent rebuilding efforts for which cement was badly needed, Murali signed a barter deal with the Lafarge Cement Company to provide cement in return for his endorsements of their products. Subsequently, with the support of Bryan Adams, the Canadian pop music star, Murali raised funds to build a community swimming pool in Seenigama, where hundreds had died needlessly because of their inability to swim.

With the ending of the war in 2009, Murali was able to extend his charitable work to the Tamil-dominated areas of the north and is building a sports complex, information technology and English training centres, and other facilities in Mankulam. And in June 2004, Murali was appointed by the United Nations World Food Programme as an ambassador to fight hunger among schoolchildren.[34]

Sanga has also been involved in charitable work, giving freely of both his time and his money. For some time, he has been an ambassador for the ICC's Think Wise campaign, a partnership with the Joint United Nations Programme on HIV/AIDS (UNAIDS) and the United Nations Children's Emergency Fund (UNICEF) that works to eliminate stigma and discrimination and promote HIV and AIDS awareness. The Test-playing nations are home to around a third of the world's population living with HIV.[35]

In Sri Lanka, Sanga has also been helping to bridge the ethnic gap, often in joint efforts with Murali. Large crowds of Tamil people in the north crowded to meet Sanga and get his autograph when he attended the 2014 Murali Harmony Cup cricket tournament in Jaffna. The Murali Harmony Cup tournament is a reconciliation T20 tournament to promote community building and friendship in post-war Sri Lanka and is organised by the Foundation of Goodness—the charity that now involves Murali, Sanga, their cricket teammate Mahela Jayawardene, and other friends and colleagues. In this tournament, cricket is played between schools and clubs, both men's and women's, from the Sinhalese-dominated south and the Tamil-dominated north. The matches are held in the north, which was deprived of sporting activities for decades during the war.

Beyond the Pitch

Murali and Sanga, two all-time greats in the world of cricket, were both born in Sri Lanka but came from two often antagonistic ethnic groups and from two very different social milieus. Playing cricket for the same team but with decidedly opposing skills and facing common adversaries over many years no doubt reinforced their mutual respect for each other and their joint efforts for national reconciliation.

Together, Murali and Sanga helped build Sri Lankan cricket from its infancy into a world cricketing power. For twenty years, they were the two most dominant faces of Sri Lankan cricket while becoming ambassadors for the game. Today, with their sporting careers behind them, they are widely admired and represent the hopes and strengths of a country once divided by war that today appears to be on its way to harmony and greater prosperity.

In terms of how they will be remembered, it is worth noting that Sri Lanka's written history stretches back two thousand years, and that Sri Lankans love to evoke memories of their heroes. We believe that Murali and Sanga will be remembered as two of the greatest cricketers of all time, but somehow they transcend the status of celebrity athlete as we have come to recognize them today. As Sanga remarked to the *Guardian* in 2011: "It is always going to be something like sport that brings people together.... [C]ricket has been the heal-all of social evils, the one thing that held the country together during 30 years of war."[36]

Perhaps this is their greater legacy. Through their sheer excellence and accomplishments, Murali and Sanga provided a diversion for people during difficult times. And their role in uniting the country is not likely to be underestimated by those in the know.

Notes

1. An over consists of six balls delivered by a bowler to batsmen. In a fifty-overs match (as in one-day cricket), the maximum number of allowable overs by one bowler is ten. Thus, Sri Lanka showed great confidence in their young star Murali by allowing him to bowl ten overs in the World Cup final.
2. A wicket, also known as a "dismissal," is the baseball equivalent of an out. In one-day cricket, a team's batting innings terminates when either ten wickets have occurred or fifty overs (i.e., three hundred balls) have been bowled.
3. K. M. de Silva, *A History of Sri Lanka* (Berkeley: University of California Press, 1981).
4. "First class" in this context refers to a match between two international teams. In modern parlance, "first class" means a match played by two teams of eleven players each over a duration of three days, usually the highest level of cricket in any country.
5. In terms of international play, where lasting reputations are forged, a cricket Test match is the original and longest version of the game. Test matches can last up to five days, often with no winner, which may sound strange to those more familiar with North American sports. The term "Test" comes from fact that the five-day contest is a gruelling test of skill and endurance.
6. *Wisden Cricketers' Almanack*, ESPN Cricinfo Online Archive, 1864–2014, at http://www.espncricinfo.com/wisdenalmanack/content/story/almanack/index.htm.
7. David Hopps, "The Speech That Set Free Sri Lanka Cricket and Glued a Troubled Nation," *Guardian*, May 18, 2011, at http://www.theguardian.com/sport/blog/2011/may/18/sri-lanka-cricket-speech.
8. Rowland Ryder, "Nothing is Certain in Cricket Except Its Uncertainty, 1974: The Glorious Uncertainty," *Wisden Cricketers' Almanack*, ESPN Cricinfo, at http://www.espncricinfo.com/wisdenalmanack/content/story/152487.html.
9. Peter Roebuck, "The Kandy Man," *Age*, November 5, 2010, at http://www.smh.com.au/sport/cricket/the-kandy-man-20101104-17fsj.html.
10. P. L. de Silva, "The Growth of Tamil Paramilitary Nationalisms: Sinhala Chauvinism and Tamil Responses," *South Asia: Journal of South Asian Studies* 20 (1997): 97–118.
11. A. C. de Silva, "Murali Won Observer Schoolboy Cricketer of the Year Title in 1991," *Sunday Observer* (Colombo), March 16, 2008, at http://www.sundayobserver.lk/2008/03/16/sp001.asp.
12. "Murali Is a Unique Bowler in Modern Cricket: Moody," DNA India, December 3, 2007, at http://www.dnaindia.com/sport/report-murali-is-a-unique-bowler-in-modern-cricket-moody-1136961.
13. "Muralitharan No-Balled by Hair," *People's Ground*, December 17, 2007.
14. Roebuck, "The Kandy Man."
15. Ravi Goonetilleke, "Biomechanical Tests Done on Muttiah Muralitharan at Hong Kong University of Science and Technology," at http://www-ieem.ust.hk/dfaculty/ravi/murali01.html.
16. *Wisden Cricketers' Almanack*.
17. René E. D. Ferdinands and Uwe G. Kersting, "An Evaluation of Biomechanical Measures of Bowling Action Legality in Cricket," *Sports Biomechanics* 6, no. 3 (September 2007); and "ICC Relaxes Bowling Regulations," BBC Sport, February 5, 2005, at http://news.bbc.co.uk/sport2/hi/cricket/4238403.stm.

18. Sriram Veera, "Murali Gets 800, Sri Lanka Win by Ten Wickets," ESPN Cricinfo, at http://www.espncricinfo.com/sri-lanka-v-india-2010/content/story/468370.html.

19. "Principal Delighted with Former Student Sangakkara," *Cricket World*, July 14, 2007, at http://www.cricketworld.com/principal-delighted-with-former-student-sangakkara/12329.htm.

20. Upananda Jayasundara, "Sangakkara Receives 'Super Lions' Award," *Daily News* (Colombo), February 12, 2005, at http://archives.dailynews.lk/2005/02/12/sp006.html.

21. Ibid.

22. Ibid.

23. Andrew Fidel Fernando, "My Father, My Critic," ESPN Cricinfo, December 20, 2013, at http://www.espncricinfo.com/magazine/content/story/701961.html.

24. Premasara Epasinghe, "Kumar Sangakkara's Long Journey to World's Leading Batsman," *The Island*, September 29, 2010, at http://pdfs.island.lk/2010/09/30/p12.pdf.

25. Mohammad Isam, "Bangladesh News: Mushfiqur Bags Masters Degree in History," ESPN Cricinfo, December 25, 2012, at http://www.espncricinfo.com/bangladesh/content/story/598478.html.

26. George Dobell, "A Degree in Life, Not Just Cricket," ESPN Cricinfo, June 22, 2012, at http://www.espncricinfo.com/mcc/content/story/569454.html.

27. "South Africa Tour of Sri Lanka, 1st Test: Sri Lanka v South Africa at Galle," ESPN Cricinfo, July 20–23, 2000, at http://www.espncricinfo.com/ci/engine/match/63893.html.

28. A century is a cricket term that denotes scoring at least one hundred runs in a match.

29. Andrew Miller, "Reluctant Sangakkara Admits Captaincy Headache," ESPN Cricinfo, June 15, 2011, at http://www.espncricinfo.com/england-v-sri-lanka-2011/content/story/519173.html.

30. S. R. Pathiravithana, "Kumar Says Test Cricket Is the Pinnacle," *Sunday Times* (Colombo), September 18, 2011, at http://www.sundaytimes.lk/110918/Sports/spt09.html.

31. "Kumar Sangakkara's 2011 MCC Spirit of Cricket Cowdrey Lecture in Full," *Telegraph*, July 5, 2011.

32. Peter Roebuck, "Sangakkara's Challenge to Cricket," ESPN Cricinfo, July 5, 2011, at http://www.espncricinfo.com/magazine/content/story/522022.html.

33. "Statistics / Statsguru / KC Sangakkara," ESPN Cricinfo, at http://stats.espncricinfo.com/ci/engine/player/50710.html?class=1;type=allround.

34. Charlie Austin, "Murali Leads from the Front," ESPN Cricinfo, January 5, 2005, at http://www.espncricinfo.com/srilanka/content/story/145035.html.

35. "Cricket Unites for People Living with HIV on World Aids Day," UNICEF, November 29, 2010; and Andy Bull, "Kumar Sangakkara Focuses on HIV Charity Work after Test Debacle," *Guardian*, June 2, 2011, at http://www.theguardian.com/sport/2011/jun/02/kumar-sangakkara-hiv-charity.

36. Bull, "Kumar Sangakkara Focuses on HIV Charity Work."

Grete Waitz
The Art of Hurrying Slowly

—Theresa Walton-Fisette

Introduction

In 1986, Olympian and writer Kenny Moore noted of Oslo's renowned Bislett Stadium:

> This is what astronauts say: The multitude below boosts a few up, to go where no one has ever gone before, and to draw the rest of us up there as well. Bislett's runner or skater, driving toward a record, is equally an extension of his audience. The act of separating oneself from history's pack becomes the act of affirming one's inseparability.[1]

He may well have been writing about one of the running stars of Oslo, Norway's own Grete Waitz.

Variously titled the "Queen of the Marathons"[2] and the "Maker of the Marathon"[3] by historians of running and women's sport, Waitz came to women's marathoning at a transformative time in the sport, and she played a central role as a transformative figure for its growth. She held world records in distances from 3,000 meters to the marathon. She won the inaugural track and field World Championship marathon in 1983, the prestigious New York City Marathon a record nine times, and the World Cross Country Championships five times. Most importantly, in accomplishing all of her success, she redefined women's possibilities in distance running by bringing her considerable track speed onto the roads, particularly in the marathon.

A reluctant superstar, modest and humble in her interactions with the press and colleagues, the unflinching Norwegian distance runner became an accidental pioneer as she ran longer and longer distances, finally emerging as the premier women's marathon runner at a time when the sport was still developing. Waitz's victory in her first marathon propelled the nascent women's sport to new heights, lending it legitimacy by demonstrating to a typically skeptical running world that women could be competitive in the 26.2-mile event. Waitz's emergence in the women's marathon, running parallel as it does to the development of the sport, marks her as a transformative athletic figure whose reach moves beyond her own unprecedented career and points to a future for equally gifted female distance runners to come.

Future Champion

Born Grete Andersen on October 1, 1953, to John and Reidun Andersen, the woman who would become Grete Waitz developed her talent in running at an early age. She joined Oslo's Vidar Sports Club at the age of twelve. Terje Pedersen, a javelin world record holder, lived in her neighborhood and inspired her to participate in track.[4] Waitz said of Pedersen, "He was my hero. I joined the same club. I wanted to please him so much."[5] Early on she participated in many running, jumping, and throwing events. She did not find success in running until she had the opportunity to run longer distances, a theme that developed over her running career.

In 1969, at age sixteen, Waitz won the Norwegian 400-meter and 800-meter Junior Championship titles. By 1971 she won the open Norwegian Championship 800-meter and 1,500-meter runs, beginning her reign as one of Norway's most elite runners. Yet in her first international competition at the 1971 European Championships in Helsinki, Waitz first experienced the pressure from the Norwegian press that would follow her through her tenure as an elite runner. Moreover, Waitz felt that she was unsupported by the Norwegian coaches and officials when she "ran terribly."[6] As she wrote, "Worse than my performance was the reaction of my countrymen. When I stepped off the track, the coach and team officials kept their distance.... I had lost before, but never had losing been so painful."[7] She said that this early experience fueled her competitive drive and her desire to compete well internationally. Yet it also created a need for her to become more independent of her national sport federation.

However, tragedy struck in Waitz's personal life in 1972. As she wrote, "At age 18, I was in love with one of my older Vidar club mates, who was my training partner and coach. When he became ill and went to the hospital, I just assumed that he would get well and we would live happily ever after."[8] When he died of cancer, Waitz, inconsolable for many months, noted that she used running to help her deal with her grief and heal:

After my boyfriend died, I lost the desire even to eat.... I felt devastated, empty. I saw no reason to do anything, let alone run.... It was my boyfriend's group of friends from the Vidar Club who eventually pulled me out of my slump.... I used that running to help me forget, to help me begin to do other things, to try to live normally again.[9]

She also began seeing the man who was to become her husband, Jack Waitz. Six years older than Grete, Jack Waitz became her coach, mentor, and sometimes training partner for the rest of her life.

In that same year, Waitz made the Norwegian Olympic team in the 1,500-meter run. Although she was one of Norway's best runners, she did not make it out of the preliminary rounds, even as she ran a personal best for the distance at 4:16.[10] For her, just the experience of being at the Olympic Games was the most important thing.[11] It also opened her eyes to the serious politics sometimes infused in sport with the murder of the Israeli athletes and coaches at the Munich Games. At the age of eighteen, she did not fully understand the magnitude of the tragedy, leaving her "perplexed, sad and frightened."[12] Thus, she was, sadly, in some way prepared for more political maneuverings with the Olympic boycotts in 1976, 1980, and 1984.[13]

In 1972, Waitz also started a winning streak in Norway that would last twelve years. She settled into her relationship with Jack, moving in with him in 1973 and marrying him in 1975. Waitz went to school to become a teacher, not seeing running as a viable career with her running days set to expire quickly. Still, at the 1974 European Championships, she was a surprise bronze medalist in the 1,500 meters, bringing her honors as Athlete of the Year in Norway.[14] Waitz credited her success to her husband: "With the help of Jack's coaching advice, I was ranked number one in the world in 1975 for the 1,500 and 3,000 meters, and ran my first world record in the 3,000."[15]

With her continued success in Norway, the expectations for Waitz were high heading into the 1976 Montreal Olympic Games. Her public predictions that a medal was not guaranteed were interpreted as modesty. She feared the Eastern European women in particular. Adding to the pressure was the Janteloven effect. Janteloven, or the Law of Jante, a concept created by Danish-Norwegian author and poet Aksel Sandemose, stereotyped the feeling that Norwegians are "not good enough." As one of Waitz's training partners, former Olympic 1,500-meter runner Arne Kvalheim, explained, "You shouldn't think you are anyone special."[16] Or, as Jack Waitz described it, "In Norway, there's an unwritten law that you shall not think yourself better than someone else, even if you are."[17] As Waitz commented, "I nearly fainted at the sight of the DDR on the East Germans' sweats the first time I had to face them. It was little me from little Norway."[18] Or, as she told *Ms.* magazine, "I feel so very simple and normal myself; I want to be like everybody else, not special."[19] Another story, often told in media accounts, explained how Waitz kept her Olympic and World medals in her kitchen cupboard. Thus, Waitz's modesty ironically made her even more beloved by the Norwegian media and people. For example, she received more votes than Norway's well-liked King Olav V in a Norwegian popularity poll.[20]

Yet the enthusiasm and adulation also created more pressure on Waitz. With a very competitive semifinal field in the 1,500 meters in Montreal, Waitz did not make the finals.

Rising Star

Much of Waitz's limited success early on must be understood in the context of the limited opportunities offered to women runners. The 1,500 meters was the longest distance offered for women at the Olympic Games, and it was not added until 1972. Not until 1984 were the 3,000 meters and the marathon added for women. The 10,000 meters was added in 1988, with the 5,000 meters in 1996 and the steeplechase in 2008, finally bringing women a full slate of distance running opportunities equal to the men's.[21] As Waitz noted of her ability:

> As a child I understood I was better in the 800 than the 400. As I trained[,] I got no faster, only stronger. By 1972 I was running the 800 and 1,500, and I saw I was better in the 1,500, so I trained more and more but still got no faster, just stronger.[22]

Runner and writer Amby Burfoot noted of the buildup to the Montreal Olympic Games, "For an entire year she tried to whip herself into 1500-meter condition. It was purely mind vs. body. Mind had won many training battles. But training was not alchemy. She could not change her body to that of a 1500-meter racer."[23] However, this early building of her speed did impact Waitz's success on the roads, shattering the assumed limits of women's abilities over long distances and building her lasting legacy in the sport.

As writer Kenny Moore, himself an Olympic marathoner, noted: "The element that has allowed Waitz to so embarrass prior long-distance records is her speed, not necessarily raw sprinter's power—that she doesn't have—but an ability to sustain a high percentage of her maximum pace over all kinds of distances."[24] Thus, had Waitz been afforded the opportunity to move up to distances that better suited her, her track career would have been even more impressive. However, this lack of opportunity on the track led Waitz to turn to the roads and eventually dominate the marathon. She may never have stepped off the track competitively had she been born in a different era and been able to contest the 5,000 and 10,000 meters. As Waitz herself remarked in 1985:

> If I hadn't run the New York City Marathon in 1978, I don't know if I would have been running at all today. Road racing really kept me going. I'd been running international track for eight years and I was thinking about quitting. I won the World

Cup, 3,000 meters. I won the World Cross-Country and ran fast times. I was pleased with what I had achieved. I was thinking about quitting because the longest distance for women on the track at that time was only three thousand meters.[25]

Yet the marathon was not her favorite, as she did not like running longer than an hour, using this as an explanation for why she ran all of her workouts so fast. In 1986 she wrote:

> This may come as a complete surprise, but the truth is I really don't like running marathons. Twenty-six and two-tenths miles is definitely not my favorite distance. The five- to ten-mile range is more like it, and it's probably the distance at which I am best.... Despite what the press says, the marathon has never been easy for me.[26]

She ran the marathon because that was what was available to her to continue her athletic career. In doing so, she rewrote the record books and inspired a generation of runners, raising expectations for women's running overall.

After the Montreal Games, Waitz decided she needed a break. She had not taken a day off between 1974 and 1976. Meanwhile, she was working full-time as a teacher with a two-hour commute, training twice a day. As she wrote: "I was tired from training and leading such a busy life, tired of having to bear the pressure and come through for others. I decided to run on my own without the support of the Norwegian Federation scholarship, responsible only to myself."[27] After this break and with her newfound independence, she came back more enthusiastic for her training and ran her fastest times to date. She became a world champion, winning the 3,000 meters at the inaugural International Association of Athletics Federations World Cup in 1977 in Düsseldorf, followed by a win at the 1978 World Cross Country Championships in Glasgow. She earned the bronze medal at the 1978 European Championships in the 3,000 meters.[28] While the Norwegian media was disappointed with the latter third-place finish, these international accomplishments showed how the increased distance boosted Waitz's chances for success.

At this point in her career, Waitz began to seriously consider retirement. She wrote:

> Track had been a wonderful career, but an erratic one as well. There were months and years I trained so hard—at one point running as many as 125 miles in one week—that I'd cry from fatigue.... At this time I felt that no matter how much I trained I wasn't going to get any faster on the track, nor was I going to avoid getting outkicked by the Eastern Europeans.[29]

Fortunately, unbeknown to Waitz at the time, she was about to enter her second running career. Waitz's friend and sometime training partner Knut Kvalheim talked about his experiences with the New York City Marathon. He advised Waitz to consider New York if she planned to run a marathon. Jack Waitz had been trying to get his reluctant wife to run one for some time. With Kvalheim's suggestion and Jack's prompting, she finally decided to do it.[30] Her first New York City Marathon remains one of the most frequently told stories about Waitz.

The New York Marathon

Jack Waitz, who kept himself informed on all types of competitive running, had been reading about elite women in the marathon. He said: "I was one of the guys who talked [Grete] into the marathon. I had to work very hard at it. I told her that her training was as good as or better than the other girls. I was pretty sure she could beat them."[31] Yet the lure of winning was not what swayed Waitz. She thought it might be her only opportunity to visit New York City.

The race came after the track season and before the start of her cross country training. It seemed a good time for an adventure in the United States. The stipulation was, however, that the race organizers would also have to pay for her husband to travel with her. In turn, Jack Waitz sold the entire venture to his wife as a getaway, a second honeymoon, for the two of them. Of course, at this stage in her career, Waitz was virtually unknown in the United States, having never run a marathon before.[32]

When New York City Marathon coordinator Pat Greene got a letter from Waitz requesting expenses for her husband as well, she rejected it. Yet when she ran this decision by Fred Lebow, the race's director, he told her to send them the tickets. He knew of Waitz's success on the track and especially her World Cross Country Championships win. Lebow definitely did not expect her to do particularly well in the marathon, but he did think that given her speed, she might put up an early fast pace that would create the likelihood of a women's world record. Lebow also thought that a world record might help the marathon earn more publicity.[33] One of the top contenders, Marty Cooksy, planned to try to run under 2:30, more than four minutes under the world record. The then-current world record holder, Christa Vahlensieck (2:34:48) of West Germany, was in the race, as was another top US runner, Julie Brown.[34] The race looked to be competitive, which was not always the case during the early years of women's marathon running.[35]

Part of the lore of this story is how well prepared for the race Waitz was—or was not. As she said before the race, "I've never run more than 20 kilometers. I came because I wanted to see New York."[36] Certainly she had never raced any longer distances. Thus, while her talent was known, her ability to handle 26 miles and 385 yards remained a huge question mark. Meanwhile, the honeymooning couple, intent on enjoying their time in New York City, spent the days before the marathon exploring the city on foot.[37] Waitz recounts asking Fred Lebow where to stand at the start, unused to the hundreds of runners lining up for a road race. As she wrote, "The New York City Marathon start on the Verrazano-Narrows Bridge was a virtual sea of people, an overwhelming sight for someone used to standing with a handful of runners on the track."[38]

Waitz started slowly, keying on Vahlensieck and Brown. She did not see Cooksy get out ahead in the lead. The early part of the race went smoothly. Or, as Waitz acknowledged, "I was used to running so much faster. It felt so slow."[39] She stayed with Brown and Vahlensieck until mile 16 and then left them behind, feeling that the pace was too easy. She also eventually caught Cooksy at the mile 18 mark and "startled male marathoners by the score."[40] She was running twenty seconds per mile faster than she had in the first half, though by mile 21 she began to feel the effects of the distance and speed, recalling: "My thighs were getting so sore. And I got a stitch in my side. I almost stopped to walk—I wanted to walk so bad—but I thought I might not start up again if I did. I was sore all over. But I kept going to get it over as fast as possible."[41]

For the last five miles she kept looking for signs of Central Park, trees, greenery, to signal that she was near the end. She began to experience the roller coaster of emotion that the marathon can induce. She wrote:

> By now it had really begun: the pain. I hurt all over—my legs, my side, my shoulders. Never had I hurt so much. I was almost crying. Odd feelings overtook me: anger, frustration, depression, then anger again. When I finally crossed the finish line, it wasn't with a sense of joy and ease, the way the media portrayed it, but with sheer relief and a lot of anger.[42]

Waitz not only won the race, but she did it in world record time—2:32:30—two minutes under the previous best. However, far from thrilled, Waitz threw her shoes down and told her husband, "I'll never do that again!"[43]

The media enthusiastically surrounded her at the finish, asking who she was, how she ran so fast, and, as Amby Burfoot wrote, given the win and world record, asking "Why aren't you even smiling?" To which Waitz replied: "Maybe I'm too tired. The race was very hard. We Norwegians are not as emotional as you. Maybe it's our long, dark winter. And I do not consider this a new world record. Only track races can be official records."[44] Yet 1978 was just the start for Waitz and the New York City Marathon. She came back again in 1979 to win in world-record time (2:27:33) and in the process became the first woman to run under two hours, thirty minutes. She also went on to win the race a record nine times over the course of her career. Her time in 1979, as noted in *Ms.* magazine, was "fast enough to have won every male Olympic marathon up to 1952."[45] Moreover, Waitz placed 102nd out of 9,875 runners—meaning that she beat most of the men in her first attempt at the marathon. Her highest overall place came in 1984 when she came 57th, meaning that she beat 14,533 people, including more than 12,000 men.[46] It was hard to argue that women did not belong. Waitz had ultimately carved out a space for women among the elite of distance running, while also garnering respect for women's distance running overall.

In 1978, after her first win at New York, Waitz had yet to understand the significance of what she had done. But others did, such as the press who surrounded her, which was exactly what Fred Lebow had hoped for, although he had not anticipated Waitz herself to become the new world record holder. Even more enthusiastic were the women who competed with Waitz that day and who watched her run. One spectator was Patti Lyons (later Catalano), who had run 2:41:31 just six weeks earlier to become the eighth-fastest woman in the marathon. She stood along the course, late in the race:

> At about 2:25 into the race we started hearing applause. People were shouting that the first girl was coming. Then I saw her[;] I went absolutely crazy. I was so happy to see a woman going so fast. I saw how thin her body was. She had no cellulite. Her rear didn't shake when she went past us. She looked so pretty running. I kept cheering her on.[47]

Two years later, Catalano followed Waitz to the finish as a competitor, becoming the second woman to run faster than 2:30. Waitz had set a new bar that other women were eager to reach and surpass. During Waitz's subsequent marathon career, she would get faster, but so would the rest of the field, changing the nature of women's marathoning into a globally competitive endeavor. Once women were running faster than two hours, thirty minutes, there was no denying their elite status. This, along with global competition, became a leading impetus for adding the women's marathon to the Olympic Games in 1984. As Patti Hagan wrote:

> While her times caused some very fast men to drop out of those early marathons when they realized they were being beaten by a woman, they helped cause the men of the International Olympic Committee to include a woman's [sic] marathon in the 1984 edition of the Games.[48]

Reluctant Celebrity

By this time, the running boom in the United States was well under way. Already in 1978, Waitz's first year in the New York Marathon, nearly ten thousand people completed the race, almost one thousand of them women. When she ran her last New York Marathon in 1992, there were almost thirty thousand runners, and nearly six thousand of them were women. The marathon meant a great deal in the United States at that time (and has continued to grow in participation since then). As Michael Sandrock argued:

> It was more than her world bests that made those early New York wins some of the most significant in the sport; it was also the world-wide exposure they received. The races were televised, and audiences saw the seemingly calm, cool, nonplussed Waitz run through "the wall" to set records, showing that women could do more than finish a marathon; they could race it.[49]

This opened doors for Waitz that did not exist on the track and that she did not really understand until she became more familiar with the meaning of the New York City Marathon and the running boom in the United States. Yet the marathon running boom was primarily white and middle to upper class and still primarily male. Kenny Moore reported that in the 1978 New York Marathon, 85 percent of the participants "had college degrees. Half had *graduate* degrees. There were 767 lawyers, 547 doctors, 977 teachers. There were 98 company presidents."[50] The doors began to open a bit, at least for women. Yet Waitz also presented a running aesthetic that was not necessarily healthy for women's running. While Waitz herself emphasized her strength, some of her competitors, such as Catalano, attributed her success to her thinness. While her size was natural for Waitz, it introduced an aesthetic not necessarily natural or healthy for other runners.

With media exposure, prize money was growing, along with more open sponsorship opportunities. While Waitz earned nothing but cab fare (and other travel expenses) for her win in 1978, this was an era of "shamateurism" whereby athletes were rewarded for their efforts but not openly so in the form of prize money per se, thus keeping intact their amateur status with national governing bodies and the International Association of Athletics Federations (IAAF). Therefore, it is difficult to determine how much in earnings Waitz took in with her early New York City Marathon wins. One report in 1980 claimed that in 1979 the men's winner earned $10,000 and the women's $5,000.[51] Bill Rodgers, who won the men's race, said that he declined the purse. But Jane Leavy reported that Rodgers received that money as part of his "expenses," and Waitz could not be reached for comment. While under-the-table payments had been disbursed for years, this was believed to be the first time a prize structure had been formulated to award, in decreasing amounts from top to bottom, the top ten finishers for the men and the top five for the women. Some athletes admitted receiving payment, though not on record, since they ran the risk of losing their amateur status and becoming ineligible for international competitions.[52]

Historian Pamela Cooper could claim accurately that by 1982, the New York Marathon was paying out awards totaling in excess of $150,000, with $18,000 going to the men's winner and another $14,000 being awarded to the women's, although this was all done clandestinely.[53] The race reportedly paid $200,000 in 1983, which race director Fred Lebow revealed in his autobiography in 1984.[54] In 1984 the New York Marathon began openly awarding prize money. Waitz won the marathon in 1978, 1979, 1980, 1982, 1983, 1984, 1985, 1986, and 1988, placing fourth in 1990. By the time she won in 1985, she earned $25,000 and a $30,000 Mercedes-Benz for first place, plus $70,000 in appearance fees. Thus, she came to the marathon at a time of change with regard to prize money.

In 1980, Waitz took a one-year leave of absence from her high school teaching job, which ended up being permanent retirement.[55] Clearly she was able to make a living at running soon after her initial wins at New York. Her wins in New York and a few endorsements, especially Adidas, which also hired Jack Waitz, were a big part of it.[56] Thus, this became another area in which Waitz exerted considerable influence, as she helped open up opportunities for women's marathoning at exactly the time that it was becoming possible to run marathons professionally.

In Norway, as in the United States, the agreed-upon solution for this dilemma concerning the viability of traditional amateurism was to set up trust funds through the national governing bodies, which were ratified by the International Olympic Committee (IOC) and the IAAF in 1981. Three years earlier, in 1978, the IAAF had also allowed athletes to be sponsored by companies so long as the national governing body was also sponsored by that company. Thus, in the United States, if a company sponsored an athlete, it had to also pay the Athletics Congress (TAC) $25,000. Some argued that this was equal to extortion, since the athletes were the ones who earned this money and received very little support from TAC.[57] Jeff Darman, the former president of the Road Runners Club of America, admonished:

> The system serves the people in power. You have so many organizations perpetuated not because they provide a service but because they operate out of fear. They can always take away the one thing they control: amateur status. It demeans the athlete and forces them to bargain under the table.[58]

Indeed, when Waitz turned down a sponsorship offer from one of the largest milk producers in Norway, the president of the Norwegian Amateur Athletics Federation, Hans Skaset, merely rolls his eyes just the tiniest bit when he thinks about it. The federation could have used the money it would have received for acting as the go between in any endorsement contract. "And, after all, it is not a bad product, milk," he observes. "We would have had no difficulty with one of our athletes endorsing milk. But Grete said she couldn't do it because she doesn't like milk."[59]

Clearly, Waitz did not take full advantage of the sponsorship opportunities that were opening up to her and other international elite runners at this time. Indeed, she often said that money was not a motivating factor for her. Waitz argued that her life would not change whether she won a medal at the Olympic Games or not, to which an interviewer in *Runner's World* magazine replied, "Surely, if you win an Olympic gold medal, there are going to be an awful lot of financial opportunities for you." The exchange ensued as follows:

> WAITZ: Yes, my life will change if I'm willing to jump on all these commercial things that maybe I would be offered, but I'm not interested.
> RW: You would actually turn them down?
> WAITZ: Yes, but I don't think money's the key to happiness in life.... If you want to do an endorsement or things like that, you have to be in focus, and obviously I don't feel comfortable with that. I like privacy and I think to have too much money will not make you any happier. But it's very hard to say these things in the United States because people here seem to believe that a lot of money is equal to happiness. But to me it's not.[60]

Waitz had always felt enormous pressure from the media, particularly in Norway. This was another reason not to accept more endorsements, and thus bare oneself to even more exposure. The pressure especially came into focus whenever she had what was considered a disappointing performance. The best example of this is likely the 1984 Los Angeles Olympic Games, when Waitz earned the silver medal behind American Joan Benoit. Waitz had suffered some back problems in the days leading up to the race and was relieved that she was physically able to participate on the day of the race. But the worries over her back had mentally taken their toll.[61] So when she finished second, she was happy with the result, even though the Norwegian press painted it as a failure—particularly because her countrywoman, Ingrid Kristiansen, came in fourth place. These pressures fueled Waitz's longing for retirement, even when she continued to improve and run well. She said of the expectations, explaining why she cried on the medal stand:

> I cried, that's right, but for more than one reason. In Norway the media had made it quite clear that Ingrid Kristiansen and I would take gold and silver. Which of us

won the gold didn't matter. All this attention had been a bit of a burden, so when I finished the race, my crying was due to a combination of winning the silver, pain in my legs and back, and—more than anything—relief that it was over.... I often experience that people around me expect much more than I do; they're more disappointed than me. It almost makes me laugh. I think "Why are you disappointed? You haven't run. I'm the one who has run, and I'm satisfied, so why can't you be satisfied as well?"[62]

On the other hand, these changes that fueled increased media coverage and exposure that led to additional pressure on Waitz also allowed her to become a full-time professional runner, which would not have been possible earlier in her career. However, Waitz spoke many times of not wanting to be the center of attention and the difficulties that fame brought her. Her agreeing to sponsorships marked a balance between the need to make a living while working not to lose all sense of privacy. If there were a way to be a professional runner without also being a media celebrity, she would have preferred that. Yet the reason that so much money was coming into distance running at this time was precisely because of the increased media exposure and attention. Thus, many of her victories in the New York Marathon came in front of thousands of fans and millions of television viewers in one of the biggest US markets.[63]

Pioneering Changes in Women's Sport

In terms of further development of the sport, this time period also marked a shift in women's training as well as in their bodies—with the expectation that both would become more like men's. In 1979, Patti Lyons said of her own transformation that Waitz made "girls realize that they can't work out like girls. They have to work out like athletes."[64] And the athletic standard of marathon running at that time was the conditioning of men, who had been hard at it since the late 1800s. Waitz was held up as an ideal, given that she was certainly athletic while remaining demonstrably feminine, given her thin stature. As Moore so eloquently put it, describing her win at the inaugural World Championship in 1983:

> Her stride was balanced and light; she still had the control to run two inches from curbs, to nimbly avoid potholes, to run even faster. As she held the long blue line down Mannerheim Street toward the stadium, she seemed born to be an expression of this kind of endurance.[65]

As Robert Condon wrote, "Waitz is characteristically serene, confident and modest. She is the primary reason women's distance running is taken seriously."[66]

Waitz was especially known for the intensity and consistency of her training. Until 1980, she worked full-time as a secondary school teacher, teaching courses in Norwegian, English, and physical education at Bjölsen School "in one of Oslo's tougher neighborhoods."[67] She would run her first workout at 5:00 a.m., followed by a long commute to work, a full day of teaching, and then run her second and more demanding workout in the evening. Both workouts were done in the dark—particularly during Oslo's long, snowy winters. Even after she stopped teaching to focus on running full-time, she continued her early-morning workouts to avoid traffic, which would interfere with her ability to run at a good pace. Arne Kvalheim, Knut's brother and also a former Olympic 1,500-meter runner, who trained with Waitz, warned Kenny Moore: "Don't run with her in the morning. She runs too fast. 5:45 right out the front door,"[68] meaning 5:45 per mile. Sandrock wrote: "When she and [Australian world champion marathoner] Rob de Castella trained together in the days leading up the 1983 World Championships, Deek [Castella] recalls having to slow Grete down, because she ran faster on many of her runs than he did."[69] Waitz did not see such training as a hardship:

> There is no sense of sacrifice, except sometimes in the summer. When it's warm and sunny it's hard for me to run. I'd rather go on holiday instead. But in the winter, I go early to bed, I get up and run. I like it, the way I live, but I find I can't explain the satisfaction to people who do not run.[70]

Transition

Like all athletes, Waitz knew that her days of being an elite runner could not last forever. She began talking of retirement as early as 1974, with the final decision hinging upon whether she thought she could continue to improve. By beginning to run the marathon and other road races in 1978, a whole different set of athletic challenges materialized for Waitz with new distances, new goals, and lots of room for improvement. However, she did feel that all the running was taking a toll on her body. She also feared that if she stopped, she might not start again, which is why she never took days off from training. As she once claimed, "One day doesn't count, but it's a principle. I don't feel it is a big sacrifice. I'm afraid I'll find out that I like it [time off] so much that I'll do it more often."[71] Her conflicted feelings about training and racing were becoming by now more clear:

> Pleasure/dread, love/hate—I feel the all for this sport, this life. And I've always lived with them both. In one way I look forward to retiring because it's tough to go out

there and train every day, twice a day. But in another way I'm afraid of that day, because it will be like a house in which the fourth wall just falls down.[72]

She credited her husband with keeping her competing and consistent, proclaiming: "Throughout all my ambivalence, it's been Jack who's kept me steady. He's let me have things my way, accommodating my needs and the mood swings I experience when I'm under pressure. He's been very patient and understanding."[73]

Waitz remained a dominant figure, particularly in the marathon and cross country, during the late 1970s and throughout the 1980s. As Sarah Pileggi of *Sports Illustrated* put it:

> Ever since Waitz, the former schoolteacher from Oslo, ran her first marathon in New York in October 1978, breaking the world record by 2:18, the rest of the world's women have been running for second place. Last year, also in New York, Waitz lowered her record by an almost unbelievable five minutes, to 2:27:33, and still she is thought to be far from her full potential as a marathoner.[74]

Along with her record-setting nine New York City Marathon wins, Waitz won the World Cross Country Championship five times (1978, 1979, 1980, 1981, and 1983), the inaugural Track and Field World Championships marathon (1983), the London Marathon twice (1983 and 1986), and the Stockholm Marathon (1988), setting multiple world records from 3,000 meters to the marathon and enjoying a stellar road racing career at shorter distances. She earned a silver medal at the inaugural women's Olympic marathon in Los Angeles in 1984. Most importantly, she did all of this at time when women's competition in the marathon grew to be very strong, running times that a quarter century later remain world class.[75] While she was able to win the 1978 New York Marathon with no specific marathon training, that quickly changed as other women began training and competing at a much higher level than previously thought possible.

Along with 1984 Olympic gold medalist, Joan Benoit of the United States, and bronze medalist Rosa Mota of Portugal, there were other talented runners from other parts of Europe, New Zealand, and Australia. Indeed, Waitz held the world record for the marathon with four different times, but it decreased thirteen times over the course of her career, one of the most competitive periods in women's marathon history. The first recognized world women's best, 3:40:22, was run by Violet Piercy of the UK in 1926. It took until 1971 for the record to get under three hours. But by 1979 Waitz brought the record for the first time under 2:30. In 1984, one of Waitz's countrywomen and main competitors, Ingrid Kristiansen, brought the record to 2:21:06, a time that stood until 1998 when Tegla Loroupe of Kenya lowered it to 2:20:47. Since then it has dropped five times to the current standard, 2:15:25, set by Great Britain's Paula Radcliffe in 2003.

Waitz also worked to increase women's participation in running. She started the Grete Waitz five-kilometer Lopet in Oslo in 1984, an all-women's event poised to demonstrate the extent of women's interest and ability in running.[76] Moreover, after a statue was built of her outside Bislett Stadium and there was money left over from the installation, Waitz suggested that it be used to sponsor a women's run, which has been an annual event since then. The event started big, with six thousand women in the first year, and it got bigger, eventually reaching forty-five thousand participants, the largest women's-only event in the world. This drive to encourage others to get involved in running can also be seen in the three books that she coauthored with Gloria Averbuch in 1986, 1997, and 2007. These works aimed at encouraging current and prospective runners while highlighting the coaching that she did in Norway with promising young female runners as well as her work with Scottish runner Liz McColgan in what became the Grete Waitz Project. Waitz also worked with Chase Corporate Challenge, a series of 3.5-mile races in cities around the United States and a few in other countries in which runners compete for their company team.[77]

Legacy

In 1990, Waitz ran her last New York City Marathon, which would also be her last competitive race. There, she placed fourth before finally retiring after two decades as an elite competitive distance runner.

Her career remains impressive not just for the speed of her times and number of wins, but for the longevity of her sustained success. Waitz's overall approach reflects her philosophy of "hurrying slowly," in which she suggests that to succeed, one must "work hard, but be patient and take time to build."[78] She was also governed by the idea that one should be "dedicated and disciplined and work hard, but take your time. Move ahead but be patient."[79]

She credited her success in her early years of running shorter distances with honing her abilities with the necessary speed training, which later made her more efficient and stronger over longer distances. She argued that not being able to earn a living at running made her pursue other endeavors, such as college and teaching, which made her a more well-rounded person. She tried to always focus on overall improvement rather than reaching specific times or chasing records. All of these approaches exemplify the "hurrying slowly" leitmotif that so underscored her life and legacy. She lived her life with the purpose of becoming the best distance runner she could, but not at the expense of only being a runner, leading her to reconcile at the peak of her career: "I am a runner, but that's not all I am. I have always tried to live a normal, ordered life, filled with as many other activities as possible."[80]

After her retirement, Waitz completed one final New York City Marathon with race director Fred Lebow, the man who first gave her a start in marathoning. Lebow was diagnosed with brain cancer and wanted to experience as a participant the very race he had built into such a huge success. Waitz, who had become his friend over the years, agreed to run it with him. For someone who had just two years earlier run it in less than two and a half hours, the run was painfully slow at 5:32:35. But worse than that, it was emotionally difficult, knowing that Lebow was so sick. Waitz noted that it felt like her tenth victory at the marathon because it meant so much to her. Lebow died only a few months later.[81]

Sadly, in April 2005, Waitz was herself diagnosed with cancer. She never disclosed what type of cancer she had, wanting to maintain her privacy. She created a cancer care foundation in Oslo, Aktiv mot Kreft (Active against Cancer), in 2007. She remained active in her work promoting running, health, and fitness until she died from cancer on April 19, 2011, at the age of fifty-seven.[82] But despite her premature death, Waitz's unprecedented career and enormous successes would in the end set the pace for generations of women marathoners still to come.

Notes

1. Kenny Moore, "Hot Times in a Northern Clime," *Sports Illustrated*, July 7, 1986, 68.
2. Michael Sandrock, *Running with the Legends: Training and Racing Insights from 21 Great Runners* (Champaign, IL: Human Kinetics, 1996).
3. Robert J. Condon, *Great Women Athletes of the 20th Century* (Jefferson, NC: McFarland, 1991).
4. Sandrock, *Running with the Legends*.
5. Kenny Moore, "In the Long Run, It's Grete," *Sports Illustrated*, October 22, 1979, 43.
6. Grete Waitz and Gloria Averbuch, *World Class: A Champion Runner Reveals What Makes Her Run, with Advice and Inspiration for All Athletes* (New York: Warner Books, 1986), 14.
7. Ibid.
8. Ibid, 12.
9. Ibid, 15.
10. Ibid, 16.
11. Stefan Bakke, "Grete Waitz: Part 3," *Athletics Weekly*, January 4, 1986, 16.
12. Waitz and Averbuch, *World Class*, 16.
13. Allen Guttmann, *The Olympics: A History of the Modern Games*, 2nd ed. (Urbana: University of Illinois Press, 2002).
14. Ibid, 17.
15. Ibid.
16. Moore, "Hot Times in a Northern Clime," 48.
17. Gloria Averbuch, "Grete Waitz," *Ultrasport*, March–April 1985, 20.
18. Moore, "Hot Times in a Northern Clime," 50.

19. Patti Hagan, "Setting the Pace," *Ms.*, August 1985, 28.
20. Craig Neff, "They Showed the Way in Norway," *Sports Illustrated*, July 5, 1982, 28–31.
21. Olympic Games (official site), at http://www.olympic.org/olympic-games.
22. Moore, "In the Long Run, It's Grete," 43.
23. Amby Burfoot, "Grete," *Runner's World*, March 1981, 48.
24. Moore, "In the Long Run, It's Grete," 43.
25. Hagan, "Setting the Pace," 30.
26. Waitz and Averbuch, *World Class*, 131.
27. Ibid, 18.
28. Moore, "In the Long Run, It's Grete," 43.
29. Waitz and Averbuch, *World Class*, 19.
30. Stefan Bakke, "Grete Waitz: Part 1," *Athletics Weekly*, December 21, 1985, 9.
31. Burfoot, "Grete," 46.
32. Bakke, "Grete Waitz: Part 1."
33. Burfoot, "Grete," 47.
34. Ibid.
35. Annemarie Jutel, "'Thou Dost Run as in Flotation': Femininity, Reassurance and the Emergence of the Women's Marathon," *International Journal of the History of Sport* 20, no. 3 (2003): 17–32.
36. Kenny Moore, "All Around the Town," *Sports Illustrated*, October 30, 1978, 27.
37. Waitz and Averbuch, *World Class*.
38. Grete Waitz and Gloria Averbuch, *Run Your First Marathon: Everything You Need to Know to Reach the Finish Line*, 2nd ed. (New York: Skyhorse Publishing, 2010), 2.
39. Burfoot, "Grete," 48.
40. Ibid.
41. Ibid.
42. Waitz and Averbuch, *World Class*, 130.
43. Ibid.
44. Burfoot, "Grete," 48.
45. Hagan, "Setting the Pace," 30.
46. New York City Marathon results, New York Road Runners, at http://web2.nyrrc.org/cgi-bin/htmlos.cgi/mar-programs/archive/archive.search.html.
47. Burfoot, "Grete," 48.
48. Hagan, "Setting the Pace," 3.
49. Sandrock, *Running with the Legends*, 232.
50. Moore, "All Around the Town," 28.
51. Jane Leavy, "$50,000 in Prizes Awarded to Some in N.Y. Marathon," *Washington Post*, April 7, 1980, A1.
52. Ibid.
53. Pamela Cooper, *The American Marathon* (Syracuse, NY: Syracuse University Press, 1999), 155.
54. Ibid.
55. Waitz and Averbuch, *World Class*, 1986.
56. Burfoot, "Grete."

57. Leavy, "$50,000 in Prizes Awarded."
58. Ibid.
59. Burfoot, "Grete," 51.
60. Ibid, 38.
61. Stefan Bakke, "Grete Waitz: Part 2, My Problems in Los Angeles," *Athletics Weekly*, December 28, 1985, 29–33.
62. Ibid, 29.
63. Janet Woolum, *Outstanding Women Athletes: Who They Are and How They Influenced Sports in America*, 2nd ed. (Phoenix: Oryx Press, 1988).
64. Hagan, "Setting the Pace," 31.
65. Kenny Moore, "Splendor and Agony in Helsinki," *Sports Illustrated*, August 15, 1983, 29.
66. Condon, *Great Women Athletes*, 151.
67. Moore, "All Around the Town," 43.
68. Moore, "In the Long Run, It's Grete," 43.
69. Sandrock, *Running with the Legends*, 233.
70. Moore, "In the Long Run, It's Grete," 43.
71. Hagan, "Setting the Pace," 30.
72. Waitz and Averbuch, *World Class*, 40.
73. Ibid.
74. Sarah Pileggi, "No. 1 Is No. 2 . . . and Closing," *Sports Illustrated*, October 27, 1980, 40.
75. Sandrock, *Running with the Legends*.
76. The event translates in English as the Grete Waitz Run.
77. Gordon Bakoulis, "Where Are They Now? Grete Waitz," *Running Times*, no. 245 (January–February 1998): 56–57.
78. Waitz and Averbuch, *World Class*, 45.
79. Grete Waitz, cited in Sandrock, *Running with the Legends*, 233.
80. Waitz and Averbuch, *World Class*, 46.
81. Jack McCallum and Richard O'Brien, "A Course Well-Run," *Sports Illustrated*, October 17, 1994, 13–14.
82. David Willey, "Graced by Grete," *Runner's World*, November 2011, 6.

Rodney Marsh
The Making of a Maverick Footballer
—Dominic Standish

Introduction

Rodney Marsh played professional soccer[1] for several teams in England and the United States during the 1960s and 1970s, before becoming a football coach and media pundit. While a player, he gained a reputation as a maverick footballer.[2] Mavericks, a term that in football circles dates back to the late 1960s, were distinguished by their flagrant rejection of authority within football and wider society. Maverick footballers have been infamous for heavy drinking, gambling, womanizing, driving fast cars, and throwing their money around. Yet mavericks have also set themselves apart from the mainstream by speaking out and ignoring societal demands to conform.

Marsh was associated with the first wave of maverick footballers in the 1960s and 1970s, a group that would include greats such as George Best and Stan Bowles, two men whose off-color reputations often underscored their extraordinary athletic accomplishments. Best was widely regarded as one of the most gifted British players of his generation, reaching the apogee of his career in 1968. In that year, Best starred on the Manchester United team that won the European Cup, he was the top goal scorer in the English First Division,[3] and he was voted European Player of the Year. Best also won the English First Division and Charity Shield Trophy in 1965 and 1967. However, problems with gambling, womanizing, and alcoholism sent his career tumbling downhill, and Best left Manchester United in 1974. He went on to play for the Los Angeles Aztecs, Fulham F.C., the Fort Lauderdale Strikers, Hibernian F.C., and the San Jose Earthquakes and made a number of guest appearances for other clubs. But he never returned to the form he achieved at Manchester United. Undoubtedly, the maverick side of his character had severely hindered his playing ability, and his short football career was essentially finished by 1974. In 2005, Best died aged fifty-nine of organ failure related to alcoholism.

By comparison, Stan Bowles had an enduring career and played more than five hundred matches for eight different football clubs over seventeen years. His sublime skills at dribbling with the ball made him a fans' favorite at a number of clubs. It was at London football club Queen's Park Rangers (QPR)[4] where he had seven very successful years and inherited the coveted number 10 shirt previously worn by Rodney Marsh. Yet Bowles similarly came into conflict with team coaches[5] and managers at several of his football clubs, including Tommy Docherty at QPR and Brian Clough at Nottingham Forest. But Bowles was never known as a womanizer or heavy drinker; gambling was his problem. At QPR, he frequently turned up to play matches at the last minute after sprinting from the nearby betting shop. Reportedly, the QPR manager tolerated this because, as one instance illustrates, after arriving twelve minutes before one match started, Bowles went onto the field and scored a goal within two minutes.[6] As Ernie Tagg, Bowles's boss when Bowles played for the English team Crewe Alexandra, once opined: "If Stan Bowles could pass a bookmaker's like he could a football, he'd have no problems at all."[7]

While many of his peers attempted to play through the lure of alcohol and gambling, Marsh crossed the Atlantic to play soccer in the United States, continued playing until he was forty-four years old, and ultimately progressed to successful careers in sport management and then the media. Marsh's reputation was enhanced as the role of the mass media in sport flourished, and he cultivated his colorful personality to become a leading soccer pundit. Marsh's maverick character provided genuine spontaneity and moments of controversy that sport media found refreshing. But he also had a tendency to be provocative, and this got him dropped from most football clubs for which he played. Eventually, this tendency led to a significant setback in his media career; in 2005, he was fired from a leading British television sport network for a joke that was considered to be distasteful. This event signified a wider cultural clash: the 1970s-era maverick's disdain for authority had come into conflict with twenty-first-century conformity against saying things considered to be offensive. More than any of his other on- or off-the-field accomplishments, it is this flaunting of contemporary convention that informs Marsh's place within the culture of sport.

The 1960s and 1970s in Cultural Context

In a 2013 interview, Marsh was asked why so many perceived maverick players had become notorious during the 1960s and 1970s. He replied:

> From a retrospective point of view, it wasn't unique to football. If you look across fashion and music and writing and from every aspect probably of society, the 60s and 70s in that 20 year period was quite unique. Right now, I could probably give

you 20 or 30 names outside of football who were fantastic characters and who live on in the memory because of their loose cannon approach to life.[8]

In considering Marsh, both the man and the sporting icon, thus, it is imperative that we consider the emerging phenomenon of maverick footballers within the cultural context of this period. The 1960s marked the era of civil rights rebellions, hippy communes, mods and rockers, and a widespread cultural rejection of authority.[9] Culturally, the 1960s were indeed a tough act to follow given the diffuse nature of the countercultural movements and any accompanying subcultures that emerged.

In comparison, the 1970s risked cultural drabness, but new forms of cultural rebellion emerged nonetheless. England led the punk rock reaction, but there was a distinctly artificial character to this hedonistic, two-fingers-to-the-establishment leitmotif.[10] Punk rocker turned media darling Jonathan King, a leading UK media success before his convictions for sexual assault, understood that 1970s punk was largely about fake marketing. He declared: "Punk was fake. I was the original punk because I believed you could sell the public anything, from the *Rocky Horror Picture Show* to Terry Dactyl and the Dinosaurs. Malcolm McLaren, Johnny Rotten and Sid Vicious were all actors."[11]

Like punk musicians, 1970s comedians Monty Python similarly challenged establishment norms and institutions, as most graphically illustrated by their movie satire of Jesus Christ, *Monty Python's Life of Brian*, a film that was effectively banned in most of the UK, Ireland, and Norway. Yet Monty Python also appeared to be limited in terms of cultural change. "I really don't know if we've done anything that changed anything, ultimately,"[12] reflected American Monty Python comic Terry Gilliam, a consideration that looks back on the sporting environment of the time.

As with punk and period comedians, the football mavericks represented a cultural reaction against the establishment rather than precipitating change. But the mavericks' comments and antics differed insomuch as they arrived at a time of growing media enchantment with football. Indeed, during the late 1960s, the role of media in football in England grew significantly. The staging of the World Cup in England in 1966 and the subsequent victory for the English team propelled public interest and media engagement. As journalist and author Rob Steen observed:

> In 1964, an NOP [National Opinion Polls] survey indicated that 44 per cent of Englishmen over the age of 16 watched football at least once a week. The World Cup almost doubled that even before TV multiplied the options. Enter ITV's Sunday regional answer to *Match of the Day*, *Star Soccer*, subsequently rechristened *The Big Match*. By the early Seventies, a week in the life of armchair anoraks and purists

alike could comprise six weekend League fixtures—usually all Division One—plus midweek League Cup, FA Cup and/or European ties.[13]

Meanwhile, newspapers, magazines and even comics for kids glamorized football. In 1969, the popular British newspaper the *Sun* went tabloid and featured numerous pages of football gossip six days a week, often alongside pictures of scantily clad women—the since controversial Page Three girls. Magazines like *Goal, Football Monthly*, and *Shoot!* engaged a wider range of football-mad audiences. By the 1970s, British sport and media were poised to capture some great moments provided by the football mavericks, both on and off the football pitch.

Maverick Footballers

English football in the late 1960s and 1970s was renowned for two types of players: hard men and skillful footballers. The hard men were usually defenders and were quite different from today's tough players. As Marsh explains: "What is a hard player? He is different today from when I played. Men like Norman Hunter, Tommy Smith and Ron 'Chopper' Harris just went through you at every opportunity.... They would not get into teams today because they didn't have the skills. I laugh when I hear some players today called hard men. There aren't any in football now because the game has changed so much, for the better I might add."[14]

The hard men often played very violently and in a manner that would be considered unacceptable today. Marsh did later confess to some violent incidents that would certainly be considered scandalous in a more modern context: "Apart from a few teenage scraps, my life has not been physically violent. Playing football, I have been sent off for head butting, and once lost my rag at school and hit a boy with a cricket bat, but that's not me. It is probably because I had too much experience of it as a child growing up."[15] Indeed, Marsh grew up in a tough working-class area in the East End of London, and he played his best years during the late 1960s and 1970s, when English football was considerably more violent than it is today. He was sent off five times in his career, mostly, as he noted, for head butting and punching in retaliation.[16]

Although Marsh was frequently impulsive, he more often employed verbal rather than physical retaliation. A distinctive feature of the mavericks has been their tendency to make abrupt comments and gestures. These men came from working-class neighborhoods where they learned as kids that they had to be quick and have their wits about them to get on in life. Those who managed to develop sharp, impulsive skills were the ones who might escape from their disadvantaged background and achieve great things. As Marsh recalled, "I was surrounded by violence, and that's the way it was on my street in those days. You had to live on your instinct and wits. As kids, we all learned how to look after ourselves. We were all rascals."[17]

The maverick footballers were the kids who were fast and intuitive; who got away and continued to be rascals. Sometimes this required a quick physical reaction, while at other times a witty, apposite comment was more appropriate. These characteristics tended to get them into trouble with football coaches, authorities, and sometimes even the police and courts. Mavericks felt that they were up against these establishment figures and institutions. Marsh explains:

> I was anti-establishment because of my parents, and this was the James Dean era, I was a rebel without a clue. I hate the "establishment" telling me what I can and can't do. That was a challenge and always has been; I have been out to beat the system.[18]

Even though mavericks had the capacity to resort to violence, they were distinguished more for their sharp, rough comments. As the lure of football grew for the media, these comments fed the appetites of commentators, journalists, and their audiences. Mavericks had not been raised to respect the middle-class, bourgeois etiquettes of establishment institutions, including the leading media organizations. When they deployed their impulsive tendencies, mavericks usually entertained but were often also reprimanded by football or legal authorities.

Marsh displayed these characteristics on many occasions and definitely fell into the category of skillful footballer rather than violent, hard man. Indeed, most mavericks were known for being flamboyant showmen as much as anything else. Their exceptional skills meant that they were usually picked to play matches for their national teams. But their maverick character meant that they could never be trusted to play more than a handful of matches. Marsh played nine times for England, while some other mavericks won a few more "caps"[19] for the national side. Regarding other renowned mavericks, Tony Currie played seventeen times in three spells spanning eight seasons for England, while Frank Worthington played eight times, Stan Bowles five times, Peter Osgood four times, and Alan Hudson only twice. These were all immensely talented footballers, yet they played for England on fewer occasions than many mediocre players. Why is it that so many great players were sidelined by England's coaches and the Football Association (FA), the established body that runs English football and the England team? Marsh's comments on the FA are especially damning:

> The Football Association is an entity that is fundamentally a self-serving, self-perpetuating membership. In my personal belief, and I've always believed this going back 50 years, I don't think the FA actually, truly, cares about football. It's a sweeping

generalization, and I'm sure in doing that I will drag in some people into it who probably do care. But, as a generalization, the FA is not an association or a membership that particularly cares about the purity of football in my opinion.[20]

This appears to be demonstrated by the unwillingness of the FA to tolerate the antics of some superb players if they refused to follow established etiquette or respond to the instructions of coaches. Marsh typified this maverick behavior during his involvement with the England team. For instance, he once outlined how challenging he found it to follow the instructions of England coach Sir Alf Ramsey for what he should do during a match.[21] He claimed to have found it difficult to take Ramsey seriously, as "he had to speak all posh because he was something special," adding, "It was obvious that he'd taken voice lessons."[22] Ramsey represented the FA; he had been knighted by the queen and risen to join the ranks of the British cultural and football elites. In spite of Ramsey's accolades and standing, Marsh, in classic maverick fashion, responded not with deference but rather with sharp wit. When Ramsey asked the England players to wear bow ties to an official event at an embassy, Marsh provoked Ramsey's disapproval by turning up wearing a bow tie and dinner jacket, but no socks and flip-flops. Before Marsh's final England match against Wales in 1973, Ramsey told Marsh, "Rodney, I will be watching you in particular, and if you don't work hard, then I will pull you off at half-time."[23] "Christ, Alf," responded Marsh, adding that while at his domestic club, Manchester City, "we normally get a cup of tea and an orange!"[24] This prompted a swift if not ignominious end to Marsh's England career.

While it was unusual for mavericks to become regular players for the national side, presumably because of their caustic attitudes, it was even rarer for 1970s maverick footballers to become managers. There were some maverick managers in English football during the 1970s and 1980s, including Malcolm Allison and Brian Clough. These managers had been football players before the 1970s and displayed many of the characteristics typical of 1970s maverick players. Both Allison and Clough were successful and admired managers. But they were also known for their free, independent approaches to football management and life. When Marsh was asked why neither of them had become managers of the England team, Marsh replied with reference to the management style of the FA: "The Football Association is such an oppressive group of people that somebody like, as an example Malcolm Allison or Brian Clough, are not going to be the kind of people that are going to get offered the job because they want to do it in their own way and they want to make their own decisions and make their own agenda."[25]

Although Allison and Clough were famous for their independence (as well as their hard drinking), the 1970s maverick players were renowned for being even more outrageous, including not only hard drinking but also womanizing, splurging money on flashy cars, and being flagrantly rude in public and to the media. As the often notorious George Best was quoted in the British media, "I spent 90% of my money on women, drink and fast cars. The rest I wasted!"[26] In comparison, Marsh claims to have been careful with his money: "I have always looked after my money and thought of the future. I may have done outrageous things on the pitch, yet when it came to finances I've done the right things."[27] But Marsh's success goes beyond astute investments. Of the 1970s maverick football players, Marsh was one of the few who made the transition from being a player to a coach before ascending to media pundit and businessman.

When I asked Marsh what made him different from the 1970s mavericks who fell afoul to alcohol and gambling, he initially replied with: "I identify with the question directly because one of my pals, George Best, would fall into that category directly."[28] Then he went on to reveal what helped his success to progress beyond playing:

> I think possibly it's because I had a grounding in life, which paralleled with football, and my grounding in life served me later in my life and that was my immediate family [who] were incredibly supportive of me both as a footballer, but also as a person. And while that wasn't so much in a loving way, because of the stark, poor background I had, it was supportive in the way of "this is the way that you should lead your life." I could think of one phrase that would sum it all up and that was "don't put all your eggs in one basket." I was never that way; I was always looking for other things in my life.[29]

Marsh the Footballer

Looking at Marsh's developmental years paints a portrait of a young man transcending place while similarly bucking convention. As a boy, Marsh trained with the youth team of the East London First Division club West Ham. But he was never offered a professional contract. He then had trials with the West London First Division side Fulham and eventually signed a contract. Marsh knew that this was a great opportunity to escape, yet his impulsive reactions immediately caused a setback: "I wanted to see what was on the other side, not just in terms of football but life itself. That was my first thought when I signed, here was the opportunity I had been waiting for. My escape route. I had been given the chance. Within a week I had my first fight with a player called Freddie Callaghan."[30] Marsh and Callaghan were both fined by the Fulham general manager, but Marsh rose through the youth and reserve teams and into the first team by the time he was eighteen years old.

Even though Marsh was successful with the Fulham team, the arrival of new coach Vic Buckingham, who had a decidedly different background from Marsh, led to a personality clash: "He came from Ajax, was half Dutch, thought he was a public schoolboy[31] and was right up his own arse in every way. I was from the East End, a cockney, playing wonderful off the cuff football and scoring goals, yet he didn't accept me from day one. This was a working man's sport and yet he wanted to change my approach. No chance."[32] Marsh was soon to be put on the transfer list despite having scored twenty-two goals in sixty-three appearances for Fulham between 1962 and 1966. Adding to that, he was eventually sold off—cast away, in no small measure—to Fulham's West London rivals Queen's Park Rangers.

During his playing career at QPR, however, Marsh's maverick character and colorful demeanor on the football pitch reached their pinnacles. In contrast to his final period of playing at Fulham, Marsh found in QPR manager Alec Stock a man who was prepared to allow him to play freely and a chairman in Jim Gregory who came from a rogue working-class background like Marsh's own. Gregory was brought up in Shepherd's Bush, where QPR are based, and his father ran a fish stall that Gregory took over at the age of fourteen when his father joined the army. Gregory and Marsh developed a very close relationship, and Marsh was given considerable freedom on and off a pitch where his maverick character thrived in the cultural climate of the late 1960s and early 1970s:

> I played for Queen's Park Rangers from 1966 to 1972, when England was alive with the air of the swinging sixties, and things were changing. I was in my early twenties and establishing myself as a top footballer. Rodney Marsh fitted the image of what was happening in the country: enjoyment, flamboyance and fun. A carefree attitude. What I quickly came to realise was that beneath the surface, football attracted some extraordinary characters. People who loved to attach themselves to the game, for all the wrong and right reasons. It was the greatest time for music, for rock and roll, many people say the seventies were the wildest times ever.[33]

This climate of cultural freedom reinforced Marsh's wild, free role on the football pitch, and success came quickly. Marsh's first season as a player at QPR went especially well: "My first season, 1966–67, was remarkable. It could not have gone any better and I didn't do a thing wrong. Everything I touched turned to gold, and there was a huge amount of publicity being given to the club. We won the League Cup against West Brom at Wembley, got promoted and I scored forty-four goals."[34]

Queen's Park Rangers rose from the Third to the First Division in three successive seasons, from 1966–1967 to 1968–1969, as Marsh banged in the goals. But then Marsh was injured and missed eighteen matches in one season, and

QPR were subsequently relegated from the First to the Second Division in 1969. Also, Gordon Jago replaced Alec Stock as the QPR coach in 1971, which changed matters considerably. To be sure, Marsh reacted harshly against Jago as he felt that his new coach was too closely aligned to league administrators. As Marsh recalled, "[Jago] was an excellent coach but an FA man, an establishment man and not my cup of tea at all."[35] At the end of Jago's first meeting with the QPR players, Marsh stood up and proclaimed that "we were all forty percent behind him."[36] When Marsh recovered from injury, and QPR did not get promoted back to the First Division, he went to see Gregory. Marsh had an agreement with Gregory that if the team did not get promoted again in one season, he could move on to fulfill his ambitions of playing in the First Division. Manchester City came in with an offer of £200,000 to buy Marsh, cash that Gregory believed he could use to buy five or six new players. Regardless, it is important to note that between 1966 and 1972, Marsh scored 106 goals in his splendid QPR career.

While Marsh had certainly contributed to making QPR a bigger club, at Manchester City he was expected to help make a big club the best. Marsh claimed that his move to Manchester City vastly increased the number of people watching the team: "After the first few games the lads were all over me, because the average crowd had been about 32,000 before I'd arrived, and then suddenly it was around 53,000, which was a massive, massive increase. There were 20,000 more people watching the games, and the rest of the players were also on a crowd bonus, so they loved it. I unashamedly take the credit for that."[37]

And yet, despite the renewed enthusiasm of Manchester City fans for their team, and despite the team's new scoring threat, results in matches took a turn for the worse, a matter for which Marsh readily assumed responsibility: "I accept the blame for losing the First Division title in 1972. That season was a nightmare for me.... It was my fault because I completely upset the balance."[38] Marsh did not start well, partly due to his physical condition: "I was eating the wrong kinds of foods in the hotel and snacking, instead of having a proper diet. I was also carrying a groin strain that I'd got at QPR about three weeks earlier, which had forced me to miss a couple of games, so I wasn't fit."[39]

In the following season, the results were even worse. This was Marsh's first full season at Manchester City, and the team finished halfway up the First Division table, which was a disaster given expectations. Nevertheless, Marsh was made Manchester City team captain for two seasons, although the coaching staff was divided on Marsh holding this title, ultimately causing a rift within club management. As Marsh acknowledges, "Later in life, I've come to realise that I'd caused, unwittingly, a division through the football club."[40]

Marsh's problems at Manchester City were widely discussed in the media and precipitated his move to the United States via a rather unusual chain of events. Marsh received a telephone call from one of pop star Elton John's managers, who explained that John, an unabashed football fan, had heard about Marsh's problems at Manchester City. He learned that John, who had recently bought a stake in the North American Soccer League's (NASL) Los Angeles Aztecs, was keen to have Marsh play for him there. Management then arranged a private plane and flew Marsh out to Los Angeles for what amounted to a recruiting trip, which included an Elton John concert to be held at Dodger Stadium. While Marsh was being sold on the idea of taking his game to the United States, he received another phone call from Beau Rogers IV, the general manager of the Florida-based Tampa Bay Rowdies soccer club, who offered to fly him to Florida to come and look at *that* team and its setup.

When Marsh arrived at the airport, hundreds of Rowdies supporters, along with approximately fifty media people, were there to greet him. In what was so blatantly an attempt to win him over to the fledgling American circuit, Marsh faced a level of media captivation like never before, but his maverick character was up to the challenge. Dick Crippen from NBC's Channel 8 affiliate interviewed Marsh live from the airport, asking him: "Rodney, you're known as the Clown Prince of Soccer. We understand you are the white Pelé?," a thinly veiled reference to the most widely regarded and beloved footballer of his generation whose career stood—then as now, perhaps—in sharp contrast to Marsh's more colorful legacy. Marsh responded with one of his classic wisecracks: "No, that's not quite true. Pelé is the black Rodney Marsh."[41] After Marsh signed with the Rowdies, this comment only fueled the rivalry between his new team and the New York Cosmos, led by an aging but still captivating Pelé.

Marsh and the Rowdies faced Pelé and the Cosmos in an NASL match at Tampa Stadium on June 6, 1976. To provoke Pelé during this match, Marsh sat on the ball, then signaled to Pelé to come and get it.[42] The Rowdies slaughtered the Cosmos 5–1. In a subsequent Rowdies-Cosmos match, Marsh's Rowdies again prevailed, this time 3–1, in a match that Marsh boldly pronounced to be "the game that put the North American Soccer League on the map."[43] This was also the first regular-season game televised live on the ABC network. The scene had certainly been set for a fiery match, and Tampa Stadium was sold out weeks before. To wind up the famous Pelé, according to Marsh, "tens of thousands of provocative signs saying, "Pelé who?" were plastered round the stadium."[44] During their next match, held in the Cosmos' home pitch, Yankee Stadium, Marsh describes how "Pelé kicked lumps out of me because of what I did to them in Tampa Bay."[45]

Despite their rivalry, Pelé, Marsh, and indeed many of the other foreign players then in the league helped lift the football standards of the NASL. When Marsh began playing in the United States, he quickly realized that the standards of football were far below those of England's First Division: "It was clear to me that I was far better than all the other players. I'd make a 20 yard pass and a guy was running backwards instead of forwards."[46] But a collection of international football stars imported into American soccer would make the NASL momentarily very exciting: "Look at the people I was playing against: Pelé, Franz Beckenbauer, Eusébio and Carlos Alberto. Finally, the world started looking and said, 'Christ almighty, it's for real.' And some of the games were magnificent. The 5–4 game we lost to the Cosmos in New York when Pelé scored a hat-trick was one of the finest games I played in my life."[47]

Marsh and the Rowdies certainly contributed to the improving international profile of American soccer. The Rowdies staged some notable victories against touring teams, including beating top English side Manchester United 2–1 in Tampa Stadium in front of a sellout crowd. The Rowdies also won against a strong Dynamo Moscow team. Marsh remembers his first season at Tampa Bay as his best in the United States.[48] The Rowdies developed a reputation that suited Marsh's maverick character and became part of the club's brand image. As he recalled:

> Going to a Rowdies game was going to an extravaganza; it wasn't just about going to watch soccer. It was promoted as a big event and it was a big event. We were the talk of the town. "Soccer is a kick in the grass" was the Rowdies song, and it was about branding that image and then bringing over a lot of young single Brits to play who were drunk and fighting and chasing all the local women. We had that Rowdies image, but on the flip side, we were always there for the kids with the camps and the clinics. All the kids wanted to be Rowdies.[49]

But it would also appear that Marsh's maverick appeal was ultimately too much for some people within American soccer in general and Tampa Bay Rowdies management in particular. Rowdies coach Eddie Firmani especially disliked Marsh, and when Marsh returned home to the UK between the 1976 and 1977 seasons, Rowdies general manager Beau Rogers phoned him to say that Firmani did not want Marsh back with the club despite a fantastic first season.

This conflict was resolved by Firmani leaving to join the New York Cosmos. But one consequence was that on-the-field results went downhill for the Rowdies. Then, for the 1978 season, in something of an ironic twist, Gordon Jago arrived in Tampa Bay as the Rowdies' new coach. Jago had been recommended by Marsh despite Marsh's earlier personal dislike of Jago when they were both under contract with QPR. And indeed, Jago's coaching improved the performance of the Rowdies team, which reached the conference championship against the Fort Lauderdale Strikers. This encounter consisted of a first- and a second-leg match, with the second one at home in Tampa. With the score level at the end of the match, the contest continued with a short, deciding overtime period. It was still level at 3–3 with five minutes remaining when the Strikers' coach, Ron Newman, substituted George Best, who then could not take part in the final shootout. Best responded in typical maverick style; he left the field and threw his rain-soaked shirt into Newman's face. Without Best's participation in the shootout, the Rowdies had the advantage. It was left to Marsh to take the fifth and final shootout kick. Marsh scored to win the match, and the forty-seven-thousand-person crowd went wild.[50] However, Marsh had suffered an injury during the match that got worse afterward, meaning that he could not play in the Soccer Bowl final against archrivals New York Cosmos five days later, a match that the Cosmos won 3–1.

The Rowdies also made it to the 1979 Soccer Bowl. But with eight minutes remaining in the match, with the Rowdies trailing 2–1 against the Vancouver Whitecaps, in something of a repeat of the Best incident from the year before, Jago substituted Marsh out of the game, meaning that like Best, Marsh would also be ineligible to participate in any subsequent shootout. Marsh responded by cursing Jago as he left the field. Unfortunately, Verne Lundquist, broadcasting the game for ABC Sports, was standing next to Marsh at the time and struggled unsuccessfully to cover the microphone; Marsh's language, broadcast for all to hear, caused an uproar in typically staid American television circles and certainly within team management.[51] Marsh, nearing the end of his contract, had clearly worn out his welcome and predictably received word from the team that his days with the club were indeed numbered. To ease the transition and minimize any negative publicity that might ensue given Marsh's popularity with the fans, the franchise hosted a testimonial match against the Fort Lauderdale side so that Marsh could leave the club he helped build into a powerhouse on a high note. This event also came with a modest payout from the proceeds. Marsh, who went on to score two goals in the match, also characteristically added fuel to an already combustible atmosphere when he cracked a joke at coach Jago's expense during the well-attended postgame dinner.[52]

The background to the punch line supposedly derived from Jago's stint as a young player at Charlton Athletic in England. Evidently, the Charlton team was playing an important quarterfinal FA Cup match against Chelsea; the score was 0–0 in the last minute of the game and the ball was heading in the direction of the Charlton goal. Jago was on the goal line and attempted to shut his legs and block the ball from going into the goal, but he failed. The ball ended up going between his legs and into the goal, and Charlton ended up losing the match 1–0. Marsh, recounting the story for a rapt dinner audience, explained that in the dressing room after the match, a dispirited Jago avowed to his coach, "I'm sorry boss. That was completely down to me. That was my fault. I should've kept my legs shut," to which the dismayed manager was said to have replied, "Not you Gordon, your mother!"[53]

Marsh parted company with the Tampa Bay Rowdies shortly thereafter. A few years earlier, the Rowdies had loaned him to Fulham, the club of his youth, for the 1976 season, a move that in British football circles marked something of a unique chapter in the sport given who else was with the club at the time. George Best also transferred to Fulham from the Los Angeles Aztecs at the same time. These changes revived a special maverick relationship. Marsh first came across Best when they played against one another in a charity match in 1972 while Best was playing for Manchester United and Marsh was at Manchester City. Marsh described a caustic encounter between them in the bar after the match, which was largely precipitated by the rivalry between the clubs and their players. Nevertheless, as Marsh outlines, things soon changed between them once they left their rival Manchester clubs: "We later would go on to become good friends. We played for different clubs in America, were at Fulham together at the end of our careers in English football, did the hugely successful Best and Marsh road show in front of live audiences up and down the country, and drank, laughed and cried as one."[54]

At Fulham, Marsh and Best were joined by another great English player, Bobby Moore, on a team of ageing stars. For the first twelve matches with this lineup, the team played attractive football and drew considerable media attention. But soon "hard men" defenders targeted these stars with some tough tackling. Unsurprisingly, the team performed poorly as the weather turned cold. After their playing days in Florida and California, Marsh and Best had aged to the extent that they were now simply unable to withstand tough tackles in the harsh English winter. "Football in England is a grey game, played on grey days by grey people," moaned Marsh.[55] By February 1977, Marsh asked the Fulham manager, Bobby Campbell, if he could return to Tampa.

Marsh would play a final two seasons for Tampa Bay from 1977 to 1979 before his departure from the franchise after that tumultuous 1979 season as described above. But even this estrangement would be short lived. In 1984, Marsh would be brought back to the Rowdies as a coach, even making twenty appearances as a player during the 1986–1987 season for the club, which was now playing as much indoors as it was outdoors due to dire NASL finances. And it is to Marsh's coaching career that we now turn.

Marsh as Coach

After 1979, the Tampa Bay Rowdies and the NASL in general fell into difficult financial straits. World-class players departed and were not replaced, and the NASL was forced to tinker with the game in order to suit American tastes, eventually abolishing the thirty-five-yard line for offside.

As a working alien, Marsh needed another job to remain in the United States for visa reasons when his playing career was over. But help arrived from the most unlikely quarters when a former Rowdies teammate offered Marsh a six-week contract as general manager of the Saint Petersburg (Florida) Thunderbolts, a new club playing in the Southern Soccer League. Following that gig, Marsh was offered a coaching role with New York United, a semiprofessional team in the American Soccer League (ASL). Marsh only coached the team during the summer months, playing in about a dozen matches himself, before he was recruited by the Carolina Lightnin' in Charlotte in 1981, which was to become Marsh's first proper managerial job. He signed contracts as both general manager and coach, and the Lightnin' won the championship in his first year. The maverick was making the transition into the managerial ranks, a move that few might have imagined given his admittedly checkered history. And yet this transition appears to have been quite a successful one.

The Lightnin' reached the semifinals of the ASL championship in Marsh's final year with the team, although losing in that round. The day after this semifinal, Marsh was contacted by his former club, the Tampa Bay Rowdies, which had fallen into a mess over players' contracts and budgets. Marsh returned to Rowdies as a coach in 1984 at a time when the NASL was spiraling further into decline, thanks to new policies such as requiring teams to field a minimum of seven Americans on the pitch simultaneously and encouraging indoor soccer to the extent that the Rowdies were forced to play a full season indoors. This changed the game significantly; Marsh recalls taking the Rowdies to play archrivals Cosmos in New York, and only about two hundred people turned up to watch. This contrasted with crowds of seventy thousand for outdoor Cosmos matches in the 1970s when Pelé and Franz Beckenbauer were their stars.

Marsh found coaching the Rowdies difficult during this period, and he admits to the same weaknesses that have plagued other talented players attempting to make the leap into coaching. As he recounts, "The biggest problem I had as a manager was asking players to do things that I had found easy as a player. The fact that many players didn't understand, or couldn't carry out my instructions frustrated and annoyed me.... At forty years old I couldn't cope with it, even if in my first year in Charlotte, we won the whole thing."[56] As the Rowdies struggled on the pitch, Marsh continued to move up the managerial ranks from coach to chief executive, all while the NASL was slowly disbanding. In a bold move, he brought in the flamboyant Malcolm Allison, his erstwhile manager at Manchester City, to coach the team. But in spite of the buzz it created, the move was ultimately a bust as Allison, well known as a great coach as well as a maverick in his own right, was arrested for drunk driving after driving the wrong way over the Howard Frankland Bridge connecting Tampa with Saint Petersburg. Allison returned to England before the end of the 1986 season. Coincidentally, the NASL collapsed shortly thereafter, and the Tampa Bay Rowdies struggled to stay in business.

Still, Marsh used his English links to keep the Rowdies going and invited Queen's Park Rangers to train at Tampa for six weeks. Eventually, as chief executive, Marsh had to do what was best for the team, enrolling the Rowdies in the American Indoor Soccer Association (AISA). Then, between 1988 and 1992, the Rowdies played in the third incarnation of the American Soccer League and its successor, the American Professional Soccer League (APSL). Marsh managed to get some quality players from England, but only about four thousand people were coming to matches in Tampa Stadium, which made it exceedingly difficult to attract top talent.

Marsh finally left the Rowdies in 1994, but he claimed to have learned a lot. Playing, coaching, and eventually managing American soccer had given Marsh exposure to methods of marketing and media relations that were more advanced than in the UK. As he recalls, "My understanding of marketing, promotion, public relations, [and] advertising was almost zero until I came to America, and I realized the value in public relations and marketing of a product."[57] Marsh's experiences in the United States were indeed formative as his media career took off.

Marsh the Media Pundit

Rodney Marsh worked as a studio and live guest exclusively for the British ITV network during the 1990 World Cup finals in Italy. Similarly, he presented for CNN in the United States during the 1994 World Cup. He participated in many different television programs for British Sky TV.

Marsh's big breakthrough came as a daily highlights commentator on Sky's *Gillette Soccer Saturday*. One of the reasons the show became successful was the spontaneous and controversial comments made by pundits, a flow of live banter that certainly allowed Marsh to parlay his untethered personality into something larger, though not without generating controversy. For instance, when the show's anchor, Jeff Stelling, asked Marsh what he thought about the pressure on Liverpool manager Gérard Houllier when the team was not doing very well, Marsh set off a bit of a firestorm with his response. Marsh explained:

> Jeff Stelling threw me a question, which I didn't know was coming. He said, "Rodney, do you think that Gérard Houllier is under extreme pressure at Liverpool?" I just openly said, "I bet he is—he just had a heart attack," which he had. Everybody went apoplectic that I said that just because it's the kind of thing I say in the pub on a Sunday morning. It created so much of a stir within Sky Sports, that Vic Wakeling, who was the Chief Executive of Sky, called in the producer of the program and Jeff Stelling.[58]

Marsh, who later wrote a letter of apology to Houllier stating that he hoped the coach had not been offended, was charged in the press with making light of a serious medical condition. Interestingly, Houllier's own response was that he found the exchange amusing and was not at all offended, but the public perception continued to suggest otherwise. Still, the public was thought to be growing weary of Marsh's off-the-cuff style of reporting, although people tuned in just to see if he would, in the spirit of his maverick nature, offer further prurient or otherwise off-color insight. In this regard, Marsh's media reputation was informed by the quick-witted street talk he had grown up with in London's East End. Throughout his playing career, his wisecracks and unscripted comments had brought him into conflict with soccer coaches and other players. Ironically, perhaps, his media career, fueled as it was by much of the same tactics, flourished as his jibes entertained, although his maverick style clashed with increasingly concerned media managers whose adherence to emergent cultural policies, namely what had come to be referred to as "political correctness," feared whom he might offend next.

Unsurprisingly, Marsh finds many contemporary British TV soccer shows very tame due to the pressures not to offend: "You ask me a question, and I'm going to answer the question completely honestly. I watch programs now like *Match of the Day* and *Soccer Saturday*, and you can just tell that they are all so guarded they don't want to say anything in case they offend somebody."[59]

In the context of the growing pressure not to offend, it was almost inevitable that Marsh's prominent role at Sky would come to an end. Despite this pressure, he continues to uphold his conviction in saying what he thinks, even if his statements are controversial: "In my media career, I have always been someone to say what he feels and if people don't like me, so what? If they don't like what I say, who cares? But often, people did like what I said and my controversial, straight-talking image was an attraction for television and radio when I quit playing. I became a pundit and loved every minute, before it eventually ended in tears."[60]

This last comment refers to yet another "offensive" moment in Marsh's often turbulent career. While appearing on the nightly phone-in TV show *You're on Sky Sports*, soon after the tsunami that caused widespread devastation in Asia at the end of 2004, there was a discussion about the Newcastle football team in England. Newcastle's fans are nicknamed the Toon Army. A Newcastle fan called the show and asked about the prospect of the star player David Beckham joining Newcastle. As Marsh describes it, "I answered the call by saying that Beckham would never sign for Newcastle because of all the trouble the Toon Army . . . had caused in Asia."[61] Marsh knew this quip would create a reaction, but he also maintains he did not mean to offend anyone: "When I was sacked by Sky it was a moment of madness, the Loose Cannon striking once more. I absolutely never had any intention of causing offence to anyone but knew it was inflammatory."[62] Andy Melvin, the deputy head of sport at Sky, explained to Marsh that they were terminating his contract "because it had caused too much controversy."[63] After he had spent eleven years as a leading panelist on the prominent *Gillette Soccer Saturday* show, Marsh's firing from Sky became a story itself, as demonstrated by it becoming an item on BBC News.[64]

Following Marsh's sacking from Sky, he was immediately hired by TalkSport radio on a two-year contract. There, he continued to build on his maverick media reputation by interviewing controversial figures, including former heavyweight boxing champion Mike Tyson. It appeared that asking Marsh to interview a controversial star like Tyson would create the kind of conflict and audience interest that TalkSport craved. Tyson even arrived with an army of fifteen bodyguards for the interview. If Marsh provoked Tyson, maybe he would need the bodyguards more than the boxer, though in actuality, the interview went very smoothly with Marsh asking some challenging questions about boxing history without any serious provocation. Had Marsh finally learned there are some people who should not be provoked, and did he avoid controversial questions to Tyson? "Not at all," he responded. "I was intimidated. But I was really only interested in getting him to talk.... He just loved talking about boxing, and he didn't want to talk about anything else.... We got so many people afterwards saying how brilliant it was that Mike Tyson was actually, genuinely talking about his love of boxing."[65]

And yet when he was offered a new two-year contract by the managers at TalkSport radio, Marsh walked away because he felt annoyed with "the way they manufactured controversy."[66] In an interview with this author, Marsh also said that programs were increasingly prepared by copying stories from the more edgy, popular newspapers, proclaiming:

> We would have preproduction meetings.... The reason I got so frustrated was that all we were doing was a radio version of what was in the *Sun* newspaper.... I said why are we doing this? Why can't we have original programing?[67]

The reply was a rather straightforward, "Well, because this is what's popular."[68]

The sort of maverick-related controversy that swirls about Marsh's broadcasting style does indeed come from spontaneity rather than studied attempts to set people up for controversial moments or copy popular stories, which the show's directors encouraged more and more. And while he explored other opportunities to work in situations in his home country that were similarly conducive to his style, he continued to work for a variety of media outlets, though typically outside the UK. For example, Marsh worked exclusively for TalkSport in Germany during the 2006 World Cup and was then hired by Yahoo! to be their football expert with weekly predictions for the English Premier League, the European Champions League, and the 2006 World Cup. He aired a series for America's NBC network called *Countdown to the World Cup* in which he interviewed players, managers, and coaches, including Bob Bradley, the former coach of the US and Egyptian national teams.

Marsh has also appeared on numerous TV shows outside of sport, including *Come Dine with Me*, *The Alan Titchmarsh Show*, *Ready Steady Cook*, and *I'm a Celebrity, Get Me Out of Here*, the latter requiring a stint in the Australian jungle with other celebrities. Perhaps true to form, Marsh was voted off the latter show after accusations of sexist jokes. But as with other instances, he remained adamant that it was unnecessary to issue an apology—private or otherwise—although ultimately he would do so if only as an expedient. As he insists, "I act like a five year old kid sometimes. I don't apologise. What you see is what you get."[69]

Marsh's media career also includes film appearances and the occasional guest column. He starred in an award-winning movie titled *Once in a Lifetime*, which was narrated by Matt Dillon and focused on soccer in the United States during the 1970s. He filmed an exclusive DVD titled *Soccer Heroes: The Glory Years*, which was released in the UK in 2007. And during the 2013–2014 Football League Championship season, Marsh wrote a punchy guest column for the QPR match day program *Hoops*. But Marsh continues to appear in the broadcast media, including a recent return to TalkSport for a regular slot on *Andy Goldstein's Sports Bar*, which Marsh describes as "unrehearsed, unstructured, and they change it during the show,"[70] just the style of show to suit a maverick.

Marsh continues to work as a media pundit, even though he appreciates that growing media pressures mean that sportspeople are prone to severe criticism if they do not conform to expectations, explaining:

> Globally, sportsmen today are massive, massive icons. And yet, as soon as anything goes slightly wrong, using Tiger Woods as an example, the whole world is trying to slaughter Tiger Woods, the whole world is trying to slaughter and has slaughtered Paul Gascoigne and George Best. As time goes on, that becomes more and more acute.[71]

Still, despite the pressures of modern media work, Marsh rejects being coached or guided to conform: "Rodney Marsh the pundit; I was untaught, uncoached, and just 100 percent real. I only ever do it under my terms and conditions. So if somebody says, 'well Rodney, we want you to talk about England, but we don't want you to talk about this.' I go, 'well okay, we're not going to talk,'"[72] signaling that it can be inadvisable to attempt to censor a maverick.

Marsh and the Role Model Debate

To understand why Marsh has been labeled a maverick rather than a role model, it is useful to consider how the role model has evolved over time. Role model athletes have been understood very differently in relation to specific social priorities and dominant frames of reference. The origins of the model heroic athlete can be traced back to ancient Greece, especially the powerful Heracles (Hercules) myths. Such heroes of Greek myths were regarded as models for achieving glory and immortality, which were key cultural values in ancient Greece, as the historian David Lunt outlines.[73] Alternatively, in nineteenth-century Britain the role model athlete was adapted to Christian morality and the need to steel characters to fight for the British Empire. The ideal sporting hero was molded by the British to lead his team out to conquer the opposition on the playing field, which resembled a battleground.[74] As William Skidelsky points out,[75] the belief that sportspeople have a moral duty to behave was fundamental in nineteenth-century English public schools. In prestigious public schools like Rugby, which was run by headmaster and historian Thomas Arnold between 1828 and 1841, character was regarded as a repository of Christian virtue. The combination of vigorous moral instruction and games playing led to the belief that physical robustness and moral purity were connected.

This empire model of the Christian athlete is evidently inappropriate today. In the journal *Leisure Studies*,[76] Gill Lines suggests that few contemporary sportspeople can live up to the image of the Victorian sporting hero: "It is questionable whether modern day sports stars can be perceived as heroic in the traditional sense, for few can live up to 'Muscular Christian' imagery of the Victorian era, where male sporting heroes were admired for high morals and exemplary sporting behaviour, displaying courage, loyalty and bravery."

Even though the Victorian sporting hero was partly mythical, this narrative set the tone for idealizing sporting role models and distinguishing them from badly behaved sportspeople in the twentieth century. However, after the Second World War, Britain gradually withdrew from its colonies, and the moral absolutes of the Victorian Empire became increasingly irrelevant for many British people. Postwar Britain witnessed the emergence of rebels and social movements that rejected traditional authority. As the eminent sociologist Stanley Cohen explained in his seminal book originally published in 1972,[77] in the 1960s individuals or groups who deviated from middle-class moral codes risked being labeled folk devils. In 1960s Britain, there were repeated moral panics about mods and rockers, which Cohen analyzes in his study.[78] The late 1960s and 1970s bore witness to the football mavericks who rejected middle-class etiquette and as a result became notorious. Despite the further unraveling of established moral codes in the late twentieth century, elites continued to moralize about personal behavior. Indeed, even more than rock and roll aficionados or wayward athletes, teenage mothers were a frequent target of reproof in 1990s Britain.

Compared with the 1960s and 1970s, there is in the early twenty-first century a decided lack of moral consensus in Western societies, and moral panics cannot, therefore, be promoted with direct reference to an established moral code. For example, today it is inconceivable that there could be a moral panic about youth subcultures as happened in 1960s Britain with mods and rockers. Instead, contemporary moral regulation is less coherent and is often promoted indirectly through role models. It is in this context that the athletic role model has taken on new meaning. As politics has become more personalized, politicians and senior media people find it easier to promote role models than an explicit moral agenda. That is why the role model sportsperson continues to endure, and mavericks are shunned.

As exemplified in Rob Steen's book *The Mavericks*,[79] Marsh has been frequently identified as one of the core maverick English footballers. Marsh himself says, in his autobiography: "I have been coupled with players like Frank Worthington, Eric Cantona, Stan Bowles, Tony Currie, Peter Osgood and Alan Hudson. It's like being called a role model. If people want to see me as someone who did his own thing, fine. Is that a maverick? It's how others see you, nothing else."[80] Marsh's comments, while certainly meant to inflame, also suggest that the distinction between mavericks and role models remains unclear and is merely a matter of perception. Yet he rejects the concept of role models: "I don't believe in role models. What does that even mean? That you try to be something and someone you're not? My motto in life has always been 'just be yourself.'"[81]

It is instructive to compare Marsh's rejection of footballers as role models to the comments of his maverick successor at Queen's Park Rangers, Stan Bowles. After Marsh left QPR for Manchester City, Bowles became the star QPR player as the team rose back to the English First Division in 1973. I interviewed Bowles in 1996, and he was similarly skeptical of attempting to fulfill the media's demands to behave as a role model to be admired by others. For Bowles, footballers are footballers who should be judged on their playing ability rather than on what they do outside football. This is one reason why Bowles found he could develop positive relationships with sport journalists, but he was also uncomfortable when nonsports journalists asked questions about his life beyond football: "You might not want the media, but it is there. You just learn to live with it. I got on very well with the sports media. I had more problems with other journalists," revealed Bowles.[82] Likewise, Marsh is critical of the media and how football's role models are now treated:

> Society has changed so dramatically over the last forty years that role models today are looked at in terms of how can we make these people fail, rather than saying isn't

it great that a kid from the gutter has grown up and become a famous world-class footballer and he's got a lovely, great big house and nice cars and wouldn't it be great to be that. I think that everybody and including the media, especially the media, look at "hasn't he slipped" and what can we do and surreptitiously find out "what he's doing wrong" so we can slaughter him.[83]

Both Bowles and Marsh exemplified the maverick counterculture, although Marsh believes that "maverick" is little more than a label: "You went to Rangers to watch Marsh and then Bowles. It seems that if you are even a little bit away from the norm, the game labels you as a rebel, a maverick or, most significantly, a failure."[84] So how does a maverick differ from a role model? As previously explored in this work, mavericks came from working-class neighborhoods. There, they learned that if they were to escape to better lives, they needed to be quick, both physically and verbally, which certainly helps explain how and why Marsh's impulsive behavior and comments have become defining features of his personality and, hence, his reputation.

Mavericks are also distinguished by their upbringings, which understandably lack instruction in middle-class expectations of manners and behavior. In other words, mavericks did not attend the expensive public schools that often continue to instill Victorian sporting manners and social politeness. Moreover, mavericks tend to distance themselves from people who have been educated at elite institutions, leading to inevitable clashes and sharp disagreements about decorum and what it means to be an adored public figure.

On numerous occasions, Marsh provided examples of how he reacted to people closely associated with the establishment or governing institutions of bourgeois society. Some of these individuals are connected with the institutions organizing football (the English FA); others are senior media managers. Similarly, prominent politicians are representatives of establishment institutions, which helps explain why when Marsh was in their company, he typically felt more comfortable among those who were more familiar seeming. For instance, in 1979, he was invited to meet Henry Kissinger, former American secretary of state and national security adviser, at the American Soccer Bowl final, although in hindsight the outcome of this tryst may have been predictable. As Marsh later remarked, "Yes, he wanted to talk football. However, despite being a person who spent his life as a peace envoy around the world, he turned out to be one of the most boring individuals I have ever met. After three minutes I made my excuses and left to go and talk to the tea lady instead."[85] Unlike role models, mavericks are not known for ingratiating themselves with the great and good of society.

By contrast, footballers who have adapted to the expectations of becoming role models have typically worked hard to please establishment figures within football and in politics. Undoubtedly, the English footballer who is the most perfect media and establishment illustration of this is David Beckham; he personifies the promotion of the contemporary role model by political and cultural elites. Beckham became a star footballer at Manchester United and Real Madrid before joining the American Major League Soccer (MLS) team LA Galaxy. He might not have had the flair of Marsh on the pitch, but Beckham has pop idol looks, a celebrity marriage, and a penchant for supporting the right causes while routinely steering clear of controversial positions. Beckham has achieved the ultimate role model status, to the extent that he has become an ambassador for British sport and a United Nations spokesperson. He was invited to 10 Downing Street in July 2008 for a chat with Prime Minister Gordon Brown about sporting and political matters; they discussed England's bid to host the World Cup in 2018. He even acted as an official representative in the negotiations for this bid. Moreover, he was a goodwill ambassador to the United Nations Children's Emergency Fund (UNICEF) and returned to 10 Downing Street in 2012 to put pressure on the new prime minister, David Cameron, to address child hunger. He would later publish an article in the popular British newspaper the *Daily Mirror* about this visit and his work with UNICEF,[86] consciously underscoring his role model reputation in such a visible forum.

But Beckham's integration into the British establishment was sealed by his role in promoting London's Olympic Games in 2012. He was a prominent participant in the opening ceremony, which was broadcast worldwide. Queen Elizabeth recognized Beckham's official membership of the British establishment by granting him the Order of the British Empire (OBE).[87] Even though Beckham is married to a pop star, he never fails to respect the etiquette of both the business media and various bodies of authority. Crucially, his career has been devoid of disrespectful wisecracks, and his minor slipups, including kicking a ball at an opponent and crashing a car that he was driving too fast, are generally ignored as isolated incidents. Beckham is widely respected as displaying the right qualities for boys to emulate. In a poll of 601 British boys by Disney XD, Beckham was chosen as the number one role model, beating Bill Gates (who finished in sixth place), Barack Obama (eighth), and many others.[88]

Marsh, who certainly occupies a very different space, nonetheless admires Beckham as a footballer but is much less convinced of his social role:

> I think he's missed the boat on what he could've done for the game. . . . I think later in his life he will regret that he had that opportunity, and he chose to ignore it. . . . If you look at the history of the world, most, if not all, of the big changes that have happened in the world have happened because of revolution and not evolution. David Beckham had the chance to be a revolutionary because of his worldwide stature. He could've put on the James Dean jacket and jeans and had a cult following forever, based on wanting to change the football world. Instead, he comes on

the stage with Prince William and David Cameron with a straight bat[89] and a nice smile and in my opinion it's completely meaningless, from Rodney Marsh's point of view. Whereas, he could've been so powerful for changing the game.... He could've done so much for the revolution of football in my opinion.... When you're given a license to do things positively, sometimes you have to be outspoken and sometimes you have to not play the straight-bat.[90]

Certainly, Beckham is not like Marsh in terms of daring to be outspoken. Like Marsh, Beckham comes from a London East End working-class neighborhood. However, Beckham was born in 1975, whereas Marsh was born in 1944, which leads some to conclude that their respective ages account for the differences between these two public figures. Beckham grew up some thirty years later than the mavericks who became notorious in the 1960s and 1970s; his formative years were in the late 1980s and 1990s, when distinctions between British working-class and middle-class identities had significantly eroded. As sociologist Frank Furedi posits, declining working-class solidarity through trade union membership between 1979 and 1996 in Britain was indicative of weakening trust in institutions across British society that maintained class solidarities.[91]

Beckham was raised during this period, whereas Marsh grew up in Britain at a time when a range of institutions created a strong sense of "them and us." It was simply easier for Beckham than for Marsh to adapt to bourgeois expectations. Indeed, researchers from the University of Manchester analyzed Beckham's changing speech patterns over time and concluded that he has even largely dropped his working-class cockney accent for a more standard, middle-class English accent.[92] In comparison, although Marsh wanted to witness "the other side,"[93] he reacted against establishment types and never wanted to integrate into establishment institutions or middle-class society.

Lasting Notoriety

When I asked Marsh if he would have ever worked for the Football Association as England manager or accepted an OBE from the queen, he answered "no" to both questions.[94] I pressed him as to why he would refuse such honors, and he replied, "I think there's no value in it—absolutely no value in it whatsoever. Let me tell you why. I'll explain it. If you revere and reward and make famous people that have done heroin and cocaine and sold stuff and committed crimes—if you revere those people and give them awards, as happens, and still happens, I have no value for that."[95] Marsh elaborated on why he rejects such establishment rituals: "I am not anti-establishment for the sake of being anti-establishment.

The only reason I am is if there is a cause to be and a real issue. I'm not just antiestablishment for the sake of damning the establishment."[96]

However, for Marsh, not wishing to become England manager, avoiding establishment recognition, and distancing himself from the role model cliché do not mean shirking responsibility. He does believe in taking responsibility when offered the opportunity, as demonstrated by his adopting management positions with several American soccer clubs. In addition, he was team captain of QPR, Manchester City, Fulham, and his teams in America. Despite these achievements, Marsh reflected that possibly he wasn't an ideal team captain: "Marsh the Captain: doesn't sound right, does it? You're right, I should never have been captain, but I seemed to get the nod for political reasons. I was always going to have my say, be creative, constructive and critical."[97]

Maybe it was these qualities combined with not being afraid to tell it like it is that earned Marsh his captains' armbands. Indeed, an important difference between Marsh and many role model footballers is his consistent commitment to saying what he believes is true rather than attempting to tell journalists and the public what they might want to hear. "Why do we try and pull the wool over the eyes of the public?" he asks. "You should tell it as if you were in the pub with your mates, just tell the truth."[98]

Speaking his mind, whether he entertained or offended, is undoubtedly the final defining feature of Marsh the maverick. Many people in sport and beyond could learn from Marsh's motto: "How do you describe a Loose Cannon? That's easy: someone who doesn't really care about anything except the things they love. Say what you think, do what you believe in and live with the consequences. I have taken that motto with me through a wonderful life in football."[99]

Marsh's determination to speak out and not conform contrasts with contemporary role models and is certainly the defining characteristic of a maverick. Unlike imperial Victorian role models, today's role models promoted by political and cultural elites speak to a climate bereft of moral absolutes. The modern construction of the role model is a desperate attempt to encourage socially conservative behavior in the absence of a prevailing ideology. Similarly, modern mavericks are not reacting against a dominant moral code as they were in 1960s and 1970s Britain. Yet, like Marsh, those who do not conform to being role models and who speak out still risk being labeled mavericks.

Former Manchester City, AC Milan, and Italian national team attacker Mario Balotelli has recently been labeled a maverick.[100] Balotelli has made many provocative comments and been involved in some strange incidents, although these have tended to make him seem foolish rather than someone deliberately challenging authority and morality.[101] But Balotelli is also not afraid to speak his mind. He has been identified as a role model for Italy's immigrant community since becoming the first black player to score a goal for Italy's national team.[102] And so it does indeed remain difficult to distinguish between role models and mavericks in terms of behavior, especially in societies that lack agreement about what we should aspire to. As Marsh himself described, some people might consider a maverick to be a role model. It would be helpful if we could only judge footballers by their playing ability and challenge attempts by political and media elites to endorse sporting role models like David Beckham as public authority figures.

Marsh has evidently taken a very different approach to his life in sport and the media when compared with David Beckham or any other athletes who have won favor with middle-class observers. To be sure, one vital distinction between a David Beckham and a Rodney Marsh is the impulse to either conform or speak out. While this provides us with a real distinction between role model and maverick athletes, we should also keep in mind that both are part of the myths we construct about sport that are fundamental to sport's attraction for us. Similarly, in ancient Greece, victory odes by the lyric poet Pindar (fifth century BC) explored sporting myths, political repercussions, human frailty, and immortal aspiration. As English professor Brian Cummings recently discussed, maverick George Best probably offered a contemporary version of the ancient Greek interplay between mortality and immortality: "[H]e found his immortal moment at a point too young for him to understand, and then found that while making him immortal it did not in any way save him from mortality."[103] Marsh's legacy is that mavericks can achieve lasting notoriety by speaking their minds instead of conforming.

Notes

1. The American word "soccer" is "football" in British English. The terms are used interchangeably in this text and should be distinguished from American football.

2. Rob Steen, *The Mavericks: English Football When Flair Wore Flares* (Edinburgh: Mainstream Publishing, 1994), 132.

3. The First Division was the highest tier of the Football League from 1888 until the creation of the Premier League in 1992. Then, the First Division became the second tier in English and Welsh football, and in 2004 it was rebranded the Football League Championship.

4. Author's note: as a matter of full disclosure, I am a QPR fan.

5. American soccer uses the term "coach" for the role of "manager" in English football. Both terms are used interchangeably in this chapter.

6. Dominic Standish, "Confessions of a Footballer," *Living Marxism*, no. 96 (December 1996–January 1997): 17.

7. Stan Bowles, *Stan Bowles: The Autobiography* (London: Orion Publishing, 2004), 1.

8. Rodney Marsh, interview by the author, June 25, 2013.

9. Andrew Calcutt, *Arrested Development: Pop Culture and the Erosion of Adulthood* (London: Cassell, 1998), 171–76.

10. I use the term "establishment" throughout this chapter. It refers to the established institutions that, through their relationships, govern society and perpetuate the form of economy in the interests of elites. The "establishment" was defined by founding social theorist Max Weber as "a technical category which designates the continuity of the combination of certain types of services with each other and with the material means of production"; see Max Weber, *Essays in Economic Sociology* (Princeton, NJ: Princeton University Press, 1999), 274.

11. Steen, *The Mavericks*, 25.

12. Ibid, 26.

13. Ibid, 51–52.

14. Rodney Marsh with Brian Woolnough, *Rodney Marsh: I Was Born a Loose Cannon* (Knutsford, Cheshire, England: Optimum Publishing, 2010), 146.

15. Ibid, 29.

16. Ibid, 159.

17. Ibid, 1.

18. Ibid, 29.

19. A small hat, or cap, displaying the England badge is given to a footballer each time he plays for the national team.

20. Marsh, interview by the author.

21. Marsh and Woolnough, *Rodney Marsh*, 107–12.

22. Ibid, 108.

23. Ibid, 111.

24. Ibid, 112.

25. Marsh, interview by the author.

26. John May, "The Best and Worst of a Legend," BBC Sport, November 25, 2005, at http://news.bbc.co.uk/sport1/hi/football/4312792.stm.

27. Marsh and Woolnough, *Rodney Marsh*, 40.

28. Marsh, interview by the author.

29. Ibid.

30. Marsh and Woolnough, *Rodney Marsh*, 33.

31. A public schoolboy in Great Britain refers to a boy who attends a privately funded, elite school.

32. Marsh and Woolnough, *Rodney Marsh*, 38.

33. Ibid, 21.

34. Ibid, 41.

35. Ibid, 44.

36. Ibid.

37. Ibid, 66.

38. Ibid, 69.

39. Ibid, 66.

40. Ibid, 68.

41. Ibid, 88.

42. Ibid, 89.

43. Ibid.

44. Ibid, 88.

45. Ibid, 89.
46. Ibid, 82.
47. Ibid, 91.
48. Ibid, 90.
49. Ibid, 91.
50. Ibid, 92.
51. Ibid, 94.
52. Travis Puterbaugh, "Rodney Marsh Testimonial, 9/14/79," Tampa Sports History, September 14, 2009, at http://tampasportshistory.blogspot.com/2009/09/rodney-marsh-testimonial-91479.html.
53. Marsh and Woolnough, *Rodney Marsh*, 96.
54. Ibid, 51.
55. Ibid, 60.
56. Ibid, 148.
57. Marsh, interview by the author.
58. Ibid.
59. Ibid.
60. Marsh and Woolnough, *Rodney Marsh*, 124.
61. Ibid, 125.
62. Ibid.
63. Ibid.
64. "TV Pundit Sacked for Tsunami Joke," BBC News, January 26, 2005, at http://news.bbc.co.uk/2/hi/entertainment/4208135.stm.
65. Marsh, interview by the author.
66. Marsh and Woolnough, *Rodney Marsh*, 134.
67. Marsh, interview by the author.
68. Ibid.
69. "'Sexist' Rodney Marsh Is Shown the Red Card by I'm a Celebrity Viewers," *Daily Mail*, November 26, 2007, at http://www.dailymail.co.uk/tvshowbiz/article-496374/Sexist-Rodney-Marsh-shown-red-card-Im-A-Celebrity-viewers.html#ixzz2X2jfBzn0.
70. Marsh, interview by the author. Marsh also helps his son Jonathan with property development in Florida and is executive ambassador to Optimum Business Solutions in Manchester.
71. Ibid.
72. Ibid.
73. David J. Lunt, "The Heroic Athlete in Ancient Greece," *Journal of Sport History* 36, no. 3 (2009): 379.
74. Richard Holt, "Champions, Heroes and Celebrities: Sporting Greatness and the British Public," in *The Book of British Sporting Heroes*, ed. James Huntington-Whiteley (London: National Portrait Gallery Publications, 1999), 10–25.
75. William Skidelsky, "The Trouble with Boys," *New Statesman*, October 20, 2003, at http://www.newstatesman.com/node/158526.
76. Gill Lines, "Villains, Fools or Heroes? Sports Stars as Role Models for Young People," *Leisure Studies* 20, no. 4 (2001): 286.
77. Stanley Cohen, *Folk Devils and Moral Panics* (Abingdon, Oxon, England: Routledge, 2011).

78. Ibid, 56–60.
79. Steen, *The Mavericks*.
80. Marsh and Woolnough, *Rodney Marsh*, 146.
81. Ibid, 144.
82. Standish, "Confessions of a Footballer," 18.
83. Marsh, interview by the author.
84. Marsh and Woolnough, *Rodney Marsh*, 146.
85. Ibid, 24.
86. David Beckham, "David Beckham: Millions of Children Go Hungry Every Day But We Can Stop It if We All Act Now," *Daily Mirror*, June 2, 2013, at http://www.mirror.co.uk/news/world-news/david-beckham-join-unicefs-fight-1937123.
87. "Beckham's Pride at OBE," BBC Sport, June 13, 2003, at http://news.bbc.co.uk/sport2/hi/football/2988104.stm.
88. "Beckham Is Top Role Model for British Boys," *Metro*, January 12, 2011, at http://metro.co.uk/2011/01/12/david-beckham-is-top-role-model-for-british-boys-625753/.
89. A "straight bat" is an English cricketing metaphor for someone who exhibits traditional, conservative behavior and beliefs.
90. Marsh, interview by the author.
91. Frank Furedi, *Culture of Fear* (London: Continuum, 2002), 129–30.
92. "David and Victoria Beckham 'Getting Posher,' Study Finds," BBC News, April 17, 2013, at http://www.bbc.co.uk/news/uk-england-22179969.
93. Marsh and Woolnough, *Rodney Marsh*, 33.
94. Marsh, interview by the author.
95. Ibid.
96. Ibid.
97. Marsh and Woolnough, *Rodney Marsh*, 103.
98. Ibid, 162.
99. Ibid, 1.
100. Brian Homewood, "Soccer-Maverick Balotelli Tired of Being in 'Eye of Cyclone,'" Reuters, October 14, 2013, at http://www.reuters.com/article/2013/10/14/soccer-italy-balotelli-idUSL3N0I421120131014.
101. Cameron Macphail, "Mario Balotelli: Manchester City's Outspoken Striker Shoots His Mouth Off," *Telegraph*, April 1, 2013, at http://www.telegraph.co.uk/sport/football/teams/manchester-city/8271646/Mario-Balotelli-Manchester-Citys-outspoken-striker-shoots-his-mouth-off.html.
102. James Taylor, "Mario Balotelli a Role Model for Italy's Immigrant Community," World Soccer, posted by Jamie Rainbow, March 10, 2013, at http://www.worldsoccer.com/blogs/mario-balotelli-a-role-model-for-italys-immigrant-community.
103. Brian Cummings, "Pelé, Cruyff, Best, Maradona, Zidane—and Pindar," *Times Literary Supplement*, June 18, 2014, at http://www.the-tls.co.uk/tls/public/article1423715.ece.

Ayrton Senna

The Legacy of a Global Racing Icon

—Viral Shah

Introduction

It was only after tragedy at Imola that the wider world realised how greatly revered Ayrton Senna had become. Even those who knew Senna personally were surprised at his global popularity. Julian Jakobi, Senna's manager and business adviser, remembered from his youth witnessing state funerals as diverse as John F. Kennedy's in 1963 and Winston Churchill's some two years later, but somehow this ranked and felt different. As he recalls, "I'd never seen anything like this. The Senna funeral in Brazil was just quite something."[1] At the time, Senna, a three-time Formula One (F1) world champion, was also the recognised second-highest-paid sportsman in the world behind the National Basketball Association's Michael Jordan.[2]

In 1994, Brazil had only recently freed itself from the shackles of a technocratic military-style dictatorship, as the historian David Aarão Reis described it, and was still in financial crisis, struggling to bring down inflation.[3] In tough economic times, the citizens of this fledgling democracy saw Senna as a symbol of hope. As historian Joel Wolfe couches it: "Brazilians did more than mourn Senna's death at his funeral; they celebrated their modernity through his life."[4]

President Itamar Franco declared a three-day period of mourning, including a day off for all schoolchildren. Millions of people lined the streets to catch a glimpse of Senna's coffin as it was carried on a fire engine into São Paulo from the airport escorted by a police motorcade. The *Guardian*'s Richard Williams aptly described the scene:

> Now banners and freshly sprayed graffiti were everywhere, dangled from every bridge, painted on every blank surface: *Obrigado Senna* (thank you, Senna), *Senna não morreu, porque os deuses não morrem* (Senna isn't dead because gods don't die). And *Obrigado, Senna por fazer nossos domingos felizes* (thank you, Senna, for making our Sundays so happy).[5]

To put this moment into greater historical perspective, more people waited in line to view Senna's coffin than for Tancredo Neves, the nation's first civilian politician after twenty-one years of the dictatorship.[6]

But while he was beloved in Brazil, Senna was also a highly divisive figure abroad, starting several feuds with multiple rivals and thus becoming a hero to some and a villain to others. His multifaceted character was full of dichotomies until his untimely death canonised him. Here was a man who fought persistently for driver safety, yet always raced at full pelt, often taking accident-inducing and life-threatening risks. He was a philanthropic multimillionaire star living through all the trappings and all the hallmarks of celebrity culture while remaining a family man at heart. And it is perhaps these contradictions alongside his undeniable talent behind the steering wheel that help define who Senna was and how he is still remembered both abroad and at home.

The Early Years

Little has been written about Senna's pre-fame years, but what is clear is that his family had the wealth and resources to allow his interest and natural talent in racing to flourish. The Senna da Silva family lived in Santana, a prosperous Italian neighbourhood in north São Paulo. Senna's father, Milton da Silva, was a successful businessman, the owner of a number of farms while also running a car parts firm that employed a staff of nearly one thousand employees.[7]

Tom Rubython's immense biography of the Brazilian contains the most comprehensive collection of observations regarding Senna's formative years, although he is prone to romanticizing the life of the young Brazilian who was raised in privilege and in a decidedly conservative atmosphere.[8] Perhaps unsurprisingly, similar circumstances enabled other racing legends to pursue their talents, including Nigel Mansell, whose father was an aerospace engineer; Graham Hill, whose father was a stockbroker; and certainly Stirling Moss, whose father was a dentist who actually had a background in motorsports himself.[9]

Yet in Brazil, motor racing was considered a sport that was free from the class antagonism that otherwise riddled Brazilian society as Brazilians cheered the best drivers their country had to offer against talent from around the world.[10] Unlike domestic Brazilian soccer, where rivalries were often dominated by racial, ethnic, and social tensions, the Brazilian motor racing driver was always considered in a global context to be competing against drivers from richer, more developed nations. A 1951 nationwide survey found that people generally believed that luxury car owners (specifically Cadillac owners) had worked hard and earned and deserved their expensive vehicles. Given this, cars were seen as the ultimate symbol of independence and selfhood. This perception of cars as typifying the democratization of consumerism in Brazilian society can be described as *automobility*.[11] In turn, it fuelled how racing drivers such as Senna were perceived in the public eye.

While his personal circumstances helped inform the earliest days of his career, Senna's early years were neither perfect nor necessarily conducive to star making. As a three-year-old, Senna had been diagnosed with a motor coordination problem that caused him to amble slowly, making it difficult for him to, for instance, run or climb stairs. An electroencephalogram showed nothing unusual, but the symptoms persisted, a matter that made it necessary for the family to adapt accordingly.[12] By most accounts, these unfortunate circumstances led directly to the moment a young Senna first experienced a modicum of success behind the wheel. For his fourth birthday, his father built him a go-kart complete with a lawnmower engine and a plastic bucket seat.[13] The youngster poured his concentration into driving. He was soon able to drive a jeep around the farm, expertly changing gears by listening to the engine sound,[14] for he could barely reach the clutch. As he progressed, concerns for his health dissipated.

In 1968, an eight-year-old Senna's motoring jaunts came to an abrupt halt when he was stopped by local police while driving the family car on São Paulo's busy roads.[15] Similar tales litter the childhoods of other racing greats, but for most Brazilians, being stopped by the police in 1968 would be an enormously worrisome experience, given that the military dictatorship running the country was intensifying its repressive policies due to an increase in street protests and the emergence of armed opposition groups.[16] It is possible that the Senna da Silva family may have been unperturbed by the police, given Milton da Silva's technocratic occupation, but it is also important to note that there are no references to their political affiliation in any literature about the family.[17]

Senna's father was instrumental in providing the best possible environment for his son's talent to flourish, contacting Lucio Pascual Gascon, a mechanic nicknamed Tchê, who had emigrated from Spain in 1960. Tchê's pedigree was clear, having, as Williams asserts, "propelled [Emerson] Fittipaldi to his boyhood karting triumphs ten years earlier."[18] Spending all his spare time working on his kart with Tchê, Senna began to absorb the intimate technical knowledge that would allow him to converse fluently with engineers later in his career. He won five successive South American karting championships from 1977 through 1981. But the competition in Europe was much tougher, and Senna failed to win any of the three world championships he entered, coming closest in 1979 but losing out on lap difference.[19]

Having seemingly plateaued in his development, Senna found himself at a crossroad; his father, who never seemed quite convinced that his talented son would be able to punch through that last wall, went so far as to try to persuade his ambitious son to enter the family business. In hindsight, this offer could be perceived as an attempt to provide the young man with something of a fallback position in case his development as a driver continued to stall, but Milton da Silva's pragmatism regarding his son's chances of reaching Formula One, the pinnacle of competitive racing, while commendable, proved nonetheless to be superfluous.[20] While the young man, perhaps cast in the role of the dutiful son, reluctantly enrolled in a business course at the University of São Paulo, he could only ignore his own dreams for so long. Three months later, in November 1980, Senna headed off to Great Britain to secure his first drive in a car.[21]

Speaking of this transition in young Senna's life, Tchê maintained that if Senna had won the karting world championship, he would have ceded to his family's pressure and ended up back in São Paulo selling screws and bolts in the family's auto parts store. It was that early failure to win that forged Senna's iron will to win.[22]

England and Formula Ford 1600

Prior to leaving for England, Senna married his long-time girlfriend Lilian de Vasconcelos Souza, a glamorous blonde who was also part of the São Paulo aristocracy. Both spoke barely a word of English. And yet Senna chose the prestige of England rather than the Italian or German Formula Ford championship, because, as Williams explains, since the 1960s, "England's club racing scene [had] represented the most effective finishing school for new talent around the world."[23]

Senna excelled in a test drive for the Van Diemen team, in what was his first time in a single-seater racing car. Ten laps later, no less than Ralph Firman, the team principal, was impressed enough to give the young Brazilian what is known as a *works drive*, defined as any racing opportunity that is officially sanctioned and has financial support from a manufacturer, alongside Argentinean Enrique Mansilla and Mexican Alfonso Toledano. But Senna's forthright nature didn't immediately endear him to Firman. Having been given the old car of the 1980 champion Roberto Moreno while his teammates raced with the new RF 81, Senna was frustrated.[24] During the first test drive at Brands Hatch, he smashed the car completely at the Druids corner. Toledano recalls: "[H]e'd been promised a new car [but only] after the first three races. . . . I could've bet some big money he did it on purpose."[25] Having run Brazilian drivers before, including the aforementioned Moreno, a furious Firman told Toledano after the incident: "[T]his is the biggest Brazilian wanker I've ever had in my life!"[26]

Still, Senna won him over with a stunning debut season, emphatically capturing both the RAC and Townsend Thoresen championships. It was expected that the Brazilian would progress to Formula Ford 2000 or even Formula Three (F3) the following year, but at the end of the 1981 season, he decided to return to Brazil, ostensibly to save his failing marriage to Lilian, for whom, it was thought, the shift from a houseful of servants in sunny Brazil to a modest life in miserable Norfolk near the Van Diemen factory had proven to be too much—which ultimately it was.

Personal matters notwithstanding, there was a pending professional matter to which Senna needed to attend: his inability to rein in a sponsor. The success of other Brazilians, from Robert Moreno and Raul Boesel in Formula Three to Formula One champion Nelson Piquet, at higher, more prestigious levels of competition meant that Senna's exploits weren't getting much media coverage in Brazil.[27] And when coupled with a decided lack of newspaper attention, sponsorship itself was becoming increasingly difficult to come by as Brazil plunged into recession. Between 1981 and 1983, income had declined, unemployment had risen sharply, and inflation soared to over 200 percent in 1983, a result of American deflationary measures ruining Latin American petrodollar loans,[28] which resulted in the drying up of many potential suitors for Senna's professional aspirations.

Image and Publicity

Another challenge to Senna's climb in the sport was his ability to affect just the right persona to further his ambitions. From his earliest days in England, it was clear that Senna was aware of the importance of image management and publicity as a means to secure suitable and sustainable sponsorship. While most professional sportspeople today are conscious of this aspect of their career in the present-day corporate environment, it had yet to become ubiquitous in the early 1980s. At Brands Hatch, in just his third race, Senna approached a young photographer named Keith Sutton, who had been taking pictures of him for Brazil's *Auto Esporte* magazine the previous week at Thruxton, and asked him to send photos and press releases back home as well as to influential people in Formula One.[29]

As Senna continued to rise in stature, people in Brazil tended to compare the young contender (to some, perhaps, pretender!) to Nelson Piquet, who by 1987, well before Senna won his first world title, was a three-time Formula One world champion. But while this was seen by many as potentially problematic, the comparison also advantaged the emergent star as in the public eye; the differences between the two racers actually seemed to work in Senna's favour—at least in part. Indeed, Senna was everything the average Brazilian might be: he was from a Catholic background, he was a fan of the well-supported Corinthians football club,[30] and he had a strong aversion to politics. Even his surname was common: da Silva. Comparatively, the Rio-born Piquet was raised in the abhorred political class. His father, Estácio Gonçalves Souto Maior, was the health minister in João Goulart's government in the earlier 1960s.[31] Prior to the 1964 military coup that ousted Goulart, Piquet's father joined Aliança Renovadora Nacional (ARENA), the party of the subsequent dictatorship, with whom he served until he was impeached in April 1969 under the controversial Institutional Act no. 5. Yet despite what appears to have been a privileged upbringing, Piquet was in some ways more a self-made man than Senna was perceived to be. For instance, in order to hide his racing career from his disapproving family,[32] Piquet took to competing under his mother's maiden name (albeit spelled "Piket"[33]). And in order to fund his racing dream, Piquet had to drop out of university in 1974—two years into an engineering course—and take a job in a garage.[34] Thus, while Senna was living in reasonable comfort in his first year as a professional racer, renting a small bungalow near Norwich in the village of Eaton, Piquet lived in a bus when first competing in Formula Three in 1977.[35] These differing paths to the top led to a divergence in character that fuelled the duo's intense rivalry.

Senna's character and success were strong factors in his popularity; it helped that he cultivated both through good media relations. Piquet, on the other hand, was far more laissez-faire when asked about his popularity: "No. I don't give a shit for that!"[36]

Newly single, a much more polished Senna returned to England in 1982, signing for Rushen Green to compete in the British and European Formula Ford 2000 competitions, winning both and dominating the field with a stunning win percentage of 78 percent. One astonishing performance at Snetterton in the fifth race of the season saw Senna drive a large portion of the race without front brakes, which had been cut by a shard of debris from an earlier crash. Having fallen back to seventh, he clawed his way past the other drivers to victory, despite being only able to use his rear brakes.[37]

It was at Zolder in May that Senna finally tried to introduce himself to Piquet. The Formula Ford 2000 race was one of the support races for the F1 Belgian Grand Prix. It was a dramatic weekend, with fan favourite Gilles Villeneuve dying in a crash during qualifying. It was amid these tense circumstances that Senna first chose to reach out to Piquet.[38] Trying to focus on the race ahead, Piquet ignored his intense young compatriot,[39] an act of gamesmanship on the part of the veteran racer that ultimately sowed the seeds of a poor relationship that would only worsen over time.

Fast-forwarding to the start of the 1988 Formula One season, Piquet was the reigning world champion. But soon he would be on the decline—in both a sporting sense and in popularity with the Brazilian public. Senna was at McLaren and finally set to fulfil his potential, but Piquet saw him as a threat. Prior to the opening race in Rio, Piquet insinuated that Senna was homosexual and that his well-publicised flings with women, not to mention his earlier marriage, were a facade.[40] To be sure, given the focus and intensity he put on his racing career, Senna rarely had a steady girlfriend, a fact that Piquet had decided to crassly exploit, although it did little to stop Senna from blowing by him in success both on and off the track. Also, just around the same time, Senna had begun a relationship with Xuxa Meneghel, a well-known figure from the Brazilian television channel TV Globo and with whom he would have an on-again, off-again relationship for the next five years. Indeed, as Senna's track success grew, so did his global popularity. This relationship with one of Brazil's most beautiful women only heightened his fame. Yet, as Meneghel recalls, it just wasn't meant to last: "We were pretty much the same. But I knew that the logistics of one career centred in Brazil, and one in Europe made life impossible. I wanted a person like him, and I thought everything he did was a lot, but he was choking me."[41] It was clear that between his early marriage with Lilian Souza and his last love, Adriane Galisteu, Xuxa Meneghel was the only serious relationship Senna had. As he himself would later acknowledge, "Only one time in my life, I thought about having a family, with children, and it was with her, with Xuxa."[42]

Rising Star

After two fine years in England, Senna was in high demand. He had offers from McLaren and Toleman to finance a year in Formula Three in exchange for a long contract. A driver with less faith in his own ability would doubtless have snapped up such a deal. Eventually, he chose Dick Bennetts's West Surrey Racing team. Senna's first experience with intense competition was in 1983. Martin Brundle, who was with Eddie Jordan's team, trailed in Senna's wake during the first half of the season as the Brazilian won nine races in a row. At that stage, anything other than a Senna procession to the title was inconceivable. In subsequent races, the Brazilian was surprisingly inconsistent, alternating between wins and accidents. This inconsistency was such that after the penultimate round, Senna was behind in the championship for the first time, trailing Brundle, who had 123 points, by 1 point.

But when the pressure was on, Senna would not buckle, winning the championship in the final race at Thruxton. He innovatively took the risk of warming up the engine faster on the opening laps "by taping up the oil radiator,"[43] which meant that later in the race he had to unbuckle his seatbelt and lean out of the cockpit to remove the tape, almost losing control of the car. With many of the best drivers in the world having passed through the doors of West Surrey

Racing, Bennetts felt that Senna was the most accomplished, comparing him to of all things "a mobile computer."[44]

Senna felt that he had served his time in the lower rungs of British motorsport, testing for a number of Formula One teams in the summer of 1983. Williams, McLaren, and Bernie Ecclestone's Brabham were all interested, as was Toleman, with whom he eventually signed. Politics, circumstances, and sponsor pressure meant that other potential openings went to other drivers.[45] He took up the offer from Alex Hawkridge, the managing director at Toleman, really after he had exhausted all of the other options. The length of the deal was three years,[46] but most importantly it included a £100,000 buyout clause.[47] A Formula One drive was the most important factor for Senna; he did not want to be trapped by a long contract. In this regard, Toleman was the perfect stepping stone, a perspective that became clearer in Senna's overall demeanour after he signed with them. Indeed, while celebrating with his newest driver over the new contract, Hawkridge noted the clear dichotomy between Senna's public and private personas. On one hand, there was the intense professional focused purely on racing. On the other, there was the genuinely warm, family-oriented man who at times would remove his steely facade and crack jokes with his new team.[48]

Brazil on the World Stage

The careers of Luis Pereira Bueno, José Carlos Pace, Emerson Fittipaldi, and Nelson Piquet had all helped establish Brazil as a force in what had typically been the Eurocentric world of motor racing. By the time Senna reached Formula One, Brazilian drivers were considered to possess talent and money, although not always in tandem.[49]

As the playwright Nelson Rodrigues wrote in the 1950s, Brazilian society was affected by a sense of inferiority, something he called "complexo de vira-lata" or "the mongrel complex,"[50] a point that Western media commentators continue to trumpet with regard to Brazil's national character. As the *New York Times*' Larry Rohter explains, "Brazil has always aspired to be taken seriously as a world power by the heavyweights, and so it pains Brazilians that world leaders could confuse their country with Bolivia, as Ronald Reagan once did."[51] This Brazilian aspiration has led some to argue that in reality, Brazilians don't value any one sport especially but that they want victories that can boost national pride and validate the nation's identity in the world.[52] Senna gave them exactly that (in a period when the Brazilian national football team was at a relatively low point), wearing the national colours with pride on his instantly recognisable yellow helmet. Through automobility, Brazilian drivers weren't entirely stereotyped "according to clichés of national temperament,"[53] as their footballing counterparts had been. Quite the contrary, they were seen as individuals tied to the culture regardless of their status as solo sportsmen.

Motor racing was seen by the military-technocratic dictatorship as a key aspect of promoting automobility throughout the nation (continuing a policy advocated by the 1956–1961 Juscelino Kubitschek administration).[54] In the early years of the dictatorship, a similar plan was put into action for football.[55] Soon enough, the government's technocratic ideals crept into the preparatory culture of the sports they were trying to promote. Senna's own success on the world stage was a clear vindication for the key components of the sporting technocratic ideal—attention to detail in terms of technical, physical, and even dietary preparation.

After a fitting debut in Rio de Janeiro for Toleman,[56] Senna's second Grand Prix was in South Africa, where he struggled with the physical endurance needed to complete an entire Formula One race, suffering from heat exhaustion and cramps in his neck and shoulders. Having finished sixth, which won him his first point at the highest level, Senna went to the medical centre, where he met Professor Sid Watkins, the International Automobile Federation (FIA)'s medical director, for the first time. The two would gradually forge a close friendship, rallying together to try to improve driver safety. To improve his endurance levels, Senna brought in fitness trainer Nuno Cobra, who referred to the emergent Formula One star in glowing terms: "In 1984, we had a skinny, highly motivated young guy ... but he gradually became an athletic performer who could run 40 or 50 laps with incredible endurance."[57]

It was at Monaco[58] that Senna gave the first clear signal that he was destined for greatness. In only his sixth Grand Prix, Senna was sensational in monsoon conditions, steadily picking off competitors from his starting position at number thirteen. By the thirty-second lap, he had passed Frenchman Alain Prost to take the lead with weather conditions ever worsening. At that point, race clerk Jack Ickx raised the red flag, halting the race. Senna, believing that he had won his first Grand Prix race, celebrated accordingly, only to learn that the rules backdated the result one lap from when the flag was raised. Understandably furious, he and others raised accusations of a French conspiracy, given Prost's nationality, French domination of the FIA, and Monaco's proximity to France.[59] But even in defeat, Senna's performance in an inferior car highlighted his achievement while having the added effect of beginning the career-long misconception that he loved racing in the wet. As Rubython notes, Senna hated the rain, but his competition hated it even more.[60] Nevertheless, the rest of the season did not match up, with technical and engine issues causing six retirements.

Another year at Toleman did not entice Senna, who, although later renowned for tough negotiating skills,[61] handled his contract situation badly. He had undertaken negotiations secretly with Peter Warr to join Lotus Renault for

1985. Before Senna could invoke the £100,000 buyout clause, however, Lotus announced the deal in August at the Dutch Grand Prix in Zandvoort.[62] Furious at this poor conduct, Hawkridge punished Senna in the one way that would truly hurt—he suspended him from racing in the following round at Monza in Italy, acknowledging: "I wanted him to leave us knowing there is a price to pay for everything you do in life. It shook him rigid."[63] What was made crystal clear was that Senna's desire to be competitive took precedence over all else. As David Tremayne wrote in *Motor Sport* magazine, "Either you were with him all the way or you weren't. For or against. If you were critical, he became suspicious of your motives. The trust began to break down."[64]

Money versus Morality

The move to Lotus saw Senna's earnings rocket to well over $1 million annually. A resulting increase in his public profile also led to a change in management, with Independent Motorsports Group (IMG)'s Julian Jakobi taking over from long-time associate Brazilian Armando Botelho Teixeira, who had up to then only worked on a part-time basis. More importantly, Lotus brought Senna his much-anticipated first Grand Prix win. At the second race of the season at a rain-soaked Estoril, Senna dominated from start to finish, finishing a full minute ahead of Ferrari's Michele Alboreto. The rest of the season saw a number of retirements but also a fine run of five consecutive top three finishes, which allowed Senna to finish fourth in the World Championship.

The penultimate race of the 1985 calendar was at Kyalami in South Africa on October 19, which, given the period, proved to be problematic both on and off the course. Indeed, there was a tremendous amount of unrest in South Africa under the apartheid nationalist government, and a state of emergency had been announced three months earlier, the first since the Soweto uprisings of 1976.[65] With renewed global focus on the violence, the suggestion that Formula One racing join the sporting boycott of South Africa arose for the first time in 1985, although South Africa had been ostracised from several international sports for over two decades.[66]

Prior to the race, Senna stated, "I am personally against the regime. I would not like to go there, but I have a commitment to my team."[67] There was pressure from the French, Finnish, and Swedish governments to force the president of the Fédération Internationale du Sport Automobile (FISA), Jean-Marie Balestre, to hold the race elsewhere, but ultimately money prevailed, to the chagrin of many commentators and drivers alike. As *Autosport* columnist Nigel Roebuck posited, "It is the hypocrisy of it that I can't stomach. It is the selective morality, the careful removal at Kyalami of certain sponsors' names from the cars—despite the fact that their products are readily available down the road, widely advertised beyond the TV cameras' reach."[68]

Nigel Mansell of Williams was victorious, while Senna retired after suffering engine failure on the eighth lap, but that was hardly the legacy of the race. Rather, its location continued to be the source of often fierce debate that culminated the following year as Formula One pulled out, but only after television networks, whose unions staunchly refused to acquiesce further, refused to broadcast the race.[69] Senna biographer Tom Rubython, often guilty of sycophancy to Senna, attempted to justify Senna's presence at the race. He suggested that Senna's relative youth in the sport clouded his political ideals, noting: "Perhaps a few years later Senna would have stuck by his principles and defied his team and the governing body, but in 1985 he was still in the early stages of his career and did not have the clout of a world champion. It was too much of a risk."[70]

To Senna, the South African Grand Prix was a strong example of how morality and sport's idealistic purity too often clashed with corporate interests and politicking. Years later at the Loretto School in Scotland, which the sons of his close friend Sid Watkins attended, Senna addressed these issues when one pupil asked how Senna could take money from a tobacco company when the health implications of smoking are well known. Senna took a long time to answer before attempting to explain what looked to be contradictory elements of his personality and professional bearing: "Look at it like this: the tobacco company pays me a great deal of money that I can use to help a large number of children in Brazil, hospitals, and clinics. I'm able to help a lot of people who otherwise wouldn't get help."[71] When compared to the present-day grid (involving, for example, the Bahrain Grand Prix controversy in 2012 in which the race took place even while activists protesting against human rights abuses clashed with government forces[72]), with Formula One drivers utterly prohibited from possessing opinions outside the specific context of motor racing, Senna and some of his fellow drivers showed some autonomy, limited though it was.

Victory or Nothing

Lotus were thought to have the capabilities to aid Senna in a title challenge, but the team was left behind as McLaren and Williams moved into new high-tech facilities.[73] In 1986, Senna became the team leader, as Elio de Angelis left for Brabham. The perception that a ruthless, cold, manipulative personality was at work grew when it was learned that Senna had vetoed the choice of British driver Derek Warwick as de Angelis's replacement; Warwick had been the choice of Lotus's British sponsor, John Player Special.[74] Warwick recalls: "When he screwed me out of a job in 1985 [with Lotus] he had already worked out in his mind that the team was not capable of running two number one drivers[;] that would have weakened his chances of becoming World Champion and he would stop at nothing in order to be that. It wasn't personal at all. I got a Christmas card from him the same year."[75]

Ironically, Senna would find himself in Warwick's situation in 1993, when Alain Prost, perhaps his greatest rival, blocked his proposed move to Williams. Competitive desire was always Senna's foremost motivation, but such comments would not have endeared him to sections of the foreign—particularly British—press. Simon Barnes of the *Times* suggested that the Brazilian's commitment might have been perceived by many as monomania.[76]

To the further dismay of the British press, Senna found a new rival in Englishman Nigel Mansell. On the first lap of the opening race of the season in Rio, Mansell was furious after he spun off trying to overtake the Brazilian: "If I hadn't backed off, we would both have hit the Armco, and it could have been a serious accident."[77] For such fierce competitors who shared so much on the track, the two would always have differing standards when it came to the line separating competitiveness from recklessness.

In the following round at Jerez, Senna hung on to beat Mansell by just 0.014 seconds—or just ninety-three centimetres on the track. In hindsight, this photo finish cost Mansell the 1986 title, which he eventually lost to Prost by a mere two points. Mansell would have to wait until 1992 to claim his maiden World Championship, a moment during which a candid Senna said to him: "It's such a good feeling, isn't it? Now you know why I'm such a bastard. I don't ever want to lose the feeling or let anybody else experience it."[78] As for the frustrated Brazilian, his frustration continued to grow as his second season at Lotus saw eight hard-fought pole positions translate into just two wins, the second in Detroit.

Having been immersed in the corporate world of Formula One for three years, Senna learned to foster relationships with the right names accordingly. With Renault leaving F1, Lotus lacked an engine supplier. Senna helped foster a deal with Honda, the beginning of a wonderfully successful six-year partnership between the driver and the Japanese manufacturer. And yet, despite the optimism, 1987 proved to be another false dawn. At the third race of the year, Mansell and Senna resumed hostilities at Spa-Francorchamps in Belgium, colliding and spinning off on the first lap at the Fagnes curve after the Englishman tried to overtake. Both blamed each other. A furious Mansell confronted Senna, who retorted with the now infamous sound bite: "When a man holds you around the throat, I do not think he has come to apologise."[79] Senna finished third overall as compatriot Nelson Piquet, who by now perceived Senna as a serious threat and was beginning the mind games, took his third world championship.[80]

Another unsuccessful season at Lotus saw Senna once again looking elsewhere. Given the fallout from his departure from Toleman, the Brazilian attempted a move to McLaren in the proper fashion, sending a formal letter to inform Peter Warr of his intention to leave.[81] Instead, Warr, knowing that Nelson Piquet would see little incentive to remain at Williams, which was in the process of losing the team's Honda engines, outmanoeuvred Senna and quickly signed the newly crowned world champion. Senna, furious at losing the upper hand in negotiations with McLaren, told *O Globo*: "My goal is to win while Lotus's is merely to survive,"[82] a point that, at the time, didn't sound entirely convincing as he was in the midst of being replaced by a triple world champion. Eventually, Senna struck a deal with McLaren's Ron Dennis worth $7.5 million annually. And it was at McLaren where the central narrative of Senna's story in Formula One began—especially as it pertained to the developing rivalry with his new McLaren teammate Alain Prost.

Senna's well-documented rivalries with the likes of Mansell and Piquet, certainly fine competitors in their own right, were tame when compared to the level of vitriol generated by Senna's rivalry with Prost, a feud that came to dominate the headlines. The Frenchman, already a double world champion in 1985 and 1986, had the McLaren team gradually built around him during his four years there. But Senna's close relationship with Honda allowed him to quickly level the competition for team supremacy. Although it brought McLaren unprecedented success, the rivalry made life difficult for team principal Ron Dennis, created internal divisions in the team, and monopolised the Formula One administration's full attention. Even from an early exchange between the two at the McLaren motor home, one could note the underlying competitive tension in their words. When Prost asked his teammate, "Is it possible to be equal?," Senna, with nary a hint of irony, replied: "No." Prost amusingly concluded, "Shit."[83]

In 1988, Senna and Prost raced in the McLaren MP4/4, which *Top Gear* presenter Jeremy Clarkson observed was "the last of the turbocharged monsters, one of the greatest racing cars ever made."[84] With Honda providing the best engine and McLaren pulling out all the stops, including hiring physical therapist Josef Leberer to keep the drivers in the best physical shape, all signs pointed to a year of dominance. And indeed it was, with Senna and Prost together winning fifteen of the 1988 season's sixteen races, though in no sense was there any togetherness in their efforts. They were a team in name only.

Religion, Prost, and Politics

Early in the season, it dawned on Senna that Prost's experience and superior race-craft would enable him to capitalise on any mistakes. It seemed that the Brazilian was up to the challenge, notching pole position in Monaco ahead of Prost by a massive 1.427 seconds. Afterward, he spoke about the performance in spiritual terms: "I realised I was no longer driving the car consciously. I was driving it by a kind of instinct, only I was in a different dimension."[85] Senna continued this good form into the race, taking a lead of just under fifty seconds. With twelve laps left, Ron Dennis radioed him to ease off. Prost, showing why he was nicknamed Le Professeur, cut the gap by six seconds with a swift lap. The Brazilian seemingly panicked. At the sharp right-handed Portier corner, Senna turned in too tightly, glancing the trackside wall, and was thrown across the track straight into the barrier. As Prost stormed past to take the points, Senna, furious at himself, walked back to his seafront apartment and locked himself in, refusing to talk to anyone.[86]

After Monaco, Senna began to publicly refer to God in terms of mental preparation and the psychological battle of motor racing. In one press conference, he was frank in laying out his beliefs: "I have always been religious, because of my family, but I was what I would call a superficially religious person. However, over the past year and a half, two years, I have started to devote more of my time to my psychological side, my spiritual side, and tried to learn more about this way of life."[87] It was clear that this was belief on the Brazilian's own terms, and although Senna relied on scripture for his understanding of the spiritual, it owed nothing to organised religion.[88] A year later in Suzuka, when the two were barely on speaking terms, Prost exploited Senna's religious beliefs as a crude explanation for his ruthless, often aggressive behaviour on the track: "He feels sustained by God[,] and he is capable of taking every risk because he thinks he is immortal."[89] The accusation stung, with Senna retorting: "Just because I believe in God, just because I have faith in God, it doesn't mean that I'm immune. It doesn't mean that I'm immortal."[90]

The manner in which Senna could compartmentalise his personality into (1) the compassionate son, boyfriend, and philanthropist and (2) the ruthless, competitive racing driver was no more evident than in the years of his greatest successes. At Estoril in 1988, the two McLaren drivers had their first falling-out of many. At the end of the first lap, Prost made a typical overtaking manoeuvre only to find Senna squeezing him dangerously close against the pit wall. A fantastic display of car control saw Prost somehow pull off the move and take the lead to eventually win. However, the Frenchman was in no mood to celebrate, bluntly stating: "If he wants the world championship that badly, he can have it." Sportswriter Richard Williams emphasised how close the two were to disaster: "Had the cars touched at Estoril, the great crash at Le Mans in 1955 might have looked like a minor affair."[91] The rift became worse when FISA president Jean-Marie Balestre, arguably the most autocratic ruler in sport at the time, got involved and made the feud his own personal business.[92]

Ahead of the Japanese Grand Prix, Balestre had written a letter to Honda's president, Tadashi Kume, with the controversial implication that Honda engineers were giving Prost, compared to Senna, inferior specification engines. The political interference was ultimately ineffective as, despite stalling on the starting grid and falling back to fourteenth place, Senna fought his way to the front, overtaking Prost on the twenty-seventh lap. And as it began to rain, the Brazilian passed the chequered flag. He had finally won his first world championship at the age of twenty-eight.

Despite having achieved his dream, Senna could not relax ahead of the new season. He would face a far more competitive field in 1989. Yet the predominant struggle was again with Prost, as the two fell out over all manner of things, from pre-race agreements to quotations fed to the media.[93]

The rivalry became caricatured as fans of both drivers vilified the other. At Silverstone, "British fans cheered when Senna spun out of the lead early on."[94] Well over a decade after Senna's death, his Formula One career was still considered by many to be defined in terms of the rivalry with Prost. The 2010 documentary directed by Asif Kapadia entitled *Senna* fell into this trap. The choice of footage taken from Formula One's extensive archive formed a simplistic dramatic arc that practically cast Prost as the villain to Senna's heroic protagonist. Senna also exploited his relationship with Honda to become the focus of the team, sidelining Prost. Before Monza, Prost was eleven points ahead and had already announced a move to Ferrari for 1990. The Frenchman recalled that at Monza,

> Senna had two cars, with 20 people around him, and I had just one car, with maybe four or five mechanics working for me. I was absolutely alone, in one part of the garage.... In practice, Ayrton was nearly two seconds quicker than me—OK, as I said, he was certainly a better qualifier than I was, but two seconds? That was a joke.[95]

The difference in performance even prompted an admission from Ron Dennis, who revealed that "[f]uel consumption, for example, has been different from one engine to the other."[96] To those who presumed open season on all aspects of Formula One to leverage a competitive advantage, this was normal, but for many, Senna was practically handed a head start.

Senna needed a victory at the 1989 Japanese Grand Prix to remain in contention for the title. Having lost the lead from pole position, he was unable to force the experienced Frenchman into a mistake, eventually attempting an inside pass on lap forty-six. Prost moved his car across to block the gap, resulting in a collision as both slid onto the Suzuka chicane escape road with wheels locked. Desperate to remain in contention for the title, Senna was aided with a push-start from the marshals to drive to the pits to replace the damaged front of the car. Footage in Kapadia's documentary curiously cuts to show Prost, assuming the race to be over, jumping out of his car and rushing immediately to the racing steward's office. Against all odds, Senna demolished the five-second lead of Benetton's Alessandro Nannini to win. His joy was short lived, however, as the FIA disqualified Senna for rejoining the Suzuka track at the wrong point (i.e., skipping the chicane where the collision happened),[97] meaning that Prost had won his third title but this time under controversial circumstances.

Prost would later reflect: "As for the accident between us at the chicane, yes, I know everybody thinks I did it on purpose. What I say is that I did not open the door, and that's it. I didn't want to finish the race like that—I'd led from the start, and I wanted to win it."[98] Due to his public defiance of his disqualification, Senna was then fined $100,000 and had his license temporarily suspended by Balestre,[99] which only served to reinforce the hero-villain narrative and embolden inaccurate notions that Prost was in alliance with Balestre.

With sections of the press demonising Senna in favour of the "immediately agreeable personality"[100] of Prost, the Brazilian became furious at the lack of balance, asking, "I am supposed to be a lunatic, a dangerous man breaking all the rules, but people have the wrong impression. What happened at Suzuka reflects the political situation in the sport. I'm prepared to fight to the end for my values, for justice."[101] And indeed, as McLaren appealed the undemocratic ex post facto decision, Balestre's dictatorial nature was typified in a press release relating to the crash in which he suggested that the ruling was unchallengeable.[102]

To be issued a license for the 1990 season, Senna was forced to publicly retract his allegation against Balestre and the FIA that the 1989 championship result had been "manipulated by economic and political groups."[103] With Prost joining Nigel Mansell at Ferrari, Austrian Gerhard Berger came in as the second driver at McLaren. The two got along famously as Berger accepted his role as number two while befriending the Brazilian with his penchant for practical jokes, one of which involved replacing Senna's passport photograph with that of a gorilla.[104] The season was reasonably free of incidents between Senna and Prost, with the two even publicly reconciling. It was on Senna's terms, but Prost seemed to accept it: "We are both professionals and what happened last year really doesn't matter anymore."[105] But then came the Japanese Grand Prix, again at Suzuka. Like the previous year, the pole position was not on the racing line,[106] thereby eradicating any advantage the best qualifier had. Senna was adamant that the rightful advantage would be restored to the pole winner:

> I did a fantastic job to be on pole. It was important to be on pole for the race. Then what happened? Balestre gave an order. We told them "we agreed before the race meeting, and you know that the pole position should be on the left side." It was an order from Balestre, because I know from inside. And this is really shit, you know. And I tell myself "OK, you try to work clean, you try to do your job properly"; and

you get fucked all the time by stupid people. If on Sunday, at the start, because I'm in the wrong place, Prost jumps at the start and beats me off the line, at the first corner I'm going for it. And he had better not turn in ahead of me, because he is not going to make it.[107]

It transpired in exactly that fashion, and Senna had won his second world championship.

The media deemed it a cynical act of revenge for the previous year's crash, while Prost fumed: "I am not prepared to fight against irresponsible people who are not afraid to die."[108] While it was clear that Senna attacked a nonexistent gap, the act can be perceived more a reaction to the infuriating meddling of Balestre than against Prost himself. Senna's entire racing philosophy and style of driving had come under attack, especially in one extraordinary interview the following weekend in Adelaide with former world champion Jackie Stewart. The Scot questioned the number of collisions in which Senna had been involved over the span of his Formula One career. Senna was highly defensive: "If you no longer go for a gap that exists, you're no longer a racing driver."[109] Stewart, also a three-time F1 champion and safety advocate, continued to disagree over what he felt was overly aggressive driving by Senna. This fearless attitude to competitive racing was perceived by others, such as Damon Hill, his teammate at Williams in 1994, to have caused a wider cultural shift in the style of Formula One racing. As Hill remembered it: "He started being very aggressive when he came in and everyone else has copied him. It has been the same for everyone since 1984."[110]

Driver Safety

Senna's aggressive style and propensity to give every lap maximum effort and concentration most likely fuelled his fight to improve driver safety. After Martin Donnelly's shocking accident while qualifying at Jerez in 1990,[111] Senna admitted to an epiphany of sorts, recalling: "In the end, I realised I was not going to give up my passion, even just having seen what I had seen. And I had to put myself together, and walk out, go to the racing car, and do it again. And do it again, and do it better than before, because that was the way to kind of cover that impact it had on me."[112] Opinion among commentators was split as to whether it was true bravery or ruthless competitiveness, but the fight for safety and sheer will to win typified the doublethink in Senna's mindset.

At Spa, Belgium, in 1992, Senna finally put to rest the criticism that he valued victory over life when Ligier's Érik Comas suffered a crash at the Blanchimont corner during qualifying. Senna stopped mid-lap to run over to Comas's car and hold his head up in a stable position until medical support arrived. FIA medical director Sid Watkins said of the incident: "We'd talked about what to do for a driver in such circumstances but only once or twice. Yet when I arrived at the scene, Ayrton had done everything we had discussed ... perfectly."[113] Qualifying for the 1991 Mexico Grand Prix, Senna suffered a dangerous accident on the notorious Peraltada turn.[114] The car skidded into the tyre barrier, which rather than acting as a safety mechanism flipped the car and trapped him under it. Senna was unhurt and even more compelled to fight for higher safety standards. Later in the season, at the drivers' meeting prior to the German Grand Prix, Senna requested that the tyre walls at the chicanes be replaced by traffic cones and run-off areas.[115] A heated discussion ended with FIA president Jean-Marie Balestre proudly declaring: "The best decision is my decision,"[116] before surprisingly opting for a vote among the drivers, who unanimously sided with Senna's suggestion.

The season itself was equally challenging; Senna won seven races, including his first-ever home victory at Interlagos in São Paolo despite driving the final laps with the car stuck in sixth gear, causing excruciating muscle spasms. Afterward he claimed: "God gave me the race."[117] The decider was again at Suzuka, and the Brazilian won the title after challenger Mansell spun off early on. At thirty-two, Senna had become the youngest-ever triple world champion.

Over the following two seasons, McLaren lagged far behind Williams on engine development. Senna had learnt that Honda, whose founder, Soichiro Honda, died the previous year, was planning to abandon Formula One at the end of the 1992 season. This led him to plan a move to Williams. Alain Prost, who had been fired by Ferrari for criticising the car, was also in talks for the same seat. Despite manoeuvring for a seat in the best car, Senna was still critical of Williams's technical progress, perceiving it as marginalising the driver's role: "No matter who you put in the car, the electronics will do the work and not the driver."[118]

Williams signed Prost, prompting 1992's champion, Mansell, to leave for IndyCars, a move that recalls his animosity toward the Frenchman at Ferrari. Another spot was open there as well, but Prost didn't want to work with Senna again: "The only thing I asked in the contract was that I don't want to be a teammate with Ayrton."[119] Despite having done the same to Derek Warwick at Lotus, the Brazilian didn't take it well: "The way he is doing it, he is behaving like a coward."[120]

The 1992 season had seen Senna retire seven times out of the sixteen races, highlighting the unreliability of the McLaren engine. At the British Grand Prix in July, he admitted: "I will stop if I don't find a competitive car. There is no reason to risk my life for third place."[121] Stuck at McLaren, Senna signed on a race-by-race basis, earning $1 million per race. The new McLaren Ford MP4/8 engine was far better than Senna had anticipated and led to some of his greatest form.[122]

Despite a fine start to the 1993 season, with two victories in the first three races, Senna was never confident of challenging Prost consistently for the championship. This included a second home victory in Brazil, where Senna met nineteen-year-old model Adriane Galisteu, a Shell Oil publicity girl. Senna won the final race of the season in Adelaide, which doubled as four-time winner Alain Prost's farewell race—easing the path for Senna to move to Williams. It also meant that McLaren had broken Ferrari's all-time record of 103 victories. More importantly, it turned out to be the final victory of Senna's illustrious career.

The Final Lap

With his future sorted out for 1994 in what all considered to be the most competitive setup at Williams, Senna was looking forward to a new challenge after six years and three championships with McLaren. This would appear to include changes in his personal life as well, as his relationship with Adriane was blooming. As he was to exclaim, "She carries my happiness."[123]

By now, Senna's business ventures were also growing. The foundations for a life post–Formula One had been set. An import-based economic strategy[124] had filtered into the Brazilian entrepreneurial consciousness during the dictatorship, even though it increased the country's dependence on key foreign inputs, as the 1973–1974 oil shock highlighted. Senna himself had begun an import business in 1993, bringing the German Audi car range, Ducati motorcycles, and Mont Blanc writing pens into Brazil.[125] His entrepreneurial drive also saw him create his own range of Senna-branded products, including a video game called *Ayrton Senna's Super Monaco Grand Prix*, which sold eight hundred thousand copies.[126]

Senna was also the only world champion left as Prost, Piquet, and Mansell had all retired. The closest challenger was thought to be a young Michael Schumacher of Benetton and Senna's new teammate Damon Hill. Even Senna's relationship with the retired Prost began to soften in the final months of his life. Yet, as the season began, Senna's focus was scattered. As Prost recalled: "He was very worried about safety—he asked me several times to raise it with the Grand Prix Drivers' Association—and he was convinced that [Flavio Briatore's] Benetton were cheating."[127] Senna also felt that the cars were unstable due to the new ban on electronic driver aids, which had thrown the Williams engineers: "It's going to be a season with a lot of accidents and I'll risk saying we'll be lucky if something really serious doesn't happen."[128]

After retiring in the first two races of the season at Interlagos and at Aida in the Pacific Grand Prix, the pressure for victory in the San Marino Grand Prix at Imola was on. Senna's older sister Viviane later suggested that her brother's mind was also preoccupied with personal matters in the week prior to Imola: "We talked for a long time. He was very low, though I will not say why. It was the last time I talked to him."[129]

Many have since suggested that Senna's relationship with Adriane Galisteu had caused a rift in the Senna da Silva family. In his unauthorised biography *Ayrton, o herói revelado* [Ayrton, the hero revealed], Ernesto Rodrigues, a former London bureau chief with TV Globo, reveals details of intimate phone calls between Galisteu and a former lover. Rodrigues claimed that Senna's brother Leonardo played the tapes to Senna on the eve of the Imola Grand Prix.[130] The Senna family refuted these claims, as did Galisteu on the twentieth anniversary of Senna's death: "It never happened, no. I was 100 percent honest with Ayrton."[131] Galisteu was from a poor background, had a drug-addicted brother who died of HIV months after Senna's death,[132] and had posed nude in men's magazines, which were all apparent points of contention for the conservative Senna family. Two days prior to Imola, Senna appeared in a magazine spread with Galisteu for *Caras*, Brazil's top celebrity magazine, something he had never done with previous girlfriends.[133] Many felt that Senna was set to marry Galisteu, but others, such as Senna's manager Julian Jakobi, disagreed: "[Senna] told me categorically at Imola that he had no immediate plans to marry her."[134]

The weekend of the San Marino Grand Prix began ominously. There was a serious accident involving Senna's compatriot Rubens Barrichello, along with the tragic death of Simtek's Austrian driver Roland Ratzenberger in qualifying. It was the first death in Formula One in a generation—since Senna's former Lotus teammate Elio de Angelis in 1986. As TV Globo commentator Reginaldo Leme put it: "I'd never seen Senna as tense as I did that weekend. At no moment did I see him smile. He was constantly focused, annoyed, saddened really."[135] Despite the tense atmosphere and his struggles with the Williams car, Senna managed to put it on pole position. Manish Pandey, writer and producer of the documentary film *Senna*, reflected on Senna's psychological state in an interview with Professor Sid Watkins:

> For me, the salient points are that Ayrton cried on Prof's shoulders after Roland Ratzenberger's death on Saturday and Prof told him: "You're a three-times world champion, you're the fastest man in the world and you've got nothing to prove." Today, Prof continues: "He liked fishing so I told him, 'Why don't you quit and I'll quit and we'll both go fishing.' But Ayrton chose to race."[136]

On the morning of the race, Senna recorded a lap for TF1, the French television station for whom Alain Prost was commentating. In a sign that their relationship had mellowed, Senna sent the following message over his radio: "I would like to say welcome to my old friend Alain Prost. Tell him we miss him very much."[137] He also had discussions with former world champion Niki Lauda regarding the potential for reforming the Grand Prix Drivers' Association to improve safety in the sport. At the start of the race, Pedro Lamy hit the back of JJ Lehto's stalled Benetton on the grid. A wheel was ripped off, injuring eight spectators and a policeman in the crowd. The crash also left debris over the track, despite the best efforts of the stewards to clear it. This led to the deployment of the safety car, a feature borrowed from the IndyCars series in America. Senna had previously raised concerns about their use, worrying "that making the cars hold station at low speed would allow their tyres to cool down, making them inefficient and possibly dangerous in the moments after racing resumed."[138] Senna led from the restart on the sixth lap, setting what was to be the third-quickest lap time of the race. So, obviously, low tyre temperatures were not an issue.

On lap seven, Senna entered the high-speed Tamburello corner at 192 miles per hour, suddenly veering off to the right. Despite Senna's best efforts to regain control, the Williams Renault crashed into the concrete wall at 131 miles per hour and rebounded into the run-off area. Senna's head slumped to the right as his car came to a stop. Galvão Bueno of TV Globo was the first of the watching media to realise that the crash had likely been fatal: "Ayrton has hit [the wall] badly. It's serious, it's very serious."[139] As journalist Timothy Collings would report, at the point of impact, "a steel suspension arm from the front right wheel snapped away and punctured his yellow helmet and his right temple."[140]

What caused him to go off the track initially still remains unsolved. Tamburello was not a corner where a driver's skills were challenged. Most concurred that something had to have gone wrong with the car, rather than that a three-time world champion had made such an amateur mistake. Several theories have been raised—from a faulty steering column, a failure in the power steering, a tyre puncture from the debris of Lamy-Lehto crash,[141] to the bottom of the car hitting a bump in the tarmac. Maurizio Passarini, the investigating magistrate in Bologna, focused his case on the car's steering column. Williams's car designer, Adrian Newey, and technical director Patrick Head were charged with manslaughter, but after a long-winded appeals process that passed the statute of limitations, the case ended with zero prosecutions in 2007.[142]

The depth of feeling that was unearthed in people from around the world after Senna's death surprised even Senna's family. His sister Viviane recalled, seven months after his passing:

> In Brazil, Japan and Europe, we knew he was important. But we have had letters from Lithuania, Pakistan and Afghanistan where they can know very little about Formula One. We have had letters from children of seven and grandmothers of 80,

works of art from all over the world, all coming straight from the heart. We had no idea how passionately people felt about him.[143]

Such emotion seemed to validate a career of intense commitment spanning sixty-five pole positions, forty-one race wins, and, of course, three world championships.

Interestingly, in the months prior to his death, Senna seemed to be transitioning into something of an elder statesman in the sport, particularly with regard to charitable concerns. He had discussed the possibility of starting a foundation with his sister: "We agreed to talk again when he came back home. After the accident, I had no choice." Senna was also becoming much more conscious of the social and economic inequality that plagued his country: "Wealthy men cannot live in an island that is encircled by poverty. We all breathe the same air. We must give a chance to everyone, at least a basic chance."[144] The millions made from projects such as his Senninha comic book series and his other business ventures were to be channelled into a foundation to help Brazil's children. Focusing on education, the Instituto Ayrton Senna now directly benefits around two million children annually.[145] Taking cues from Senna's own business acumen, the foundation is funded entirely from donations and partnerships with the private sector. It has created a social legacy even greater than the brilliance of Senna's own extraordinary racing career.

Notes

1. Tom Rubython, *The Life of Senna* (Croydon, England: Myrtle Press, 2011), 431.
2. Julian Jakobi, "My Century," BBC World Service, June 30, 1999, at http://www.bbc.co.uk/worldservice/people/features/mycentury/transcript/wk26d3.shtml.
3. Tim Vickery, "The Rise of the Technocrats," *Blizzard: The Football Quarterly*, no. 6, ed. Jonathan Wilson (September 2012): 89.
4. Joel Wolfe, *Autos and Progress: The Brazilian Search for Modernity* (New York: Oxford University Press, 2010), 3.
5. Richard Williams, *The Death of Ayrton Senna* (London: Penguin Books, 2010), 3.
6. Wolfe, *Autos and Progress*, 3.
7. Rubython, *The Life of Senna*, 19.
8. Ibid. Despite his conservative, Catholic family background, in a 1990 interview with the Brazilian edition of *Playboy*, Senna admitted that he had lost his virginity at the age of thirteen to a tall, blond prostitute. See Agência Estado, "Senna: os deslizes de um herói que foi pessoa comum," Diário do Grande ABC, 2004, at http://www.dgabc.com.br/Noticia/160056/senna-os-deslizes-de-um-heroi-que-foi-pessoa-comum; and "Senna Interview from 1990," *Autosport*, April 2009. The original interview appeared in 1990; see Mônica Bergamo, "*Playboy* Entrevista Ayrton Senna," *Playboy* (Brasil), August 1990, 139–57, at http://www.insideplayboybr.com/#!entrevista--ayrton-senna/c1jv6.

9. Williams, *The Death of Ayrton Senna*, 43.

10. Wolfe, *Autos and Progress*, 101.

11. Ibid., 115.

12. Williams, *The Death of Ayrton Senna*, 42. Electroencephalography is a technique that records the brain's electrical activity. An electroencephalogram (EEG) is the name of the reading that is produced.

13. Rubython, *The Life of Senna*, 20.

14. Ibid., 21.

15. Ibid.

16. Archdiocese of São Paulo, *Torture in Brazil: A Shocking Report on the Pervasive Use of Torture by Brazilian Governments 1964–1979*, ed. Joan Dassin, trans. Jaime Wright (New York: Vintage, 1986), 51–52.

17. Ibid., 63: "Citizens also collaborated [with the dictatorship]. The Permanent Group for Industrial Mobilization, initiated before the coup in contacts between the insurgent military officers and businessmen, was founded in April 1964."

18. Williams, *The Death of Ayrton Senna*, 44.

19. Senna finished sixth in his European debut in the 1978 world championship, aged eighteen. He raced with the Italian DAP company, with his father footing the bill. He followed this initial promise with two frustrating second-placed finishes in the following two years.

20. Rubython, *The Life of Senna*, 25.

21. Ibid.

22. Christopher Hilton, *Memories of Senna: Anecdotes and Insights from Those Who Knew Him* (Sparkford, Somerset, England: Haynes Publishing, 2011), 20.

23. Williams, *The Death of Ayrton Senna*, 46.

24. Hilton, *Memories of Senna*, 27.

25. Ibid., 28.

26. Ibid.

27. Rubython, *The Life of Senna*, 35–36.

28. Frances Hagopian and Scott Mainwaring, "Democracy in Brazil: Origins, Problems, Prospects," Working Paper no. 100, Helen Kellogg Institute for International Studies, University of Notre Dame, September 1987, 5, at http://kellogg.nd.edu/publications/workingpapers/WPS/100.pdf.

29. Giles Richards, "Ayrton Senna: F1 Photographer Keith Sutton Recalls a Remarkable Journey," *Guardian*, April 30, 2014, at http://www.theguardian.com/sport/2014/apr/30/ayrton-senna-photographer-keith-sutton-f1.

30. "Big Names, Big Passion," FIFA, February 2009, at http://www.fifa.com/newscentre/features/news/newsid=1033135/index.html.

31. "Estácio Gonçalves Souto Maior," in *Dicionário Histórico Biográfico Brasileiro pós 1930*, 2nd ed. (Rio de Janeiro: Centro de Pesquisa e Documentação de História Contemporânea do Brasil; Fundação Getulio Vargas, 2001), at http://cpdoc.fgv.br/producao/dossies/Jango/biografias/estacio_goncalves_souto_maior. Souto Maior was the minister of health from September 1961 until June 1962. He died of a heart attack in 1974, five years after being removed from ARENA.

32. Herb Zurkowsky, "From Karts to Grand Prix, Nelson Piquet Defied Father to Race," *Montreal Gazette*, September 26, 1981, at http://news.google.com/newspapers?id=4oAxAAAAIBAJ&sjid=9KQFAAAAIBAJ&pg=2518,2645430&dq=nelson+piquet&hl=en.

33. Marcos Júnior, "Nelson Piquet: F1 Tricampeão," Terceiro Tempo, 2013, at http://terceiro tempo.bol.uol.com.br/que-fim-levou/nelson-piquet-4275.
34. Zurkowsky, "From Karts to Grand Prix," 105.
35. Rubython, *The Life of Senna*, 29.
36. Keith Collantine, "'In Our Day We Got Paid to Drive': Mansell and Piquet on Modern F1," F1 Fanatic, January 27, 2013, at http://www.f1fanatic.co.uk/2013/01/27/nigel-mansell-nelson-piquet-brazilian-tv-interview/.
37. Williams, *The Death of Ayrton Senna*, 53.
38. Rubython, *The Life of Senna*, 48. As Dennis Rushen recalled, "Ayrton said to me 'I'm going to introduce myself to Nelson Piquet because I want to be like him.' He was so excited, just like a boy.... But Piquet snubbed him and he took it personally—you do at that age. He was very angry and said 'I'm going to beat him one day.' And he did."
39. Williams, *The Death of Ayrton Senna*, 53.
40. Rubython, *The Life of Senna*, 162. A BBC profile described Piquet as "a notorious womaniser, [who] lived a simple life, avoiding PR work and preferring to spend his time away from races on his boat.... The remarks [insulting Senna] served no purpose other than to diminish further Piquet's reputation. It escaped no-one that he was making these remarks about men who had by then established themselves as better drivers than him." See Andrew Benson, "Formula One's Greatest Drivers: Number 16, Nelson Piquet," BBC Sport, May 8, 2012, at http://www.bbc.co.uk/sport/0/formula1/17871420.
41. Rubython, *The Life of Senna*, 203.
42. Ibid.; see also Senna and Xuxa together on her TV show during Christmas, 1988, at http://www.youtube.com/watch?v=H3WXmuiBq_M.
43. Williams, *The Death of Ayrton Senna*, 58.
44. Rubython, *The Life of Senna*, 67.
45. Ibid., 90.
46. Williams, *The Death of Ayrton Senna*, 65.
47. Rubython, *The Life of Senna*, 94.
48. Ibid., 93.
49. Williams, *The Death of Ayrton Senna*, 68.
50. Rodrigues coined the phrase after Brazil lost 2–1 to Uruguay in the final of the 1950 World Cup, which Brazil hosted. But in this context, Brazil's maiden World Cup win in Sweden in 1958 put to bed such an idea.
51. Larry Rohter, "If Brazil Wants to Scare the World, It's Succeeding," *New York Times*, October 31, 2004, at http://www.nytimes.com/2004/10/31/weekinreview/31roht.html?_r=0.
52. Vickery, "The Rise of the Technocrats," 86.
53. Williams, *The Death of Ayrton Senna*, 68.
54. Wolfe, *Autos and Progress*, 167.
55. Vickery, "The Rise of the Technocrats," 89: "Brazilian football was able to develop in harmony with the dictatorship. The establishment of the National Championship in 1971, for example, was an explicit part of the regime's plan to unify the giant country."
56. Senna's debut at Jacarepaguá lasted just eight laps after a turbocharger malfunction.
57. Rubython, *The Life of Senna*, 199.
58. In Brazil, Senna was known as the "Rei de Monaco" (the king of Monaco) after winning six races at the track over his career.

59. Williams, *The Death of Ayrton Senna*, 70.

60. Rubython, *The Life of Senna*, 300–301.

61. In 1991, McLaren team principal Ron Dennis commented that Senna "is a hard and totally inflexible negotiator who will use all the methods at his disposal to maximise his position." See Rubython, *The Life of Senna*, 205.

62. "Prost Dominant as McLaren Seals Constructors' Crown," ESPN, August 26, 1984, at http://en.espnf1.com/f1/motorsport/story/145225.html.

63. Rubython, *The Life of Senna*, 98.

64. David Tremayne, "The Man in the Yellow Helmet," *Motor Sport*, June 1994, at http://www.motorsportmagazine.com/halloffame/ayrton-senna/the-man-in-the-yellow-helmet/.

65. Philip Bonner, "The Soweto Uprising of June 1976: A Turning Points Event," South African History Online, at http://www.sahistory.org.za/pages/governence-projects/june16/extract-soweto-uprising.html.

66. Tom Prankerd, "The 1985 South African Grand Prix: Hot Air, Cold Choices," Counter-X, at http://counter-x.net/f1/1985/review/south_africa/index.html. South Africa was barred from the Olympics in 1962, FIFA banned their football team in 1964, and the ICC suspended their cricket team in 1970.

67. Rubython, *The Life of Senna*, 122.

68. Keith Collantine, "1985 South African Grand Prix Flashback," F1 Fanatic, February 5, 2008, at http://www.f1fanatic.co.uk/2008/02/05/f1-and-racism-the-1985-south-african-grand-prix/.

69. Terry Lovell, *Bernie Ecclestone: King of Sport* (London: John Blake, 2008), 94.

70. Rubython, *The Life of Senna*, 122.

71. Jessamy Calkin, "Senna: The Driver Who Lit Up Formula One," *Telegraph*, May 20, 2011, at http://www.telegraph.co.uk/culture/film/8524259/Senna-the-driver-who-lit-up-Formula-One.html. As Sid Watkins said: "There was no bullshit about him. Zero.... The year he was killed I got a project going whereby if I could raise $1 million from a private source, I would get funding from the European Union and these two sums would go towards a scheme for educating medical assistants in the upper Amazon in Brazil. I said to Ayrton, I need a million, and he said OK, just like that. He put the money up and we set up the training school at the beginning of 1994—at the end of that year he and I were going up the Amazon to inspect how the scheme was going, but of course he got killed."

72. John F. Burns, "Bahrain Race Is Not First Controversy for Formula One," *New York Times*, April 21, 2012, at http://thelede.blogs.nytimes.com/2012/04/21/bahrain-race-is-not-first-controversy-for-formula-one/.

73. Rubython, *The Life of Senna*, 110–11.

74. Ibid., 129.

75. Hilton, *Memories of Senna*, 192.

76. Simon Barnes, "Senna Rising to Challenge after Phoenix," *Times* (London), March 24, 1990.

77. Cari Jones, "25 Years Ago Today: Senna Beats Mansell by 0.01s," F1 Fanatic, April 13, 2011, at http://www.f1fanatic.co.uk/2011/04/13/25-years-today-1986-spanish-grand-prix/.

78. David Tremayne, "Lewis Hamilton: World Leader Driven to Get Back to Front," *Independent*, March 22, 2009, at http://www.independent.co.uk/sport/motor-racing/lewis-hamilton-world-leader-driven-to-get-back-to-front-1651220.html.

79. Rubython, *The Life of Senna*, 146.
80. Ibid., 149.
81. Ibid., 150.
82. Ibid., 151.
83. Asif Kapadia, dir., *Senna*, Universal Pictures, 2010, at 19 minutes, 25 seconds.
84. Jeremy Clarkson, *Top Gear*, episode 5, season 15, BBC 2, July 25, 2010, at http://www.youtube.com/watch?v=7kUNTtvMOtQ. The year 1988 was the last year in which turbochargers were allowed by Formula One regulations.
85. Williams, *The Death of Ayrton Senna*, 87.
86. Ibid., 89.
87. Rubython, *The Life of Senna*, 362.
88. See Hilton, *Memories of Senna*, 42. John Connor, a marketing manager at Marlboro, reminisces: "I was joking, because my brother is a Catholic priest. The reaction I got from Senna made me realise he wasn't Catholic. To begin with I'd assumed he was Catholic, because that's what Brazil is, but when they didn't want the cross at the funeral that made me think it was a bit more. However, the Bible definitely came into his beliefs."
89. Rubython, *The Life of Senna*, 189.
90. Manish Pandey, "Ayrton Senna: The Faith of the Man Who Could Drive on Water," *Huffington Post*, January 8, 2011, at http://www.huffingtonpost.com/manish-pandey/ayrton-senna_b_909096.html.
91. Williams, *The Death of Ayrton Senna*, 92. The crash at the twenty-four-hour, 1955 Le Mans race saw the death of Mercedes driver Pierre Levegh along with 83 spectators, while 120 others were injured. Levegh's car made contact with the back of the car of Lance Macklin, who had tried to overtake Mike Hawthorn after the latter had made a late decision to slow down and make a pit stop. Levegh's car, engulfed in flames, was thrown into the crowd, while Macklin's hit the barrier on the opposite side. See "Le Mans Disaster (1955)," at https://www.youtube.com/watch?v=RMoh5hZAaZk, uploaded by British Pathé, July 27, 2011.
92. Simon Barnes, "The Turbo-Charged President Fuelled by Driving Ambition: Jean-Marie Balestre, Interview," *Times* (London), February 14, 1991.
93. Simon Taylor, "Lunch with Ron Dennis," *Motor Sport*, November 2012, at http://www.motorsportmagazine.com/halloffame/ron-dennis/lunch-with-ron-dennis/.
94. Williams, *The Death of Ayrton Senna*, 96.
95. Nigel Roebuck, "Ayrton Senna, by Alain Prost," *Motor Sport*, October 1, 1998, at http://ayrton-senna.co.uk/eternity/ayrton_senna_by_alain_prost.html.
96. Rubython, *The Life of Senna*, 185.
97. As Nelson Piquet, who was hardly a fan of Senna, put it in a drivers' meeting at Suzuka in 1990: "There was a big fuck up last year with Ayrton. Why do we have to repeat the same thing? The safest thing is, if you miss the chicane, the stewards stop you. If there's no traffic, they can let you go. If you have to turn around, if you have to go backwards that's much more dangerous because if another car comes and also misses the chicane, it will knock into you." See Kapadia, *Senna*, at 41 minutes, 44 seconds.
98. Roebuck, "Ayrton Senna, by Alain Prost."
99. Hugh Hunston, "Anger over FISA Bid to Fine Senna," *Herald Scotland*, October 31, 1989, at http://www.heraldscotland.com/sport/spl/aberdeen/anger-over-fisa-bid-to-fine-senna-1

.605210. As Hunston writes, "Dennis said FISA's document presented eight [previously unpunished] counts on which Senna should have been excluded, including an allegedly dangerous manoeuvre which resulted in the collision with team-mate Alain Prost."

100. David Miller, "Senna Foiled in Potentially Fatal Formula!," *Times* (London), November 4, 1989.

101. Williams, *The Death of Ayrton Senna*, 99.

102. Miller, "Senna Foiled in Potentially Fatal Formula!" Tom Rubython adds: "In those days the governing body had the right, if an appeal was made against a Steward's decision, to impose further penalties. It was legally barmy, of course, but the FISA under Balestre's leadership was run under wild west rules"; see Rubython, *The Life of Senna*, 195.

103. John Blunsden, "Senna Considers Abandoning His Grand Prix Career," *Times* (London), November 10, 1989.

104. Williams, *The Death of Ayrton Senna*, 100.

105. Rubython, *The Life of Senna*, 205–6.

106. The racing line is the quickest path around a track, the one with the least resistance—as opposed to the "dirty side" of the track.

107. Rubython, *The Life of Senna*, 208. These comments were made by Senna a year after the incident.

108. Ibid, 209.

109. "Ayrton Senna's Famous Interview with Sir Jackie Stewart," at http://www.youtube.com/watch?v=pdCWDSpwv9U, uploaded by F1gameshowsradio4, July 3, 2012. The interview was first broadcast on Australia Channel 9, November 4, 1990. See also Ayrton Senna, *Ayrton Senna's Principles of Race Driving* (London: Hazleton, 1993), 152; Senna reiterated: "The driver must actively create chances for overtaking and pressurise his opponent into a mistake. This duelling is the real fascination of Formula One races. . . . A successful overtaking move means you have studied your opponent and discovered his weaknesses."

110. Rubython, *The Life of Senna*, 293–94.

111. "Martin Donnelly Horrific Crash 1990," at https://www.youtube.com/watch?v=1hSF6_4UDTo, uploaded by Raplapeno60, January 24, 2009. The crash occurred on September 28, 1990.

112. Kapadia, *Senna*, at 38 minutes, 52 seconds.

113. Rubython, *The Life of Senna*, 220.

114. "F1 1991 Ayrton Senna Mexico City Crash," at http://www.youtube.com/watch?v=7ixxWrSmoa4, uploaded by ID343, April 24, 2010. The crash occurred on June 16, 1991.

115. The 1991 German Grand Prix at Hockenheim was on July 28, a few races after Senna's accident in Mexico, and Senna's objections to contemporary safety measures were typical of his actions as he became a senior member on the grid.

116. Kapadia, *Senna*, at 1 hour, 1 minute, 55 seconds.

117. Alan Baldwin, "Interview, Motor Racing: Senna More Life than Death for Movie Maker," Reuters, April 29, 2014, at http://uk.reuters.com/article/2014/04/29/motor-racing-senna-pandey-idUKL3N0NK3ZS20140429.

118. Kapadia, *Senna*, at 1 hour, 9 minutes, 27 seconds.

119. Ibid., at 1 hour, 1 minute, 13 seconds.

120. Rubython, *The Life of Senna*, 263.

121. Ibid., 261.

122. Ibid., 282.

123. Ibid., 297.

124. Wolfe, *Autos and Progress*, 163.

125. Rubython, *The Life of Senna*, 344.

126. Rubython, Ibid., 372.

127. Keith Collantine, "Alain Prost on the Death of Ayrton Senna," F1 Fanatic, February 11, 2008, at http://www.f1fanatic.co.uk/2008/02/11/alain-prost-on-the-death-of-ayrton-senna/. Senna felt that Benetton was still using traction control to eliminate wheel spin; see Rubython, *The Life of Senna*, 380–81. Later, Benetton was found to have a program called "launch control" hidden in the onboard computer, which could "control the clutch, gearshift and engine speed fully automatically to a predetermined pattern" (Rubython, *The Life of Senna*, 494), but the FIA was unable to prove that it had been used.

128. Rubython, *The Life of Senna*, 376.

129. Andrew Longmore, "Senna's Driving Ambition Lives On," *Times* (London), December 8, 1994.

130. Ashling O'Connor, "Suffering of the Girl He Left Behind," *Times* (London), April 22, 2004, at http://www.thetimes.co.uk/tto/sport/formulaone/article2333582.ece.

131. Jonathan McEvoy, "Adriane Galisteu: I Didn't Cheat on Ayrton Senna ... The Day He Died My World Stopped," *Daily Mail*, April 29, 2014, at http://www.dailymail.co.uk/sport/formulaone/article-2616230/Adriane-Galisteu-I-didnt-cheat-Ayrton-Senna-day-died-world-stopped.html.

132. Gisele Vitória, "Eusentinapele a dor," *Istoé Gente*, December 2009, at http://www.terra.com.br/istoegente/edicoes/536/eu-senti-na-pele-a-dor-adriane-galisteu-comemora-158437-1.htm.

133. Zina Saro-Wiwa, "Brazil's Bland and Beautiful," BBC News, December 9, 2004, at http://news.bbc.co.uk/2/hi/entertainment/4080263.stm.

134. O'Connor, "Suffering of the Girl He Left Behind."

135. Kapadia, *Senna*, at 1 hour, 18 minutes, 37 seconds.

136. Manish Pandey, "Ayrton, Prof and Me," *Institute Quarterly* 2 (October 10, 2011), at http://www.ayrton-senna.net/ayrton-prof-and-me/.

137. Williams, *The Death of Ayrton Senna*, 127.

138. Ibid.

139. Rubython, *The Life of Senna*, 384.

140. Timothy Collings, "Day the Music Died Haunts Imola," *Telegraph*, April 23, 2004, at http://www.telegraph.co.uk/sport/2377510/Day-the-music-died-haunts-Imola.html.

141. "Puncture a Likely Cause for Senna's Accident: Newey," ESPN, May 17, 2011, at http://www.espn.co.uk/f1/motorsport/story/48681.html.

142. Donald McRae, "Ayrton Senna's Death 'Changed Me Physically,' Says Adrian Newey," *Guardian*, May 16, 2011, at http://www.theguardian.com/sport/2011/may/16/adrian-newey-ayrton-senna-death.

143. Andrew Longmore, "Senna's Driving Ambition Lives On," *Times* (London), December 8, 1994.

144. Rubython, *The Life of Senna*, 373.

145. Instituto Ayrton Senna, "Who We Are," at http://senna.globo.com/institutoayrtonsenna/quem_somos/index.asp. Alain Prost and Ron Dennis are both trustees of the institute.

Katarina Witt
The Many Faces of a Showcase Athlete
—Annette R. Hofmann

Introduction

In the months just prior to the fall of the Berlin Wall in 1989, the famous American ice skating show *Holiday on Ice* featured an East German performer—a rare subject for an American show, given the lingering East-West tensions. It was not easy for East German athletes to leave their socialist country to live, compete, or even perform in the capitalist West. Only those who could demonstrate that they were extremely loyal to their state were allowed to do so. The figure skater Katarina Witt, who was considered "*the* symbol of the former GDR," was just such a unique athlete.[1] Although time has shown her to fall more on the side of expediency than any specific loyalty, she nevertheless was one of a mere handful of former communist bloc celebrities who achieved not only local but also global fame because of their ability to transcend the challenges of the times both at home and abroad.

Tracing Witt's life to the present day, one can see the often contradictory elements that seem to have followed her career path. Well past her athletic prime, she remains in the early twenty-first century an international sporting figure of some renown. First and foremost, she is the embodiment of an athlete, one of international acclaim and deservedly so. And yet she also represents so much more than that. Her undeniable physical prowess, her beauty, glamour, commercialization, and even eroticism, bring a unique dimension to her stature among other luminaries. But perhaps just as palpably she has also evolved into an individual whose place in the cultural zeitgeist links a modern Germany to its recently divided past. In this regard, she has become a face of a reunited Germany.

Through Witt's career, we can examine the life of a hard-working athlete who, despite the challenges and prejudices of the Cold War, became one of the world's best known and admired figure skaters. Even more telling, and often to the chagrin of sport's commentators and critics, given her Hollywood-esque air and supermodel appeal, she also became something of a phenomenon beyond her sport. That she was a citizen of East Germany before she conquered the West makes her story all the more remarkable. Still, this degree of success came at a cost, namely that her talent, a broad and often diverse skill set that extends beyond the rink, is thought to have ultimately been overshadowed by her mass appeal, this transition playing out amid lingering suspicions regarding her level of political involvement throughout the period.

This chapter, then, seeks to offer insight into Katarina Witt's public life and disputed legacy with regard to the various roles she played within the systems that continue to mark German and world sport. A special focus will be placed on Witt's connections to certain sectors within the GDR itself, a spectrum that runs the gamut from state officials and coaches to the press, and the roles these connections continue to play in terms of her career and influence as it is expressed worldwide. Of particular importance to this examination will be how the former skating star uses her physical appeal in a way that theorist Pierre Bourdieu would term "body capital," a circumstance that allows her to move beyond the confines of mere athletic success into the realm of often unprecedented economic accomplishment.[2]

Toward this, we must traverse Witt's two autobiographies, various media accounts, and a wide range of Internet sites that have proven to be helpful in tracing her competitive and postcompetition career. Particularly useful are her autobiographies, in which she analyzed East German Secret Service (Stasi) documents that were collected about her life that reveal the pressure under which she lived, trained, and competed—at least until the fall of the Berlin Wall.[3]

The Rise of Women's Figure Skating

To fully engage the significance of Katarina Witt as athlete, it is essential to review, at least in part, the evolution of competitive women's figure skating as it is today more broadly conceived. At the turn of the twenty-first century, figure skating was the most popular televised women's sport in the United States.[4] It is also a sport to which women had an early entrance. Ice skating on frozen lakes, ponds, and rivers has been a pastime in Europe and North America for centuries, as can be seen for instance in the winter paintings of the sixteenth-century Belgian painter Pieter Bruegel the Elder.[5] More than merely gliding along on the ice, skaters also enhanced their movements through directional changes, leaps, twists, and other athletic maneuvers that made their tasks much more difficult, if not exciting to watch. In this regard, figure skating developed as a sport that combined elements of dancing and gymnastics. It was also one of the early sports that was considered "sex-appropriate"[6] for women, meaning that women could perform and compete while still retaining the ideal feminine image.

Much earlier than in most sports, the first international ice skating competitions for women took place at the beginning of the twentieth century. The first world championship competition was held in 1906 in Davos, Switzerland. Olympic competition preceded the establishment of the 1924 Winter Games in Chamonix, France, with contests at the Summer Games in 1908 in London and 1920 in Antwerp, which, as Adams notes, "brought figure skating to a large public, the first time, turning it into a commercial entertainment with mass appeal,"[7] a trend that continued unabated through the interwar years.[8] World War II, however, interrupted international competition for much of the 1940s.[9]

As it developed, modern figure skating, particularly the women's side of the sport, was defined by its exceptional female athletes, who displayed a sense of style that enhanced their athleticism while remaining closely associated with the feminine ideal of the times. The popular appeal of this combination of femininity and ice began with the Norwegian figure skater Sonja Henie, whose skill displayed through elegance "captivated audiences as well as judges."[10] Henie won ten world championships in a row, as well as three Olympic gold medals in the 1920s and 1930s. After her athletic success, she became an actress in Hollywood, skated in a Hollywood Ice Revue, and appeared in advertisements as well. According to the Norwegian sport sociologist Gerd von der Lippe, "Henie's seemingly endless triumphs, her athletic but flowing style, her showmanship and glamorous outfits and her blond looks transformed the sport to one based on style and glamour as well as athleticism." Before Henie, long skirts and the color black were preeminent in figure skating.[11]

Decades before Witt, Henie, still regarded by some as among the greatest skaters of all time, was lifted to an iconic status, a media-driven style of celebrity treatment that was still in its infancy. Henie is therefore an early example of the growing alliance among sport, the media, and profit-making ventures through celebrity. Her body became a form of capital, commercialized above and beyond her athletic performances, which in turn placed a nascent ideal of female beauty squarely in the marketplace.

Playing with femininity and gender roles is central to the performance of women's ice skating. This is frequently the case in any aesthetics-driven sports in which the margin of victory is defined not by numbers but rather by the subjective judgments of third-party observers. As is typically the case in such traditionally gendered affairs, female athletes are forced to highlight their femininity and play to gender roles to please the judges as well as the audiences. Through their cosmetics, clothes, and physical attributes, athletes have to turn their physical capital into erotic capital to maintain an expected level of attractiveness,[12] which noted sport historian Allen Guttmann calls "erotic athleticism."[13] Besides the exposure of a certain erotic dimension, aesthetic sports also demand a high degree of heteronormativity and self-determination.[14] Katarina Witt, who all these years later is still called "the prettiest face of socialism"[15] or "Marx's pretty daughter" by the press,[16] became one of many who followed Henie's lead in terms of both recognizing and exploiting female gender roles as they continued to develop in women's sport well into the twentieth century.

Multidimensional Star

Katarina Witt, or "Kati" as she was known in East Germany, grew up in Karl-Marx-Stadt, which has since reverted to its traditional name of Chemnitz. Born in 1965, Witt claims to have taken up skating at the age of five, becoming a member of the figure skating section of the city's highly regarded sports club known for its many champions.[17]

Witt was seven years old when she won her first competition. By age nine, her talent caught the eye of Frau Jutta Müller,[18] the East German skating coach whose reputation extended well beyond East Germany and who would accompany Witt throughout her amateur skating career. Although it was not always an easy relationship between coach and budding star given Müller's lofty expectations for highly disciplined trainees, she worked with young Katarina through many problematic areas, and they found common ground that eventually paid handsome dividends for them both. Among Müller's most challenging rules was her insistence on a strict regimen of diet and training that eschewed the sorts of activities that would be second nature to most young girls growing up in modern times. Such prohibitions precluded the consumption of junk food of any sort, alcohol, and generally anything that would otherwise impede an athlete's training regimen.

Although she may have balked at some of these rules, from her early teenage years Witt had dreams of becoming a world champion,[19] and in order to fulfill such aspirations she had to agree to eschew her youthful tendencies and bow before Frau Müller's expectations. Toward these aims, most of Witt's adolescence would indeed consist of ambitious daily training sessions that included, among other matters, keeping a near-constant watch on her ideal weight. It would appear, thus, that any difficulties she might have once experienced in keeping to such a strict regimen paid off in the end, given how many superb moments she and her coach would share. Included among these would be eight national titles, six European titles, four world championships, and the Olympic gold medals she brought home to East Germany in 1984 and 1988.

Shortly after Witt ended her amateur career, she turned professional. Already an emergent international star coming off her successes in the Olympics, the twenty-three-year-old phenom had several offers and performed at various ice shows in the West, something quite unusual for an East German athlete before

Glasnost- and Perestroika-style policies were finally adopted by the East German state.[20] By ascending to the various show circuits available to her, Witt's popularity rose even more, especially in the United States, though not always with the skeptical press (see below). But she also seemed to long for the challenges of international competition and performed commercially always with an eye toward a triumphant return to competitive skating.

Witt was ineligible to compete at the 1992 Albertville games, as it was not until 1993 that the International Skating Union (ISU) opened up eligibility to professional skaters. But in 1994, at the age of twenty-eight, she made her return to Olympic competition at Lillehammer,[21] though this time under the flag of a reunited Germany. Despite her long break, she finished in a respectable seventh place.

After that, Witt, who never again appeared in an Olympic event, returned to the show circuits, making the most of every opportunity to again vie for international titles before eventually settling into a post-ice career that would see her through forays into a wide range of interests including modeling, show business, commerce, and a range of social causes for which she would garner even more acclaim through her Katarina Witt Foundation.[22] She was by every measure a unique sort of international athletic celebrity: made in the often inaccessible East but heralded by the West, though with some well-publicized reservations.

Elite Sport in the GDR

Witt's on-ice success offers a glimpse of how GDR state officials once fostered elite sport through the achievements of gifted and loyal athletes. Elite sport was of great importance to the ideology of the GDR, and the state deliberately harnessed it because its popularity offered political impact throughout much of the Cold War. Elite sport and the advancement of such talent were hierarchically structured and kept under close surveillance. The government provided enormous financial support to ensure success in such high-profiled competitions as world and Olympic championships.[23] Those sports in which they were able to best countries deemed hostile to the East German state, including (and perhaps especially) the Federal Republic of Germany, among other Western nations, were amply funded and nurtured beginning in the late 1950s. Through its successful sport programs, the GDR sought to gain international prestige, demonstrate the superiority of socialism, and strengthen the self-confidence of its populace, reflecting to the world the power of its political system.

To be successful, East Germany constructed a very detailed plan and invested in it accordingly. Talented children were coached in the Kinder und Jugendsportschulen (KJS), special boarding schools for children and youth in which they were physically trained but also educated to embody the typical ideal of the socialist personality. These schools were also called "Die Schmiede der DDR,"[24] meaning "blacksmith" foundries where coaches aimed to forge top athletes. Sport sciences also strongly focused research on the demands and problems of elite sports, ensuring the scientifically and psychologically based optimal development of the athletes.[25] As Kai Reinhart notes, the elite sports of the GDR were characterized by comprehensive recruiting mechanisms, spatial and social insularity, the full support of athletes, and massive physical and psychological access and monitoring by the Stasi.[26]

Witt attended just such a KJS in Karl-Marx-Stadt from the age of eight years onward. There she became one of a mere few who participated in developing their ice skating talents. Her academic lessons were adjusted to her training times and competitions, often resulting in private academic lessons, though of questionable rigor. This of course came at a cost, namely her pursuit of an education beyond the ice. As an athlete whose attention was focused predominantly within that domain, Witt was unable finish her high school degree until she was twenty years old, which was some three years longer than it would have taken the average student. Moreover, she would never achieve the highest degree (*Abitur*) that would have enabled her to attend university.[27]

Regardless of such consequences, however, it was obvious that the GDR's deliberate support of its athletes appeared to be a success, as this nation of only seventeen million beat the United States and West Germany in the Olympic medal count in the Summer and Winter Games in 1976 and later in 1988 despite the population deficit.[28] Even greater was the success in its ongoing rivalry with West Germany. Beginning in 1968, East Germany regularly managed to beat its Western counterpart by winning more medals in high-profile international contests. After the Sarajevo Winter Olympics in 1984, Egon Krenz, a member of the GDR politburo and secretary of the Central Committee of the Sozialistische Einheitspartei Deutschland (SED) party, which was responsible for sport development, addressed the successful GDR Olympic team in East Berlin. He emphasized that through their success, the athletes had contributed to the thirty-fifth birthday of their nation, arguing that the role of sports within the overall political system "expresses a close relationship between the athletes and the working-class party, between the athletes and our GDR, our socialist fatherland."[29]

Krenz went on to say that, from a socialist point of view, the Olympic arena was a "showplace of peaceful coexistence." He then focused on the quarrel between socialism and imperialism, agreeing with the West German tabloid *Bild*:

> Olympic Games are in fact one of those areas where the better should be proven. However, not in the individual case—otherwise it wouldn't be a sport of many surprises with winners and losers—but rather in the amount of wins.

Here, Krenz was clearly referring to the leading position of his country in the Olympic medal count. According to an interview with German sport historian Joachim Teichler, the East German government was riding a wave of success brought about through its athletes' emerging international reputations.[30] The country invested millions in elite sport but hardly any money in sports programs for the general public.

Katarina Witt was just such an example of this investment trend. As Krenz made clear, she was a "talent of the people who is equipped with all liberties and assets of socialism." He also called her a trademark for the GDR "by which the perception of the East in North America"[31] had been altered.

Witt, as pretty as she was successful, was clearly an asset in the GDR's objective of competing politically through success in international sport. She had also demonstrated a strong degree of loyalty to her state, which elevated her to the level of GDR darling—their showpiece athlete whose reputation and appeal would be used by her government as propaganda to demonstrate, if not celebrate, the successes of the socialist order. As one commentator appearing in the 2005 TV documentary *Goodbye DDR* could claim, Witt had become the GDR's biggest national treasure.[32] But again, this development came at a cost, particularly after the cessation of hostilities between East and West brought about through the end of the Cold War.

National Treasure

It is important to note here that one of the West's chief complaints against Witt as she emerged on the world skating circuits was that her politics was at odds with her presence in Western venues. After the fall of the Berlin Wall in 1989, Witt was often accused by the Western press of having been at the very least a Stasi collaborator. This assumption, which turned out to be inaccurate, was nevertheless exploited by the press and Witt's detractors throughout the 1990s. Ironically, it marked the extent to which she became in a sense victimized by both sides, a situation that extends beyond the Cold War itself. While she was in her own way loyal to the GDR, Witt, like many other state-supported athletes, was also closely observed by the Stasi, and the extent of this surveillance was found to have been well documented once the state fell.

In all, more than three thousand pages[33] chronicling Witt's experiences as a closely watched state asset were found spread out over twenty-seven files of Stasi documents. These papers speak to the close scrutiny she endured through such state projects as OV Flop (Operative Process Flop),[34] later to be called OPK Flop (Operative Person Control).[35] Such intense analysis of the skater's private and public life began when she was only eight years old.[36] Not only were listening devices hidden in her various residences but even people with whom she had close relationships, including teachers, training partners, and even personal friends, were enlisted by the Stasi as collaborators to spy on her. She was able to read accounts of people visiting her tucked neatly away in her secret service files, finding as well recaps of her phone conversations, the names of her romantic partners, and even sordid descriptions of her sexual activities including the duration of sexual encounters.

To be sure, fighting this propaganda war on so many fronts took its toll on her, as detailed in her 1994 autobiography *Meine Jahre zwischen Pflicht und Kür*. Witt reacted to the press coverage about her life and to the various accusations by the Western press after the fall of the Wall. She used excerpts from these Stasi reports and tried to refute them. Her aim was to present a more authentic Katarina Witt to a world that had so easily tagged her as a "Stasi whore" or an "SED Ziege" (goat), as she was derogatorily called in the Western press.[37] Thus, while the sanctioned office in charge of the Stasi documents after the dissolution of the GDR government could accurately declare that she was among the favored few, having received all sorts of perks from the East German government for the role she played,[38] it does not offer a full accounting of the toll that serving in this capacity as a sort of GDR ambassador to the world took on her.

This sort of dual treatment afforded important celebrities at the hands of the East German state was hardly unusual. In East Germany, athletes were strategically utilized as what some have deemed "diplomats in sweatsuits."[39] It is evident from many of Witt's comments to the media that she was one of them. She spoke positively about the socialist state where she had grown up, which had supported her athletic career and allowed her a life with many privileges not only during the existence of the GDR but also after German reunification.

Throughout this stretch, Witt seemed to have willingly followed the party line. During her youth she was a member of the communist youth group Freie Deutsche Jugend (FDJ; Free German Youth), and later she was a member of the SED and a representative of the GDR parliament, the Volkskammer. In an interview, she mentioned that she believed in her country and its political goals. She engaged in political affairs because she was thankful for the government's collective efforts to train her to perform in her sport and to allow her to travel the world as freely as she had because of her success on the ice.[40]

In a 1988 article in the East German sport newspaper *Deutsches Sportecho*, Witt offers a defense of national policies. She particularly praised the "constant endeavor of her country to preserve peace and guarantee the right to work."[41] Witt maintained that both were essential elements of human rights.[42] She officially announced that she would never have been able to become such a great ice skater in a capitalist country because her family would not have been able to afford it financially.[43]

But a closer look at Witt's comments suggests that not all of them were always entirely pro-state either. Indeed, in a note found in Stasi files dated some three weeks before the final breaking apart of the GDR, she expressed disappointment with both GDR politicians as well as those in West Germany, citing in particular the television coverage of the demonstrations that were occurring in those chaotic days on the streets in the East. In order not to lose such a high-profile and seemingly loyal athlete during such turbulent times, the Stasi met often with her and routinely impressed upon her to remember who the real enemies of the state actually were.[44] In this regard, it appears as if GDR officials continued to think of her as having influence over the East German population because of her public standing. And yet her position in such affairs left her vulnerable. To be critical of the GDR would have been tantamount to career suicide, a rejection of all the advantages she enjoyed in the GDR spotlight. But in trying to establish where her true interests lay and to then act accordingly, she was also setting the stage for the full-throated condemnation of her as a sort of pawn of the East that she expected would come her way by a decidedly unforgiving West, precisely at a time when anticommunism had moved from fiery Cold War rhetoric to post–Cold War eulogies to a malignant past. In this regard, it would appear that she was positioned in the middle of an enduring propaganda war that had nothing to do with her while it had everything to do with her and her success on the international stage.

To be sure, Witt, the GDR's showcase athlete and proclaimed "national treasure,"[45] could be seen on special occasions in the company of leading politicians such as the aforementioned Krenz and a few times with Erich Honecker, general secretary of the ruling party. These men of power enjoyed her company, but at the same time they wielded enormous power over her life. In many interviews, she praised socialism and how it defined strength collectively, as was also chronicled in the West German newspaper *Frankfurter Allgemeine Zeitung* (*FAZ*), which noted: "For the GDR and the working-class party, Katarina Witt on occasion sings choruses of praise. After all, she was considered as a future companion and since November 1985 a candidate for the SED."[46] Similarly, her place within the broader confines of the GDR, where she had many privileges, is described by a West German journalist as "capitalistically tinted social status and socialistically dyed (extra-)class consciousness."[47]

Witt of course understood her place and how her accomplishments ultimately tied her to the East German state. As a means to maintain her standing, she often acted according to the script, particularly when it came to the perks associated with her fame. She once proclaimed, for example, that "even after winning my first Olympic Gold medal—I was still able to successfully manage my time. There were no endorsement deals to distract me. It was forbidden."[48] It was also not necessarily accurate. Even though it was officially forbidden, Witt had indeed received lavish gifts including a Volkswagen Golf (at the time a very popular West German vehicle[49],) various apartments, and, according to the West German political journal *Der Spiegel*, a passport that allowed her to travel to the West.[50] Clearly she was able to demand certain privileges as a result of her celebrity. She was even granted her wish to attend acting school despite her difficult schedule and her own admitted lack of talent.[51] But as *FAZ* journalist Roland Zorn would note, Witt's smile and aura were a sort of ticket to freedom and privilege, albeit limited, within the GDR's rigid order:

> She is only allowed to be [an] advertiser on her own account and for the good of her patron, the GDR. Katharina [sic] Witt—within one's reach but yet so far, a fairy-tale character of sports. Seducible, "western" habit, open—but yet bound to the brazen rules of her community, when the outward projected self-conception of socialist ideals are at stake. At the same time she is a fairy-tale character on call. If she ends her career, which could happen any year, she might have to go back to the pleasant surroundings of Karl-Marx-Stadt. Even for her, liberty is not boundless.[52]

Behind the scenes, however, Witt's life was not always as detached from the repressive order as her lifestyle might suggest. Like so many other national treasures of her generation, she too experienced tremendous pressure and deprivation despite her advantages. Witt had to fulfill certain expectations in order to preserve whatever creature comforts her efforts had afforded her. She was required to demonstrate through her performance the superiority of East Germany's political system, and, as such, Stasi files reveal just how concerned state officials were about Witt when she did not train with the necessary earnestness, when her performances lacked urgency, or when she exceeded her so-deemed perfect skating weight. In one of the documents, she was offensively referred to as "Dicker Mops" (fat pug dog) because she had recently weighed in a few kilos over what was deemed to have been her ideal performance weight. As revealed in a 1983 document, state officials were generally in a heightened state of alert when it came to her day-to-day deportment, noting: "She does not fulfill the performance mandate. It would be possible for her to beat the class enemy in elite sport, but she does not have the right attitude."[53] But these concerns did not necessarily end with the state.

Witt's compatriots displayed public shock and dismay when, after her 1988 Olympic victory in Calgary, she announced her intention to become a professional and skate in American ice shows.[54] Her decision was seen by many as a betrayal of their notions of the perfect athlete, who should not earn any money for his or her success in sport but rather relish the opportunity to represent the state accordingly.[55] Strangely enough, however, it would be politicians who allowed her to pursue these opportunities in the decadent West, a decision that begs many questions:

- Were GDR politicians really so sure of Witt's loyalty that she would not betray her country and remain in the capitalist West?
- Was the outstanding ice skater just lucky because it was only a few months before the political change in 1989?
- Did someone pay the GDR government to let Witt perform in the West, or was the government merely comfortable receiving portions of her income from those shows?

The answers to the above questions appear to at least hint at the economic and political windfall that these appearances brought in return to the GDR itself. According to Witt's 1995 autobiography, this was not the first time the East German government gained financial advantages through her success. She further claims that she was only allowed to keep a portion of the money she earned on these ventures, which was also the case with the salary she earned performing with *Holiday on Ice* from November 1988 to April 1989. The arrangement appears to have been one in which the skater could keep only a meager 20 percent for herself. The rest of the money was supposedly impounded by the umbrella organization of GDR sports, Deutscher Turn- und Sportbund (DTSB).[56] So in this regard, many of the perks she received came in the form of less tangible (although certainly valuable in their own way) indulgences to be granted from the central seats of state power.

"Sex on Skates"[57] (aka "Sex Komma Null für Kati"[58])

Witt was in Spain when the GDR finally collapsed. She had not anticipated such a dramatic change and was caught by surprise, as she acknowledges in her 1995 autobiography. Still, after the fall of the Berlin Wall, the now twenty-five-year-old international superstar would find herself poised to enjoy freedoms once thought unimaginable. And yet there remained other kinds of pressure before her.

The Western press, for example, continued its onslaught against Witt for her supposedly naïve views on politics. Reporters questioned why she had not left her country earlier, or why she had been unable to anticipate the changes ahead or even publicly denounced the socialist system. Of this period of transition, Witt remembers the difficulty she had coping with the West, especially the press, which continued to harass her even though she had once been the darling of the Western—especially West German—media earlier in her career. Now they not only questioned her political past but also watched her private life very closely, which, for someone already used to the prying eye of the Stasi, must have felt oddly familiar yet nonetheless discomfiting. But instead of emanating from once hidden state files, stories about various love affairs with male celebrities, many of which, according to Witt, were fabricated, now appeared regularly in the tabloids. Without the GDR to run interference from Western criticism, she had to learn to fend for herself.

Due in large part to her competitive nature, Witt was eventually able to make peace with the press. Over time she learned how to present herself professionally, winning over both the public as well as a highly critical media as she quickly became ubiquitous for both her talent and her star power. In addition to appearances on American television, she could be seen on a number of German screens—large and small—showing her affection for the past while becoming a central icon of an *Ostalgie-Welle*, a wave of nostalgia for former East German culture. For some time in the mid-1990s, Witt even moderated a so-called *Ostalgie-Show* on a private TV channel. According to her, it was her striving for perfection and her ability to perform in sports that helped her adjust to life in the capitalist West,[59] although according to others, it was her undeniable appeal as a sex symbol that aided her in the transition.

Indeed, long before Witt ran afoul of the press, reporters had made her attractiveness the cornerstone of their coverage of her. Certainly, she was not alone in this kind of treatment. During Witt's prime, the press spent considerable column inches describing the skater's attractiveness. The American sprinter Florence Griffith Joyner (aka Flo-Jo) was similarly covered, as would be auto racer Danica Patrick and tennis player Gabriela Sabatini, whose physical attractiveness often informed the quality of their athletic accomplishments. Particularly in women's figure skating, in order to be successful, it is necessary that the athlete display a discernible aura of heterosexual femininity and sexuality. Certainly Witt was initially fêted because of her athletic prowess, but her physical beauty helped keep her in the public eye long after the spotlight of competitive skating gave way to the glitz and glamour of show business. For many, she was as much a sexual icon as she was a sports champion, as her sexuality continued to underscore public accounts of who she was, a matter that she herself was able to exploit, especially once she was freed from the grip of the GDR.

During her competitive years, Witt captivated judges and spectators with her technical skills and her way of performing with a highly sexualized artistry highlighted by her selection of sheer and revealing skating costumes. The Stasi noted in their files that as early as puberty, Witt had already figured out that she was quite attractive and could use this advantage to influence people, often to the chagrin of purists and rivals.[60] At the 1988 Olympic Games in Calgary, for example, American rival Debi Thomas's coach Alex McGowan voiced concern that the predominantly male judge panel was swayed by Witt's appearance more than by her performance. She wore a short, sequined dress—and a tiara—while Thomas wore a less revealing and perhaps less stylish bodysuit adorned only with sequins.[61] Of course, this was not the only time Witt's appearance rankled those in the sport. Witt's costumes would eventually lead the ISU to rule that costumes could not be "excessively theatrical," a standard that the figure skating world came to call the "Katarina Rule."[62] Despite the consternation over her clothing choices, her unique mix of looks and talent landed Witt on the cover of *Time*, Germany's first female athlete to be so featured.[63]

The trajectory of Witt's career reveals the skater to be complicit in the sexualization of her own reputation, an issue that continues to expand in her postathletic endeavors.[64] Upon her retirement from skating in 1998, Witt was able to find new ways to capitalize on her looks. The former "ice princess" posed not once but twice in *Playboy*, the first time in 1998, for which she was paid one million dollars. Completely nude in many of the shots, Witt's images were a hit with readers, leading to a sellout of the issue for only the second time in the publication's history (the first being the inaugural issue in 1953 featuring a nude Marilyn Monroe).[65] When asked about the reasons behind her decision to pose nude, Witt explained:

> *Playboy* had been asking me to pose for them for almost ten years, since 1988. I wasn't interested at the time because it didn't fit into my career. But when they asked again in 1998, I thought, "Why not?" I had a successful professional career that was getting better and better, so it wasn't like I was taking off my clothes to jump back into the public eye. I did it to be little rebellious, I suppose. I'd been the ice princess, the little girls' idol. I thought, "The heck with it, let's do something more controversial."[66]

Witt also mentioned that while she did not necessarily want to pose for erotic photos just for the sake of having done it, her ultimate goal was "to show a woman celebrating her own body, comfortable with her femininity. Pure. Not lustful."[67] Three years later, however, Witt appeared in the German edition of *Playboy*. Again Witt was able to use her body as capital, an issue that became much more commonplace in subsequent years as more and more female athletes from a range of countries opted to have their nude photos printed in various magazines, calendars, and other media to gain publicity and earn substantial amounts of money.[68] In this way, these women were able to parlay their athletic and fit bodies into erotic capital, as the German media and sports scholar Daniela Schaaf writes in her analysis of self-marketing among female athletes.[69] Witt was among the first to do so, and she continues to maintain that she did it without regret. She also maintains that her family and friends accepted her decision while noting that German standards of modesty and decorum are relatively lax, making it less of a scandal to display one's fit body in such a fashion.[70]

The Face of the German Olympic Bid[71]

Well past her athletic prime, Witt has managed to stay connected to German sport in other ways. Most notably, nearly ten years after Witt retired from her active life as an ice skater, she was selected by the Munich Olympic Organizing Committee for the Olympic Winter Games 2018 as the chairperson of the Kuratorium 2018. In this capacity, she served as an ambassador, presenting Germany's bid for the 2018 Winter Games.

Witt was a brilliant choice, given that she represented many aspects of German life that exemplify how far the country has progressed since the Cold War. Not only was she a renowned Olympic athlete but she was also a woman, a former citizen of East Germany, and a representative of winter sport. Moreover, Olympic organizers could be sure that she had enough experience to deal with the harsh press while she once again put to use her looks and charm as a mechanism for gaining votes.

Again, we see Witt serving in multiple capacities to help sway minds and curry favor. By this time well into middle age, although still attractive and charismatic, she was an optimal choice to represent the German effort to bring the Olympic Games back to Bavaria for the first time since the ill-fated 1972 Summer Games. But not all aspects of her involvement were well received. In particular, there was the matter of tradition running clumsily into the face of commercialism; instead of displaying Witt in the usual short skating skirt, the bidding committee outfitted the world famous Olympian in a typical Bavarian dress known as a dirndl. This traditional garment, with its low neckline that favors the female contours, is normally worn only by Bavarians and other Alpine peoples. While this choice of attire was discerned throughout Germany, no one in the international community seemed to notice (or perhaps even care) that Witt was not actually Bavarian! And yet, for Germans, this was seen as a faux pas, as it underscored the fact that Witt was not an authentic representative for the region. Adding this discrepancy to other suspicions that continue to swirl about her regarding her ties to the GDR and affiliated matters made her an even less attractive ambassador in the eyes of her fellow citizens, who seemed unconvinced that her selection was even right for the country.[72]

For international voters, however, Witt's dirndl was a nonissue as Munich made it to the final round of voting, though in the end the city's bid came up short. Neither the ecological concept presented by the bidding committee nor the beauty and charm of the former skating champion were enough. Money won out, and Germany, or more specifically Munich, lost to the South Korean city of Pyeongchang. This loss was a great disappointment for the German Olympic movement and winter sport enthusiasts in the country, though not so much for some opposing citizens such as local farmers who did not want to give up or even lend out their land for new Olympic facilities. Witt, who had put so much energy and effort into the bid, could hardly hide her disappointment, nor could the rest of her team. It was one of the few public battles in her life that she lost.[73]

A Legacy Wedged between Past and Present

One can certainly see many parallels to Katarina Witt when looking at the storied career of the Norwegian Olympic champion Sonja Henie, although the political realities of the respective times manage to obscure some of these similarities. Perhaps, like no other German female athlete before or since, Witt, the "West-Östliche Diva" (Western-Eastern Diva), could present herself both as a symbol of athletic excellence and as an international sex symbol whose glamour transcends national and even political boundaries. And yet, despite having represented a reunited Germany all these years hence, Witt somehow remains a controversial symbol of a disunited German past.[74]

During Witt's prime, the East German government had put tremendous pressure on her to perform successfully in the international sporting arena. In this regard, they utilized her international celebrity as a means to soften their often unflattering image in other contexts. In return, she received various advantages and had fewer restrictions in her daily life than many other citizens of the GDR, including the freedom to travel to the West, although the costs of such freedoms were indeed quite high.

In addition to a challenging and at times merciless training regimen, Witt also had to cope with the prying eyes of an unforgiving state. With few exceptions, no one knew that Witt's steps were being so closely watched by state security—something she discovered after the political system broke down. Regardless, for East German politicians, she was a valuable property that the state could ill afford to lose, treating her more as commodity than the international champion she grew to be.

By virtually every measure, Witt's life can be seen as a series of compromises: she gave of herself as freely as the state demanded, but she also demonstrated that she knew how to play the game while the system continued to game her. In this regard, then, Witt's life can be viewed as a series of reciprocal exchanges taking place between her and the many constituencies that harnessed her celebrity for causes well outside the sporting environment.

Notes

1. See the 2005 TV documentary *Goodbye DDR* by authors Peter Hartl and Henry Köhler, in four parts. One part was specifically on Katarina Witt, subtitled "Kati und der schöne Schein" [Kati and the nice shine]. Shine (or glamour, or appearance) has an ambiguous meaning in this context. It not only is connected to glimmer and success but also can be interpreted as acting or show. The film was produced by Phoenix and shown on the German public TV channel ZDF.

2. Pierre Bourdieu, "Ökonomisches Kapital, kulturelles Kapital, soziales Kapital," in *Soziale Ungleichheiten*, ed. Reinhard Kreckel, 183–93 (Göttingen: Otto Schwartz, 1983). Witt's biography could also be analyzed using a Foucaultian lens. Her life shows all the aspects of power that he addresses in his research. However, that will not be the purpose of this chapter.

3. Although first published in 1994, I will refer in this chapter to the 1995 paperback edition of Katarina Witt, *Meine Jahre zwischen Pflicht und Kür* (Munich: Goldmann Verlag, 1995). According to Alexander Osang, it was written by a ghostwriter rather quickly and as a result lacks quality. See Alexander Osang, "Die Akten aus der Eiszeit," *Der Spiegel* 18 (2002): 72.

4. Mary Louise Adams, "Skating," in *International Encyclopedia of Women and Sports*, vol. 2, ed. Karen Christensen, Allen Guttmann, and Gertrud Pfister (New York: Macmillan Reference, 2001), 1021.

5. Roland Renson, "From Pieter Bruegel to Hendrik Avercamp: Winter Sport Scenes as Genre Paintings in the Low Countries in the 16th and 17th Centuries," paper presented at the North American Society for Sport History Conference, Halifax, Nova Scotia, May 27, 2013; also see Adams, "Skating," 1016–21.

6. Adams, "Skating," 1016.

7. Mary Louise Adams, "From Mixed-Sex Sport to Sport for Girls: The Feminization of Figure Skating," in *Women in Sports History*, ed. Carol A. Osborne and Fiona Skillen (London: Routledge, 2011), 40.

8. James R. Hines, *Figure Skating: A History* (Urbana: University of Illinois Press, 2006). The British skater Madge Syers entered the men's figure skating world championships in 1902 and placed second. Syers and others pushed the International Skating Union (ISU) to include women, which it finally did in 1906.

9. Hines, *Figure Skating: A History*.

10. Gerd von der Lippe, "Henie, Sonja," in *International Encyclopedia of Women and Sports*, vol. 2, ed. Karen Christensen, Allen Guttmann, and Gertrud Pfister (New York: Macmillan Reference, 2001), 501.

11. Ibid., 502.

12. Daniela Schaaf, "Der Körper als Kapital: Sportlerinnen im Spannungsfeld zwischen Selbstvermarktung und Selbstermächtigung," in *Die Sexualisierung des Sports in den Medien*, ed. Daniela Schaaf and Jörg-Uwe Nieland (Cologne: Herbert von Halem Verlag, 2011), 117–23.

13. Allen Guttmann, *The Erotic in Sports* (New York: Columbia University Press, 1996), 75.

14. Robert Gugutzer, "Körperpolitiken des Sports: Zur sportiven Verschränkung von Körper, Geschlecht und Macht," in *Die Sexualisierung des Sports in den Medien*, ed. Daniela Schaaf and Jörg-Uwe Nieland (Cologne: Herbert von Halem Verlag, 2011), 41.

15. In German, "Das schönste Gesicht des Sozialismus"; see Hartl and Köhler, *Goodbye DDR*.

16. Steffen Winter, "West-östliche Diva," *Der Spiegel* 2 (2009): 88.

17. Witt, *Meine Jahre zwischen Pflicht und Kür*, 125.

18. Jutta Müller is perhaps the most famous and successful figure skating coach in the world. She trained her daughter Gabriele Seyfert, who won two world championships for the GDR in 1969 and 1970. Afterward, she became coach to Günter Zöller, Jan Hoffmann, Sonja Morgenstern, Marion Weber, Anett Pötzsch, Constanze Gensel, Simone Lang, Evelyn Großmann, and Ronny Winkler. Witt was her best-known athlete. In 2004, Müller was admitted to the World Figure Skating Hall of Fame. See Katarina Witt and E. M. Swift, *Only with Passion: Figure Skating's Most Winning Champion on Competition and Life* (New York: Public Affairs, 2005); and Witt, *Meine Jahre zwischen Pflicht und Kür*.

19. Hartl and Köhler, *Goodbye DDR*.

20. Henry Kamm, "Glasnost Debate Divides East Germany's Officials," *New York Times*, March 8, 1989, at http://www.nytimes.com/1989/03/08/world/glasnost-debate-divides-east-germany-s-officials.html.

21. [The two years between the 1992 and 1994 Winter Olympics can be attributed to the reformatting of the Winter and Summer Games, which are now held at alternating two-year intervals rather than both being held in the same year every four years as was customary. To wit, after 1994, subsequent Winter Games were held in 1998, 2002, 2006, and so on, while the Summer Games embarked on a trajectory that took them to 1996, 2000, 2004, etc.—eds.]

22. Witt and Swift, *Only with Passion*, 145.

23. Hans Joachim Teichler, "Herrschaft und Eigensinn im DDR-Sport," in *Transformationen des deutschen Sports seit 1939*, ed. Michael Krüger (Hamburg: Czwalina, 2001), 233–49.

24. Hartl and Köhler, *Goodbye DDR*.

25. Kai Reinhart, "*Wir wollten einfach unser Ding machen*": *DDR-Sportler zwischen Fremdbestimmung und Selbstverwirklichung* (Frankfurt: Campus Verlag, 2010), 136.

26. Ibid., 182.

27. Witt, *Meine Jahre zwischen Pflicht und Kür*, 34ff., 176.

28. The Moscow Olympics (1980) and Los Angeles Olympics (1984) are excluded since not all nations participated as a result of political boycotts.

29. The original is as follows: "Es drückt eine enge Verbindung zwischen den Sportlern und der Partei der Arbeiterklasse, zwischen den Sportlern und unserer DDR, unserem sozialistischen Vaterland, aus . . ." See "Festlicher Empfang für unsere Olympioniken im Hotel 'Stadt Berlin,'" *Deutsches Sportecho*, February 22, 1984, 3.

30. The interview with Teichler can be found in Hartl and Köhler, *Goodbye DDR*.

31. Dieter Wales, "Tagebuch," *Deutsches Sportecho*, February 29, 1988.

32. Hartl and Köhler, *Goodbye DDR*.

33. Witt mentioned this number. However, it is not really known how many pages existed. In 1993, Alexander Osang believes that there must have been around 4,500 pages, and in 2002 only 1,354 pages were left. What happened to the rest is unknown. See Osang, "Die Akten aus der Eiszeit," 69.

34. In German, Operativer Vorgang Flop. This Stasi method of observation was very intense and used on persons who were believed to be a danger to the GDR.

35. In German, Operative Personen Kontrolle.

36. Witt, *Meine Jahre zwischen Pflicht und Kür*, 24–29, 126, 131.

37. This title translates as "My years between duty and freestyle." See Witt, *Meine Jahre zwischen Pflicht und Kür,* 7, 204.

38. This office is called Behörde für die Unterlagen des Staatssicherheitsdienstes. The Birthler Behörde was in charge of Witt's documents. See Osang, "Die Akte aus der Auszeit," 72.

39. The German term is *Diplomaten im Trainingsanzug.*

40. Hartl and Köhler, *Goodbye DDR.*

41. The original is as follows: "ständige Bemühen ihres Staates um die Erhaltung des Friedens und die Garantie des Rechts auf Arbeit."

42. "Ich finde unsere Politik richtig," *Deutsches Sportecho,* February 18, 1988, 3.

43. Ibid.

44. Witt, *Meine Jahre zwischen Pflicht und Kür,* 197–98.

45. Dave Anderson, "Olympics Take a First Step on the Road to Reality," *New York Times,* February 7, 1988, S3.

46. The original is as follows: "auf die DDR und die Partei der Arbeiterklasse singt Katarina Witt bei Gelegenheit Lobeshymnen. Schließlich ist sie Genossin in spe, seit November 1985 Kandidatin für die SED."

47. The original is as follows: "kapitalistisch getönter Sonderstatus und sozialistisch gefärbtes (extra-) Klassenbewusstsein."

48. Witt and Swift, *Only with Passion,* 103.

49. It should be noted that people had to wait for years for a permit to buy a car in the GDR. They were then typically only able to buy the state-manufactured car (a Trabant) or another car manufactured in a socialist country. To have a Western car was a great privilege that was granted only rarely.

50. Osang, "Die Akten aus der Eiszeit," 72–73.

51. Witt denied having some of the privileges that were mentioned in the press. She admitted that she did receive a dishwasher and an apartment. But she also said that she had to pay the rent. And after the fall of the Berlin Wall, she vehemently denied a statement made by the federal officer responsible for Stasi documents that she had appeared in the Stasi files as a favored person. More about her time at the acting school can be found in Witt and Swift, *Only with Passion,* 176ff.

52. The original is as follows: "Werbeträger darf sie nur in eigener Sache und zum höheren Wohl ihres Mäzens, der DDR, sein. Katharina Witt—zum Greifen nahe und doch so fern, eine Märchenfigur des Sports. Verführerisch, "westlich" im Habitus, unverkrampft—und doch an den ehernen Spielregelns ihrer Gesellschaft immer dann gebunden, wenn das nach außen behauptende Selbstverständnis sozialistischer Ideale auf dem Spiel steht. Dabei ist sie eine Märchenfigur auf Abruf. Beendet sie ihre Karriere, womit jährlich zu rechnen ist, muss sie vielleicht für immer in das Provinz-Amiente von Karl-Marx-Stadt zurückkehren. Selbst für sie ist die Freiheit nicht grenzenlos..." Roland Zorn, "Eine Märchenfigur auf Abruf: Sozialistisches Leitbild und privilegierter Star," *Frankfurter Allgemeine Zeitung,* March 19, 1986, 22.

53. Witt, *Meine Jahre zwischen Pflicht und Kür,* 84, 138. The original is as follows: "Sie erfüllt den Leistungsauftrag nicht. Sie wäre in der Lage, den Klassengegner im Leistungssport zu schlagen, habe aber nicht die richtige Einstellung hierzu."

54. In one instance, Witt was met with open hostility while emceeing a rock concert in East Berlin in 1988. See Witt, *Meine Jahre zwischen Pflicht und Kür,* 182. There are two explanations for this hostility. Perhaps it was simply because she was not wearing the official dress of the

GDR state youth organization, the FDJ. The other explanation is quite the opposite: perhaps she was booed off the stage because she still represented the GDR state. Only a few weeks before the fall of the Berlin Wall, East Germans were growing increasingly critical of their government. See "Hausmitteilungen" [House notes], *Der Spiegel* 18 (2002): 5.

55. Thomas Fetzer, "Die gesellschaftliche Akzeptanz des Leistungssportssystems," in *Sport in der DDR: Eigensinn, Konflikte, Trends,* ed. Hans Joachim Teichler (Cologne: Sportbuch Strauß, 2003), 358–422.

56. Witt, *Meine Jahre zwischen Pflicht und Kür,* 182.

57. "Dancing On Ice's New Judge Katarina Witt on Posing Naked, Being Spied On and Romance on the Rink," *Daily Mirror,* January 12, 2012, at http://www.mirror.co.uk/3am/celebrity-news/dancing-on-ices-new-judge-katarina-157644.

58. "Sex Komma Null für Kati," *Bild Hamburg,* February 27, 1988, 12. This title would be translated as "Sex Comma Zero," but in German it is a play on the number 6.0. In German, the number six (*sechs*) is pronounced almost like the English word "sex."

59. Winter, "West-östliche Diva," 88.

60. Witt and Swift, *Only with Passion,* 42–49.

61. Michael Janofsky, "Thomas Leads Skating; Witt Second," *New York Times,* February 26, 1988, B11, 15.

62. Ellyn Kestnbaum, *Culture on Ice: Figure Skating and Cultural Meaning* (Middletown, CT: Wesleyan University Press, 2003). For more details about the competition between Thomas and Witt, see Alison Wrynn and Annette R. Hofmann, "Debi Thomas vs. Katarina Witt Rivalry: 'The Battle of the Carmens: The Social Construction of a Skating Rivalry,'" in *Rivals: Legendary Matchups That Made Sports History,* ed. David K. Wiggins and R. Pierre Rodgers (Fayetteville: University of Arkansas Press, 2010), 133–46.

63. Witt, *Meine Jahre zwischen Pflicht und Kür,* 164.

64. Guttmann, *The Erotic in Sports,*160.

65. "Dancing On Ice's New Judge Katarina Witt."

66. Witt and Swift, *Only with Passion,* 90.

67. Ibid., 91.

68. Gertrud Pfister, "Die Darstellung von Frauen im Mediensport: Kontinuitäten und Veränderungen," in *Die Sexualisierung des Sports in den Medien,* ed. Daniela Schaaf and Jörg-Uwe Nieland (Cologne: Herbert von Halem Verlag, 2011), 75ff.

69. Schaaf, "Der Körper als Kapital," 117.

70. Witt and Swift, *Only with Passion,* 91.

71. This heading is from the article "Olympia 2018: Durban und das Dirndl," *TZ* (Munich), June 23, 2011, at http://www.tz-online.de/aktuelles/olympia-2018/olympia-2018-durban-dirndl-1294653.html.

72. Gerhard Pfeil, "Mountain Revolt: Bavarian Farmers Threaten Bid for Olympic Games," *Spiegel Online International,* January 4, 2011, at http://www.spiegel.de/international/germany/mountain-revolt-bavarian-farmers-threaten-bid-for-olympic-games-a-737654.html.

73. "Persistence Pays as Pyeongchang Is Awarded 2018 Winter Olympics," *Deutsche Welle,* July 6, 2011, at http://www.dw.com/en/persistence-pays-as-pyeongchang-is-awarded-2018-winter-olympics/a-15216411.

74. Schaaf, "Der Körper als Kapital," 126; and Winter, "West-östliche Diva," 88.

Afterword: The Wide Worlds of Sport Text
What Can a Global Perspective on Sports Bring to a Life-Long New York Yankees Fan?

—Jack Lule

Introduction

Often in academic life, we encourage our students to develop what we now call a global perspective. We perhaps assume that there is value in situating ourselves and our students—intellectually, perhaps even physically—outside of national and cultural boundaries. Indeed, at my university in the United States, I am part of a faculty group that created a new interdisciplinary major we call Global Studies. We require interdisciplinary coursework on the study of globalization. We require language study. We require study abroad. We do all this with the hope that our students attain in the classroom, in careers, and in daily life a global perspective. But this is not just an American educational phenomenon. Around the world, millions of students leave their nations and families for an opportunity at global study.

The study of sport, however, may seem to resist the benefits of a global perspective. And one must admit: sport can be exceedingly local. For many people, sport begins at the most insular level—the family. Knowledge of and passion for the home team—be it nation or city—are a birthright. Infants are swaddled in team colors. Family rituals often have relatives gathering around television sets or at stadiums. Wins and losses are occasions of shared joy and sorrow. Sport eventually becomes a subject in which people earn deep, historical, and comprehensive "local knowledge," as Clifford Geertz has posed it, gained over decades of study, observation, participation, and practice, handed down from generation to generation.[1] The local sport fan may seek deep and abiding knowledge of other teams—rival or "enemy teams" in particular—but the learning of others is undertaken to better support the home team. "Like sailing, gardening, politics, and poetry, law and ethnography are crafts of place:

they work by the light of local knowledge," Geertz says.² I would certainly add sport to that eclectic list.

America's Games

Perhaps more than most, fans of American sport can seem especially local, and even parochial. It is by now a truism that American fans are primarily passionate about their own sports—created by Americans and certainly bearing a "made in the USA" stamp—football, baseball, and basketball, with some at times offering a begrudging nod to Canada's game, hockey, located somewhere in the mix. It is of particular interest that the most popular American sport carries the name of the world's most popular sport—but is an entirely different sport. Yet *football* offers one way for us to understand the value of a global perspective. *Football* and/or *fútbol* pose similarities and differences, comparisons and variations, and correspondence and contrasts in terms of the various ways that people and their sports are the same and, yes, different.

Ultimately, that may be the fundamental value of a global perspective: we not only come to better understand others; we come to better understand ourselves. The present volume—a global study of sport celebrities from around the globe—exemplifies and confirms the wisdom and value of a global perspective. Scholars from around the world bring local knowledge to bear on local sport stars and the local issues their presence suggests. Each reader in turn brings to each chapter his or her own local knowledge, ignorance, memories, passions, divergence, and convergence. And in that meeting between the two locales—a local text and local reader, a chapter on cricket stars and a reader who knows only baseball stars—a new and global perspective is born.

Paul Ricoeur, a philosopher of hermeneutics—the close reading and interpretation of texts—sees this confluence of reader and text as noble and powerful. He calls the moment "appropriation" and says that "what has to be appropriated is nothing other than the power of disclosing a world" opened up by the text.³ He contends further that the power of disclosing a world will be a very personal transaction. The text, he proffers, will disclose a world, but that world will be a different one for me than for you and for my colleague who grew up with cricket and *fútbol* in India. We all will learn, but we will learn—we will appropriate— different things. In different language, Ricoeur borrows from fellow philosopher Hans-Georg Gadamer the concept of a "fusion of horizons" and argues that in reading and interpretation, "the world horizon of the reader is fused with the world horizon of the writer."⁴ Through the work, generosity, and knowledge of the writers presented here, and through the texts they have generated, I learn of people I had never before heard, and I get new ways of looking at issues I have known my entire life.

From Local to Global

More than most edited volumes, this collection of pieces comes to have a collective, cumulative effect. Each chapter offers its own world, but together the chapters offer an ever more complex world, adding bit by bit to my knowledge, giving me different ways, sometimes contradictory ways, of comprehending a sport, such as *fútbol*, as well as comprehending an issue, such as racism.

I will try to capture below a small sample of what I have learned and the global perspectives I have gained from this text. Perhaps it will be similar to your own. In the hermeneutic spirit, in which the reader acknowledges his or her own reflexive position to the texts, I offer the *ragbag* of local knowledge that I bring to my reading.

I am a lifetime New York Yankees fan and, more broadly, a lover of baseball whether it is played in Boston, Williamsport, Japan, or Cuba. I am an interested television viewer of the spectacle of the US National Football League and college football but suspicious of the role that sports plays in US universities, a role that one does not see in universities around the world. I watch the National Basketball Association and the National Hockey League during the playoffs, when the games matter most, and the tension is palpable even without close knowledge. I knew about Yao. I am a jealous admirer of the worldwide passion for *fútbol*, which I have seen from Indonesia to Cuba to Italy, but of which I know only a little. I am ignorant of Formula One racing, ice skating, sumo wrestling, cricket, and more. I think sport has and can capture the most important issues of our day, from racism to terrorism to sexism, but it can also capture humankind at its finest. I came to the text with this local knowledge and a desire for more.

Athletes as Ambassadors

In America, we often have debates on whether athletes should be role models. Seemingly each time a high-profile athlete is involved in some tawdry scandal or is in trouble with the law, commentators will say that, whether they like it or not, athletes are given high status and privilege in our society, are looked up to, even worshipped, by youth, and must accept that responsibility. Nonsense, say others. These athletes are often young people themselves, grappling with newfound fame and fortune, and are the least likely figures to be role models. A touchstone in this debate often is a 1993 Nike advertising campaign built around basketball star Charles Barkley's belief that athletes should not be role models.[5]

However, many of the global athletes profiled in this volume, willingly or not, became much more than role models. They became cultural icons and national ambassadors. I felt this as a significant difference from the American scene. In the United States, Babe Ruth, Muhammad Ali, Michael Jordan, Tiger Woods, and more have surely been understood as US sport stars and celebrities of the highest order and are known worldwide. They may even represent the United States to people of other lands. But I am not sure Americans feel that these figures represent them or their nation. Yet, time after time in this volume, the words *icon* and *ambassador* appear and capture a complex and powerful relationship. It is as if the people of a nation have felt slighted, ignored, or left out of international conversations. And then a local athlete succeeds and bursts forth on the global stage, bringing attention and acclaim to the homeland, and the people of that nation respond with intense pride, admiration, and even love. The athletes are understood by themselves and by others as representing an entire nation and people.

We learn, for example, that skater Katarina Witt was a face of beauty, a face of commercialization, a face of glamour, and, last but not least, a face of Germany: both for the East but also for a reunited Germany. We learn that basketball star Yao Ming was invited by President George H. W. Bush to attend a luncheon for visiting Chinese president Jiang Zemin and given a chance to speak. He even received an award in 2009 for his contributions to the Sino-US relationship. We learn that after Ayrton Senna, the Formula One driver, died in a racing accident, Brazil declared a three-day period of national mourning. MotoGP motorcycle rider Valentino Rossi is a legend in Italy and an international ambassador for his sport. Sumo wrestler Chad Rowan from Hawaii became Japan's most important cultural symbol in the 1990s as Yokozuna Akebono and was chosen to help inaugurate the 1998 Nagano Olympic opening ceremonies. Aquatic athlete Duke Paoa Kahanamoku was Hawaii's beloved goodwill ambassador in the mid-1900s. In chapter after chapter, we see that the *transaction* between athlete and fan—athlete and nation—is of the highest magnitude.

Oddly, in my reading and ruminations on star athletes as cultural icons and ambassadors, I found myself intrigued by the few stories of great athletes who, despite their huge success on international stages, were not embraced by their nation or people. British sport in particular seems beset by such difficulties. Maverick football player Rodney Marsh, for example, as big an international star as there was in the 1970s, who went on to a turbulent broadcasting career, pointedly pushed back against the idea of being a role model or cultural icon, speaking his mind on controversial topics and refusing to adapt to team, sport, and cultural expectations. British tennis star Andy Murray, despite a historic victory at Wimbledon in front of his victory-starved nation, remained largely unloved and unappreciated at home. Viewed as petulant, surly, sulky, humorless, and competing not on court but on television networks and tabloids against the legacies of previous tennis personalities such as Björn Borg, John McEnroe, Vitas Gerulaitis, Ilie Năstase, and Jimmy Connors, Murray was found wanting. He achieved great success in his sport without finding the admiration, pride, or respect of his people, many of whom barely claim him as one of their own, and he seems unlikely to become an ambassador or icon anytime soon—or ever, for that matter.

The social, cultural, economic, and political powers of sport are well known. But the complex, special, and powerful relationship between the global sport figures discussed here and their nations is remarkable to observe. It makes the US social conversation about athletes as role models seem smaller in comparison.

Sports as Sites for Social Struggle

I am accustomed to the idea that sports can be situated where troubling social issues, such as terrorism and racism, are dramatized and sometimes confronted. The archetypal American example is Jackie Robinson "breaking the color line" and enduring vitriol and hatred as he became the first African American to play baseball in the modern era. Other examples abound in US culture and include sprinters John Carlos and Tommie Smith raising their fists in what continues to be called a "black power" salute at the 1968 Olympic Games in Mexico City, just a few years after boxer Cassius Clay refused to go to war in Vietnam, having become a Muslim and changing his name to Muhammad Ali.

Parochial and local, I too often think of the confluence of sport and social struggle in an American context. It is of great interest to see that issues of race, gender, class, and more play out on pitches, rinks, and fields around the world. The great Cameroonian *fútbol* star, Samuel Eto'o, endured racist taunting by European football fans, including some making monkey sounds and throwing bananas on the field. Katarina Witt was called a "Stasi whore" and an "SED Ziege" (the goat of the Socialist Unity Party) in Germany. Duke Paoa Kahanamoku, as a native Hawaiian, overcame racism, which saw him as a racially colonized foreigner, to represent the United States and win gold and silver medals in swimming at the 1912, 1920, and 1924 Olympiads.

And what a powerful scene has been portrayed in this book of the 1996 World Cup in cricket. The militant group, the Tamil Tigers, seeking an independent state for the minority Tamils in Sri Lanka, had recently bombed the Central Bank in Colombo, killing 91 people and injuring 1,400 more. Yet the World

Cup would go on in nearby Pakistan with underdog Sri Lanka playing Australia in the final match. And who emerged as the hero and led Sri Lanka to the upset victory: twenty-three-year-old Muttiah Muralitharan—"Murali"—a member of the Tamil minority. Murali would then go on to partner with Kumar Sangakkara—"Sanga"—a member of the Sinhalese majority, to provide the nation with an example of partnership between Tamil and Sinhalese and a model for ethnic conciliation. It is a fabulous story and a reminder of sport's power to dramatize exemplary models.

The Heroic Journey

Finally, it is impossible to read this volume and not be struck by the power of the human spirit to strive, persevere, and triumph—and to recognize in its chapters the mythic narrative of the Hero. In *The Hero with a Thousand Faces*, another volume dedicated to the local and global, Joseph Campbell finds that the mythic story of the Hero is told in every human culture and takes similar form in every culture: the Hero is born into ordinary, sometimes humble, circumstances, receives a calling to adventure or journey, leaves home, endures initiation, trial, and adversity, but ultimately returns home triumphant.[6] The myth appears in every culture, Campbell maintains, because it offers "living inspiration," a hopeful model for living.[7] The hero, he writes, "is the man or woman who has been able to battle past his personal and local historical limitations" and "to return then to us, transfigured, and teach the lesson" of life renewed.[8]

Mircea Eliade argued that the Hero embraces one of the chief characteristics of myth, "the creation of exemplary models for a whole society." And, he said, "[i]n this, moreover, we recognise a very general human tendency; namely, to hold up one life-history as a paradigm and turn a historical personage into an archetype."[9] Myth, Eliade said, "supplies models for human behavior and, by that very fact, gives meaning and value to life."[10]

Each chapter here in some measure narrates the myth of the hero, offers us models for human behavior, and provides us with glimmers of insights into the meaning of life. Each athlete received a calling, pursued distinction in sport, prevailed in trials and competition, and returned home, often in triumph. Some endured truly compelling trials. Eto'o, Kahanamoku, Witt, Murali, and others overcame barriers of gender, class, and race. Suzanne Lenglen broke through the gender and ethnocentric stereotypes of the post–World War I era and became the first woman to find global fame in tennis while conceivably ushering in the age of sport as spectacle. Marta overcame crushing poverty and gender stereotypes to elevate women's *fútbol* in Brazil. Norwegian distance runner Grete Waitz underwent personal tragedies, such as the death of a young boyfriend, and political machinations, including the Olympic boycotts of 1976, 1980, and 1984, before ultimately finding worldwide success as a marathon runner. Chad Rowan—a gaijin, a foreigner, from Hawaii, although ethnically Samoan—stoically endured the political, cultural, and economic pressures of an ethnocentric system to become a sumo legend in Japan as Yokozuna Akebono. Surely an essential characteristic of this text is that, as Joseph Campbell affirmed, the myth of the hero continues to be told in cultures around the world, and its lessons can carry across eras as well as boundaries. I learn as much from Kahanamoku's trials in the early 1900s as I do from Murali's triumphs in the late 1900s.

The Wide World of Sports

When I was young, my local, parochial sports interests sometimes were pierced by an innovative ABC television show, *ABC's Wide World of Sports*. First hosted by Jim McKay, the program ran from 1961 to 1998 and was sometimes revisited in later years. The show's concept and conceit were to broadcast sporting events not typically seen on American television, such as auto racing, rodeo, surfing, powerlifting, and cliff diving, as well as sports usually televised only during the Olympics, such as skiing and figure skating. The show featured a stirring, perhaps melodramatic introduction:

> Spanning the globe to bring you the constant variety of sport—the thrill of victory—and the agony of defeat—the human drama of athletic competition.[11]

The words were accompanied by vivid video clips, including a spectacular skiing crash to dramatize the agony of defeat.

I found myself thinking of the show as I read and reread this volume. We indeed have been offered in this collection a wide world of sports through global perspectives not often gathered in one self-contained location. My conception of a "world," though, has deepened considerably since my adolescent years. Interests in reading and writing led me to theories of interpretation—hermeneutics—and the generous visions of Ricoeur and Geertz. My studies can be simply put: how do we interpret and understand written work, especially written work from other times and places, such as ancient Greece, colonial America, the antebellum South, or even Cold War Europe? We do not seek really to understand disparate *authors* of those eras. We seek to understand *their worlds*. "If we can no longer define hermeneutics in terms of the search for the psychological intentions of another person which are concealed *behind* the text, and if we do not want to reduce interpretation to the dismantling of structures, then what remains to be interpreted?" Ricouer asks. His answer: "I shall say: to interpret is to explicate the type of being-in-the-world unfolded *in front of* the text."[12] What is this strange world? Ricoeur suggests, "what must be interpreted in a text is a *proposed world* which I could inhabit."[13]

You and I have found ourselves in front of this text that surely offers *proposed worlds* for us to inhabit—France in Fitzgerald's Jazz Age, Sri Lanka in 1996, Hawaii in 1912, Japan in the 1990s, Germany in 1989, China in the new millennium. The world is wide and the text ambitious, spanning not only the globe but also time. Although many of the sports and the countries were first "foreign" to me, I have inhabited those worlds and gained much. Across time and space, I have viewed a shared love of, passion for, and devotion to sport. I have admired those who have heard a call and taken on the heroic quest. I have been repelled by the cruel vitriol and hatred that some are forced to suffer. But ultimately, I am inspired by the stories of those who endure to become ambassadors of sports and nations as well as humankind.

Notes

1. Clifford Geertz, *Local Knowledge: Further Essays in Interpretive Anthropology* (New York: Basic Books, 1983).

2. Ibid., 167.

3. Paul Ricoeur, *Interpretation Theory: Discourse and the Surplus of Meaning* (Fort Worth: Texas Christian University Press, 1976), 92.

4. Ibid., 93.

5. Claire Smith, "The Debate: Athletes as Role Models," *New York Times*, last modified July 23, 1993, at http://www.nytimes.com/1993/07/23/sports/sports-of-the-times-the-debate-athletes-as-role-models.html.

6. Joseph Campbell, *The Hero with a Thousand Faces*, 3rd ed. (Novato, CA: New World Library, 2008).

7. Ibid., 1.

8. Ibid., 14–15.

9. Mircea Eliade, *Myths, Dreams, and Mysteries: The Encounter between Contemporary Faiths and Archaic Realities*, trans. Philip Mairet (New York: Harper & Brothers, 1960), 32.

10. Mircea Eliade, *Myth and Reality*, trans. Willard R. Trask (New York: Harper & Row, 1963), 2

11. *ABC's Wide World of Sports*, IMDb, at http://www.imdb.com/title/tt0190895/.

12. Paul Ricoeur, *Hermeneutics and the Human Sciences*, ed. and trans. John B. Thompson (Cambridge: Cambridge University Press, 1981), 141.

13. Ibid., 142.

Contributors

Editors

Dr. Joel Nathan Rosen is associate professor of sociology at Moravian College in Bethlehem, Pennsylvania. His research focuses primarily on the relationship between human activity and stratification as informed by cultural idioms such as music and sport. He is the author of *The Erosion of the American Sporting Ethos: Shifting Attitudes toward Competition* (McFarland) and *From New Lanark to Mound Bayou: Owenism in the Mississippi Delta* (Carolina Academic Press); and coauthor with Roberta J. Newman of *Black Baseball, Black Business: Race Enterprise and the Fate of the Segregated Dollar* (University Press of Mississippi). He is also the author and coauthor of several book chapters and peer-reviewed journal articles, and the coeditor with David C. Ogden of *Reconstructing Fame: Race, Sport, and Evolving Reputations*; *Fame to Infamy: Race, Sport, and the Fall from Grace*; and *A Locker Room of Her Own: Celebrity, Sexuality, and Female Athletes* (all University Press of Mississippi).

Dr. Maureen M. Smith is a professor in the Department of Kinesiology and Health Science at California State University, Sacramento, where she teaches sport history and sport sociology. She is the past president of the North American Society for Sport History, and an active member of the North American Society for the Sociology of Sport and the International Society for the History of Physical Education and Sport. Dr. Smith's work has appeared in *Sport and Society*, the *Journal of Sport and Social Issues*, the *Journal of Sport History*, the *International Journal of the History of Sport*, and several edited collections.

Contributors

Dr. Lisa Doris Alexander is associate professor of African American studies at Wayne State University in Detroit. She is the author of *When Baseball Isn't White Straight and Male: The Media and Difference in the National Pastime* (McFarland). Dr. Alexander is a Chicago sports fan whose work has also appeared in *NINE: A Journal of Baseball History and Culture*, *Black Ball: A Negro*

Leagues Journal, the *Journal of Popular Film and Television*, and the *Journal of American History*.

Sean Bell is a founder of the Brighton Salon, an experimental meeting place for live, free public discussion that has been running for ten years in England. He was a local newspaper journalist and worked on the British national editions of the magazines *Campaign* and *Computing* and still occasionally contributes to less-mainstream publications, particularly on the subject of cultural perceptions of the general public (whatever that is). He has a degree in fine art and a master's degree in journalism and society. An avid biker, Sean has been riding motorcycles on- and off-road for more than thirty years and has a unique knowledge of the sport and its machinery but has never raced. He is married with two children.

Dr. Benn L. Bongang is a professor of political science and chairman of the Department of Political Science and Public Affairs at Savannah State University. He is an alumnus of the Executive Leadership Institute (ELI) of the University System of Georgia. He was a 1992–1993 Hubert H. Humphrey Fellow and earned degrees in journalism and international studies from Boston University and the University of South Carolina. He worked for several years as a radio journalist and a TV producer/director for the Cameroon Radio and Television Corporation (CRTV). He also worked for United Nations Radio and the UN Office for Disarmament Affairs in New York. He is author of *The United States and the United Nations: Congressional Funding and UN Reform* (LFB Scholarly Publishing).

Dr. Dong Jinxia received her bachelor's and master's degrees from Beijing Sports University in 1982 and 1985, respectively, and her PhD from the University of Strathclyde in 2001. She worked at Beijing Sports University between 1985 and 1996. While she was studying her PhD program in Scotland between 1996 and 2000, she also coached the Scottish girls' gymnastics team. Since 2001, she has been working at Peking University, lecturing and researching in the fields of Olympic culture, gender and sport, sports sociology, and physical education. She is the founding director of the Peking University Research Center for Gender, Sports, and Society, deputy director of the Peking University Research Center for Sport, Society, and Culture, and member of the Peking University Academic Evaluation Committee for Social Science. She has also authored hundreds of articles in both Chinese and English on sport, the Olympics, culture, and gender, including the internationally acclaimed book *Women, Sport and Society in the New China* (Frank Cass, 2003).

Dr. Joel S. Franks received his bachelor's and master's degrees in history from San José State University and his PhD from the Program in Comparative Culture at the University of California, Irvine. The author of several publications in the fields of sport studies and ethnic studies, he teaches Asian American and American studies at San José State University.

Dr. Silvana Vilodre Goellner is professor of physical education at the University of Rio Grande do Sul, Brazil. She coordinates the Center for Memory of Sport (Porto Alegre) and has several publications that examine women, history, and gender.

Annette R. Hofmann is a professor of sports studies at the Ludwigsburg University of Education in Germany. She is the president of the International Society for the History of Physical Education and Sport (ISHPES) and vice president of the German Gymnastic Federation (Deutsche Turner-Bund). She is an academic editor of the *International Journal of the History of Sport* and book review editor of the *Journal of Sport History*. She holds several other positions on national and international academic boards. She has published more than thirty papers on the American Turners, including the book *The American Turner Movement: A History from Its Beginnings to 2000* (Max Kade German-American Center, 2010). She is a coeditor with Marit Nybelius of *License to Jump! A Story of Women's Ski Jumping* (Beijbom Books, 2015).

Cláudia Samuel Kessler is a Brazilian anthropologist. She has a bachelor's degree in social sciences and a master's degree in social sciences from Universidade Federal de Santa Maria (Brazil). Her main areas of research are gender (especially women's studies) and the sociology of sports. She writes about gender-based violence, gender, and sports.

Dr. Jack Lule is professor and chairman of the Department of Journalism and Communication and founding director of the Global Studies Program at Lehigh University. His research interests include digital media, globalization and media, international communication, and cultural studies of news. He is the author of three books: *Globalization and Media: Global Village of Babel* (Rowman and Littlefield); *Daily News, Eternal Stories: The Mythological Role of Journalism* (Guilford); and *Understanding Media and Culture: An Introduction to Mass Communication* (Flatworld). Dr. Lule is also the author of more than fifty scholarly articles and book chapters and a frequent contributor to numerous newspapers and periodicals, and he has served as a commentator about the news on National Public Radio, the BBC, and other media outlets.

He has been awarded grants from the New York Times Company Foundation, the National Endowment for the Humanities, and others. He is the recipient of numerous teaching awards, including the Deming Lewis Faculty Award and the Donald B. and Dorothy L. Stabler Foundation Award for Excellence in Teaching. A former reporter, he earned his PhD from the University of Georgia and received the Distinguished Alumni Scholar Award from the university's Henry W. Grady College of Journalism and Mass Communication. He has been teaching at Lehigh since 1990.

Li Luyang is a graduate student at Peking University. She earned her BA from Jilin University, China. Her main research interests are sports culture and media strategy. She has presented in international conferences and has published numerous articles in Chinese on sports media.

Dr. Mark Panek is associate professor and department chair of the University of Hawai'i at Hilo's English Department. He is the author of *Gaijin Yokozuna: A Biography of Chad Rowan* and *Big Happiness: The Life and Death of a Modern Hawaiian Warrior* (both University of Hawai'i Press), both of which examine the cultural moves required of young men from Hawai'i who attempted careers in professional sumo, a centuries-old cultural touchstone as well as Japan's national sport.

Dr. Roberta J. Park is Professor Emerita of Integrative Biology at the University of California, Berkeley. A pioneering figure in sport history, her intellectual contributions to sport history and physical education studies are extensive and integral to the broader field of kinesiology. Moreover, she has influenced entire generations of sport historians through her many individually authored works as well as through her many collaborations with J. A. Mangan.

Dr. Gamage Harsha Perera received his BSc (Hons) (2008) from the University of Peradeniya, Sri Lanka, and his MSc (2011) and PhD (2015) degrees in statistics from Simon Fraser University, British Columbia. A keen cricketer, his research interests are in cricket analytics.

Dr. Nancy E. Spencer is associate professor in the Sport Management Program at Bowling Green State University in Ohio. Her scholarship focuses on intersections of gender, national identity, and race in professional women's tennis, and her work has appeared in the *Sociology of Sport Journal*, the *Journal of Sport and Social Issues*, the *Journal of Sport Management*, and *Sport Marketing Quarterly*. She has written chapters in *Asian American Athletes in Sport and Society*, edited by C. Richard King (Routledge, 2015); and *Bodies of Discourse: Sports*

Stars, Media, and the Global Public, edited by Cornel Sandvoss, Michael Real, and Alina Bernstein (Peter Lang, 2012).

Professor Tim B. Swartz received his BMath in statistics and computer science from the University of Waterloo in 1982, and his MSc (1983) and PhD (1986) degrees in statistics from the University of Toronto. He is a full professor in the Department of Statistics and Actuarial Science at Simon Fraser University, where he has worked since 1986. His research interests include inference, computational statistics, Bayesian methodology, and the application of statistics in sport. He is coauthor with Michael Evans of *Approximating Integrals via Monte Carlo and Deterministic Methods* (Oxford University Press, 2001). He has also published more than eighty peer-reviewed articles.

Viral Shah is a journalist and writer based in London. He was previously the English language–edition editor of cafébabel, a pan-European online magazine in Paris, and he is currently working for a financial newswire. He recently completed his master's in journalism at Aarhus University, Denmark, and City University London, having previously studied English literature at Warwick University. He has contributed to *Spiked,* the *Huffington Post UK,* and the *Independent,* writing predominantly on sport and specifically football.

Dr. Dominic Standish is a faculty member at the University of Iowa and lectures at its Italian campus (CIMBA/CUIS). He has had articles and chapters published in numerous books, journals, and websites, which can be accessed from his website at dominicstandish.com. His book *Venice in Environmental Peril? Myth and Reality* was published by the University Press of America in 2012. Dr. Standish is a season ticket holder at the English Football club Queen's Park Rangers.

Dan Travis is a freelance writer whose journalism centers on the politics of sport, health, and education policy. His research interests focus on the shifting notions of the public sphere, the political subject, and attitudes toward competition. These themes have been explored in both his MSc in social and political theory and a variety of published articles. His copywriting and social-networking advice work includes building audiences and producing copy for a range of clients in the medical, financial, and creative industries.

Dr. Theresa Walton-Fisette is an associate professor in the School of Foundations, Leadership and Administration at Kent State University. Her work centers on critical examinations of sport and physical activity, keeping in mind both theoretical and practical concerns. She is the author of *Pinned by Gender*

Construction? A Critical Analysis of Media Coverage of Women's Amateur Wrestling in the United States (Lambert Academic Publishing) as well as many book chapters and journal articles.

Zhong Yijing is CEO of an educational startup in Beijing that promotes children's participation in sport and brain development. Previously, she worked at CG/LA Infrastructure Consultancy, the Brookings Institution, the World Bank, and China Central Television Sports Channel, among others. She got her BA from Peking University and her master's from Johns Hopkins University, and she has published articles in Chinese and English on new energy strategies and the educational system in China.

Index

AC Milan, 245
Adams, Bryan, 200
Adams, Mary Louise, 280
Adelaide Race Track (Australia), 266, 268
Adelaide Test match (Australia), 195
Adidas AG, 213
Africa Cup of Nations, 167
African Player of the Year, 167–68
Africa Top Sports, 172
Age, 191, 194
Agostini, Giacomo, 25, 48
Aida (Okayama International Circuit) (Japan), 268–69
ajauda de custos (small stipend), 150
Aktiv mot Kreft (Active against Cancer), 219
Alan Titchmarsh Show, 239
Albacete Balompié (Spain), 177
Alberto, Carlos, 232
Alboreto, Michele, 259
Ali, Muhammad, 26, 41, 48, 300–301; refusal to go to Vietnam, 301
Aliança Renovadora Nacional (ARENA), 255
Allison, Malcolm, 227, 235
Amateur Athletic Union (AAU), 102, 105, 109, 115
Ambrose, Greg, 116
American Broadcasting Company (ABC), 231, 233
American Grand Prix, 33
American Indoor Soccer Association (AISA), 236
American Major League Soccer (MLS), 243
American Professional Soccer League (APSL), 235–36
American Soccer Bowl, 242–43
Andy Goldstein's Sports Bar (TalkSport), 239

Angelis, Elio de, 260, 269
ANTA Sports Products Ltd. (China), 88
Anthony, Carmelo, 93
Antongo, 169
Anzhi Makhachkala (Dagestan), 179; training in Moscow, 180
Apple Inc., 83, 91–92
Arnold, Thomas, 240
Artest, Ron (Metta World Peace), 88
Asahi Shimbun, 136
Asashōryū, 141–42
Asian Games, x
Association of Tennis Professionals (ATP), 62, 66
Athletics Congress (TAC), 213
Atisanoe, Saleva'a, 127
Audi (German), 268
Australian Open, 66
Australian Rules Football, 34
Auto Esporte, 254
Automobility, 252, 257–58
Autosport, 259–60
Averbuch, Gloria, 218
Ayrton Senna's Super Monaco Grand Prix, 268

Bahrain Grand Prix, 260
Baker, Brad, 32
Bales, Jean-Marie, 259–60, 263–67, 276n
Balotelli, Mario, 245
Bangladesh, 189, 197, 199
Banjul, The Gambia, xv–xviii
Barker, Sue, 69
Barkley, Charles, 80, 300
Barnes, Simon, 261
Barra, Lindsay, 62
Barrichello, Rubens, 269

311

Barry, Chuck, 33
Baseball Hall of Fame, 140–41
Basketball Digest, 92
Basketball Hall of Fame (US), 75, 80, 82
Bata Schoolboy Cricketer of the Year (1990–1991), 192
Bates, Jeremy, 68
Battier, Shane, 88
Beatlemania, 124
Beckenbauer, Franz, 232, 235
Becker, Boris, 66
Beckham, David, 237, 242–44, 246
Beckham, Victoria, 243
Benetton Formula Ltd., 265, 268, 270, 277n
Ben-Hur (1959), 33
Benmayor, Rina, 100
Bennetts, Dick, 256–57
Benoit, Joan, 214, 217
Berlin, Germany, 283
Berlin Wall, 57, 278–79, 284–85, 288, 295–96n
Best, George, 222, 228, 232, 234, 239, 246
Beveridge, Bob, 134–35, 137
BDA Sports Management, 82
Biaggi, Max, 39
Big Brother (UK), 45–46
"Big Matches," 189
Bild (West Germany), 283–84
Billington, Henry, 57
Biri Biri (Alhaji Momodu Njie), xiii, xv–xxi
Bislett Stadium, 204, 218
Biya, Paul, 164, 171, 173–74
Björsen Skole (Oslo), 216
"black power" salute, in Mexico City, 301
Blanchimont Spa (Circuit de Spa-Francorchamps) (Belgium), 266–67
Bloomberg Business Week, 91
Bodo, Peter, 66
Boesel, Raul, 254
Bogalusa Enterprise (Los Angeles), 107
Bohn, Michael, 16
Boney, Philippe, 166
Bongben, Leocadia, 171
Borg, Björn, 63, 301
Bourdieu, Pierre, 279

Bowles, Stan, 222–23, 226, 241
Boxing Day Test (1995), 193–96
Boxing Day tsunami, Seenigama (2004), 200
Brabham Racing (Project Brabham) (UK), 257, 260
Bradman, Don, 194, 196–97, 199
Brands Hatch (UK), 253–54
Briatore, Flavio, 268
British Anglican Church, 192
British Broadcasting Corporation (BBC), 62, 67, 69, 171, 177
British Empire, x
British Lawn Tennis Association (BLTA), 59
British Sky TV, 236
British Superbikes (BSB), 35
Brown, Gordon, 243
Brown, Julie, 209–10
Browne, Mary K., 12
Bruegel, Pieter (the Elder), 279
Brundle, Martin, 256
Bucher, Ric, 87, 92
Buckingham, Vick, 229
Buddhism, 187, 192
Bueno, Galvão, 270
Bueno, Luis Pereira, 257
Bueno, Maria, 3
Bungeishunju, 127
Burfoot, Amby, 207, 210
Burger, Gerhard, 265
Burgher Recreation Club (BRC), 188
Burghers, 187
Bush, George H. W., 125, 300

California Feed Company, 115
Callaghan, Freddie, 228
Cameron, David, 68, 243–44
Cameroon Professional Society (US), 178
Campbell, Bobby, 234
Campbell, Joseph, 302
Cantona, Eric, 241
Cape Verde national football team, 171
Capriati, Stephano, 5
Caras, 269
Carlin, John, 164, 168

Carlos, John, 301
Carlton Tennis Club (Cannes), 10
Carolina Lightnin' (ASL), 235
Carrillo, Mary, 5
Castella, Rob de, 216
Catalano, Patti (nee Lyons), 211–12, 215
CD Leganés (Madrid), 165
Celebrity Big Brother (UK), 45–46
Central Park (New York), 210
Centro Sportivo Alagoano (Brazil), 150
Ceylon Cricket Association, 188
Ceylon Missionary Society, 192
Chamberlain, Wilt, 116
Chambers, Dorothea Lambert, 8–9, 13–14, 16
Chan, Jackie, 93
Chan, Susan, 13
Charlton Athletic F.C., 233
Chase Corporate Challenge, 218
Chelsea FC (UK), 175–76, 182
Chicago Athletic Association (CAA), 105
China Central Television (CCTV), 84, 92
Chinese Basketball Association (CBA), 77–78, 85
Chinese Grand Prix Formula One World Championship (2004), 79
Chinese National (Basketball) Team, 78–79, 85
Chinese People's Political Consultative Conference (NCCPPCC), 91
Chock Full o' Nuts, 90
Chongqing Fu Yuan (China), 91
Christianity, 44, 187, 240
Churchill, Winston, 250
Circuit Terlemen (Circuit Zolder) (Belgium), 255
Clarkson, Jeremy, 262
Clemente, Roberto, 99
Cleveland, Grover, 101
Cleveland Cavaliers, 61–62
Clough, Brian, 223, 227
Club de Regatas Vasco da Gama, 150–51
Coakley, Jay, 77
Cobra, Nuno, 258
Coca-Cola, 90

Cockney, 229, 244
Cohen, Stanley, 240–41
Cold War, 278, 282, 284, 286, 291, 303
Colero, Fermin, 165
Collings, Timothy, 270
Colombo, Sri Lanka, 187–90, 197, 199–200
Colombo Cricket Club, 188
Come Dine with Me, 239
Comes, Érik, 266–67
Command, Bobby, 116
Committee to Protect Journalists (US), 166
Commonwealth Games (British Empire Games), xi
Communist Party (Sri Lanka), 191
Condon, Robert, 215
Connan, Clifford, 83
Connes, Leonard, 106
Connors, Jimmy, 301
Constantine, x
Cook, James, 100
Cooksy, Marty, 209–10
Cooper, Pamela, 213
Cooperstown, New York, 140–41
Corinthians football club (Brazil), 149, 254–55
Coubertin, Pierre de Frédy (Barron de Coubertin), x
Countdown to the World Cup (NBC), 239
Crewe Alexandra F.C. (UK), 223
Cricket World Cup, 198–99; Australia–New Zealand (2015), 199
Crippens, Dick, 231
Crutchlow, Cal, 25, 32, 48
Cuju, x
Cummings, Brian, 246
Curran, Thomas, 109, 110
Currie, Tony, 226, 241

Daft Punk, 68
Dagestan (Russian Caucasus), 179
Daily Mail (UK), 15
Daily Mirror (UK), 15, 67–68, 243
Daily Record (UK), 55–56

Dare to Compete: The Struggle of Women in Sports (1999), 5
Darman, Jeff, 213
Davis, Baron, 93
Davis, Ralph, 106
Davis Cup (tennis), 59
Davos, Switzerland, 280
Day Book (Chicago), 106–7
Dean, James, 226, 243
Dempsey, Jack, 8
Dennis, Ron (Le Professeur), 262–64
Derby County Football (UK), xvi
Der Spiegel (West Germany), 287
Deutscher Turn- und Sportbund (DTSB), 288
Deutsches Sportecho (East Germany), 285
Dickens, Charles, *A Tale of Two Cities*, 55
"Dicker Mops" (fat pug dog), 287
Didrikson, Mildred Ella "Babe," 9
Diffousso, Kadgi, 165
dirndl (Bavarian dress), 291–92
Disney XD, 243
Dissanayake, Gamini, 190
Djokovic, Novak, 55, 62, 67
Dobell, George, 197–98
Docherty, Tommy, 223
Dodger Stadium, 231
Donnelly, Martin, 266
Dravidians, 187
Drogba, Didier, xviii
Druids corner (Brands Hatch), 253
Ducati, 37–38, 43, 47, 268
Duffy, Bill, 82
"Duke Kahanamoku Fund," 114
Duke of Edinburgh, 101
Duke-UNC basketball rivalry, 61
Duluth News Tribune, 107–8
Dunblane, Scotland, shooting, 58, 67–69; "Fred West," 65; "Hamilton, Thomas," 65

East Asian Games, x
East Berlin, Germany, 283
East German Secret Service (Stasi), 279, 283–87, 289, 294n

Easy Rider (1969), 32
Ecclestone, Bernie, 257
Ederle, Gertrud, 8
Edgren, Robert, 108
Eliade, Mircea, 302
Emperor's Cup, 124–25, 129, 131, 136–37
Engelmann, Larry, 6
Engeltine Cottage, 199
English Premier League, 175–76, 179, 182
Entertainment and Sports Programming Network (ESPN), 55, 62, 66, 196; Cricinfo, 196; Star Sports (China), 84; Walt Disney Company, 84
Equinoxe (Cameroon), 166
ESPN the Magazine, 92
Eton School, x
European Champions League (ECL), 165
European Council of Tolerance and Reconciliation (ETCR), 178
Eusébio (da Silva Ferreira), xvii, 232
Everton FC (UK), 176, 182
Exeter School, x
exoticism, 16, 99–100, 103–5, 107–10, 116–20
Everet, Chris, xx, 3
Evergreen Sports Agency, 79

Fame to Infamy: Race, Sport, and the Fall from Grace, 174
FC Barcelona (Spain), 165–67, 175
FC Dynamo Moscow, 232
FC Gold Pride (US), 154
FC Inter Milan (Italy), 167, 179
FC Rosengård (Sweden), 154
Federal Republic of Germany (West Germany), 209, 282–83, 286. *See also* FRG
Fédération Camerounaise de Football (FECAFOOT), Article XXVIII, 171
Fédération Internationale de Football Association (FIFA), ix, xi, xix, 64, 66, 145, 151, 164, 167–70, 172–76, 182, 224
Fédération Internationale du Sport Automobile (FISA), 259
Federation of Real Madrid Fan Clubs, 165
Federer, Roger, 55, 62, 66–67

Ferrari Formula 1 (Scuderia Ferrari), 259, 265, 267–68
FIFA Women's World Cup, ix
FIFA World Cup, ix, xi, xix, 164; Brazil (2014), 145, 170, 172–76, 182; China (2007), 151; England (1966), 66, 224; Germany (2006), 64; Italy (1990), 164, 172, 181; South Africa (2010), 167–70
Finke, Volker, 173–74
Finland, 112
Firman, Ralph, 253
Firmani, Eddie, 232
Fittipaldi, Emerson, 252, 257
Fitzgerald, F. Scott, 4; *The Great Gatsby*, 16; Jazz Age, 304
500 cc two-stroke Grand Prix, 26, 32, 37
Flappers, 16
Flavian Amphitheater (The Colosseum), x
Flores, William, 100
Fonda, Peter, 32
Fong, Hiram, 115–16
Football Association (FA), 226–27, 230, 242, 244; FA Cup, 233
Football Monthly, 225
Forbes, 91
Ford, Gerald R., 90
Ford Model T, 31
Foreign Correspondent's Club (Japan), 130
Formula Ford, 253–55
Formula One (F1), 31–32, 38, 40–41, 47, 79, 250, 253–55, 257–64, 266–71, 299–300
Formula One Grand Prix: British, 267; Dutch, 259; German, 267; Japanese, 263–65; Monaco, 258, 262–63; Portuguese, 259, 263; South African, 258–60
Formula Three (F3), 254–56
Fort Lauderdale Strikers (NASL), 222
Foundation of Goodness, 200
Franco, Itamar, 250
Frankfurter Allgemeine Zeitung (FAZ), 286–87, 295n
Freeth, George, 106, 112
Freire Deutsche Jugend (Free German Youth), 285

French Open, 19, 63
Friess, Steve, 79
Fry, Stephen, 46
Fulham F.C., 228–29, 234, 245
Furedi, Frank, 244
futebol, 145, 149, 151, 298–99, 301–2

Gadamer, Hans-Georg, "fusion of horizons," 298–99
Gaijin, 123, 127–28, 130–32, 134, 136–42, 303
Galisteu, Adriane, 256, 268–69
Gallico, Paul, 15
Gaman, 128–29, 141
Garber, Greg, 66
Garmin Ltd., 91
Gascoigne, Paul, 239
Gates, Bill, 243
Gatorade, 92
Geertz, Clifford, xxi, 303; "local knowledge," 297–98
Geladinho, 148
Genovese, Vincent, 102, 104–5, 112
German Democratic Republic (East Germany), 206, 278–79, 281–89, 291–92; politburo, 283
German Touring Car Masters (2010), 79
Germany (reunited), ix, 64, 151, 239, 278, 282, 290–92, 300–301, 304
Gerulaitis, Vitas, 301
Gibernau, Sete, 39
Gilbert, Brad, 62–63
Gilbert, Dan, 61
Gilbert, David, 14
Gillette Soccer Saturday, 236–38
Gilliam, Terry, 224
Glasnost, 281–82
Goal, 225
Golden Age of Sport, 4, 8–10, 19
Goodbye DDR (2005), 284
Goodie, Jade, 45–46
Google, 48, 90
Gone With the Wind, 33
Goolagong, Evonne, 3
Gopalan Trophy, 188
Goulart, João, 255

Gould, Chris, 130
Grand Prix Driver's Association, 268
Grand Slam (tennis), 7, 10, 34–35, 55–57, 62, 65–71
Grange, Harold "Red," 8
Grayson, Harry, 115
"greatest of all time" (GOAT), 26, 36, 47–48
Greene, Pat, 209
Greenslade, Roy, 67
Gregory, Jim, 229
Greta Waitz 5-kilometer Lopet (Oslo), 218
Greta Waitz Project, 218
Graf, Peter, 5
Graf, Steffi, 3
Guardian, The (UK), 67–68, 89, 180, 201, 250
Gunasekara, Kushil, 200
Gupa, Amit, xi
Guttmann, Allen, 280–81

Habermas, Jürgen, 28
Hagan, Patti, 211
Hagiography, xx
Hair, Darrell, 193–95
Hakuhō, 141
Hall, Stuart, 119
Hall of National Sport, 124, 126, 129, 138–39, 142
Haoles, 101, 111, 118–19
Hardy, Jamison, 105
Hargreaves, Jennifer, 13
Harlem (New York), 104
Harley Davidson, 32–33
Harris, Ron "Chopper," 225
Harrow, x
Harumafuji, 141–42
Hawaiian Gazette, 111–12, 114–15
Hawaiian Promotions Committee, 111
Hawaiian Star, 111
Hawkridge, Alex, 257, 259
Haye, David, 68
Head, Patrick, 270
Helsinki, Finland, 205
Henderson, Lew, 112
Henie, Sonja, 9, 280, 292

Henman, Tim "The Tiger," 35, 56–58, 60, 64–65, 67–68
Henry, William, 106
Heracles (Hercules), 240
Hermeneutics, 298
Hero with a Thousand Faces, The, 302
Hibernian F.C. (Scotland), 222
Hill, Damon, 265, 268
Hill, Graham, 251, 266
Hill, Grant, 83
Hinduism, 187
Hinkaku, 130–32, 137–38, 141
Hodgkinson, Mark, 60
Hold, Oliver, 67–68
Holiday, Billy, 16
Holiday on Ice, 278, 288
Hollingsworth, Hank, 116
Hollywood, xix, 12, 16, 30, 103, 109, 131, 278, 280
Hollywood Ice Revue, 280
Home Box Office (HBO), 5
Honda (Repsol Honda), 42–43, 47, 261–64, 267
Honda, Soichiro, 267
Honecker, Erich, 286
Hong Kong University of Science and Technology, 195
Honolulu, Hawaii, 100, 102–5, 111–15
Honolulu Harbor, 104
Honolulu Advertiser, 137
Honolulu Star Bulletin, 112–13
Hoops (UK), 239
Hoppe, Willie, 109
Hopps, David, 190
horse racing, 39–40
Hospital of Laquiquinne (Douala), 178
Houllier, Gérard, 236, 237
House of David, 9
Houston Chronicle, 87
Houston Rockets, 75, 79–83, 85, 87–89, 92
Howard, Ron, 38
Huang Shen Fund (China), 91
Hudson, Alan, 226, 241
Hughes, Rob, 177
Hui Nalu Club, 112, 118

Huizinga, John, 82
Hunt, James, 38, 43
Hunter, Norman, 225
Hytner, David, 180

I Am a Celebrity, Get Me Out of Here, 239
Ickx, Jack, 258
Independent Motor Sports Group (IMG), 259
Independent Television Authority (ITV), 224, 236
Indomitable Lions (Cameroon National football team), 163, 167, 170, 172–74, 181
IndyCars (US), 34–35, 42, 270
Inmola (IT) Grand Prix, 269
Inouie, Daniel, 116
Inside Stuff, 92
Institutional Act no. 5 (Brazil), 255
Instituto Ayrton Senna, 271
Interlagos (Autódromo José Carlos Pace) (Brazil), 267–69
International Association of Athletics Federations (IAAF), 212–13
International Automobile Federation (FIA), 258
International Basketball Federation (FIBA), 85; Japan World Championships (2006), 86; US World Championships (2002), 85–86
International Cricket Council (ICC), 189, 195; International Cricketer of the Year, 199; Think Wise campaign, 200
International Journal of the History of Sports, xi
International Olympic Committee (IOC), ix, 78, 211, 213
International Skating Union (ISU), 282, 290
Ishihara, Shintaro, 125, 129
Islam, 179–80, 187
Israeli athletes, murder of, 206
Israel-Palestine, 178–79

Jago, Gordon, 230, 232–33; Rodney Marsh joke, 233–34

Jakobi, Julian, 259, 269
Jaksa, Kari, 180
James, Cyril Lionel Robert (C. L. R.), xii
James, LeBron, 61–62
"Japan bashing," 130–31
Japan Sumo Association, 130–31, 140
Japan That Can Say No, The, 125
Jarvie, Grant, ix, 199
Jayawardene, Mahela, 199, 201
Jerez (Circuito de Jerez) (Spain), 261, 266
Jerusalem Post, 179
Jiang Zemin, 89, 300
Jim Crow, 105
John, Elton (Reginald Dwight), 231
John Player Special, 260–61
Joint United Nations Programme on HIV/AIDS (UNAIDS), 200
Jola, xvii
Joly, Janneke, 180, 182
Jones, Bobby, 8
Jordan, Eddie, 256
Jordan, Michael, xx, 81–83, 135, 250, 300
Journal of Pacific History, 116–17
Joyner, Florence Griffith (Flo-Jo), 289
"Jubilee Wimbledon disaster," 11–12
Judo, xi

Kadabbi, x
Kadgi Sports Academy (Cameroon), 165
Kaduru, 188
"Kahanamoku's Kick," 114
Kaká (Ricardo Izecson dos Santos Leite), 155–56
Kalima, George, 136, 138
Kalima, Haywood, 138, 140
Kandy, Sri Lanka, 189, 191–92, 195–96
Kantor, Moshe, 178
Kapadia, Asif, 264–65
Karl-Marx-Stadt (Chemnitz), 281, 283, 287
Karting, 253
"Katarina Rule," 290
Katarina Witt Foundation, 282
Kattoulas, Velisarios, 127

Kehai, Rabbit, 116
Kieta, Muhammed, 166
Kealana, Momi, 116
Kealana, Rusty, 116
Kenka, 129–30
Kennedy, John F., 250
Kensington Palace (London), 178
Kenya, 93, 217
Kerimov, Suleiman, 180
Kinder und jugendsportschulen (KJS), 282–83
King, Billie Jean, 12
King, Jonathan, 22
King George V (England), 17
King Gustav V (Sweden), 10
King Kahanamoku I (Hawaii), 109
King Kalakaua (Hawaii), 101
King Olav V (Norway), 206–7
Kipapa, Percy, 135
Kissinger, Henry, 242
Kissler, George, 106
Kojima, Noboru, 127–28, 130
Konishiki, 128–31, 136–38, 140, 142
Kopke, E. S., 111
Krenz, Egon, 283–84, 286
Kristiansen, Ingrid, 214–15, 217
Kubitschek, Juscelino, 258
Kuhio Beach (Waikiki), 117
Kume, Tadashi, 263–64
Künzler, Daniel, 180–81
Kvalheim, Arne, 206, 209, 216
Kvalheim, Knut, 208, 216

Lafarge Cement Company, 200
LA Galaxy (MLS), 243
Lamy, Pedro, 270
Lamy-Lehto crash, 270
Laney, Al, 15
La Parisienne Pâtisserieon, xv, xvii
Last, Jeremy, 179
Lauda, Niki, 38
Laver, Rod, 116
Leavy, Jane, 212
Leberer, Josef, 262

Lebow, Fred, 209–11, 213, 219
Lehto, JJ, 270
Leisure Studies, 240
Leitmotif, 218
Le Mans (France), 263
Leme, Reginaldo, 269
Lendl, Ivan, 62–64
Lenglen, Anaïs, 4, 6
Lenglan, Charles "Papa," 4–8, 17, 58
Lenglan, Suzanne, 19
Leppé, Samuel Mbappé, 164, 167–68
Les Brasseries du Cameron (Douala), 165
Lewis, Ferd, 137
Ligier (France), 266–67
Lima, Kleiton, 147, 155
Lindenberg, Sigewart, 180, 182
Lines, Gill, 240
Liverpool F.C. (UK), 175, 236
Lloyd, John, 68
London Marathon, 217
London's East End, 225, 229, 237, 244
Lord's Cricket Ground (St John's Wood, London), 189
Lorenzo, Jorje, 25, 39
Loretto School (Scotland), Senna tobacco controversy, 260
Loroupe, Tegla, 217
Los Angeles Athletic Club, 106
Los Angeles Aztecs, 222
Los Angeles Lakers, 80
Los Angeles Sol, 152
Los Angeles Times, 106
Lotus Renault F1 Team, 258–62, 267
Lu Hao, 82, 91
Lule, Jack, xiii, xvii, 297
Lundquist, Verne, 233
Lunt, David, 240
Lydon, John (Johnny Rotten), 224

Madison Square Garden, 12
Madras (Chennai), 188
Magic Astor, The (2009), 82
Maior, Estácio Gonçalves Souto, 254
Major League Baseball (MLB), xix

Makaossa, 164
Mallory, Molla, 10
Manchester City F.C., 227, 230–31, 234–35, 241
Manchester United F.C., 222, 232, 234, 243
Mandarin, 81–84
Mangan, James Anthony (J. A.), xi
Mankulam, Sri Lanka, 200
Man of the Match, 198
Mansell, Nigel, 251, 260–62, 265, 267–68
Mansilla, Enrique, 253
Maracanã Stadium (Rio de Janeiro), ix
Maracanã Walk of Fame (Brazil), 151
Maradona, Diego, xvi–xviii, xix
Marathon, 204, 207–13, 215–19
Márquez, Mark, 25, 32, 48
Marvin, George, 108
"Marx's pretty daughter," 281
Marylebone Cricket Club (MCC) (England), 189–90, 197
Marylebone (MCC) Spirit of Cricket Cowdrey Lecture, 198–99
Match of the Day, 234–37
Mathewson, Christy, 107
Maui News, 113
Maverick, 222–29, 231–35, 237–42, 244–46, 300
Mavericks, The (1994), 241
McCann, Kate, 45
McCann, Madeleine, 45
McCloud, Keith, 55–56
McConnell, Jack, 64
McDonald's, 83, 91
McEnroe, John, 40, 62–64, 301
McGowan, Alan, 290
McKay, Jim, 303
McKinley, William, 101
McLaren, Malcolm, 224
McLaren Racing, 255–57, 260, 262–63, 265, 267–68; MP4/4, 262; Ford MP4/8, 267–68
McShane, Robert, 115
Meiji Shrine (Tokyo), 126
Melbourne, Australia, 191, 193–94
Melbourne Cricket Ground (Australia), 193
Melvin, Andy, 238

Meneghel, Xuxa, 256
Mercedes-Benz, 213
Merriwell, Frank, 107
Mexican Grand Prix, 267
Miami Heat, 61
Michelle Akers Player of the Year Award (US), 155
Michigan–Ohio State football rivalry, 61
Middle Ages, x
Milla, Roger, 164, 167–70, 173, 182
Milwaukee Bucks, 84
"Ming Dynasty," 75, 82–83
Miyazawa, Kiichi, 130
Moadougou, Priscilla, 166
Mohamed, Iya, 172
Monroe, Marilyn (Norma Jean Baker), 290
Mont Blanc, 268
Monty Python, 224
Monty Python's Life of Brian, 224
Monza (Autodromo Nazionale Monza) (Italy), 259, 264
Moody, Tom, 192
Moore, Bobby, 234
Moore, Kenny, 204, 207, 212, 215–16
Moors' Sports Club, 188
Moreno, Roberto, 253–54
Morley, Gary, 16
Moss, Sterling, 251
Mota, Rosa, 217
Motocross, 32
MotoGP, 25–27, 29–33, 35–43, 46–47, 49–50, 300; Moto2, 36; Moto3, 36; mini-moto, 36–37
Motor Cycle News (UK), 35
Motor Sport, 259
Mottrom, Buster, 68
Mourinho, José, 175–76
Ms., 206, 210
Müller, Jutta (Frau), 281, 294n
Mumumi, Moutakilow, 172
Munich Olympic Organizing Committee for the Olympic Winter Games (2018), 291–92
Murali Harmony Cup (Jaffna), 201

Murray, Andy, "Paraguay shirt scandal," 64–65
Murray, James, 58, 60
Murray, Judy, 58–59
Murray, William, 58
"Murray Mocktail," 68
Musashimaro (Fiamalu Penitani), 141
Muscular Christianity, 240
Mutations (Cameroon), 166
Mutombo, Dikembe, 88

Nadal, Rafael, 55, 59, 62, 67
NASCAR, 31, 42
Nash, Steve, 93
Năstase, Ilie, 301
National Amateur Athletic Competition, 129
National Basketball Association (NBA), xix, 33, 61, 75, 77, 79, 250, 299; All-NBA Team, 75; All-Star Games, 75, 83; Basketball without Borders program, 93
National Broadcasting Company (NBC), 231, 239
National Football League (NFL), 299
National Hockey League (NHL), 299
Navratilova, Martina, 3, 41
Nendel, Jim, 99, 105–6, 110–11
Neves, Tancredo, 251
Newcastle United F.C., 237
Newey, Adrian, 270
Newman, Ron, 232–33
Newsweek, 92
New York City Marathon, 204, 207, 209–10, 212, 217–19
New York Cosmos (NASL), 155, 231–33, 235
New York Herald, 105–6
New York's Time Square, 86
New York Telegram, 105
New York Times, 92, 105, 130, 177, 257
New York Tribune, 107
New York United (ASL), 235
New York Yankees, 297, 299
Neymar (Neymar da Silva Santos Júnior), 155
Nice Tennis Club (France), 5, 7

Nicholas, Mark, 194
Nike, 91, 300
Nixon, Richard, 89
Nondescripts Cricket Club (NCC), 197
North American Soccer League (NASL), 155, 231–32, 234–35
Norton Motorcycle Company, 33
Norwegian Amateur Athletics Federation, 213–14
Nottingham Forest F.C. (UK), 223
Nowell, Cord, 176–77
Nykøbing Fl (Denmark), xvii

Oahu, Hawaii, 100, 113
Oates, Thomas, 89
Obama, Barack, 243
Oedipus Rex, 169–70
Official Baseball Annual, The, 115
Ogden, David C., xii–xiv, 174
O Globo, 156, 262
Oh, Sadaharu, 129
Olympic Games, ix–xii, 85; Albertville (1992), 282; Amsterdam (1928), 109; Antwerp (1920), 108, 280, 301; Athens (776 B.C.), x; Athens (2004), 85–86, 88, 90; Beijing (2008), 79, 86; Calgary (1988), 281, 283, 287, 289–90; Chamonix (1924), 280; Grenoble (1968), 283; Innsbruck (1976), 283; Lillehammer (1994), 282; London (1908), 280; London (2012), xi, 34, 55, 70, 158, 243; Los Angeles (1932), 103; Los Angeles (1984) 207, 211, 214, 217; Mexico City (1968), 283, 301; Montreal (1976), 206–8, 283; Munich (1972), 205–6; Nagano (1998), 123, 139–41, 300; Paris (1924), 10, 102–3, 301; Sarajevo (1984), 281, 283; Seoul (1988), 283; Sidney (2000), 79, 167; Stockholm (1912,) 102, 105–6, 110, 112, 117, 119, 301
Once in a Lifetime: An Extraordinary Story of the New York Cosmos (2006), 239
O'Neal, Shaquille, 83
"one child" policy (China), 76
one-day cricket, 190

One-Day International (ODI) (World Cup), 191, 195, 199; Calcutta, 186
OPK Flop (Operative Person Control), 284–85
Orca Digital (China), 90
Order of the British Empire (OBE), 243–44
"Oriental" outsider, 80, 86–87
Orwx of Douala (Cameroon football side), 164
Osgood, Peter, 226, 241
Oslo, Norway, 204–5, 216–19
Osmond, Gary, 116–17, 119
Ostalgie-Show (Germany), 288
Ostalgie-Welle, 289
Otis, Sam, 115
Outing, 108
OV Flop (Operative Process Flop), 284–85
Oxley, Matt, 37
Oyakata, Azumazeki, 132, 134

Pace, José Carlos, 257
Pacific Commercial Advertiser (Honolulu), 105, 111–14
Pacific Grand Prix (Japan), 268
Paddock, Charley, 110
Page Three girls, 225
Pandey, Manish, 269
Paris Métro, 19
Parry, Fred, 34, 57, 68
Passarini, Maurizio (Balogana), 270
Pathiravithana, S. R., 198
Patrick, Danica, 289
PEAK Shoes (China), 88
Pearl Harbor, 101, 129
Pearson, Andrew Russell "Drew," 115–16
Pederson, Terje, 205
Pedrosa, Dani, 25, 42
Pelé (Edson Arantes do Nascimento), xvii–xviii, xix, 155–56, 231–32, 235
People's Choice (2012), 199
PepsiCo, 91
Peraltada turn (Autódromo Hermanos Rodríguez) (Mexico City), 267
Peres, Shimon, 179

Perestroika, 281–82
Piercy, Violet, 217
Pikens, W. H., 11
Pileggi, Sarah, 9–10, 217
Pindar, 246
Pineapple, 104
Pines, Ophir, 179
Piquet, Nelson, 254–57, 261–62, 268
Pitt, Brad, 30
Pittsburgh, Pennsylvania, 106, 112
Plain Dealer (Cleveland, Ohio), 115
Playboy, 271n, 290
Poli, Raffaele, 180–81
Polpiti, 188
Polumbaum, Judy, 89
Porsche AG (Germany), 170
Portier corner (Circuit de Monaco), 263
precautionary principle, 27
Presley, Elvis, 33
Princess Diana, 45–46
Prince Vijaya, 187
Prince William, 244
Prost, Alain, 258, 261–70
Puma SE (Germany), 169–70
Pyle, C. C. ("Cash and Carry"), 11–15

Queen Elizabeth II (England), 68, 243
Queen Liliuokalani (Hawaii), 101
Queen Mary (England), 11, 17
Queen's Park Rangers F.C. (QPR), 223, 229–30, 236, 241

RAC, 253–54
Radcliffe, Paula, 217
Radio Tiempni Sintou (Cameroon), 166
Rahim, Mushfiqur, 197
Ramsey, Sir Alf, 227
Ranatunga, Arjuna, 193
Randall (artist), 113
Ranjitsinhji (H. H. Jam Saheb Shri Sir Ranjitsinhji Vibhaji of Nawanagar), 106
Ratzenberger, Roland, 269
Reagan, Ronald, 257
Real Madrid (Spain), 165, 243

Real Racing Club de Santander (Spain), 175
Reebok, 91
Reigate (English Cricket Side), 40
Reinhart, Kai, 283
Reis, David Aarão, 250
Reno Evening Gazette (Nevada), 115
Reno Rotary Club (Nevada), 115
Richard, Morris, xx
Ricoeur, Paul, 298, 303–4
Rijichō, Dewanoumi, 130
Rijkaard, Frank, 175
Rio de Janeiro, Brazil, ix, 150, 152, 255–56, 258, 261
Rising Sun (1992), 125
Ritchie, John (Sid Vicious), 224
Ritchie, Willie, 10
Road Runners Club of America, 213
Roberts, Kenny, 32
Robinson, Jackie, xviii, 90, 301
Rocky Horror Picture Show (1975), 224
Roddick, Andy, 62, 66–67
Rodgers, Beau, IV, 231–32
Rodgers, Bill, 212
Rodriguez, Ernesto, 269
Rodriguez, Nelson, "complexo de vira-lata," 257
Roebuck, Nigel, 259–60
Roebuck, Peter, 191, 194, 198–99
Rohter, Larry, 257
Roland Garros (France), 19
role models, 240–43, 245–46, 299–301
Roman Empire, x
Ronaldinho (Ronaldo de Assis Moreira), 155
Ronaldo (Cristiano Ronaldo dos Santos Aveiro), 155
Rosaldo, Renato, 100
Rosell, Sandro, 175
Rosen, Joel Nathan, 174
Rossi, Graziano, *Pushing the Limits*, 37–38
Royal Albert Street Bazaar, xvi
Royal College (Ceylon), 189
Rubython, Tom, 251, 258, 260
Rugby School, x, 240
Runner's World, 214

Rush (2013), 38
Russell, Bill, xx
Russian Green Racing (UK), 255
Ruth, George Herman "Babe," xx, 8, 116, 300
Ryan, Elizabeth, 17
Ryde Gold Medal, 196
Ryder, Roland, 190

Sabatini, Gabriela, 289
Saint Petersburg Thunderbolts (Florida), 235
Sampdoria (Unione Calcio Sampdoria) (Italy), 176, 182
Samuel Eto'o Private Foundation, 178
"Samuel Eto'o Reigns as Uncrowned King," 168
Samurai, 123, 133, 138–39
Sandemose, Akxel, *Janteloven* (Law of Jante), 206
Sanders, Bill, 82
Sandrock, Michael, 211
San Francisco's Athletic Club, 114
Sangakkara, Kashema, 196, 199
Sangakkara, Kumari, 191
Sangster, Mike, 68
San Jose earthquakes, 222
San Marino Grand Prix (California) (1994), 44, 268–69
Santa Cruz Futebol Clube, 151
Santos FC (Brazil), 154
São Paulo, Brazil, 250–53, 267
Schaaf, Daniela, 290–91
Schilling, Mark, 130
Schumacher, Michael, 268
Schuylkill River, 112
Scola, Luis, 88
Scottish independence referendum (2014), 68–70
"SED Zige" (Goat), 285, 301
Seles, Monica, 19
Senna (documentary), 269
Senninha comic book series, 271
Senpai, 137
Senshuraku, 138–39
Serrekunda, The Gambia, xv–xvii

Sesquicentennial Auditorium (Philadelphia), 12
Seville Futbol (Spain), xvii–xviii
"Sex on Skates" ("Sex Komma Null für Kati"), 288
"shamateurism," 212
Shanghai Public Diplomacy Association, 89
Shanghai Sharks, 77
Shapiro, David, 140
Sheene, Barry, 26, 43
Shell Oil, 268
Shepard's Bush (UK), 229
Shetty, Shilpa, 45–46
Shimon Peres Center for Peace, 179
Shinto, 124, 126, 128–29
Shoot, 225
Sierra Leone football, xvi
Silence of the Lambs, The (1999), 33
Silva, Audalio da, 147–48
Silva, José da, 147–48
Silva, Leonardo da, 269
Silva, Milton da, 251–53
Silva, Thereza da, 147–48
Silva, Viviane da, 270–71
Silverstone Circuit (UK), 264
Simtek Research (UK), 269
Sina Weibo (China), 90
Sinhalese, 186–88, 191–94, 196, 198–201, 302
Sinhalese Sports Club (SSC), 188
Sir Garfield Sobers Trophy (2012), 199
Skaset, Hans, 213–14
Skidelsky, William, 240
SLAM, 92
Slater, Michael, 194
Small, Bud, 107
Smith, Earl, xii
Smith, Tommie, 301
Smith, Tommy, 225
Soccer Heroes: The Glory Years (2007), 239
Songe, Alex, 174
Southern Soccer League, 235
Souza, Lilian de Vasconcelos, 253–54, 256
Soweto uprisings (1976), 259
Sozialistische Einheitspartie Deutschland (SED), Central Committee, 283
Spa-Francorchamps (Belgium), Fagnes curve, 261
Spanish la Liga, 165, 177
Spanish National League, 165
Speedway, 35
Sporting Life, 109
Sporting News, 92
Sports Illustrated, 92, 217
Sri Lanka (Ceylon), 186–201, 301–2, 304
Sri Lanka "A" Cricket Team, 192, 197
Sri Lanka Cricket Board, 194
Sri Lanka Test team, 190, 192, 196
Stage, Jeff, 116
Stanley Cup, 125
St Anthony's College (Ceylon), 189, 192
Stapel, Diederik, 180, 182
Star of Soccer (*The Big Match*), 224
Star Trek, 33
Stasi. *See* East German Secret Service
"Stasi whore," 285, 301
Stawell-Brown, Helen, 57
Steen, Rob, 224, 241
Stelling, Jeff, 236
Stern, David, 81–84, 87–88
Stjernholm, Staffan, 152
Stock, Alec, 229
Stockholm Marathon, 217
Stoner, Casey, 37, 39
St. Petersburg Open (tennis) (Russia), 62
St Thomas's College (Ceylon), 189
Suez Canal, 188
Sullivan, John L., 114
Sumo World, 131, 140
Sun (UK), 238
Sunday Times (UK), 198
Supermoto, 32
surf boarding, 99–100, 102–3, 105–6, 108–9, 113–17
Surfer Magazine, 116
Surtees, John, 36
Sutton, Keith, 254
Suzanne shorts (Bermuda shorts), 13

324 Index

Suzuka Circuit, 263, 265
Suzuki, Hiromi, 139
Swedish Football Association, 152

tae kwon do, xi
Tagg, Ernie, 223
taiji (tai chi), 82
Takahamada, 124–27, 129, 131–33, 135–36, 138–41
Takahashi, Yoshitaka, 128
Takamyama (Jesse Kuhaulua), 128–29
Takemikazuchi, 126
Takeminakata, 126
TalkSport Radio, 238–39
Tamburello corner (Autodromo Enzo e Dino Ferrari) (Italy), 270
Tamils, 186–88, 191–92, 197–201, 301–2
Tamil Tigers, 198–99; bombing of Central Bank, 186, 301–2
Tamil Union, 188, 192, 197
Tampa Bay Rowdies, 231–36
Tampa Bay Stadium, 231
Tandian, Moussa, 166
Tarzan, 103–4
Tavullia, Italy, 29
Taylor, A. P., 115
Taylor, Rodger, 68
Tchê (Lucio Pascual Gascon), 252–53
Teenage Mutant Ninja Turtles, 37
Teichler, Joachim, 284
Teixeria, Armando Botelho, 259
10 Downing Street (UK), 243
Terry Dactyl and the Dinosaurs, 224
Test Cricketer of the Year (2012), 199
Thatcher, Margaret, 44
Thomas, Debi, 289–90
Thorpe, Jim, 99, 102, 107
Thrum's Hawaiian Annual of 1913, 113
Thruxton Circuit (UK), 254, 256–57
Tilden, William "Big Bill," 3, 8
Time (US), 168, 290
Times, The (UK), 83, 261
Tinling, Ted, 19
Tin Pan Alley, 107

Toledano, Alfonso, 253
Toleman Racing, 256–58, 261–62
Top Gear, 262
Top100.cn (China), 90
Tota (José Júlio de Freitas), 149
Tour de France, 70
Tourist Trophy (Isle of Man), 35
Townsend Thoresen, 253–54
"Toy Department," 9
Trask, Haunani-Kai, *From a Native Daughter*, 117
Tremayne, David, 259
Trinity College (Anglican), 189, 192, 196
Trinity Lion, 196
Triumph Motorcycles L.T.D., 33
TV Globo (Brazil), 256, 269–70
Twenty-20 (T20), 190–91, 199, 201
Twitter, 47
Tyresö Fotbollsförening (Sweden), 154
Tyson, Mike, 135, 238

ukulele, 104
Umeå Ik (Sweden), 151, 153
Union of European Football Associations (UEFA), 175; Champion's League tournament, 167
United Nations Children's Emergency Fund (UNICEF), 200, 243
United Nations World Food Programme, 200
University of California, Berkeley, 10
University of Hawaii, 103
University of Manchester, 244
University of Pennsylvania, 106, 112
University of São Paulo, 253
University of Western Australia (Perth), 195
Unmack, William, 109
USA Today, 79
U.S. Open, 55; 2012 U.S. Open, 70
U.S.-Sino relations, 89, 300

Vahlensieck, Christa, 209–10
Vancouver Whitecaps, 233
Van Diemen team 253–54

Veddah, 187
Verrazano-Narrows Bridge (New York), 210
Victorian Period, 13, 18, 240, 242, 245
Vidar Sports Club, 205
Villeneuve, Gilles, 255
Virginia Slims (Tour), 12
Visa Inc., 83, 91–92
Volkskammer, 285
von der Lippe, Gerd, 280
VR 46, 36, 46, 48

Wade, Virginia, 55
Waikiki, 113
Waimānalo (Hawaii), 138
Waitz, Jack, 206, 209, 213
Wakahanada, 126, 131–32, 136–37, 141
Wakeling, Vick, 236
Wall Street (1987), 44
Wang Zhizhi, 85
Warr, Peter, 258–59, 262
Warwick, Derek, 260–61, 267
Washington Herald, 107
Washington Post, 105–7
Wasserman, Dan, 79
water polo, 99
Watkins, Sid, 258, 260, 267, 269–71, 274n
Weah, George, xviii
Weissmuller, Johnny, 103
Wembley Stadium, 229
West Bromwich Albion F.C., 229
Western New York Flash (US), 154
West Ham United F.C., 228
"West-Östliche Diva" (Western-Eastern Diva), 292
West Surrey Racing, 256–57
Wetherall, William, 128
What if I Had Never Tried It?, 36
Wicket, 34, 186, 190, 192–93, 195–96
Wicketkeeper, 199
Wide World of Sports (ABC), 303, 304n
Wiggins, Bradley, 70
Wightman, Hazel, 15
Wilbon, Michael, 85, 92
Willard, Michael Nevin, 117–19

Williams, Fred, 114
Williams, Richard, 5, 58
Williams, Richard (journalist), 250, 263
Williams, Serena, xx, 3
Williams, Venus, xx, 3
Williams Martini Racing, 260–61, 265, 267–69
Williams Renault, 270
Wills, Helen, 8–11; vs. Suzanne Lenglen, 10–11
Wimbledon (All-England Lawn Tennis and Croquet Club), 3, 7–17, 34–35, 55–69, 301; 1919 Women's Final, 16
Wire, The (2002–2008), 33
Wisden Cricket Almanack (1864), 190, 195
Witt, Katarina, *Meine Jahre zwischen Pflicht und Kür*, 285
Wittell, Ian, 61
WKS Hi-Park (China), 91
Wolfe, Joel, 250
Women's Professional Soccer (US), 152
Wood, Joe, 107
Woods, Eldrick Tont "Tiger," 116, 135, 239, 300
World Cross Country Championship, 204, 208–9, 217
World Cup Cricket, 301
World Series (baseball), 139
World Superbikes (WSB), 35, 36
Worthington, Frank, 226, 241
Wushu, xi
Wu Zhifei, 89

Yamaha, 38, 43, 47
Yang, Philémon, 171
Yanjing Beer, 84
Yao Family Wines (US), 90
Yao Ming, *Yao: A Life in Two Worlds*, 92
Yao Ming Day, 83
Yao Ming School (China), 91
Yao Qinlei, 92
Yaoundé Nsimalen International Airport, 173
Year of the Yao, The (2004), 92
Ye Li, 88, 92
Yi Jianglian, first game against Yao, 84

yokozuna, xx, 123, 125–34, 136–42, 300, 303,
    Yokozuna Promotions Council, 127–30
You're on Sky Sports, Rodney Marsh's "Toon Army" joke, 237

Zaragoza (Spain), 177
Zhang, Erik, 82
Zimbabwe, 189, 197
Zorn, Roland, 287

CPSIA information can be obtained
at www.ICGtesting.com
Printed in the USA
BVHW051552210622
640113BV00007B/14